The Scandal of Kabbalah

JEWS, CHRISTIANS, AND MUSLIMS FROM THE ANCIENT TO THE MODERN WORLD

Edited by Michael Cook, William Chester Jordan, and Peter Schäfer

Imperialism and Jewish Society, 200 B.C.E. to 640 C.E. by Seth Schwartz
A Shared World: Christians and Muslims in the Early Modern Mediterranean by Molly Greene
Beautiful Death: Jewish Poetry and Martyrdom in Medieval France by Susan L. Einbinder
Power in the Portrayal: Representations of Jews and Muslims in Eleventh- and Twelfth-Century Islamic Spain by Ross Brann
Mirror of His Beauty: Feminine Images of God from the Bible to the Early Kabbalah by Peter Schäfer
In the Shadow of the Virgin: Inquisitors, Friars, and Conversos *in Guadalupe, Spain* by Gretchen D. Starr-LeBeau
The Curse of Ham: Race and Slavery in Early Judaism, Christianity, and Islam by David M. Goldenberg
Resisting History: Historicism and Its Discontents in German-Jewish Thought by David N. Myers
Mothers and Children: Jewish Family Life in Medieval Europe by Elisheva Baumgarten
A Jewish Renaissance in Fifteenth-Century Spain by Mark D. Meyerson
The Handless Maiden: Moriscos and the Politics of Religion in Early Modern Spain by Mary Elizabeth Perry
Poverty and Charity in the Jewish Community of Medieval Egypt by Mark R. Cohen
Reckless Rites: Purim and the Legacy of Jewish Violence by Elliott Horowitz
Living Together, Living Apart: Rethinking Jewish–Christian Relations in the Middle Ages by Jonathan Elukin
The Church in the Shadow of the Mosque: Christians and Muslims in the World of Islam by Sidney H. Griffith
The Religious Enlightenment: Protestants, Catholics, and Jews from London to Vienna by David Sorkin
American Evangelicals in Egypt: Missionary Encounters in an Age of Empire by Heather J. Sharkey
Maimonides in His World: Portrait of a Mediterranean Thinker by Sarah Stroumsa
The Scandal of Kabbalah: Leon Modena, Jewish Mysticism, Early Modern Venice by Yaacob Dweck

The Scandal of Kabbalah

LEON MODENA, JEWISH MYSTICISM,
EARLY MODERN VENICE

Yaacob Dweck

PRINCETON UNIVERSITY PRESS
PRINCETON AND OXFORD

Copyright © 2011 by Princeton University Press
Published by Princeton University Press, 41 William Street,
Princeton, New Jersey 08540
In the United Kingdom: Princeton University Press, 6 Oxford Street,
Woodstock, Oxfordshire OX20 1TW

press.princeton.edu

All Rights Reserved

Library of Congress Cataloging-in-Publication Data

Dweck, Yaacob.
The scandal of Kabbalah : Leon Modena, Jewish mysticism, early Modern Venice /
Yaacob Dweck.
  p. cm. — (Jews, Christians, and Muslims from the ancient to the modern world)
Includes bibliographical references and index.
ISBN 978-0-691-14508-2 (hardcover : alk. paper) 1. Modena, Leone, 1571–1648. Ari
nohem. 2. Cabala—Controversial literature—History. I. Title.
BM526.D84 2011
296.1'6—dc22   2010049226

British Library Cataloging-in-Publication Data is available

This book has been composed in Janson Text

Printed on acid-free paper. ∞

Printed in the United States of America

10 9 8 7 6 5 4 3 2 1

For Juliana

A roaring lion: happy, mad, injurious.
 —Rashi, Berakhot 32a

Contents

List of Illustrations	xi
Abbreviations	xiii
Introduction	1
Chapter One Hebrew Manuscripts in an Age of Print	29
Chapter Two Early Modern Criticism of the *Zohar*	59
Chapter Three Guiding the Perplexed	101
Chapter Four Safed in Venice	127
Chapter Five A Jewish Response to Christian Kabbalah	149
Chapter Six The Afterlife of *Ari Nohem*	171
Chapter Seven Kabbalah and Scholarship in the Nineteenth Century	201
Epilogue History of a Failure	231
Acknowledgments	237
Works Cited	239
Index	273

List of Illustrations

Figure 1 A page from Modena's copybook. London, British Library, MS Or. 5395, 5a. — 29–30

Figure 2 Title page to *Sha'agat Aryeh*, copied by Leon Modena. Parma, Biblioteca Palatina, MS Parma 2238, 5a. — 40

Figure 3 Title Page to *Sha'agat Aryeh*, copied by Isaac Levi. New York, Jewish Theological Seminary Library, MS 10611, 2a. — 41

Figure 4 Title page to Modena's responsa, *Ziknei Yehudah*. London, British Library, MS Add 27148, 1b. — 48

Figure 5 Title page to the *Zohar*, Mantua, 1558. New York, Jewish Theological Seminary Library. — 59–60

Figure 6 Title page to Azariah de' Rossi, *Meor Enayim*, Mantua, 1573–1575. Parma, Biblioteca Palatina, St. De Rossi, 983. — 94

Figure 7 Azariah de' Rossi, *Meor Enayim*, Mantua, 1573–1575, 179b. Parma, Biblioteca Palatina, St. De Rossi, 983. — 95

Figure 8 Title page to Maimonides, *Guide of the Perplexed*, Venice, 1551. New York, Jewish Theological Seminary Library. — 101–102

Figure 9 Title page to Moses Cordovero, *Pardes Rimonim*, Krakow, 1592. New York, Jewish Theological Seminary Library. — 127–128

Figure 10 Hebrew title page to Joseph Solomon Delmedigo, *Sefer Ta'alumot Hokhmah*, Hanau, 1629–1631. New York Public Library. — 149–150

Figure 11 Title page to Yair Hayim Bacharach, *Havot Yair*, Frankfurt, 1699. New York, Jewish Theological Seminary Library. — 171–172

Figure 12 Hebrew title page to first printed edition of *Ari Nohem*, Leipzig, 1840. Private collection. — 201–202

Figure 13 Title page to Isaac Reggio's working edition of *Ari Nohem*. Oxford, Bodleian Library, MS Reggio 34, 1a — 212

Abbreviations

Autobiography	*The Autobiography of a Seventeenth-Century Venetian Rabbi: Leon Modena's Life of Judah*, trans. and ed. Mark R. Cohen (Princeton: Princeton University Press, 1988).
Letters	*Igrot Rabi Yehudah Aryeh mi-Modena*, ed. Yacov Boksenboim (Tel Aviv: Tel Aviv University Press, 1984).
AJS Review	Association for Jewish Studies Review
BT	Babylonian Talmud
HUC	Hebrew Union College
HUCA	Hebrew Union College Annual
JHI	Journal of the History of Ideas
JJTP	Journal of Jewish Thought and Philosophy
JNUL	Jewish National and University Library/National Library of Israel
JPS	Jewish Publication Society
JQR	Jewish Quarterly Review
JSJT	Jerusalem Studies in Jewish Thought
JSQ	Jewish Studies Quarterly
KH	Kerem Hemed
KS	Kiryat Sefer
LBIYB	Leo Baeck Institute Year Book
MGWJ	Monatsschrift für die Geschichte und Wissenschaft des Judentum
PAAJR	Proceedings of the American Academy for Jewish Research
REJ	Revue des Études Juives
RMI	La Rassegna Mensile di Israel
SUNY	State University of New York
SV	Studi Veneziani

The Scandal of Kabbalah

Introduction

"Nonsense is nonsense, but the history of nonsense is science." Thus Saul Lieberman, the great Talmudist of the twentieth century, introduced Gershom Scholem to his colleagues at the Jewish Theological Seminary in New York. Lieberman's apocryphal and oft-quoted remark testifies to the modern Jewish ambivalence toward Kabbalah, successfully overcome only by Scholem's scientific scholarship. No one did more to perpetuate the narrative of Scholem's rescue of Jewish mysticism from the condescension of his scholarly predecessors than Scholem himself. Enlightened scholars of the Jewish past had persisted in casting Kabbalah as primitive, antimodern, and irrational. In a word, nonsense. The demands of responsible scholarship required careful and considered criticism of Kabbalah, a task Scholem identified with the trajectory of his own career. In the preface to the first edition of *Major Trends in Jewish Mysticism*, he reflected: "More than twenty years have passed since I began to devote my life to the study of Jewish mysticism and especially of Kabbalism. It was a beginning in more than one sense, for the task which confronted me necessitated a vast amount of spade work in a field strewn with ruins and by no means ripe as yet for the constructive labours of the builder of a system."[1] For all its sarcasm, Lieberman's quip only reinforced Scholem's carefully cultivated posture as the heroic founder of historical scholarship on Kabbalah.

This book explores the substance and subsequent history of Leon Modena's critique of Kabbalah in seventeenth-century Venice as a challenge to Scholem's foundational narrative. A rabbi and a preacher in the Venetian ghetto, Modena witnessed the transformation of Jewish society, culture, and institutions through the spread of Kabbalah. In 1639 he took the unprecedented and dangerous step of subjecting this newly dominant spirituality of early modern Judaism to meticulous analysis. Part religious polemic, part cultural criticism, and part epistolary treatise, Modena's Hebrew exposition entitled *Ari Nohem* (The Roaring Lion) addressed a society saturated with Kabbalah, a condition that he sought desperately, and with utter futility, to change. Modena argued against the antiquity of Kabbalah by subjecting the origins of kabbalistic texts to rigorous analysis. He

---

[1] Scholem, *Major Trends in Jewish Mysticism* (Jerusalem: Schocken, 1941), vii. On Lieberman's remark and its variants, see Abe Socher, "The History of Nonsense," *AJS Perspectives* (Fall 2006): 32–33.

2 • Introduction

indicted the growing cults of personality that had formed around prominent kabbalists, and he objected to the proliferation of kabbalistic practices in the synagogue and in the study house. This book tells the story of Modena's *Ari Nohem*, its composition in the ghetto of Venice and its criticism of Venetian Jewish culture, its circulation in manuscript in the ensuing centuries and its appearance in print in the early nineteenth century. In this story, the critical history of Kabbalah emerged and developed alongside the spread of mystical belief and mystical praxis. Modena's counterhistory formed an integral part of the history of Kabbalah in the very period it was coming to dominate Jewish life.[2]

THE SPREAD OF MEDIEVAL KABBALAH: AN EARLY MODERN
CULTURAL REVOLUTION

In the centuries before Modena subjected it to withering criticism, Kabbalah carried a range of meanings for Jews and Gentiles. A Hebrew term one can render as "tradition" or "reception," Kabbalah referred to a mode of reading, a library of texts, a series of concepts, and a range of practices. As a mode of reading, Kabbalah encompassed a set of interpretive assumptions adopted by an initiate in the course of approaching a sacred text. Kabbalists assiduously applied these methods of exegesis to the most sacred of texts, the Bible, and relied on mystical symbolism to uncover its theological content.[3] In the thirteenth century the Jewish biblical exegete Moses ben Nahman (Nahmanides) repeatedly used the phrase "by way of truth" in his biblical commentary to indicate the kabbalistic interpretation of a particular passage.[4] Two centuries later and to very different effect, the most celebrated Christian kabbalist of the Renaissance, Pico della Mirandola, repeatedly drew on kabbalistic modes of exegesis in arriving at his theological theses.[5] Although they maintained opposing esoteric truths, Pico and Nahmanides both employed kabbalistic hermeneutics to arrive at them. Kabbalistic exegesis was most frequently applied to the Bible and

---

[2] For revisions to Scholem's portrait of prior scholarship, see Moshe Idel, *Kabbalah: New Perspectives* (New Haven: Yale University Press, 1988), 1–10; Daniel Abrams, "Defining Modern Academic Scholarship: Gershom Scholem and the Establishment of a New (?) Discipline," *JJTP* 9 (2000): 267–302; David N. Myers, "Philosophy and Kabbalah in Wissenschaft des Judentums: Rethinking the Narrative of Neglect," *Studia Judaica* 16 (2008): 56–71.

[3] Moshe Idel, "PaRDeS: Some Reflections on Kabbalistic Hermeneutics," in *Death, Ecstasy, and Other Worldly Journeys*, ed. John J. Collins and Michael Fishbane, 249–68 (Albany: SUNY Press, 1995).

[4] Elliot R. Wolfson, "By Way of Truth: Aspects of Nahmanides' Kabbalistic Hermeneutic," *AJS Review* 14 (1989): 103–78.

[5] Chaim Wirszubski, *Pico della Mirandola's Encounter with Jewish Mysticism* (Cambridge: Harvard University Press, 1989).

particularly the Pentateuch, but a range of medieval and early modern thinkers used Kabbalah to interpret later authoritative texts such as the Talmud and other classics of rabbinic literature. Some went so far as to engage in kabbalistic readings of more recent works, such as Maimonides' *Guide of the Perplexed*.[6]

The term Kabbalah was also used to refer to the objects of religious study. Medieval and early modern readers designated a range of texts such as *Sefer ha-Bahir* (The Book of Illumination), *Sefer Yetzirah* (The Book of Creation), and *Pardes Rimonim* (The Pomegranate Orchard) as kabbalistic works even if these books or their authors did not always use the term Kabbalah to describe them. By far the most celebrated work of Kabbalah was the *Zohar* (The Book of Splendor). Rather than a single book, the *Zohar* comprised a corpus of texts, most of which consisted of a running commentary on the Pentateuch. Written in the thirteenth century in a mixture of Hebrew and Aramaic, it combined exegesis of individual verses with parables, homilies, and stories. Much of this commentary recounted the wondrous deeds of Simeon bar Yohai and his colleagues and purported to describe Jewish life in Roman Palestine of the second century. Rabbinic authorities attributed the *Zohar*, like *Sefer Yetzirah* and *Sefer ha-Bahir*, to an ancient author and assumed that its kabbalistic content represented age-old Jewish esoteric traditions.[7]

Both as a mode of exegesis and a library of texts, Kabbalah reverted to a set of ideas and motifs. For example, some kabbalists used the concept of the *sefirot*, or the spheres, to refer to a division of the Godhead into multiple entities or emanations.[8] Others employed the notion of *gilgul*, or the transmigration of souls, to explain what happened to a person's soul after death.[9] Another important concept was *devekut*, which described the initiate's special relationship to knowledge of the divine.[10] Kabbalists disagreed, often passionately, over the precise meaning of these and other seminal concepts. Not all kabbalists employed the notion of the sefirot to refer to the Godhead, and many of those who did argued about their nature, division, and order. Important as these disagreements were, Kabbalah had

---

[6] Moshe Idel, *Absorbing Perfections: Kabbalah and Interpretation* (New Haven: Yale University Press, 2002); Idel, "Maimonides' *Guide of the Perplexed* and the Kabbalah," *Jewish History* 18 (2004): 197–226.

[7] Boaz Huss, *Ke-zohar ha-rakia: perakim be-hitkablut ha-Zohar uve-havnayat erko ha-simli* (Jerusalem: Mossad Bialik and Ben-Zvi Institute, 2008); Daniel Abrams, "The Invention of the *Zohar* as a Book: On the Assumptions and Expectations of the Kabbalists and Modern Scholars," *Kabbalah* 19 (2009): 7–142.

[8] Idel, *Kabbalah: New Perspectives*, chap. 6.

[9] Gershom Scholem, "*Gilgul*: The Transmigration of Souls," in *On The Mystical Shape of the Godhead:Basic Concepts in the Kabbalah*, 197–250 (New York: Schocken Books, 1991).

[10] Gershom Scholem, "*Devekut*, or Communion with God," in *The Messianic Idea in Judaism and Other Essays on Jewish Spirituality*, 203–27 (New York: Schocken Books, 1995).

emerged as a distinct theosophical system at the end of the Middle Ages, and its antiquity was consistently taken for granted by almost all of its adherents.[11]

The term Kabbalah also encompassed a series of ritual practices. One of the primary channels through which Kabbalah spread in the early modern period was by means of new religious practices. For instance, kabbalists composed new prayers and introduced them into the liturgy of various Jewish communities; they undertook pilgrimages to the actual or reputed gravesites of the virtuous dead in order to commune with the recently departed or with ancestral spirits. Kabbalists also adapted and transformed traditional Jewish practices. By endowing prayer with theurgic significance, they reconfigured the function as well as symbolic meaning of a crucial element of Jewish life. The rites of charity, penitence, and sexual abstinence were all imbued with new theological import. Torah study became a sacred rite with cosmic ramifications. In a centuries-long outburst of religious creativity, kabbalists manufactured a new Jewish discourse rich with symbols, myths, and rituals. They were the ultimate meaning makers. They sought to infuse nearly every aspect of Jewish life with theological importance and cosmic significance. And their success was astonishing.[12]

For the religious adept, however, Kabbalah also referred to something beyond these rituals of practice, modes of exegesis, bodies of literature, and new theological concepts. Throughout the medieval and early modern periods the term Kabbalah referred to a putative tradition of esotericism, to secrets that God had revealed to Moses at Mount Sinai. Kabbalists maintained that these secrets had been transmitted orally from one generation to the next or rediscovered by means of personal divine revelation in the Middle Ages.[13] The term Kabbalah encompassed both the actual content of these secrets and the process of their transmission.[14] Kabbalistic knowledge required initiation into an esotericist elite, and to use the term Kabbalah

---

[11] Gershom Scholem, *Origins of the Kabbalah* (Philadelphia and Princeton: JPS and Princeton University Press, 1987); Haviva Pedaya, *Ha-Shem veha-mikdash be-mishnat R. Yitshak sagi nehor: iyun mashveh be-kitve rishone ha-mekubalim* (Jerusalem: Magnes Press, 2001).

[12] Gershom Scholem, "Tradition and New Creation in the Ritual of the Kabbalists," in *On the Kabbalah and Its Symbolism*, 118–57 (New York: Schocken, 1996); Lawrence Fine, *Physician of the Soul, Healer of the Cosmos: Isaac Luria and His Kabbalistic Fellowship* (Stanford: Stanford University Press, 2003), chaps. 6–8.

[13] Rivka Shatz, "Kabbalah: Tradition or Innovation" (Hebrew), in *Masuot: mehkarim be-sifrut ha-Kabalah uve-mahshevet Yisrael mukdashim le-zikhro shel Prof. Efrayim Gotlib*, ed. Michal Oron and Amos Goldreich, 447–58 (Jerusalem: Mossad Bialik, 1994).

[14] Elliot R. Wolfson, "Beyond the Spoken Word: Oral Tradition and Written Transmission in Medieval Jewish Mysticism," in *Transmitting Jewish Traditions: Orality, Textuality, and Cultural Diffusion*, ed. Yaakov Elman and Israel Gershoni, 166–224 (New Haven: Yale University Press, 2000); Eitan P. Fishbane, *As Light before Dawn: The Inner World of a Medieval Kabbalist* (Stanford: Stanford University Press, 2009), chap. 3.

indicated that one had received its secrets from a source whose authority was beyond reproach. Repeatedly medieval and early modern kabbalists emphasized the authenticity of their sources, whether oral or written, in making theological claims about the nature of God or in designating a given idea as esoteric. The secrets God gave to Moses at Sinai were said to have been transmitted by master to disciple for a given period of time until the fear that they would be forgotten led a particular figure to transcribe them, the way Simeon bar Yohai recorded the *Zohar*, Akiva *Sefer Yetzirah*, or Nehuniah ben ha-Kaneh *Sefer ha-Bahir*. Kabbalists insisted that the mysteries transmitted in these books were not peripheral but essential to the theological core of Judaism.[15]

Throughout the medieval period, Kabbalah remained the preserve of a select group of learned individuals. With the possible exception of the prophetic Kabbalah espoused by Abraham Abulafia in the late thirteenth century, medieval kabbalists tended to restrict their teachings to other initiates and did not seek to propagate their theology or their writings beyond a limited circle.[16] And then something happened. Beginning in the second half of the fifteenth century, a confluence of factors—the reconfiguration of Jewish populations, the development of a new technology of textual reproduction, the rise of a new cultural center, and the intense interest of non-Jewish intellectuals in Jewish knowledge—transformed Kabbalah from an esoteric set of texts and practices into a feature of public religious life. For the Jews, this constituted nothing less than a cultural revolution.

In the late fifteenth century the Spanish and Portuguese crowns expelled or forcibly converted the Jews within their realms, effectively dissolving two of the largest Jewish communities in Europe in less than a decade. In the early sixteenth century many cities in western and central Europe expelled their Jews, leading to their exodus from large parts of the Holy Roman Empire. These expulsions resulted in mass migration and resettlement in two areas that were to become major Jewish centers for the next several centuries: the Ottoman Empire and the Polish-Lithuanian Commonwealth.[17] As the axes of Jewish life shifted from western Europe to

---

[15] Moshe Halbertal, *Concealment and Revelation: Esotericism in Jewish Thought and Its Philosophical Implications* (Princeton: Princeton University Press, 2007), chaps. 9–12.

[16] Moshe Idel, "We Have No Kabbalistic Tradition on This," in *Rabbi Moses Nahmanides (Ramban): Explorations in His Religious and Literary Virtuosity*, ed. Isadore Twersky, 51–73 (Cambridge: Harvard University Press, 1983). On Abulafia, see Moshe Idel, *Language, Torah, and Hermeneutics in Abraham Abulafia* (Albany: SUNY Press, 1989); Elliot R. Wolfson, *Abraham Abulafia—Kabbalist and Prophet: Hermeneutics, Theosophy, and Theurgy* (Los Angeles: Cherub Press, 2000); Harvey J. Hames, *Like Angels on Jacob's Ladder: Abraham Abulafia, the Franciscans, and Joachimism* (Albany: SUNY Press, 2007).

[17] Jonathan I. Israel, *European Jewry in the Age of Mercantilism 1550–1750* (London: Littman Library, 1998), 4–28; David B. Ruderman, *Early Modern Jewry: A New Cultural History* (Princeton: Princeton University Press, 2010), 23–55.

eastern Europe and the eastern Mediterranean, and as the terms "Sepharad" and "Ashkenaz" were sundered from their geographic referents of Iberia and Franco-Germany and began to refer to the new communities of the Ottoman Empire and Poland-Lithuania, medieval Kabbalah was radically refashioned. The large-scale resettlement of Jewish populations led to the increased circulation of kabbalistic texts, ideas, and thinkers.

In the sixteenth century northern Italy remained one of the only regions of western Europe with continuous if somewhat precarious Jewish settlement. Although the Polish-Lithuanian Commonwealth and the Ottoman Empire contained considerably larger Jewish populations, Italy remained crucially significant for the makings of early modern Jewish culture. In places such as Mantua, Ferrara, and Ancona, conversos fleeing the Iberian Peninsula, Ashkenazi migrants from central Europe, Sephardic merchants from the Ottoman Empire, and native Italian Jews lived in close proximity and brought their competing customs to bear upon one another. Like other cities in Italy, Venice served as a meeting point for different Jewries.[18] Situated at the crossroads between western Europe and the Ottoman Empire, a maritime power with considerable territorial holdings on the peninsula and a republic with vexed relations with nearly every European power, Venice also possessed a variegated and contentious Jewish community.[19] In Venice native strands of Italian Kabbalah mixed with Iberian and Ottoman traditions as well as Ashkenazi variants from Poland and Lithuania.[20]

One of the central points of convergence involved the production and dissemination of printed Hebrew books.[21] Jewish religious elites had quickly embraced the new technology of printing in the late fifteenth century, but they tended not to print kabbalistic books. At the turn of the sixteenth century a mere handful of kabbalistic works had appeared in print, and those

---

[18] On Rome, see Kenneth Stow, *Theater of Acculturation: The Roman Ghetto in the Sixteenth Century* (Seattle: University of Washington Press, 2001), 22– 29; Stow, *Jewish Life in Early Modern Rome* (Aldershot: Ashgate, 2007), chaps. 9–11. On Florence, see Stefanie B. Siegmund, *The Medici State and the Ghetto of Florence: The Construction of an Early Modern Jewish Community* (Stanford: Stanford University Press, 2006), 61–66.

[19] Brian Pullan, *The Jews of Europe and the Inquisition of Venice, 1550–1670* (Totowa, NJ: Barnes and Noble Books, 1983); Gaetano Cozzi, ed., *Gli Ebrei e Venezia: secoli XIV–XVIII* (Milan: Edizioni Communità, 1987); David Malkiel, *A Separate Republic: The Mechanics and Dynamics of Venetian Jewish Self-Government, 1607–1624* (Jerusalem: Magnes Press, 1991); Robert C. Davis and Benjamin Ravid, eds., *The Jews of Early Modern Venice* (Baltimore: Johns Hopkins University Press, 2001); Benjamin Ravid, *Studies on the Jews of Venice, 1382–1797* (Aldershot: Ashgate, 2003).

[20] Moshe Idel, "Italy in Safed, Safed in Italy: Toward an Interactive History of Sixteenth-Century Kabbalah," in *Cultural Intermediaries: Jewish Intellectuals in Early Modern Italy*, ed. David B. Ruderman and Giuseppe Veltri, 239–69 (Philadelphia: University of Pennsylvania Press, 2004).

[21] Jean Baumgarten, *Le peuple des livres: Les ouvrages populaires dans la société ashkénaze XVIe–XVIIIe siècle* (Paris: Albin Michel, 2010), 223–61.

emerged largely due to the initiatives of interested Christians. Only in the second half of the century did Kabbalah appear in print with consistency and frequency.[22] In the years immediately following the 1553 ecclesiastical ban on the printing of the Talmud, the dynamics of Hebrew print changed dramatically, and entire genres of Jewish literature that had hitherto circulated largely in manuscript form began to be printed.[23] With the significant exception of *Sefer ha-Bahir*, which was not printed as an individual book until the seventeenth century, nearly every major work of medieval Kabbalah appeared in print at Hebrew presses in northern Italy, and many of them in multiple editions. In the decades that followed the publication of medieval classics such as the *Zohar*, *Sefer Yetzirah*, and *Ma'arekhet ha-Elohut*, contemporary Kabbalah in the form of sermons, custom manuals, exegetical anthologies, and legal treatises began to feature regularly as part of a culture of Jewish print. This combination of medieval masterpieces with contemporary commentary vastly expanded the number and range of kabbalistic books available at the turn of the seventeenth century.

Coincident with this embrace of a relatively new technology, an innovation in Jewish theology proved to have profound consequences for the spread of Kabbalah. In the second half of the sixteenth century, Safed, a small town in northern Palestine, rapidly became an important, if not the most important, center of Jewish culture.[24] The explosion of creativity in Safed took many forms—liturgy, poetry, exegesis, and homiletics—but it was Kabbalah and Jewish law that were at the core of this short-lived but widely repercussive cultural renaissance. Isaac Luria, the most important kabbalist in Safed, generated a new kabbalistic theology that endowed the devotion of the individual with enormous religious power. Central to Luria's theology was the concept of exile, specifically the exile of the *shekinah*, or the in-dwelling of the divine presence. Luria's kabbalistic teaching placed human beings at the center of the cosmos and imbued human action, particularly the performance of the commandments, with cosmic significance.[25] If an individual performed the commandments with the proper intention, the *shekinah* would be restored from its exile and reunited with

---

[22] Isaiah Tishby, "The Controversy over the Book of the *Zohar* in the Sixteenth Century in Italy" (Hebrew), in *Hikre Kabalah u-sheluhoteha* (Jerusalem: Magnes Press, 1982), 1:79–130.

[23] Amnon Raz-Krakotzkin, *The Censor, the Editor, and the Text: The Catholic Church and the Shaping of the Jewish Canon in the Sixteenth Century* (Philadelphia: University of Pennsylvania Press, 2007).

[24] Solomon Schechter, "Safed in the Sixteenth Century: A City of Legists and Mystics," in *Studies in Judaism: Second Series*, 202–85 (Philadelphia: JPS, 1908).

[25] Scholem, *Major Trends in Jewish Mysticism*, seventh lecture; Ronit Meroz, "The Teachings of Redemption in Lurianic Kabbalah" (Hebrew), Ph.D. diss., Hebrew University, 1988; Fine, *Physician of the Soul, Healer of the Cosmos*; Shaul Magid, *From Metaphysics to Midrash: Myth, History, and the Interpretation of Scripture in Lurianic Kabbala* (Bloomington: Indiana University Press, 2008); Joseph Avivi, *Kabalat ha-Ari* (Jerusalem: Ben-Zvi Institute, 2008).

God. Luria's reputation did not rest solely on this innovative theology of exile that he developed in Palestine. After his death in 1572, Luria acquired a reputation as a miracle worker and pious ascetic that greatly enhanced his mystique. One of his elder colleagues in Safed, Joseph Karo, repackaged a summary of the Jewish legal tradition in his law code the *Shulhan Arukh* and drew on kabbalistic literature, particularly the *Zohar*, in the formulation of countless rulings.[26] His law code served as a standard reference work for rabbis and for students of Jewish law; through legal digests, customs books, and an extensive commentary tradition, Karo's mystically charged legal code entered into the fabric of Jewish religious life.

As the spread of Lurianism and the diffusion of the *Shulhan Arukh* demonstrate, the kabbalistic culture of Safed was anything but local. Even as the city's economic and cultural fortunes declined at the end of the sixteenth century, Luria's theology and Karo's law code took over the Jewish world. Karo's *Shulhan Arukh*, the first Hebrew book to be reprinted in the lifetime of its author, appeared no fewer than seventeen times in the sixteenth century. Lurianic Kabbalah traveled to Italy and from there went further north to Prague and to the Jewish communities of Poland-Lithuania, particularly via new vernacular treatises on proper Jewish conduct.[27] The direct influence of Lurianic Kabbalah, and, in particular, its relationship to the messianism of Sabbetai Zevi, remains the subject of vigorous debate.[28] By most accounts, however, the writings of Luria, Karo, and their students remained at the center of Jewish life long after Safed had returned to its former state as a cultural backwater.

By the end of the Middle Ages, then, Kabbalah was no longer the exclusive province of an elite. It was also no longer the religious property of the Jews. A range of celebrated Christian intellectuals in Europe expressed a strong interest in Kabbalah.[29] Beginning in Italy in the late fifteenth century

[26] Israel M. Ta-Shma, *Ha-Nigleh she-ba nistar: le-heker shekie ha-halakhah be-Sefer ha-Zohar* (Tel Aviv: Ha Kibutz Ha-Meuhad, 2001), 88–104. See the review of the first edition by Yehuda Liebes, "The *Zohar* as a Halakhic Book" (Hebrew), *Tarbiz* 64 (1995): 581–605; R. J. Zwi Werblowsky, *Joseph Karo: Lawyer and Mystic* (Oxford: Oxford University Press, 1962).

[27] Idel, "Italy in Safed, Safed in Italy"; Amnon Raz-Krakotzkin, "From Safed to Venice: The *Shulhan Arukh* and the Censor," in *Tradition, Heterodoxy, and Religious Culture: Judaism and Christianity in the Early Modern Period*, ed. Chanita Goodblatt and Howard Kreisel, 91–115 (Beer Sheva: Ben-Gurion University of the Negev Press, 2006).

[28] Gershom Scholem, *Sabbatai Sevi: The Mystical Messiah, 1626–1676* (Princeton: Princeton University Press, 1973); Zeev Gries, *Sifrut ha-hanhagot: toldoteha u-mekomah be-haye haside R. Yisrael Ba'al Shem Tov* (Jerusalem: Mossad Bialik, 1989); Moshe Idel, "'One from a Town, Two from a Clan,' The Diffusion of Lurianic Kabbala and Sabbateanism: A Re-Examination," *Jewish History* 7 (1993): 79–104.

[29] François Secret, *Les Kabbalistes Chrétiens de la Renaissance* (Paris: Dunod, 1964); Joseph Dan, ed., *The Christian Kabbalah: Jewish Mystical Books and Their Christian Interpreters* (Cambridge: Harvard College Library, 1997); Wilhelm Schmidt-Biggemann, ed., *Christliche Kabbala* (Ostfildern: Thorbecke, 2003).

and continuing through the early eighteenth century in northern Europe, Christians on both sides of the confessional divide interpreted kabbalistic texts in the interest of Christianity and used kabbalistic methodologies in support of Christian dogma. The efforts of these intellectuals has been retrospectively termed Christian Kabbalah, a catch-all term used to describe a range of opinions and uses of Kabbalah frequently at odds with one another. The most celebrated Christian thinker to become a devotee of Kabbalah was Pico della Mirandola, a Florentine aristocrat who lived in the second half of the fifteenth century and drew on Kabbalah as a component of his ancient theology. For Pico a single truth united all periods and cultures, and a harmony of religious insight existed among ancient Pagan, Jewish, and Christian writings. Kabbalah was ostensibly the Jewish domain of this ancient theology. For him kabbalistic texts were thus as important and as ancient as the Hermetic Corpus and the oldest Sibylline Oracles.

Pico was only the most prominent in a long line of non-Jewish intellectuals who studied Kabbalah, including Johannes Reuchlin, Pietro Galatino, and many others. As producers and consumers, Catholics and Protestants in western Europe played a crucial role in the publication and dissemination of Kabbalah beyond the Jewish elite. For centuries they initiated and oversaw the printing of kabbalistic texts in Hebrew, translated kabbalistic texts into Latin, and drew on Kabbalah when preaching to potential Jewish converts. Over and above the growing body of kabbalistic literature available in Latin, a flood of dictionaries and grammars of Hebrew and Aramaic offered a curious reader a range of tools with which to study newly printed texts.[30] The appropriation of Kabbalah that began in earnest with Pico and continued for the next several centuries was hardly a disinterested intellectual exchange between Christians—Catholic or Protestant—and Jews. These encounters fraught with conversionary pressures and uneven power relations had important consequences for the history of Jewish knowledge. After the initial phase when they served as teachers to interested Christians, Jews were no longer necessary intermediaries in the acquisition of esoteric Jewish learning.

The confluence of these factors—the reconfiguration of Jewish populations, the rise of a new center in Safed, the appearance of kabbalistic texts in print, and the interest of Christians in the esoteric wisdom of the Jews—had important consequences for the place of Kabbalah in early modern Judaism. By the turn of the seventeenth century, Kabbalah as a set of ideas, texts, and practices was no longer a secret. Printed works of Kabbalah, both medieval classics as well as more recent ones, were available for purchase. Kabbalistic rituals and doctrines had spread from Safed to much of

---

[30] Stephen G. Burnett, *From Christian Hebraism to Jewish Studies: Johannes Buxtorf (1564–1629) and Hebrew Learning in the Seventeenth Century* (Leiden: Brill, 1996).

the Jewish world. Preachers in Italy, both Jewish and Christian, quoted Kabbalah in their sermons.[31] Organizations of confraternal piety drew on Kabbalah in their elaboration of new rituals and in the formulation of new liturgical rites.[32] The spread of Kabbalah posed an enormous challenge to other forms of Judaism. Both a social force and an innovative Jewish theology, Kabbalah conquered or co-opted Maimonidean rationalism, Talmudic legalism, and ascetic pietism. According to Robert Bonfil, the spread of Kabbalah effectively served the elevation of private religious experience, a development that strikingly prefigured certain aspects of modernity.[33]

LEON'S ROAR

Leon Modena's world was inundated with Kabbalah. His greatest student, Joseph Hamiz, his beloved son-in-law, Jacob Levi, his cousin, Aaron Berekhya of Modena, and his aged mentor, Menahem Azariah da Fano, were all passionate devotees. With his Venetian colleagues and with foreign visitors, with his rivals and inside his own family, Modena encountered Kabbalah at every turn. Whether reading in the cacophony of his overcrowded home or celebrating a circumcision, Modena confronted Kabbalah as a vital force in Jewish life. At the age of sixty-eight, plagued by a range of illnesses and beset by mounting debt, stricken by grief and estranged from his loved ones, Modena penned his indictment of Venetian Jewish culture. Written in elegant Hebrew, Modena's *Ari Nohem* heaved with emotion as deep as it was self-consciously restrained. Modena criticized Kabbalah to diminish its status, not to destroy it. He paid kabbalists the devastating compliment of taking their arguments seriously and refuting them one by one. To the claim that Kabbalah represented an ancient esoteric tradition dating back to Moses at Sinai, Modena responded with a systematic analysis of the historical origins of kabbalistic texts. He sought to distinguish between Kabbalah and the Oral Torah, a concept that he maintained did have its origins in revelation. Kabbalah and its core documents, he demonstrated, had emerged only in the late Middle Ages.

Modena rejected the notion that only kabbalists possessed the hermeneutic keys to uncover the secrets of the Bible, but he never characterized their modes of exegesis as inherently worthless. To the contrary, he

---

[31] David B. Ruderman, ed., *Preachers of the Italian Ghetto* (Berkeley: University of California Press, 1992).

[32] Elliott S. Horowitz, "Jewish Confraternities in Seventeenth-Century Verona: A Study in the Social History of Piety," Ph.D. diss., Yale University, 1982.

[33] Robert Bonfil, "Change in the Cultural Patterns of a Jewish Society in Crisis: Italian Jewry at the Close of the Sixteenth Century," in *Essential Papers on Jewish Culture in Renaissance and Baroque Italy*, ed. David B. Ruderman (New York: New York University Press, 1992), 405.

repeatedly extolled the virtues of the *Zohar* as a reservoir of homiletic insight. At the same time, he resisted the attempt to designate Kabbalah as a distinctive form of knowledge or wisdom. For Modena, knowledge could be the product only of reason and understanding, and whatever was beyond reason, as kabbalists repeatedly described Kabbalah, could not be knowledge. Kabbalists maintained that belief in the sefirot constituted a crucial element of Jewish faith and branded as heretics anyone who denied their centrality to Judaism. Modena repudiated this claim and leveled a severe countercharge of his own: after an examination of the sefirot as a concept, he concluded that it pointed to a plurality within God similar to the Christian doctrine of the Trinity. To a range of thinkers who had characterized Kabbalah as the entirety of God's revelation and the totality of the Jewish tradition, Modena responded with a work of cultural criticism that reduced Kabbalah to scale.[34]

Ari Nohem thus represents an instance of what Amos Funkenstein called a counterhistory.[35] Like authors of counterhistories in antiquity and the Middle Ages, Modena systematically exploited the sources of his opponents; in his case, the very works that kabbalists adduced to prove the antiquity of Kabbalah and its centrality within Judaism. He mined the sixteenth-century editions of the *Zohar* as well as medieval and early modern Jewish chronicles to formulate a coherent account of the origins of the *Zohar* that denied its antiquity and identified it as the pseudepigraphic creation of Moses de Leon and his circle. He examined the hagiographic legends about Isaac Luria and concluded that Luria was incapable of the magical feats attributed to him by his disciples. He fought strenuously against the kabbalistic appropriation of Maimonides and sought to restore the study of the *Guide of the Perplexed* to the pursuit of philosophical wisdom. Modena's counterhistory audaciously and, as time would prove, accurately presented Kabbalah as a recent innovation within Jewish theology rather than an ancient preserve of Sinaitic secrets; it sought to separate the homiletic and exegetical elements within Kabbalah from the totalizing claims about Kabbalah as the entirety of Judaism, and it argued for a clear distinction between normative sources of the law—codes, commentaries, and rabbinic responsa—and works of Kabbalah.

---

[34] On *Ari Nohem*, see Luc Desplanches, "Le monde de la Kabbale dans l'Italie du XVIIe siècle Léon de Modène: Ari Nohem," Thèse de Doctorat, Université des Sciences Humaines de Strasbourg, 1985; Moshe Idel, "Differing Conceptions of Kabbalah in the Early 17th Century," in *Jewish Thought in the Seventeenth Century*, ed. Isadore Twersky and Bernard Septimus, 137–200 (Cambridge: Harvard University Press, 1987).

[35] Amos Funkenstein, *Perceptions of Jewish History* (Berkeley: University of California Press, 1993), 36. On later Jewish counterhistories, see David Biale, *Gershom Scholem: Kabbalah and Counter-History* (Cambridge: Harvard University Press, 1979); Susannah Heschel, *Abraham Geiger and the Jewish Jesus* (Chicago: University of Chicago Press, 1998).

But *Ari Nohem* was hardly a detached quest for truth. Much as it was a counterhistory, it was also a countertheology. Modena explicitly addressed his epistolary treatise to his student Hamiz, a kabbalist and philosopher who had studied medicine at the University of Padua and had been Modena's disciple for many years.[36] He attempted to persuade Hamiz, whom he loved like a son, to abandon his assiduous devotion to Kabbalah and to return to the *Guide of the Perplexed*. But Hamiz was hardly the only intended reader of *Ari Nohem*. Modena wanted to convince the Jews of Venice to abandon their embrace of a newfangled and irrational form of Jewish polytheism and return to the Judaism of Maimonides. Modena's appeal to reason, represented by Maimonides' *Guide*, had an important spiritual function for him: it was both a constitutive part of Jewish tradition that he valued for its own sake and a battering ram he used to demolish parallel claims to authenticity on the part of kabbalists. He pointed to the historical irony entailed in the popularization of esotericism and issued a clarion call to return to the fundamentals of Maimonidean rationalism. And in an effort to support his argument, he put together a range of medieval sources that introduced a tradition of antikabbalism into premodern Judaism. *Ari Nohem* was, in this respect, an astonishingly ambitious work, and a formidable challenge to the cultural revolution of Kabbalah.

Modena went to great lengths to invent an intellectual genealogy for his criticism of Kabbalah. He pointed to critical statements about Kabbalah in the work of medieval jurists and exegetes. He collated oppositional statements to the public teaching of Jewish esotericism in the writings of Moses Isserles and Solomon Luria, sixteenth-century rabbinic authorities in Poland, into a systematic rejection of Kabbalah. Repeatedly he pointed to Elijah Delmedigo, a fifteenth-century philosopher from Crete and tutor to Pico della Mirandola, as an important precedent for his own work.[37] But Modena's intense search for intellectual antecedents should not obscure the genuine innovation of his own work. While some may have uttered critical statements about Kabbalah and others may have opposed its dissemination, no one had ever written a sustained and comprehensive critique. In contrast to his predecessors—those he mentioned as well as those he neglected—Modena cast his own polemical net over a much wider area.[38] In terms of the range of issues it addresses and the critical approach

---

[36] On Hamiz as Modena's prized student, see *Letters*, 346; Nehemiah S. Libowitz, *Seridim mi-kitve ha-filosof ha-rofe veha-mekubal Yosef Hamits* (Jerusalem: Darom, 1937).

[37] Elijah Delmedigo, *Sefer Behinat ha-Dat*, ed. Jacob J. Ross (Tel Aviv: Tel Aviv University Press, 1984).

[38] Modena did not mention Isaac Polgar, Elijah Levita, or Judah Messer Leon. See Carlos del Valle, "La critique de la Qabbale chez Isaac ibn Polgar," in *Expérience et écriture mystique dans les religions du livre*, ed. Paul B. Fenton and Roland Goetschel, 131–141 (Leiden: Brill, 2000); Jordan S. Penkower, "A Renewed Inquiry into the *Sefer Masoret ha-Masoret* of Elijah

it adopts, *Ari Nohem* far outstrips the few disparaging comments in Elijah Delmedigo's *Behinat ha-Dat* or the passing remarks about the popularization of esotericism by Moses Isserles and Solomon Luria. To a certain degree, one can find precedent for many of Modena's criticisms in medieval and early modern Jewish thought. And Modena himself ransacked the rabbinic bookshelf to find as many such precedents as he could. But no single work before *Ari Nohem* offered a compelling alternative theory of the origins of the *Zohar*, a response to the appropriation of Kabbalah by non-Jews, a defense of Maimonides as a rationalist philosopher, and an attack on Safed Kabbalah. Furthermore, the range of sources Modena employed to make his case—kabbalistic texts as well as chronicles, letters, legal codes, and philosophical tracts—displayed a level of critical engagement with Kabbalah that was entirely new. The counterrevolutionary had closely studied the revolution.

JEWISH MYSTICISM AND JEWISH MODERNITY

In this book I attempt to reconstruct Modena's criticism of Kabbalah as a product of seventeenth-century Venice. I seek to answer a basic question in the study of early modern Jewish history: what did it mean to oppose Kabbalah in the very period when it had come to dominate Jewish life? To do so, I position the history of ideas within the study of written texts as material objects. I examine Modena's substantive criticism of Kabbalah, his analysis of the *Zohar*, its authorship and its reception, his rejection of the myth of Isaac Luria, his objection to the appropriation of Kabbalah by leading Christian theologians, and his attempt to resurrect Maimonides as a cultural hero and intellectual model. At the same time, I place Modena's criticism in its bibliographic context. Drawing on a historical model developed by Ann Blair, I reconstruct the "total history" of a single text in order to study Modena as a reader and as read.[39] I integrate Modena's annotation of printed books and manuscripts, as well as his reading extracts in his notebooks and letters, into an analysis of his ideas about Kabbalah. I pay careful attention to the medium in which Modena's ideas circulated in his lifetime and in the years after his death. As with the case of Jean Bodin's *Theater of all of Nature* studied by Blair, the production and consumption of

---

Bahur" (Hebrew), *Italia* 8 (1989): 7–73; Simha Assaf, "From the Storehouses of the Library in Jerusalem" (Hebrew), in *Minhah le-David: Sefer ha-Yovel le-David Yelen*, 226–28 (Jerusalem: Weiss, 1935).

[39] Ann Blair, *The Theater of Nature: Jean Bodin and Renaissance Science* (Princeton: Princeton University Press, 1997) 9. See also James A. Secord, *Victorian Sensation: The Extraordinary Publication, Reception, and Secret Authorship of "Vestiges of the Natural History of Creation"* (Chicago: University of Chicago Press, 2000).

Modena's *Ari Nohem* were tied so closely together that attempts to separate them analytically inevitably break down; however, in contrast to Bodin's book, which was printed in the late sixteenth century, Modena's *Ari Nohem* did not appear in print in an early modern edition, a fact that had enormous consequences for the book's history. *Ari Nohem* continued to circulate in manuscript both during Modena's lifetime and after his death until its first appearance in print in the nineteenth century.[40] In the very period that Kabbalah had shifted from closed to open knowledge, criticism of Kabbalah had become esoteric.

This book argues that Modena and later readers of *Ari Nohem* used what has been characterized as a fundamentally medieval medium—the manuscript—to promote a precociously modern position—historical and philosophical skepticism about the origins and religious significance of Kabbalah. Using the history of *Ari Nohem* as a case study, this book seeks to challenge a series of scholarly orthodoxies about the nature of modern Judaism and the critical study of Kabbalah; at the same time, it seeks to intervene in current historiographic debates about the relationship between print and manuscript and the cultural life of seventeenth-century Venice.

Inevitably these concerns bring up a still larger question: the origins of Jewish modernity.[41] Scholars have pointed to the eighteenth-century Jewish Enlightenment (Heb. *Haskalah*) as the beginning of a self-conscious and critical Jewish modernity.[42] Alternatively they have discovered a sharp break in attitudes toward the Jewish past among nineteenth-century practitioners of the Science of Judaism (*Wissenschaft des Judentums*).[43] In particular, they point to the use of philology and history to reflect upon the nature of the past as a fundamental break from prior attitudes. Whether

---

[40] Leon Modena, *Ari Nohem*, ed. Julius Fürst (Leipzig: K. Tauchnitz, 1840). A second edition appeared as *Ari Nohem*, ed. Nehemiah S. Libowitz (Jerusalem: Darom, 1929).

[41] Salo W. Baron, "Ghetto and Emancipation: Shall We Revise the Traditional View?" *Menorah Journal* 14 (1928); Michael A. Meyer, "Where Does the Modern Period of Jewish History Begin?" *Judaism* 24 (1975): 329–38; Jacob Katz, ed. *Toward Modernity: The European Jewish Model* (New Brunswick, NJ: Transaction Books, 1987); Gershon David Hundert, *Jews in Poland-Lithuania in the Eighteenth Century: A Genealogy of Modernity* (Berkeley: University of California Press, 2004); Moshe Rosman, *How Jewish Is Jewish History?* (Oxford: Littman Library, 2007), chap. 2.

[42] Michael A. Meyer, *The Origins of the Modern Jew: Jewish Identity and European Culture in Germany, 1749–1824* (Detroit: Wayne State University Press, 1967); Jonathan M. Hess, *Germans, Jews and the Claims of Modernity* (New Haven: Yale University Press, 2002); Shmuel Feiner, *The Jewish Enlightenment* (Philadelphia: University of Pennsylvania Press, 2004).

[43] Leon Wieseltier, "*Etwas über die jüdische Historik*: Leopold Zunz and the Inception of Modern Jewish Historiography," *History and Theory* 20 (1981): 135–49; Yosef Hayim Yerushalmi, *Zakhor: Jewish History and Jewish Memory* (New York: Schocken Books, 1989), 81–103; Ismar Schorsch, *From Text to Context: The Turn to History in Modern Judaism* (Hanover, NH: Brandeis University Press, 1994); Michael Brenner, *Prophets of the Past: Interpreters of Jewish History* (Princeton: Princeton University Press, 2010).

one points to the eighteenth-century *Haskalah* or nineteenth-century *Wissenschaft des Judentums* as the point of origin for modern Judaism, a critical stance toward Kabbalah marks a common feature.[44] This rejection of Kabbalah often goes hand in hand with the resurrection of Maimonides' *Guide of the Perplexed*.[45]

Jewish intellectuals at the turn of the nineteenth century used new literary forms—the essay, the monograph, and the periodical—to make their arguments; furthermore, they celebrated the new and trumpeted their own novelty, offering satirical portraits of their predecessors and railing against the obscurantism of the rabbinic elite. In their works, their own forerunners in prior centuries appear either as intellectual outliers or as isolated precursors of the enlightened modernity that they themselves ushered in with such great fanfare. Modern scholars have tended to mirror the claims of their sources: the insistence upon a radical break with the past that participants in the Jewish Enlightenment claimed for themselves has been accepted as historically accurate. One scholar has gone so far as to compare the impact of the Jewish Enlightenment on the Jews with that of the French Revolution on Europe.[46] In short, modern Judaism begins with a fundamental discontinuity with the past.

This book challenges this scholarly emphasis on rupture as characteristic of the turn toward the modern. Several of the elements that ostensibly constitute modern Judaism are clearly present in Modena's treatment of Kabbalah in the early seventeenth century: a critical attitude toward sacred texts and their origins, a skepticism about received wisdom and doctrine, and an acute awareness of the difference between the Jewish past and the Jewish present. Modena's desacralization of Kabbalah, his historicization of the *Zohar* as a text written in the Middle Ages, his rejection of Isaac Luria as a mythmaker and miracle worker, and his turn to Maimonides' *Guide*

---

[44] On Moses Mendelssohn's attitude toward Kabbalah, see Alexander Altmann, *Moses Mendelssohn: A Biographical Study* (Philadelphia: JPS, 1973), 11–12; Altmann, introduction to Moses Mendelssohn, *Jerusalem, or, on Religious Power and Judaism*, trans. Allan Arkush (Hanover, NH:Brandeis University Press, 1983), 22. For a revisionist view, see Rivka Horwitz, "Kabbalah in the Writings of Mendelssohn and the Berlin Circle of Maskilim," *LBIYB* 45 (2000): 3–24. On Kabbalah among nineteenth-century scholars, see Gershom Scholem, "Reflections on Modern Jewish Studies (1944)," in *On the Possibility of Jewish Mysticism in Our Time and Other Essays*, ed. Avraham Shapira, 51–71 (Philadelphia: JPS, 1997).

[45] James H. Lehmann, "Maimonides, Mendelssohn, and the Me'asfim: Philosophy and the Biographical Imagination in the Early Haskalah," in *LBIYB* 20 (1975): 87–108; Jay Harris, "The Image of Maimonides in the Nineteenth-Century Jewish Historiography," *PAAJR* 54 (1987): 117–39; Allan Nadler, "The 'Rambam Revival' in Early Modern Jewish Thought: Maskilim, Mitnagdim, and Hasidim on Maimonides' *Guide of the Perplexed*," in *Maimonides after 800 Years: Essays on Maimonides and His Influence*, ed. Jay M. Harris, 231–56 (Cambridge: Harvard University Press, 2007).

[46] Feiner, *The Jewish Enlightenment*, 1.

prefigure some of the most significant developments of modern Jewish intellectual history.

In highlighting these factors, I do not wish to argue that modern Judaism originated in the ghetto of Venice or to cast Modena as the first modern Jew. Rather I seek to contest a historiographic focus on rupture that has resulted in a caricature of early modern Jewish intellectuals. Like other figures in the early seventeenth century, Modena subjected the received wisdom of his day to careful scrutiny. His precariously situated critical sensibility had far-reaching consequences. *Ari Nohem* offers a telling and distinctly Jewish example of the marriage between textual criticism and religious dissent that characterized so much of European intellectual life in the early seventeenth century. Whether or not one relies on a historical model of crisis for this period, European intellectuals in the decades before and after Modena wrote *Ari Nohem* subjected almost all certitudes—religious, theological, scientific—to sustained skepticism.[47] The products of their thought were electrifying. By the time Modena composed *Ari Nohem*, his slightly elder contemporary Isaac Casaubon (1559–1614) had demolished the antiquity of much of Renaissance ancient theology. Casaubon proved that the Sibylline oracles and the Hermetic corpus were late antique forgeries rather than works contemporary to the Bible.[48] Modena's *Ari Nohem* did much the same for the core texts of Kabbalah, the Jewish component of ancient theology. When viewed cumulatively, Casaubon's and Modena's work stripped many of the core texts that had constituted ancient theology in the Renaissance of their pretensions to antiquity. Modena's contemporary in Venice, Paolo Sarpi, also challenged a series of received ideas about the history of the Catholic Church and the institution of the papacy. Sarpi dissented from traditions and practices that had become canonical, and he did so in the form historical accounts and reflections on religion.[49] Modena, who may have known Sarpi, and who excerpted his *History of the Council of Trent* in his notebooks, turned to a historical account of Kabbalah as a means of opposing the dominant and newly accepted traditions of Venetian Jews. Modena's skepticism had genuine limits. For all his sophistication as a reader and for all the intellectual archeology he performed on

---

[47] On crisis and the seventeenth century, see "*AHR* Forum: The General Crisis of the Seventeenth Century Revisited," *American Historical Review* 113 (2008); and "The Crisis of the Seventeenth Century: Interdisciplinary Perspectives," *Journal of Interdisciplinary History* 40 (2009). On early modern skepticism, see Richard H. Popkin, *The History of Scepticism: From Savonarola to Bayle* (New York: Oxford University Press, 2003).

[48] Anthony Grafton, *Defenders of the Text: The Traditions of Scholarship in an Age of Science, 1450–1800* (Cambridge: Harvard University Press, 1991), chaps. 5 and 6.

[49] Gaetano Cozzi, *Paolo Sarpi tra Venezia e l'Europa* (Turin: G. Einaudi, 1978); David Wootton, *Paolo Sarpi:Between Renaissance and Enlightenment* (Cambridge: Cambridge University Press, 1983).

Kabbalah, he never submitted the Bible to the same scrutiny as he did the *Zohar*. *Ari Nohem* was many things, but it was not Spinoza's *Theological-Political Treatise*.

In positing *Ari Nohem* as a Jewish exemplar of early modern skepticism, I follow contemporary scholarship on early modern history that rejects a view of modernity as single moment of rupture.[50] Modena did not seek to argue for something new or to celebrate secularization. He thought of himself as a defender of tradition, a tradition he identified with the spiritualized rationalism of Maimonides and the *Guide of the Perplexed*. In fact, his argument was fundamentally conservative insofar as he saw in Kabbalah a late development and an excrescence that tainted the original state of philosophical excellence exemplified by the *Guide*. He desperately hoped to preserve the patterns of knowledge transmission that had been eroded by the spread of Kabbalah and by the printing of Jewish law infected with kabbalistic teachings. But the arguments made in *Ari Nohem* about the origins of Kabbalah were repeatedly reconfigured in the ensuing three and a half centuries. Modena and later readers of his work who criticized Kabbalah did so in traditional literary forms—polemics, letters, and rabbinic responsa—rather than in monographs or essays, the genres that would come to dominate critical scholarship. Here again, comparison with Casaubon and Sarpi proves instructive. For all of the intellectual innovation of his criticism, Casaubon's debunking of the Hermetic forgeries appeared in a theological tome written as part of a polemic against a Catholic cardinal. Sarpi's innovative thinking about the possibility of a secular society appeared in notebooks on religion that circulated in manuscript only among his close associates. The generic conventions that effectively constituted and contained their work and Modena's should not obscure its intellectual ingenuity. The story told here thus contrasts with most narratives about the origins of modern Judaism: it turns out to be less a story of rupture than one of reconfiguration.[51]

THE HISTORY OF THE BOOK AND THE HISTORY OF VENICE

In addition to reconsidering existing scholarly traditions on the origins of modern Judaism, my study of Modena contributes to current debates about the history of written culture in the early modern period. The history of the book, a mode of inquiry that examines the material history of written

---

[50] Grafton, *Defenders of the Text*, introduction; Jay M. Harris, *How Do We Know This? Midrash and the Fragmentation of Modern Judaism* (Albany: SUNY Press, 1995), chap. 5; Guy G. Stroumsa, *A New Science: The Discovery of Religion in the Age of Reason* (Cambridge: Harvard University Press, 2010), 1–13.

[51] Lorraine Daston and Peter Galison, *Objectivity* (New York: Zone Books, 2007), 10.

culture, has transformed the study of early modern Europe.[52] Bibliographic analysis has been linked to contemporary concerns about the instability of texts and the mobility of meaning. Within this growing field of cultural history, scholars debate the historical impact of the invention of print. This book takes up the call by Adrian Johns to write a cultural history of print rather than a history of print culture.[53] Breaking with the assumption that certain properties such as dissemination, standardization, and fixity inhere in the technology of printing and constitute something called print culture, Johns argued that one should attempt to address the history of printing at a local level: to trace the histories of reading through the reconstruction of specific reading practices and the histories of individual texts. Crucially for this study, early modern historians have pointed to the persistence of manuscript production and circulation well into the so-called age of print. A localized cultural history of print must account for the composition and circulation of manuscripts at a given center of early modern printing.

Building upon these arguments, I reposition the history of *Ari Nohem* at the juncture between print and manuscript. The story of Modena's book—both its composition and its later circulation—offers a vivid example of the persistence of manuscript production well into the age of print.[54] It also offers important evidence about the history of printing itself. In emphasizing manuscripts for the historical reconstruction of printing, scholars have pointed to discrepancies between manuscript and printed versions of the same text or to the manuscripts used by correctors in print shops. As a work that circulated in manuscript, *Ari Nohem* offers crucial evidence about the cultural history of printing. Modena assessed the impact of printing on the transmission of Jewish culture particularly in terms of Kabbalah and Jewish law. Although his judgment was highly polemical, his argument reflected careful attention to the material form in which a given text circulated in his own time.[55]

---

[52] Robert Darnton, "'What Is the History of Books?' Revisited" *Modern Intellectual History* 4 (2007): 495–508; Andrew Pettegree, *The Book in the Renaissance* (New Haven: Yale University Press, 2010).

[53] Adrian Johns, *The Nature of the Book: Print and Knowledge in the Making* (Chicago: University of Chicago Press, 1998); Joseph A. Dane, *The Myth of Print Culture: Essays on Evidence, Textuality, and Bibliographical Method* (Toronto: University of Toronto Press, 2003).

[54] Harold Love, *The Culture and Commerce of Texts: Scribal Publication in Seventeenth-Century England* (Amherst: University of Massachusetts Press, 1998); Brian Richardson, *Manuscript Culture in Renaissance Italy* (Cambridge: Cambridge University Press, 2009).

[55] Modena's contemporaries Johannes Kepler and Francis Bacon were also interested in the cultural consequences of print. On Kepler, see Nicholas Jardine, *The Birth of History and Philosophy of Science: Kepler's "A Defence of Tycho against Ursus"* (Cambridge: Cambridge University Press, 1984). On Bacon, see Julian Martin, *Francis Bacon, the State, and the Reform of Natural Philosophy* (Cambridge: Cambridge University Press, 1992).

While Modena was keenly aware of the power of the printed word, many of his own writings, particularly his polemical works, circulated in manuscript throughout the early modern period. This phenomenon was hardly unique to Modena and constitutes a principal feature of written culture in early modern Venice.[56] For a number of reasons—fear of censorship, threat of persecution, desire to maintain proximity to a reader—an author might articulate a given argument in manuscript rather than in print. Modena understood print as a public medium that he could not completely control; he wanted to proclaim his arguments, but not too loudly. Had *Ari Nohem* appeared in print, Modena would almost certainly have been ostracized within the Jewish community. Modena may also have been afraid of censorship. Two years before he wrote *Ari Nohem*, his vernacular summary of Jewish rites, the *Riti Ebraici*, had appeared in Paris. When Modena learned of its publication, he submitted a manuscript of his work to the Venetian Holy Office for review. A second edition appeared in Venice the following year with several alterations. Manuscripts offered a hedge between the public embrace of a controversial position and the impossibility of silence. In this sense *Ari Nohem* provides the most elaborate example of a wider phenomenon: throughout the period under consideration here, most sustained criticism of Kabbalah circulated in manuscript rather than in print.[57]

Comparison between Modena and Isaac Luria on this account proves particularly revealing. Although separated by over half a century and half the Mediterranean—Modena was born in Venice the year before Luria died in Safed—both authors had remarkably similar literary profiles. Modena had one print persona—preacher, anthologist, translator, lexicographer, and apologist—and another manuscript identity—polemicist against Christianity, critic of Kabbalah, memoirist for his family, and alleged practitioner

---

[56] Marino Zorzi, "Dal manoscritto al libro," in *Storia di Venezia*, ed. Ugo Tucci and Alberto Tenenti, 4:817–958 (Rome: Giovanni Treccani, 1996); Federico Barbierato, *Nella stanza dei circoli: Clavicula Salomonis e libri di magia a Venezia nei secoli XVII e XVIII* (Milan: S. Bonnard, 2002); Filippo de Vivo, *Information and Communication in Venice: Rethinking Early Modern Politics* (Oxford: Oxford University Press, 2007).

[57] See the discrepancy between manuscript and printed versions of Joseph Solomon Delmedigo's "Ahuz Letter." A shorter version lacking critical comments on Kabbalah appeared in *Sefer Elim* (Amsterdam: Menasseh ben Israel, 1629). A longer version circulated in manuscript and appeared in Abraham Geiger, *Melo Chofnajim* (Berlin, 1840), 1–28, Hebrew section. For doubts on the authenticity of the longer version, see David B. Ruderman, *Jewish Thought and Scientific Discovery in Early Modern Europe* (New Haven: Yale University Press, 1995), 146–52. For confirmation, see Jordan S. Penkower, "S. D. Luzzatto, Vowels, and Accents and the date of the *Zohar*," in *Samuel David Luzzatto: The Bi-Centennial of his Birth*, ed. Robert Bonfil, Isaac Gottlieb, and Hannah Kasher (Jerusalem: Magnes Press, 2004), 128. For another instance of criticism of Kabbalah in manuscript, see William Horbury, "Judah Briel and Seventeenth-Century Jewish Anti-Christian Polemic in Italy," *JSQ* 1 (1993–1994): 171–92.

of pseudepigraphy. Luria in print, the Luria that Modena subjected to such merciless criticism in *Ari Nohem*, was a miracle worker, a healer, a divine oracle; but Luria in manuscript was a theologian of enormous intellectual reach. His students jealously guarded his theological writings and refused to allow them into circulation. Modena knew of some of these writings, as his discussion of Isaiah Horowitz and Christian Kabbalah makes clear, but he probably had not read them.

I examine print and manuscript as complementary to one other rather than in opposition; the invention of one technology did not replace an existing one. Here too, rupture fails to capture the relationship between the past and the present. The evidence surveyed in this book demonstrates that the boundaries between manuscript and print were as untidy chronologically as they were commercially, materially, and socially.[58] A historiographic preoccupation with the new has served to undermine and obscure long-term continuities, in this case the production and circulation of manuscripts, that can actually illuminate moments of transformation as they occurred. Manuscripts in an age of print—modern manuscripts—possess considerable significance for the historical reconstruction of how intellectuals worked, how ideas circulated, and how knowledge was produced. They offer crucial evidence for understanding the ways in which these intellectuals themselves thought about technologies they understood to be new. Only in the age of print could a manuscript take on meaningful significance as a distinct medium of communication suited to a particular set of ideas. The new hardly replaced the old: print endowed manuscripts with a cultural importance they had never had and imbued them with a sense of secrecy that retained enormous power to subvert the printed word.[59]

Accounts of early modern Venice usually focus on the sixteenth century as the apogee of Venetian culture and dismiss the seventeenth century as an era of slow but inevitable decline. This book draws on the cultural history of the Jews to challenge this decline-and-fall narrative.[60] Modena may have been the most important critic of Kabbalah in the Venetian ghetto, but he was hardly the only Venetian Jew to analyze his own society with great care. His colleague in the rabbinate Simone Luzzatto defended the political and economic privileges of Venetian Jewry in a vernacular treatise written the

---

[58] David McKitterick, *Print, Manuscript, and the Search for Order, 1450–1830* (Cambridge: Cambridge University Press, 2003).

[59] Jon R. Snyder, *Dissimulation and the Culture of Secrecy in Early Modern Europe* (Berkeley: University of California Press, 2009).

[60] For recent studies that draw on other areas of Venetian culture to make a similar claim, see Barbierato, *Nella stanza dei circoli*; Vivo, *Information and Communication in Venice*; and Edward Muir, *The Culture Wars of the Late Renaissance: Skeptics, Libertines, and Opera* (Cambridge: Harvard University Press, 2007).

year before *Ari Nohem*.⁶¹ Luzzatto's *Discorso* included a profile of contemporary Jewish knowledge that recast a medieval typology of three kinds of Jewish scholars: Talmudists, philosophers, and kabbalists.⁶² Luzzatto wrote about Kabbalah without Modena's polemical edge—hardly surprising in a printed work addressed to the Venetian Doge and Senate—but he reflected on it as a social force of considerable consequence in Venetian Jewish life. Moreover he analyzed it with critical distance, pointing to parallels between the sefirot and the Neoplatonic emanations and invoking Pico's interest in Kabbalah. For all their differences, Luzzatto and Modena were at the height of their analytical powers in the early decades of the seventeenth century, and Kabbalah was of primary importance to both of them.⁶³ The presence of these figures in Venice indicates that the decline in the cultural life of the city may not have been as precipitous or as universal as has hitherto been assumed. Historians have long pointed to a shift in creative activity away from the visual arts and toward the natural sciences and music in seventeenth-century Venice. The Jewish ghetto must be added to the opera box and the academies as a site of enduring cultural vitality.⁶⁴

A NEW FIGURE: THE CULTURAL CRITIC

Leon Modena is hardly an obscure personality in the annals of early modern Venice or Jewish history.⁶⁵ One of the most articulate of early modern Jews, Modena wrote in a number of genres on a wide range of subjects.

---

⁶¹ Simone Luzzatto, *Discorso circa il stato de gl'Hebrei et in particolar dimoranti nell'inclita città di Venetia*, ed. Riccardo Bachi (Bologna: A. Forni, 1976); Luzzatto, *Ma'amar al Yehude Venetsyah*, trans. Dan Lattes (Jerusalem: Mossad Bialik, 1950); Benjamin C. I. Ravid, *Economics and Toleration in Seventeenth Century Venice: The Background and Context of the Discorso of Simone Luzzatto* (Jerusalem: American Academy of Jewish Research, 1978).

⁶² Luzzatto, *Ma'amar al Yehude Venetsyah*, 137–48. On the typology, see Robert Bonfil, "A Cultural Profile," in Davis and Ravid, *The Jews of Early Modern Venice*, 169–90.

⁶³ See Ruderman, *Early Modern Jewry*, 2–5.

⁶⁴ H. G. Koenigsberger, "Decadence or Shift? Changes in the Civilization of Italy and Europe in the Sixteenth and Seventeenth Centuries," in *Estates and Revolutions: Essays in Early Modern European History* (Ithaca: Cornell University Press, 1971). On opera and the academies, see Wendy Heller, *Emblems of Eloquence: Opera and Women's Voices in Seventeenth-Century Venice* (Berkeley: University of California Press, 2003); Muir, *The Culture Wars*.

⁶⁵ Howard Ernest Adelman, "Success and Failure in the Seventeenth Century Ghetto of Venice: The Life and Thought of Leon Modena, 1571–1648," Ph.D. diss., Brandeis University, 1985; Talya Fishman, *Shaking the Pillars of Exile: 'Voice of a Fool,' an Early Modern Jewish Critique of Rabbinic Culture* (Stanford: Stanford University Press, 1997); Cristiana Facchini, "Una insinuante modernità: Note su Leone Modena e l'ebraismo nel seicento, Rassenga bibliografica," *Annali di storia dell'esegesi* 19 (2002): 467–97; David Malkiel, ed., *The Lion Shall Roar: Leon Modena and His World* (Jerusalem: Magnes Press and Ben-Zvi Institute, 2003).

Born in Venice in 1571, he spent much of his early life in northern Italian towns such as Ferrara, Cologna da Veneto, and Montagnana. But apart from later periods in Ferrara and Florence, Modena lived in Venice for almost the entirety of his adult life.[66] At the time of his wedding in 1590, he was invested by the Venetian rabbinate with the title of *haver*, the first stage on his way to rabbinic ordination, which he earned in 1609 at the ripe age of thirty-eight.[67] Over the next four decades, Modena served as one of several rabbis to the multiple congregations that constituted the early modern Jewish community of Venice. He also worked as secretary to the rabbinate, taught in the schools, sang as a cantor, issued legal decisions, and preached in the synagogues. In spite of the prestige he may have accrued from his apprenticeship and later participation in the institutional life of the Venetian rabbinate, Modena was quite miserable as a rabbi. Communal power among the Jews in early modern Venice lay with the wealthy merchants, not with the learned clergy. Venetian rabbis did not receive a fixed salary but were paid a fee for each of the services they performed. Modena eked out an unstable livelihood from his various rabbinic duties as well as a range of other jobs such as proofreader in print shops and private tutor. His literary works brought him some measure of fame as well as a small supplement to his income.

Upon Modena's death in 1648, his grandson Isaac Levi collected his papers and prepared several of his works for publication. Beleaguered by conflict with the leaders of the Venetian Jewish community and beset by a rapidly declining Hebrew press in Venice, Levi was unsuccessful in his attempts to print them.[68] Levi's organization and care of Modena's papers in the years after his death, however, played a crucial role in the preservation of Modena's literary legacy. Nearly all of Modena's polemical writings—on Christianity, the soul, Kabbalah, and rabbinic Judaism—as well his correspondence and his annotated books survived owing to Levi's efforts. The attempt by a relative, usually a son, to preserve the written remains of a deceased scholar was hardly new. The annals of Jewish history are replete with figures whose writings survive largely due to the efforts of their family. Levi's concern for Modena's legacy, however, went beyond the demands

---

[66] For an account of Modena's life, see Howard E. Adelman, "Leon Modena: The Autobiography and the Man," in *Autobiography*, 19–49. For a biography of his early life, see Ellis Rivkin, "Leon da Modena: Part I," Ph.D. diss., Johns Hopkins University, 1946. To the best of my knowledge, Rivkin never wrote the second half of Modena's biography as he outlined in the introduction to his thesis; for Rivkin's later work, see his "The Sermons of Leon da Modena," *HUCA* 23 (1950–1951): 295–317; *Leon da Modena and the 'Kol Sakhal'* (Cincinnati: HUC Press, 1952).

[67] On the early modern Italian rabbinate, see Robert Bonfil, *Rabbis and Jewish Communities in Renaissance Italy* (Oxford: Littman Library, 1990).

[68] Isaac Levi, *Medaber Tahpukhot*, ed. Daniel Carpi (Tel Aviv: Tel Aviv University Press, 1985).

of filial piety and approached the level of contemporary European scholars and scientists who went to great lengths to establish collections and archives of their teachers and mentors.[69]

Scholarship on Leon Modena over the last two centuries has been dominated by the discussion of two works—his autobiography, *Hayyei Yehudah* (*The Life of Judah*), and a pseudepigraphic critique of rabbinic culture, *Kol Sakhal* (*The Voice of a Fool*). Modena's autobiographical journal, composed at discrete intervals in the final decades of his life, recounts the financial and familial tribulations he faced after the death of his eldest son Mordecai in 1617 due to injuries sustained in alchemical experiments.[70] Written with arresting clarity and genuine pathos, *Hayyei Yehudah* offers a rare glimpse into the interior life of an early modern Jew. The combination of Modena's literary ability and the genuine scarcity of early modern Jewish autobiographies has attracted numerous scholars to the work.[71] For all the lurid details it offers about Modena's gambling habits, dysfunctional marriage, and failing health, *Hayyei Yehudah* offers little if any insight into his thought. In an attempt to understand Modena's mind, scholars have repeatedly turned to *Kol Sakhal*, a pseudepigraphic criticism of rabbinic culture Modena may have written.[72] *Kol Sakhal* offers a scathing criticism of rabbinic power, a mocking description of the precepts of Jewish law, and a blueprint for legal reform. Much of the scholarship on *Kol Sakhal* has dwelt on the question of the text's authorship.[73] Although a welter of circumstantial evidence points to Modena as the author, this cannot be established with absolute certainty.

---

[69] Michael Hunter, ed., *Archives of the Scientific Revolution: The Formation and Exchange of Ideas in Seventeenth-Century Europe* (Rochester: Boydell Press, 1998); Ingo Herklotz, *Cassiano dal Pozzo und die Archäologie des 17. Jahrhunderts* (Munich: Hirmer Verlag, 1999). See also the collected studies on the cultural history of archives in *Archival Science* 7 (2007).

[70] Leon Modena, *Hayyei Yehudah*, ed. Daniel Carpi (Tel Aviv: Tel Aviv University Press, 1985); Modena, *Autobiography*.

[71] Some have sought to cast it as the beginnings of a Jewish autobiographical tradition, and others have cautioned against attributing such an impact to a text hardly known before the nineteenth century. See the discussion in Marcus Moseley, *Being for Myself Alone: Origins of Jewish Autobiography* (Stanford: Stanford University Press, 2006), 103–47.

[72] The Hebrew text first appeared in Isaac S. Reggio, ed., *Behinat ha-Kabalah: Kolel Sefer Kol Sakhal ve-Sefer Sha'agat Aryeh* (Gorizia: Joh. Bapt. Seitz, 1852). For an annotated English translation and discussion of the literature between Reggio's edition and the late twentieth century, see Fishman, *Shaking the Pillars of Exile*. For work since, see Howard Adelman, "Leon Modena, *Homo Ludens*, and *Kol Sakhal*" (Hebrew), in *The Lion Shall Roar*, ed. Malkiel, 91–105; Omero Proietti "'La Voce di De Acosta [=431]' sul vero autore del Qol Sakhal," *RMI* 70 (2004): 33–54; David Sorotzkin, "The Timeless Community in an Age of Change: The Emergence of Conceptions of Time and the Collective as the Basis for the Development of Jewish Orthodoxy in Early Modern and Late Modern Europe" (Hebrew), Ph.D. diss., Hebrew University, 2007.

[73] Fishman, *Shaking the Pillars of Exile*, 5–8.

In the event that Modena was indeed the author of *Kol Sakhal*, his criticism of Kabbalah in *Ari Nohem* poses a basic question: how could the author of a pseudepigraphic attack on rabbinic culture criticize the *Zohar* as pseudepigraphic? The attribution of a text to one Amitai bar Yedaiah ibn Raz in 1500 differs quite substantially from the attribution of a book to Simeon bar Yohai, a second-century sage who appears throughout rabbinic literature as the author of legal opinions and the subject of extraordinary stories. Furthermore, the author of *Kol Sakhal* planted a series of clues that a careful reader could use to decipher its date of composition; if Moses de Leon and his colleagues had inserted a similar set of signals to their readers when they composed the *Zohar*, these hints had been lost to all but the most discerning of readers by the seventeenth century. Modena's contemporaries treated the *Zohar* as the product of rabbinic antiquity and elevated the text into a normative source of the law. Finally, *Kol Sakhal* and the *Zohar* had radically opposed cultural trajectories in the early modern period. *Kol Sakhal* was copied by Modena and again by his grandson, but the work did not circulate widely before the nineteenth century.[74] By contrast, the *Zohar* had appeared in print multiple times over the course of the early modern period and became a foundational text of Jewish culture.

Within the context of Modena's life, *Ari Nohem* was a late work.[75] But it was not a work of late style. It represents the culmination of Modena's criticism that had been mounting for several decades to a culture dominated by Kabbalah rather than an abrupt change in his opinion.[76] It was hardly an accident, however, that Modena wrote *Ari Nohem* as a man of sixty-eight. Modena had an acute sense of intellectual entitlement that had not been well served by his perpetual struggles for status and money. The Venetian rabbinate had hardly been a profession that enabled him to pursue his writing in comfort. He had watched in jealous anger as kabbalists had taken

---

[74] For the possibility that Saul Berlin (1740–1794) read it in manuscript, see ibid., 172–74.

[75] For references to *Ari Nohem* in Modena's writings, see *Autobiography*, 153. A manuscript that contains several pages of Modena's notes includes an excerpt from Elijah Delmedigo's *Behinat ha-Dat* copied in Modena's hand. Following this excerpt appears a short note: "After this I composed a long treatise against this sect [the kabbalists], I called it *Ari Nohem*." See Milan, Ambrosiana MS Q 139 Sup, 52A; *Sefer Behinat ha-Dat*, ed. Ross, 15. In responsum number 131 dated to 1645, Modena wrote: "For this wisdom [Kabbalah] ... is very distant from me, as I have explained the reason at great length in a treatise that I composed which I called *Ari Nohem*." Leon Modena, *She'elot u-Teshuvot Ziknei Yehudah*, ed. Shlomo Simonsohn (Jerusalem: Mossad ha-Rav Kook, 1956), 177; hereafter *Ziknei Yehudah* followed by number of responsum and page number. On this responsum, see Don Harrán, "*Nomina Numina*: Final Thoughts of Rabbi Leon Modena on the Essence of Sacred Music," *Italia* 17 (2006): 7–63. For reference to Harrán's earlier studies on Modena and music see 8, n. 4.

[76] See *Ziknei Yehudah*, no. 35, 50–52; for his opposition to the discussion of Kabbalah in public sermons in a text composed in 1625, see responsum in ibid., no. 55, 76–78. A substantial portion of this responsum appears in English in Marc Saperstein, *Jewish Preaching 1200–1800: An Anthology* (New Haven: Yale University Press, 1989), 406–7.

over his community and his mantle of intellectual authority. They were the ones who had combined charisma and learning while Modena had been pushed to the margins. From these margins he took up a new position, unpaid and not very prestigious, but one that allowed his wrath to pour forth in cantankerous and controlled prose. He became a critic.

Modena's criticism and its subsequent history constituted some of the very ruins evoked by Scholem at the outset of *Major Trends in Jewish Mysticism*, ruins that Scholem himself recovered with such magnificent and ruthless efficiency in the construction of his own narrative. *Ari Nohem* and its history were profoundly inconvenient to the integrity of Scholem's story.[77] It undercut two of the central and contradictory claims upon which he built his scholarly edifice: the marginality of Kabbalah and its ostensible neglect as the subject of critical inquiry. Scholem was of two minds about the place of Kabbalah within Judaism: at times he insisted upon Kabbalah as a vibrant but subterranean force within Jewish history; at other times he insisted on its absolute centrality. But he was piercingly clear about its neglect as an academic subject before he wrote his doctoral dissertation on *Sefer ha-Bahir*.[78]

The monumentality of Scholem's achievement renders suspect any discussion of Kabbalah that does not account for the originality of his work. From the most particular details of analytic bibliography to the historical reconstruction of complex ideas, no one can treat Kabbalah without confronting Scholem. One of his rare and revealing comments about Moses Cordovero—"he had the gift of transforming everything into literature"— could easily be said of his own work.[79] The scope of Scholem's historiographic vision was matched and even exceeded by the power of his prose. For all the assaults on Scholem's narrative, both in his own lifetime and in

---

[77] Scholem was remarkably silent about *Ari Nohem*. He mentioned Modena in passing in his lecture, "Did Moses de Leon Compose the Book of the *Zohar*?" (Hebrew), *Madaei ha-Yahadut* 2 (1925/1926): 16. He used *Ari Nohem* for evidence about a reputed student of Luria's in Venice in the late sixteenth century and acerbically referred to Modena as "this enemy of Kabbalah." See "Israel Sarug, a Student of the *Ari*?" (Hebrew), *Zion* 5 (1940): 224. And he responded to a bibliographic question posed by Nehemiah Libowitz, editor of the second edition of *Ari Nohem*. See *Ari Nohem*, ed. Libowitz, 157. Though a copious annotator of his own books, Scholem only lightly annotated his copy of Libowitz's edition of *Ari Nohem*. Most of his annotations pointed to texts Modena had read in manuscript. See *Ari Nohem*, ed. Libowitz, number 8855.3 in the Scholem Library at the JNUL. On Scholem and silence see Gary Smith, "'Die Zauberjuden': Walter Benjamin, Gershom Scholem, and other German-Jewish Esoterics between the World Wars," *JJTP* 4 (1995): 237–38.

[78] *Das Buch Bahir* (Leipzig: W. Drugulin, 1923). On the circumstances of its appearance in print, see Lou H. Silberman, "Scholem to Eisler on the Publication of *Das Buch Bahir*," *Studies in Bibliography and Booklore* 16 (1986): 5–12; as cited in Saverio Campanini, "Some Notes on Gershom Scholem and Christian Kabbalah," *Sefer zikaron le-Gershom Scholem bi-mlot esrim ve-hamesh shanim le-petirato*, ed. Joseph Dan, 2:15 (Jerusalem: Hebrew University, 2007).

[79] *Major Trends in Jewish Mysticism*, 249.

the decades since his death, his work endures in no small measure because of his ability to transform Kabbalah into literature. Scholem may well have been the greatest mind to study Kabbalah, but he was hardly the first. In using the history of *Ari Nohem* to challenge Scholem's scholarly self-presentation, I wish to be clear about what I am not doing: Modena was not Scholem in Baroque Venice. In one of his late pieces, Scholem perceptively pointed to Reuchlin as his intellectual ancestor.[80] Scholem may not have been a kabbalist, as he repeatedly insisted, but like Reuchlin before him he was clearly sympathetic to Kabbalah. For all his insight, Modena lacked such sympathy.

This book is divided into three sections: the first examines Modena as writer; the second, Modena as reader; and the third, Modena as read.

Chapter 1 positions Modena's writing practices within the context of early modern Venice, capital of Hebrew printing and center of manuscript production. Drawing on a range of unexamined sources, this chapter points to the collaborative nature of Modena's writing. Through the reconstruction of Modena's relationship with his grandson Isaac Levi, who served as his amanuensis in the final two decades of his life, I locate the writing of *Ari Nohem* as the product of their joint efforts, a working relationship that was typical among intellectuals—Jewish and Christian—in northern Italy in the early seventeenth century.

Chapters 2 and 3 examine Modena as a reader of medieval Jewish texts, the *Zohar* and the *Guide of the Perplexed*. Chapter 2 studies Modena's historicization of the *Zohar* as the work of Moses de Leon in medieval Castile rather than Simeon bar Yohai in Roman Palestine. Modena objected to the elevation of the *Zohar* as a source of legal and cultural authority; his criticism of the ancient origins of the work was an attempt to deflate its newly acquired status rather than a wholesale rejection of its contents. If Modena sought to counter the prestige of one medieval work, the *Zohar*, he also attempted to revitalize that of another, the *Guide of the Perplexed*. Chapter 3 examines Modena's attempt to reclaim Maimonides from his kabbalistic critics and admirers. I argue that many of Modena's most important positions in *Ari Nohem*—his understanding of tradition, his rejection of kabbalistic theology, and his attack on kabbalistic hermeneutics—were informed by his reading of Maimonides.

Chapters 4 and 5 reconstruct Modena's reactions to two important phenomena in early modern Kabbalah: the renaissance in Safed and the study of Kabbalah by Christians. Chapter 4 uses *Ari Nohem* to document the

---

[80] "Die Erforschung der Kabbala von Reuchlin bis zur Gegenwart," in *Judaica III: Studien zur jüdischen Mystik* (Frankfurt: Suhrkamp Verlag, 1973), 247. On this passage, see Campanini, "Some Notes on Gershom Scholem and Christian Kabbalah," 2:14.

transmission of Kabbalah from Safed to Venice and examines Modena's indictment of this transfer of knowledge and practice. I trace Modena's criticism through his reaction to the growing cult of personality around Isaac Luria and his detailed response to one of the most significant theological treatises composed in Safed, Moses Cordovero's *Pardes Rimonim*. Chapter 5 examines Modena's outrage at the appropriation of Kabbalah by Christians, particularly Pico della Mirandola. It examines Modena's effort to separate Christian Kabbalah from Jewish theology and to redefine Kabbalah as a uniquely Jewish realm of thought (here, too, the anticipation of Scholem's idea of Jewish mysticism as an authentically Jewish contribution to the history of religion is striking).

Chapters 6 and 7 study Modena's work as it was read by later scholars. Chapter 6 traces the circulation of *Ari Nohem* in manuscript from its composition through its first appearance in print. The different stages in the reception of *Ari Nohem* in manuscript offer an alternative history of Kabbalah in the seventeenth and eighteenth centuries, one that has largely been told through the histories of Sabbatianism and Hasidism. Chapter 7, by contrast, reconstructs the competing efforts of a group of scholars in the early nineteenth century, including Isaac Reggio, Solomon Rosenthal, and Julius Fürst, to print the first edition of *Ari Nohem*. It turns to the mixed reception given to the work by two nineteenth-century kabbalists, Elijah Benamozegh and Isaac Haver Wildmann. This later history of *Ari Nohem* points to the significance of Kabbalah as an issue of urgent concern to a broad range of Jewish intellectuals in the nineteenth century.

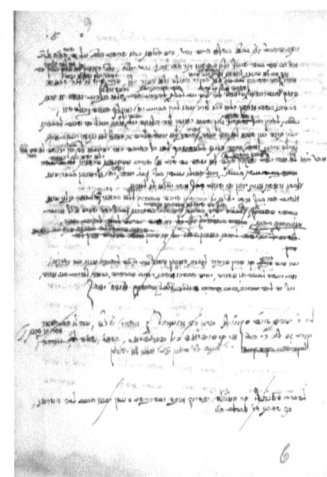

CHAPTER ONE

Hebrew Manuscripts in an Age of Print

> The three forms of literary study brought together in the making of this book might be thought to create a kind of trinity. But if so, it must be said at once that the doctrine of the literary trinity is Arian, not Athanasian. The father is bibliography, the spirit is context, but close reading is only the son. It is a later, dependent, and subordinate activity which can be practiced with safety only within the boundaries marked out for it by its senior colleagues.
> —David Womersley

> Laborants, operators, artificers, and servants did different things in making Boyle's science. Yet they had one characteristic very much in common: they were largely invisible.... The historical problem is therefore twofold: one wants to document and to clarify the significance of technicians' work, yet one also wants to explain why it was that they were largely transparent to the gaze of those who employed them—how and why, that is, such a fundamental distinction was made between the value of what they did and what their masters did, between their invisibility and their employers' authority.
> —Steven Shapin

Figure 1 (previous page). A page from Modena's copybook.
© The British Library Board. MS Or. 5395, 5a.
Modena's copybook from the late 1630s contains rough drafts of letters, poems, and responsa. A diagonal line through a letter indicates that it had been sent.

LEON MODENA was well aware of the difficulties and the consequences of turning a text from a manuscript into a printed book.¹ Over the course of his life, he had arranged for the printing of his own books, worked as an editor at Venetian printing houses, and composed approbations to the works of his colleagues and students. He was also highly conscious of the importance of being printed. The extensive list of his own writings that appeared in his autobiography focused largely on his writing in print.² In a section of his notebooks from the 1630s, he attempted to organize every Hebrew book within six different categories. This list, an illuminating exercise in the organization of knowledge, consisted only of printed books.³ Yet this same writer composed a series of works in the last several decades of his life that circulated exclusively in manuscript during his own lifetime and in the centuries after his death. These were all of a polemical nature: *Ben David*, a refutation of the transmigration of souls; *Magen ve-Zinah*, a response to criticism of the Oral Torah; and *Magen va-Herev*, a polemic against Christianity unfinished at the time of his death in 1648.⁴ Additionally, *Kol Sakhal* circulated exclusively in manuscript in this period.

In the winter of 1639, at age sixty-eight, Modena completed his Hebrew polemic against Kabbalah. Although he continued to update the list of his writings in his own manuscript of *The Life of Judah*, Modena did not add *Ari*

---

¹ Benjamin Ravid, "The Prohibition against Jewish Printing and Publishing in Venice and the Difficulties of Leone Modena," in *Studies in Medieval Jewish History and Literature*, ed. Isadore Twersky, 135–53 (Cambridge: Harvard University Press, 1979).

² *Autobiography*, 122–28.

³ Ancona, Communità Israelitica, MS 7, 5A–7B. The categories were legal decisions, biblical exegesis, homiletics, miscellaneous and grammar, philosophy and wisdom, and Kabbalah. On this manuscript as Modena's notebook, see Isaiah Sonne, "Leon Modena and the Da Costa Circle in Amsterdam," *HUCA* 21 (1948): 15, n. 29. For a description, see Simonsohn, Introduction, in *Ziknei Yehudah*, 16, n. 36; *Autobiography*, 270. Consulted on microfilm reel F 2532 at the JNUL.

⁴ For the first printing of *Ben David*, see Eliezer Ashkenazi, ed., *Ta'am Zekenim* (Frankfurt: Kauffmann, 1854), 61A–64B. For *Magen ve-Zinah*, see Abraham Geiger, *Leon da Modena, Rabbiner zu Venedig (1571–1648), und seine Stellung zur Kabbalah, zum Thalmud und zum Christenthume* (Breslau: J. U. Kern, 1856), 1A–10B (Hebrew section). Excerpts from *Magen va-Herev* appeared in the same volume, 10B–14A (Hebrew section). Later editions include Lou H. Silberman, "The Magen V'Hereb of R. Judah Aryeh of Modena (Leon Da Modena) Codex De Rossi 1141 with an Introductory Essay," Doctorate of Hebrew Letters, HUC, 1943; Leon Modena, *Magen va-Herev*, ed. Shlomo Simonsohn (Jerusalem: Mekize Nirdamim, 1960). Cf. Allen Howard Podet, *A Translation of the Magen wa-Hereb by Leon Modena, 1571–1648* (Lewiston, NY: Mellen Press, 2001).

Nohem or any of his other polemical writings to this list. In another passage of his autobiography, he somewhat wistfully remarked that *Ari Nohem* "was never printed."[5] When juxtaposed with other evidence from Modena's own writings and from those of his colleagues in northern Italy, this comment indicates that Modena had hoped to see *Ari Nohem* appear in print in his own lifetime. Irrespective of his hopes, however, more than two centuries would elapse between the composition of *Ari Nohem* and its initial printing.

The circumstances of Modena's life as well as the cultural world of early modern Venice offer some context for why *Ari Nohem* did not appear in print in the seventeenth century. This chapter, which situates the production of *Ari Nohem* within the written culture of Venice in the early seventeenth century, compares Modena's writing practices to those of contemporary Jewish and Christian intellectuals in Venice and the Veneto. The first section argues that the notion of an author's autograph fails to account for the collaborative nature of Modena's writing practices in the final decades of his life. In seventeenth-century Venice, masters and disciples frequently composed and copied works in tandem. Toward the end of Modena's life, his grandson Isaac Levi (known as Yitzhak min Haleviyyim) functioned as something of a personal secretary. Modena and Levi appear to have collaborated on the composition and copying of *Ari Nohem*.

The second section focuses on the importance given to material form within Modena's actual argument in *Ari Nohem*. Venetian writers and readers preferred manuscript books to printed ones for works on a whole range of subjects, especially religious polemics. The use of a manuscript for a work such as *Ari Nohem* was entirely in keeping with larger trends among Venetian intellectuals, Jewish and Christian. The difference between manuscript and print not only informs Modena's immediate working environment, it also functions as a crucial part of his argument. As a work of criticism *Ari Nohem* reflected upon the transmission of Jewish tradition, particularly the transmission of esoteric information and the principles of Jewish law. Modena argued that the printing of legal and kabbalistic books had effected a radical change in the transmission of Jewish tradition, a change that he decried in no uncertain terms at several points. *Ari Nohem* polemicized against one medium, print, in the form of another, manuscript.

SCRIBAL CULTURES IN SEVENTEENTH-CENTURY VENICE

Scholars have highlighted the continuous and persistent production of manuscripts throughout the early modern period. Intellectual historians, literary critics, and material bibliographers have jettisoned any notion of

[5] *Autobiography*, 153.

printing and the printed book as having replaced the production and circulation of manuscripts.[6] Printed books and manuscript books circulated in persistent tension among the same communities of readers and writers. When faced with different options for the circulation of their works, early modern writers found that print and manuscript held different advantages. Publication, however, could occur in either medium.[7] The term "author's autograph" as used by modern scholars might refer to several different types of texts within the phenomenon of scribal publication. A working copy describes a draft of a text that an author kept in his or her possession and continued to work on for a period. A manuscript for circulation indicates that the writer had authorized the text to circulate and that the text may differ from a working copy in layout and punctuation. The crucial point for this study has to do with the nature of an author's autograph. In order for the term to carry any meaning, the writing practices of the author in question must be reconstructed. In Modena's case, enough evidence survives that facilitates the reconstruction of his writing practices in extensive if only partial detail.

In addition to the term "autograph," a second issue raised by historians of the book is particularly relevant to Modena and *Ari Nohem*. Scholars have emphasized that authors might be reluctant to print a given text for a number of reasons. First, out of caution, authors might not print a work. The contents of a text might be scandalous, seditious, or prohibited, and its appearance in print might jeopardize the reputation or safety of an author, publisher, or printer. Second, an author might want to keep a closer connection between his or her text and its intended reader. While a manuscript might not offer a foolproof medium for ensuring this connection, it could ensure this relational proximity with far greater certainty than a printed book. Third, early modern authors of a particular class had contempt for printing as a process that corrupted the text, a phenomenon referred to as the stigma of print.[8] Finally, cost might have been too prohibitive to justify the printing of a given work. Modena does not seem to have felt the stigma of print, but his autobiography and responsa offer ample evidence that cost proved to be a major obstacle in his efforts to print his own work.[9] Modena may have wanted to print *Ari Nohem* in his own lifetime; however, the expense of printing, the controversial contents of the work, and the desire to maintain a closer hold on his readers all appear to have played crucial

---

[6] H. R. Woudhuysen, *Sir Philip Sidney and the Circulation of Manuscripts, 1558–1640* (Oxford: Clarendon Press, 1996); McKitterick, *Print, Manuscript, and the Search for Order*.

[7] Love, *The Culture and Commerce of Texts*, 35–89.

[8] J. W. Saunders, "The Stigma of Print: A Note on the Social Bases of Tudor Poetry," *Essays in Criticism* 1 (1951): 139–64.

[9] *Ziknei Yehudah*, no. 108a, 157. See also *Autobiography*, 141.

roles in the continued circulation of the work as a manuscript rather than a printed book.

Modena lived in one of the great centers of early modern printing.[10] Scholars have noted that in the fifteenth century more books were printed in Venice than in any other city in Europe. In the sixteenth century, over half of all books printed in Italy were printed at Venetian presses. Through the early seventeenth century, Venice was by far the most important center of Hebrew printing. Less well known is that during this same period, Venice was home to a thriving scribal culture or, more precisely, intersecting scribal cultures. Over the last several decades, scholars have called attention to the continuous composition and circulation of manuscripts in early modern Venice.[11] When viewed in aggregate, their work demonstrates that early modern Venice was a flourishing center for the production and circulation of manuscripts as well as printed books.

While a historical profile of written culture in early modern Venice is beyond the scope of this study, a sketch of some of the ways Venetians used manuscripts in the sixteenth and seventeenth centuries will facilitate greater precision in situating Modena's writing practices. In the sixteenth century, Venice was the principle market for Greek manuscripts in Europe. European diplomats as well as Venetians themselves employed ateliers of scribes to copy Greek manuscripts at the same time that the city served as the principle center for Greek printing.[12] If inexpensive labor costs enabled the copying of Greek manuscripts, the news industry depended upon handwritten newsletters to avoid surveillance and to increase the speed with which political and military information was disseminated.[13] Venice, one of

---

[10] Paul F. Grendler, *The Roman Inquisition and the Venetian Press, 1540–1605* (Princeton: Princeton University Press, 1977); Martin Lowry, *The World of Aldus Manutius: Business and Scholarship in Renaissance Venice* (Ithaca: Cornell University Press, 1979); Bronwen Wilson, *The World in Venice: Print, the City, and Early Modern Identity* (Toronto: University of Toronto Press, 2005); Lisa Pon and Craig Kallendorf, eds., *The Books of Venice* (Venice: La Musa Talìa, 2009).

[11] Dorit Raines, "Office Seeking, *Broglio*, and the Pocket Political Guidebooks in *Cinquecento* and *Seicento* Venice," *SV* 21 (1991): 137–94; Zorzi, "Dal manoscitto al libro"; Brendan Dooley, *The Social History of Skepticism: Experience and Doubt in Early Modern Culture* (Baltimore: Johns Hopkins University Press, 1999); Federico Barbierato, "Tra attori e inquisitori: Manoscritti, commedia dell'arte e diffusione delle conoscenze magiche nella Venezia del seicento," in *I luoghi dell'immaginario barrocco*, ed. Lucia Strappini (Naples: Liguori, 2001); Vivo, *Information and Communication in Venice*.

[12] Paul Canart, "Jean Nathanaël et le commerce des manuscrit grecs à Venise au XVIe siècle," in *Venezia centro di mediazone tra Oriente e Occidente (secoli XV–XVI) aspetti e problemi*, ed. Hans-Georg Beck, Manoussos Manoussacas, and Agostino Pertusi, 2:417–38 (Florence: L. S. Olschki, 1977).

[13] Dooley, *The Social History of Skepticism*, 9–44; Peter Burke, "Early Modern Venice as a Center of Information and Communication," in *Venice Reconsidered: The History and Civilization of an Italian City-State, 1297–1797*, ed. John Martin and Dennis Romano, 389–419 (Baltimore: Johns Hopkins University Press, 2000).

the great hubs of information in the early modern Mediterranean, did not have regular printed newsletters until the end of the seventeenth century.[14]

In addition to the manuscript trade in political information, texts about a variety of subjects circulated almost entirely in manuscript as their readers and writers struggled to avoid detection by religious and political authorities. The records of the Inquisition offer ample evidence of the circulation of magical texts such as the *Clavicula Salomonis* (The Lesser Key of Solomon) at the turn of the seventeenth century.[15] Attributed to King Solomon and supposedly rediscovered by Babylonian priests in the early centuries of the common era, this work of demonology contained magical secrets that enabled its readers to effect medical cures. Readers of the *Clavicula Salomonis*, including agents of the Inquisition, occasionally turned to local Jews for assistance in interpreting them.[16] In this period Venice was home to several erudite libertines who satirized the Roman curia as well as the sexual mores of their Venetian compatriots. Figures such as Ferrante Pallavicino (1618–1644) circulated scatological novellas in manuscript or printed them under false imprints.[17]

Manuscripts served as the preferred medium not only for subversive texts about magic and sex, but also for potentially seditious works about religion and politics. Several of the most distinguished intellectuals in Venice and the Veneto at the turn of the seventeenth century restricted a considerable portion of their writings to manuscript. Partially as a response to Pietro Pomponazzi's 1516 treatise *On the Immortality of the Soul*, early modern Italian intellectuals repeatedly reflected on the nature of the soul.[18] Cesare Cremonini (1550–1631), a professor of natural philosophy at the University of Padua and colleague of Galileo, expressed his most controversial philosophical positions in manuscript and remained quite cautious in his printed work.[19] Suspected of denying the immortality of the soul, he was investigated on several occasions by the Inquisition. Cremonini's suggestion that

[14] Mario Infelise, "Le marché des information à Venise au 17e siècle," in *Gazettes et information politique sous l'Ancien Régime*, ed. Henri Duranton and Pierre Rétat, 117–28 (Saint Etienne: Université de Saint-Etienne, 1999).

[15] Barbierato, *Nella stanza dei circoli*.

[16] Dorit Raines, "Judaism in the eyes of the Venetian Patriciate in the Time of Leon Modena" (Hebrew), in Malkiel, *The Lion Shall Roar*, 41. Asher Lemlin and Gedalya ibn Yahya knew of this work. See Moshe Idel, "The Magical and Neoplatonic Interpretations of the Kabbalah in the Renaissance," in *Jewish Thought in the Sixteenth Century*, ed. Bernard Dov Cooperman (Cambridge: Harvard University Press, 1983), 194.

[17] Muir, *The Culture Wars*, 106. For a Jewish text from later in the seventeenth century concerning sexual conduct and Kabbalah that did not appear in print, see Roni Weinstein, *Juvenile Sexuality, Kabbalah, and Catholic Reformation in Italy: "Tiferet Bahurim" by Pinhas Barukh ben Pelatiyah Monselice* (Leiden: Brill, 2009), 115–27.

[18] Ernst Cassirer, Paul Oskar Kristeller, and John H. Randall Jr., eds., *The Renaissance Philosophy of Man* (Chicago: University of Chicago Press, 1948), chap. 5; Martin L. Pine, *Pietro Pomponazzi: Radical Philosopher of the Renaissance* (Padua: Antenore, 1986).

[19] Muir, *The Culture Wars*, 13–60.

the soul could not survive without the body did not appear in print and was confined to manuscript.[20]

Paolo Sarpi was also suspected of rejecting the immortality of the soul.[21] A theological consultant to the Venetian government during the Papal Interdict of 1606–1607, Sarpi wrote *A History of the Council of Trent*, which was printed in London in 1619.[22] Over the course of his life, Sarpi kept a series of notebooks that recorded his thoughts on philosophical and religious themes. These *Pensieri*, as the manuscript notebooks were called, provide evidence of Sarpi's theories about the possibility of a secular society. A society that "could survive even if people did not believe that anti-social behavior would meet with divine punishment, even if people were 'atheists' who denied the existence of a providential God."[23]

Modena was well aware of Sarpi's *A History of the Council of Trent*, a work he excerpted in his notebooks and cited at an early point in his polemic against Christianity.[24] A comparison between their respective writing practices can help illuminate the composition of *Ari Nohem*. Sarpi may have confined his most controversial social theories to manuscript, but he composed them in tandem with an assistant. The *Pensieri sulla religione* survive in a manuscript copy written by an amanuensis with autograph corrections by Sarpi himself.[25] Indeed, numerous intellectuals in northern Italy, Jewish and Christian, composed their work in tandem with an amanuensis. In addition to Sarpi, Menahem Azariah da Fano (ca. 1548–1620), a leading kabbalist and rabbinic authority in northern Italy at the turn of the seventeenth century who features prominently in *Ari Nohem*, also worked with an assistant. He wrote hand in hand with his student and colleague Isaac Levi of Mantua.[26] In one instance, Isaac Levi of Mantua copied out a

---

[20] Nicholas Davidson, "Unbelief and Atheism in Italy, 1500–1700," in *Atheism from the Reformation to the Enlightenment*, ed. Michael Hunter and David Wootton (Oxford: Clarendon Press, 1992), 76. On Cremonini's manuscripts, see Maria Assunta Del Torre, *Studi su Cesare Cremonini: Cosmologia e logica nel tardo aristotelismo padovano* (Padua: Antenore, 1968).

[21] Wootton, *Paolo Sarpi*, 20–23, 41.

[22] Noel Malcolm, *De Dominis (1560–1624): Venetian, Anglican, Ecumenist and Relapsed Heretic* (London: Strickland and Scott, 1984), 55–60.

[23] Wootton, *Paolo Sarpi*, 5, 13–38.

[24] Ancona, Communità Israelitica, MS 7, 63A; as cited by Adelman, "Leon Modena," 26, n. 56. Modena referred to Sarpi as "my friar" and noted that his *History* was printed in London. See also Modena, *Magen va-Herev*, 12; as cited by Fishman, *Shaking the Pillars of Exile*, 21. In both instances, Modena cited Sarpi on Adam and original sin.

[25] On the transmission of Sarpi's *Pensieri filosofici e scientifici*, see Luisa Cozzi, "La tradizione settecentesca dei "Pensieri" Sarpiani," *SV* 13 (1971): 393–450; as cited by Wootton, *Paolo Sarpi*, 14, n. 1.

[26] To be distinguished from Modena's grandson Isaac Levi, who lived in Venice. See Joseph Avivi, "The Writings of Ari in Italy Up to the Year 1620" (Hebrew), *Alei Sefer* 11 (1984): 110; Avivi, "The Writings of R. Menahem Azariah da Fano on the Wisdom of Kabbalah" (Hebrew), *Sefunot* 4, 19 (1988): 355–56.

draft of his work, Menahem Azariah da Fano corrected the draft with annotations in the margin, and Isaac Levi of Mantua transferred his teacher's marginal corrections to a second manuscript copy of the same work. Another leading kabbalist in northern Italy and a relative of Modena's, Aaron Berekhya reported that his book *Magen Aharon* had been stolen while his student was in the midst of making a copy.[27] The literary production of these figures demonstrates that manuscript books and printed books existed in tandem with one another. All of them printed books in their own lifetime and wrote books that circulated in manuscript within limited circles of readers. Moreover they frequently wrote with amanuenses whose work was largely invisible in the seventeenth century.[28]

LEON MODENA AND ISAAC LEVI

The lives of Modena and Isaac Levi similarly demonstrate the coterminous production of works in print and manuscript. Reconstructing the relationship between Modena and his grandson offers a crucial perspective on Modena's writing practices and methods of composition in the final two decades of his life.[29] In their case family relationships and professional interests closely overlapped. Modena's daughter Diana had married Jacob Levi, a scholar and kabbalist, in the summer of 1613. Modena and his son-in-law fought bitterly over the value of Kabbalah and the authorship of the *Zohar*. In *Nahalat Ya'akov*, completed before 1620, Levi attempted to respond to his father-in-law's doubts about Kabbalah.[30] Although it did not appear in print, Levi's work circulated in Modena's circle.[31] As mentioned throughout *Ari Nohem*, Modena wrote his own polemic partially in response to his son-in-law's oral and written arguments about Kabbalah. In the spring of 1621, Levi became father to a son named Isaac. Despite their disagreements about Kabbalah, Modena felt extremely close to Levi and repeatedly described him as "a son-in-law of perfect virtues."[32] After the

---

[27] Isaiah Tishby, "The Conflict between Lurianic Kabbalah and Cordoverian Kabbalah in the Writings and Life of R. Aaron Berekhya of Modena" (Hebrew), in *Hikre Kabbalah u-sheluhoteha*, 1:208.

[28] Steven Shapin, "The Invisible Technician," *American Scientist* 77 (1989): 554–63.

[29] On Modena's earlier attitudes toward writing, see *Lev ha-Aryeh* (Venice: G. Sarzina, 1612).

[30] Moshe Hallamish, "A Document Concerning a Controversy about Kabbalah in Italy in the Early Seventeenth Century" (Hebrew), *Bar-Ilan* 22–23 (1987): 181.

[31] For evidence that Hamiz had read it, see *Ari Nohem*, MS A 5B, 22, ed. Libowitz, 2. For a list of manuscripts of *Ari Nohem*, see the works cited section of this book. Unless otherwise noted, all citations to *Ari Nohem* include a reference to the text as it appears in MS A and in *Ari Nohem*, ed. Nehemiah Libowitz (Jerusalem: Darom, 1929). MS A consulted on microform reel F 48694 at the JNUL.

[32] *Autobiography*, 132; Introduction, in *Ziknei Yehudah*, 3.

death of Modena's son Zebulun in 1622, Diana and Jacob Levi went to live with Modena and his wife, a domestic arrangement that lasted for over three years. When Isaac Gershon, a rabbi who had served as a preacher in the Ashkenazi synagogue, left Venice in the fall of 1625, Modena and Jacob Levi took over his duties and shared the task of delivering sermons.[33] In the summer of 1629, Jacob Levi died from a plague that had led to over a hundred deaths in the Jewish ghetto.[34]

Jacob Levi's death played a crucial role in fostering the relationship between Modena and his grandson. Shortly thereafter, Diana and her eight-year-old son Isaac returned to Modena's home. Three years later, Diana married a second time. Upon his mother's remarriage, Isaac continued to live with his grandfather while his mother went to live with her new husband. Modena took charge of his grandson and developed a keen interest in his education. Isaac, orphaned of his father, turned to his grandfather as a surrogate; Modena, who had seen two of his sons die and another leave Venice for the New World, looked to his grandson as his legacy.[35]

A text Modena composed in 1633 points to this closeness and offers a crucial perspective on his writing practices. More than thirty years earlier, a wealthy Levantine Jewish merchant named Joseph Pardo had commissioned Modena to produce an anthology of biblical commentaries. Pardo had asked Modena to compile the anthology from thirty printed volumes of biblical exegesis he had placed at his disposal.[36] After having completed a portion of the work, Modena lost the commission because of his gambling habit.[37] In the early 1630s Modena returned to it and prepared a short preface to the extant portion. He described the state of his rough draft in elaborate detail and indicated the precise nature of his grandson's copying:

> The aforementioned four portions remained in my possession, written down as when they had first left my pen, filled with erasures and illegible letters as is a writer's wont. More than one thing had been drawn from one of several books, that is to say, it was truly impossible to understand anything.... Until in the summer of 1632 that just passed, I called my grandson, my daughter's son Isaac, may the Lord protect him and preserve him, and I gave them to him. And I commanded him to copy them in such a way as to facilitate their being read. And the youth was young,[38] and copied them in such a way that the eye of

---

[33] *Autobiography*, 129.
[34] Ibid., 243.
[35] Carpi, "Introduction" (Hebrew), in *Medaber Tahpukhot*, 10.
[36] *Autobiography*, 101.
[37] Modena lists the pericope *Bereshit*, *Pinhas*, *Mattot*, and *Masei*. He also completed *Balak*. See ibid., 208.
[38] I Sam. 1:24.

one who reads them will behold the youthful work, but it is [now] possible to understand them.[39]

This preface concludes with Modena's signature and a date of 12 Shevat 5393 (23 January 1633).

Modena's description of his draft as filled with errors, erasures, and corrections echoed a comment made by Isaac Levi in a colophon he included in the same manuscript:

> And I, with the voice of thanksgiving, will sacrifice to the One[40] who granted me the merit to copy out the explanation of this holy portion, which was composed by his eminence, my master and teacher,[41] the crown upon my head,[42] my elder, may God his Rock protect him in His commandment. [I copied] it from the work of his own hand, filled entirely with erasures, illegible letters, and corrections as is the way of writers. I finished it on Sunday, the fifth day of Elul, 5392.[43]

Written six months before his grandfather's preface, Levi's summary of his task included an identical description of Modena's writing.

Modena's draft copy of his anthology of biblical commentaries does not appear to have survived; however, a copybook he used over a two-year period to prepare drafts of his letters, poems, and responsa is still extant.[44] The texts prepared in this copybook match Modena's description of the rough draft he had prepared of his anthology. Phrases are crossed out, individual letters or whole words have been erased, and considerable portions of the text are almost illegible. Letters that had been recopied and sent to their intended recipient bear a long diagonal line through them and a note indicating they had been sent. (See figure 1.) Responsa extant in this copybook were copied out into another manuscript containing all of Modena's responsa. Modena had prepared his rough draft of the anthology in 1601. The copybook with drafts of his letters, poems and responsa dates from the late 1630s. For much of his life Modena maintained a consistent writing practice: he would prepare a rough draft of a text, heavily edit it, and have it copied out by an assistant onto another manuscript.

In his copy of Modena's anthology, Levi's colophon concludes with the following prayer: "Thus the Lord shall grant me the merit to copy out from the remainder of his [Modena's] compositions and his wisdom for

---

[39] Oxford, Bodleian Library, Canon Misc. 204, 170B; Adolf Neubauer, "Quelques notes sur la vie de Juda Léon de Modène," *REJ* 22 (1891): 83; Mark R. Cohen, "Who Wrote the Ambrosiana Manuscript of *Hayyei Yehudah*?" in *Autobiography*, 286. Date as given in Cohen.

[40] Jon. 2:10.

[41] Abbreviated as *mem vav*, which I have taken as *mori ve-rabi*.

[42] II Sam. 1:10.

[43] August 23, 1632. Oxford, Bodleian Library, Canon Misc. 204, 159A.

[44] London, British Library, MS Or. 5395. See Yacob Boksenboim, "Introduction" (Hebrew), in *Letters*, 1–7.

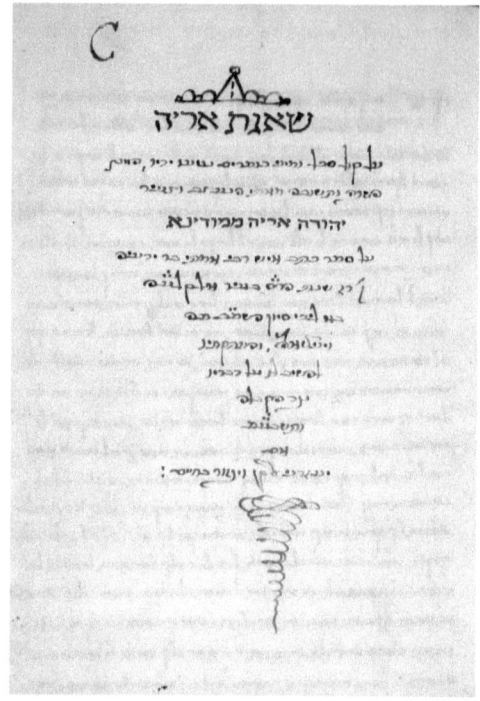

Figure 2. Title page to *Sha'agat Aryeh* copied by Leon Modena.
Parma, Biblioteca Palatina, MS Parma 2238, 5a.
Reproduced by permission of the Ministero per i Beni e le Attività Culturali.
The title page to Modena's response to *Kol Sakhal* in his own copy.

they increased in his life.... These are the words of the small and young mosquito, Isaac, son of the esteemed master and teacher, Jacob son of Kalonymous ha-Levi, may the righteous be remembered for a blessing."[45] When Isaac was all of eleven years old, he had already formulated a plan to copy out all of his grandfather's writings.

For the rest of Modena's life and well after his death, Levi remained deeply involved with his grandfather's literary production. About two years after instructing him to copy the anthology, Modena introduced Levi to printing "so that he would learn to derive benefit from working with his hands in a clean and easy craft and, at the same time, not desist from his studies."[46] Levi worked as a Hebrew editor at the Vendramin press, one of the few houses in Venice that employed Jews continually throughout

---

[45] Oxford, Bodleian Library, Canon Misc. 204, 159A; Boksenboim, "Introduction," 4. Isaac also composed a short colophon at the conclusion of the portion on *Mattot*. See 137B.

[46] *Autobiography*, 141.

Figure 3. Title Page to *Sha'agat Aryeh* copied by Isaac Levi.
New York, Library of the Jewish Theological Seminary, MS 10611, 2a.
Courtesy of the Library of the Jewish Theological Seminary.
The title page to Modena's response to *Kol Sakhal* copied by Isaac Levi from his grandfather's copy.

the seventeenth century.[47] At the press, Levi served as editor for Modena's *Bet Yehudah*, a supplement to Jacob ibn Habib's *Ein Ya'akov* designed as a reference aid for preachers printed in 1635.[48] At the conclusion of the work, Isaac included a short note: "If there are many mistakes in the first and second sections of the work, reader do not be shocked.... Apart from the many troubles experienced during printing, the composition of the printed letters was achieved entirely by one young in years and light in wisdom.

---

[47] Ravid, "The Prohibition against Jewish Printing," 145.

[48] Ten years earlier Modena printed *Bet Lehem Yehudah*, an annotated index to the rabbinic sayings in *Ein Ya'akov*, referred to as *Ein Yisrael* in seventeenth-century Italy. On the variation in title, see *Autobiography*, 226. Modena's work was intended as a thematic finding aid for preachers who drew upon Ibn Habib's collection of nonlegal Talmudic passages. In contrast, *Bet Yehudah* listed additional Talmudic passages that had not been included in *Ein Ya'akov* and was organized by tractate rather than theme. See Bezalel Safran, "Leone da Modena's Historical Thinking," in Twersky and Septimus, *Jewish Thought in the Seventeenth Century*, 392–98.

I am fourteen years of age on this day, Isaac of the Levites ... son of the esteemed author's daughter."[49] Over ten years later, Levi returned to this work and used it as the basis of his own *Ma'ase Hakhamim*. Printed in 1646, this pamphlet collected passages from *Ein Ya'akov* and Modena's *Bet Yehudah* and arranged them with Rashi's commentary.[50]

Levi moved back and forth between printer and scribe, an uncommon phenomenon among contemporary gentiles. Five years after having edited *Bet Yehudah*, Levi copied *Sha'agat Aryeh* and *Kol Sakhal* from Modena's own copy.[51] His transcription presents a fair copy of the manuscript prepared by his grandfather. Thus an interlinear annotation at the end of chapter 3 of the second part of *Kol Sakhal* in Modena's copy was incorporated into the body of the text in Levi's.[52] This pattern repeats itself throughout Levi's copy of *Kol Sakhal*. In Modena's copy a sequence of three passages at the beginning of chapter 5 appears out of order and a series of marginal notes indicates the correct order; in Levi's copy the three passages have been arranged in correct sequential order.[53]

In late February 1648, less than one month before his death, Modena completed a will whose central subject was the bequest of his literary remains: "I have no wealth or riches in my home ... my everlasting gift is my written work."[54] His grandson played a leading role: "At the end of the first month following my death, I direct my grandson Isaac Levi, may God his Rock protect him and grant him long life, to assemble all my writings and compositions and those by others than myself, and separate the Hebrew ones from those in Italian, under my curse lest he overlook anything, even one page."[55] Modena charged Levi with dividing his Italian writings into four lots and assigning them to different people, including one portion for himself. Levi served both as a primary literary executor and a primary literary heir. With some significant exceptions, Modena's Hebrew writings were bequeathed entirely to Levi. In his will Modena had stipulated that two of his Hebrew works in manuscript—his polemic against Christianity

---

[49] Leon Modena, *Bet Yehudah* (Venice: Vendramin, 1635), 48B. See Moritz Steinschneider, *Catalogus Librorum Hebraeorum in Bibliotheca Bodleiana*, facsimile edition (Hildesheim: Georg Olms, 1964), 1349.

[50] For a similar disclaimer about his own work, see Isaac Levi, *Ma'ase Hakhamim* (Venice: Bragadin, 1646), 22A.

[51] Fishman, *Shaking the Pillars of Exile*, 172–74. Levi's copy of *Kol Sakhal* formerly in the possession of the London Beth Din is now New York, JTS, MS 10611.

[52] For Modena's copy, see Parma, Biblioteca Palatina, Codex de Rossi 85 (Parma MS 2238), 22A, lines 20 and 21. For Levi's, see New York, JTS, MS 10611, 19B.

[53] Parma, Biblioteca Palatina, Codex de Rossi 85 (Parma MS 2238), 23A–23B; New York, JTS, MS 10611, 20B–21A.

[54] *Autobiography*, 174–76. The will includes several dates; the final one is February 24, 1648. Modena died on March 21, 1648. For Modena's earlier will, see the epilogue.

[55] *Autobiography*, 175. Translation slightly modified.

and his notebooks—should be given to Moses Luzzattin.[56] Levi's largely successful effort to make his own copies of these two manuscripts testifies to his continued involvement with his grandfather's literary estate after his death. These copies provide vital evidence about his habits as an adult scribe, such as his use of catchwords, signature marks, and overall handwriting. They also offer important clues to his involvement in the transcription of *Ari Nohem*.

Like his grandfather, whom he sought to emulate in so many ways, Levi composed an autobiography. In this work he recounts that Luzzattin had loaned him "a manuscript book" written by Modena shortly after his grandfather's death. Luzzattin had given him the book on condition that he not give it to anyone else. Upon learning that Levi had let Modena's book out of his possession, Luzzattin accused him of violating their agreement. Levi's autobiography includes a long and often confusing justification written in the third person of his loss of Modena's manuscript. Essentially Levi accused Modena's son, also named Isaac, of stealing it from him. According to Levi, the proceeds from the sale of Modena's possessions after his death had been split between his two living daughters, Diana and Esther. Shortly thereafter, Modena's only living son, Isaac, returned to Venice from the New World. When he learned what had happened to his father's possessions, he objected and took his sisters to court. After these costly proceedings, he turned to his nephew:

> One day the aforementioned Isaac Modena who was worthless, reckless,[57] and embittered,[58] and above all completely broke, came in search of Isaac [Levi] his nephew. Listen to me, nephew. Behold, I do not want to harm you. I know that you have seized for yourself all the papers that belonged to my father, may he rest in peace. I do not lack for people who tell me every day that were I to sell them, they would give me more than a hundred ducats. Therefore, I want a keepsake of my father's. Give me such and such a book,[59] and perhaps with it I shall abandon you without destroying you.[60] But Isaac [Levi] refused. But he [Isaac Modena] and other people threatened him and made him afraid.... And he [Levi] said to him [Modena] on a daily basis: let me first copy it for myself. And R. Isaac [Levi] began to copy it but he did not finish. One night, the Thursday before the week of the pericope *va–yeshev*, the aforementioned man [Modena] came to the house of R. Isaac Levi. He came with threats, with a mighty hand and an outstretched

---

[56] Written as Luzzattin, not Luzzatto. He appears to have been a nephew of Simone Luzzatto. Modena also bequeathed to him sermons in manuscript. Modena, *Hayyei Yehudah*, 112; *Autobiography*, 269.
[57] Cf. Jud. 9:4.
[58] Cf. Job 21:25.
[59] No title is given.
[60] Cf. Deut 20:19.

arm,⁶¹ under the pretext that the next day he planned to travel. And he [Isaac Levi] would not budge but he [Modena] seized it [the manuscript], and forcibly removed it. And he [Levi] swears, may his soul be ostracized and banned from heaven and from living creatures, if a complete copy of the work remains in his possession.⁶²

Levi had indeed taken charge of his grandfather's papers as he was instructed to do in Modena's will and went to considerable effort to protect his literary legacy. As he recounted, he was unsuccessful in completing his copy of one of the manuscripts that had been bequeathed to Luzzattin. Although he does not specify which manuscript, it appears that it was Modena's notebook.⁶³

Levi's preservation of his grandfather's literary remains was about more than filial piety. While he may have been a loyal grandson eager to honor his deceased grandfather, he was also engaged in a drawn-out struggle against the Luzzatto family to inherit Modena's position as communal scribe. Much of his autobiography functioned as an exercise in self-justification and included copious details about his ultimately successful campaign against one of the leading Jewish intellectuals in seventeenth-century Venice, Simone Luzzatto, and his family, to succeed his grandfather.

Levi was also able to copy *Magen va-Herev*. While Modena's own draft does not appear to have survived, Levi's copy, along with a title page and short introduction, is still extant. On the title page, Levi described the circumstances of his transcription: "I found it among his compositions in manuscript that he left after his death and I copied it."⁶⁴ He indicated that he copied the work within a year of Modena's death, in the month of Tevet 5409 (December 1648–January 1649). Although he claims to have found it among his grandfather's papers, one might conjecture that he made a copy for himself because Modena's own draft had been assigned to Luzzattin. Levi's introduction amounts to a necrology of his grandfather.⁶⁵ Like Modena's preface to the anthology of biblical commentaries, it reveals several important aspects of Modena's writing practices, such as his method of notetaking and composition. After describing Modena's accomplishments as a preacher throughout northern Italy and as a teacher of Jews and Christians, Levi mentioned his written works. He distinguished between

---

⁶¹ Cf. Deut. 4:34.

⁶² Levi, *Medaber Tahpukhot*, 90–91. For a twentieth-century fictional account of Isaac Modena's life, see Mikhail Krutikov, *From Kabbalah to Class Struggle: Expressionism, Marxism, and Yiddish Literature in the Life and Work of Meir Wiener* (Stanford: Stanford University Press, 2011), 306–9.

⁶³ *Autobiography*, 270. However, it may also have been the collection of sermons.

⁶⁴ Milan, Biblioteca Ambrosiana, MS Q 139 Sup., 2A. For Levi's handwriting, see Cohen, "Who Wrote," 292.

⁶⁵ See Geiger, *Leon da Modena*, 10B–11B, Hebrew section. Levi's introduction includes several phrases taken directly from Modena's own preface to his manuscript of writings by Abner of Burgos. See Parma, Biblioteca Palatina, Codex de Rossi 533 (Parma MS 2440), 1A–1B. For a partial transcription of this preface, see Reggio, *Behinat ha-Kabalah*, xiii–xiv.

those that had appeared in print and "some twenty others in manuscript." While his list of books in print includes various subjects, his list of those in manuscript focuses on biblical commentaries and does not include any of the polemical writings or responsa.⁶⁶ In his claim that "the whole world addressed him [Modena] with respect in their letters with *titles* fitting for his glory, which I have in my possession," Levi further indicated that he had taken control of his grandfather's papers. On Modena's attitude toward writing, he commented: "He used to say, truthfully swearing, that in his lifetime, the profit from his two fingers (such were his words), that is to say, from writing, was 3000 ducats. . . . Because his script was like pearls, written and spoken with clarity, as we can see from his writings." Among his many professions, Modena had served as a professional scribe, and he had evidently boasted at one point of living by his own pen.

Levi proceeded to describe the origins of *Magen va-Herev*. According to Levi, Modena had claimed that no Jew since Isaac Abravanel had gone to such lengths to defend the Jewish faith against its Christian opponents.⁶⁷ Levi characterized *Magen va-Herev* as a response to Christian polemics against Judaism, and specifically to Pietro Galatino (d. 1539), who had composed "a book of great weight in the Latin language that cites passages, both real and imagined, against our faith." Levi referred to *De arcanis catholicae veritatis*, printed first in Ortona in 1518 and reissued several times over the next century, and specified that Modena had copiously annotated "the margins of the book."⁶⁸ Modena had also annotated a work by Sixtus of Siena, presumably his *Bibliotheca Sancta*, a book that had appeared multiple times in the sixteenth century as well.⁶⁹ Levi claimed to have both volumes in his possession: "And please know, there was not a single book about any religion there might be, whether Ishmaelite or some other religion, that he [Modena] did not read and study in order to become strong in his faith. Specifically, he saw the beliefs of all their principal scholars . . . in order to

---

⁶⁶ On Modena's biblical commentaries in manuscript, see Richler, "Unknown Writings of R. Judah Aryeh Modena" (Hebrew), *Asufot* 7 (1993): 157–68.

⁶⁷ Isaac Abravanel (1437–1508), an Iberian Jewish courtier who had written extensively about Christianity. Modena had summarized Abravanel's *Mashmia Yeshua* in his notebooks. See Simonsohn, "Introduction" (Hebrew), in *Ziknei Yehudah*, 16, n. 36.

⁶⁸ On Galatino in print, see Isaiah Sonne, "Church Use of the Kabbalah in Seventeenth-Century Missionary Work" (Hebrew), *Bitzaron* 36 (1957): 57, n. 10; Saverio Campanini, "Le prefazioni, le dediche, e i *colophon* di Gershom Soncino," in *L'attività editoriale di Gershom Soncino 1502–1527*, ed. Giuliano Tamani, 45–50 (Cremona: Edizioni dei Soncino, 1997). On the work, see Alba Paladini, *Il De Arcanis di Pietro Galatino: Traditio giudaica e nuove istanze filologiche* (Lecce: Congedo, 2004). On Gershom Soncino, the prominent Jewish printer who printed the first edition, see Moses Marx, *Gershom Soncino's Wanderyears in Italy, 1498–1527: Exemplar judaicae vitae*. (Cincinnati: Society of Jewish Bibliophiles, 1969).

⁶⁹ See Clemente E. Ancona, "Attacchi contro il Talmud di Fra Sisto da Siena, e la riposta, finora inedita, di Leon Modena, rabbino in Venezia," *Bollettino dell'Istituto di Storia della Società e dello Stato Veneziano* 5–6 (1963–1964): 297–323.

respond to them." After this intensive reading in comparative religion, Levi wrote that Modena had decided to compile his thoughts about Christianity into a coherent treatise.[70]

Modena's own writings corroborate Levi's account of his working habits. Referring to *Magen va-Herev* in his autobiography, Modena indicated that he "wrote memorandum notes for some things to be written in that treatise."[71] His notebook included reading extracts from works by Abravanel, Sarpi, and Carlo Sigonio as well as other authors cited in *Magen va-Herev*. Modena also owned a compilation of polemical works against Judaism by Abner of Burgos, a fourteenth-century Jew who had converted to Christianity. While Modena's copies of Galatino and Sixtus of Sienna have not been identified, his manuscript of Abner of Burgos contains numerous annotations that contest Abner's critical comments about Judaism.[72]

At the close of the introduction, Levi declared: "Would that his [Modena's] words were written down with iron stylus and lead,[73] with the tip of a hard point kept for generations in order that people may know how to respond." The biblical phrase "iron stylus and lead" was often used to refer to printing in prefatory materials appended to early printed Hebrew books. In *Bet Yehudah*, edited by Levi at the Vendramin press, Modena used the phrase in his address to the reader. Describing the process of printing, Modena referred to publicizing his works in writing "with iron stylus and lead throughout the entire land."[74] Apart from this allusion in Levi's preface, however, no record survives of an attempt to print Modena's *Magen va-Herev* in the seventeenth century.

A year after copying *Magen va-Herev*, Levi attempted to print an edition of his grandfather's responsa *Ziknei Yehudah*.[75] This work, which contains Modena's responses to legal inquires over the course of half a

---

[70] On this work, see David Berger, "On the Uses of History in Medieval Jewish Polemic against Christianity: The Quest for the Historical Jesus," in *Jewish History and Jewish Memory: Essays in Honor of Yosef Hayim Yerushalmi*, ed. Elisheva Carlebach, John M. Efron, and David N. Myers, 35–36 (Hanover, NH: Brandeis University Press, 1998); Talya Fishman, "Changing Early Modern Jewish Discourse about Christianity: The Efforts of Rabbi Leon Modena," in Malkiel, *The Lion Shall Roar*, 159–94; Alessandro Guetta, "Anti-Catholic Apologetics in Leon Modena's *Magen va-Herev*: A Comparative Reading" (Hebrew), in Malkiel, *The Lion Shall Roar*, 69–89; Daniel J. Lasker, "Jewish Anti-Christian Polemics in the Early Modern Period: Change or Continuity?" in *Tradition, Heterodoxy, and Religious Culture*, ed. Goodblatt, and Kreisel, 473–77.

[71] *Autobiography*, 176.

[72] Parma, Biblioteca Palatina, Codex de Rossi 533 (Parma MS 2440). On Modena's annotated *Meor Enayim*, see below.

[73] Job 19:23–24.

[74] Modena, *Bet Yehudah*, 2B.

[75] On Modena's responsa, see Joseph Zeev Greenberg, "Responsa *Ziknei Yehudah* by Rabbi Judah Aryeh Modena as a historical source for the history of the Jews in Italy," (Hebrew) (M.A. thesis, Bar–Ilan University, 1976); Shlomo Simonsohn, "Halakhah and Society in the Writings of Leone da Modena," in Twersky and Septimus, *Jewish Thought in the Seventeenth Century*,

century, survives in a unique manuscript. Substantial portions were copied in Modena's own hand, and it seems likely that it was among the Hebrew writings bequeathed to Levi by Modena in his will.[76] The first page of this manuscript appears to be a title page written in block letters:

> *Ziknei Yehudah*. And they are writings that have not gone forth publicly, that
>   is they are
> the rulings, and responses to questions by the rabbi
> the great and
> eminent of his generation . . . Judah
> Aryeh Modena
> may his sacred righteous memory be for a blessing.[77]

In between the lines, an interlinear note adds: "The sweet psalmist of Israel[78] he sought the good of his people[79] the righteous and humble." The second paragraph describes Levi's involvement with the work: "Sent over the fields among the watering places[80] to grant merit to the multitudes; by his grandson and his student, who supervised the printing in order to print, and to appeal to everyone. The afflicted and the young, Isaac of the Levites, son of the esteemed master and teacher, the divine, Jacob, may his righteous and holy memory be a blessing."[81] While this text was meant to serve a frontispiece to a printed edition, *Ziknei Yehudah* did not appear in print in the seventeenth century.

The manuscript of *Ziknei Yehudah* bears certain similarities to Levi's copy of *Magen va-Herev*. The same phrase used by Levi in the interlinear note about his grandfather appears on the first page of his copy of *Magen va-Herev*.[82] Both manuscripts contain texts in Modena's hand and in Levi's hand. Levi's copy of *Magen va-Herev* contains eight unnumbered leaves in Modena's own hand that include his copy of *Magen ve-Zinah* as well as some reading notes. Finally, Levi expressed his desire to see both works appear in print.

Levi's collaboration with Modena spanned several decades and involved the preparation of draft copies, the oversight and editing of printed work, and the preservation and perpetuation of Modena's literary legacy. At least three manuscripts composed over two decades—the anthology of biblical commentaries, the responsa, and the polemic against Christianity—survive

---

435–45; Jeffrey Woolf, "The Responsa of Leon Modena: Continuity without Change" (Hebrew), in Malkiel, *The Lion Shall Roar*, 55–68.
[76] See Simonsohn, "Introduction" (Hebrew), in *Ziknei Yehudah*, 9.
[77] London, British Library, MS Add. 27148.
[78] II Sam 23:1.
[79] Es. 10:3.
[80] Cf. Job 5:10.
[81] London, British Library, MS Add 27148, 1b.
[82] For the phrase in *Ziknei Yehudah*, see ibid., lines 4 and 5. For the phrase in *Magen va-Herev*, see Milan Q 139 Sup., 2A.

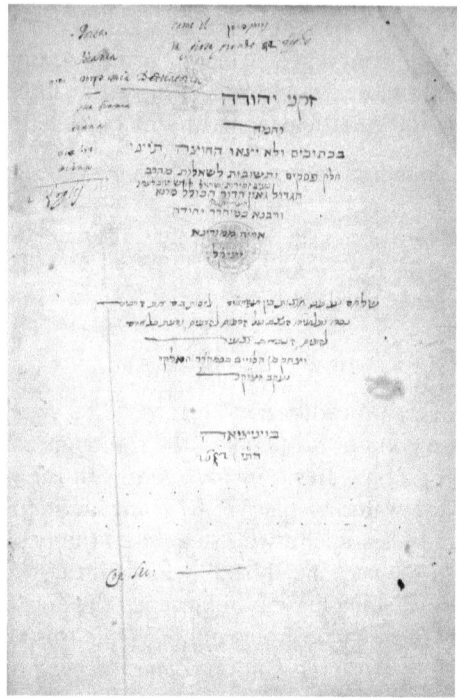

Figure 4. Title page to Modena's responsa, *Ziknei Yehudah*.
© The British Library Board. MS Add 27148, 1b.
Isaac Levi's title page to Modena's responsa that was intended to serve as the title page to a printed edition. *Ziknei Yehudah* was not printed in the seventeenth century.

with samples of both hands. Levi not only supervised the printing of Modena's work as an adolescent, he also attempted to print his grandfather's work in the years after his death. Given Modena's intense involvement in Levi's upbringing and Levi's attempts to model himself after his grandfather, it is not surprising that their handwriting was extremely similar and at certain points nearly indistinguishable.

SCRIBAL COPIES OF *ARI NOHEM*

A manuscript of *Ari Nohem* currently in Moscow has been identified as Modena's autograph of the work.[83] At issue, however, is the type of autograph: one produced solely by the author or one produced by the author

---

[83] MS A. Richler, "Unknown Writings," 169–71. Richler allows for the possibility that Levi copied it.

and an amanuensis. This manuscript appears to be a scribal copy produced by Levi and corrected by Modena. Several factors point to the hypothesis that it was produced for circulation. First, the manuscript is not a working copy. Modena's description of a working draft and an actual specimen of one offer stark contrasts to the manuscript. The Moscow manuscript of *Ari Nohem* contains relatively few revisions or cross-outs, and the writing has been carefully laid out in even lines and in justified columns. The marginal and interlinear notes appear to be corrections and later additions rather than instances of large-scale rewriting and reformulation.

The handwriting and the signatures that appear on the Moscow manuscript offer several important clues to the respective involvement of Modena and Levi. In spite of the close similarities in their handwriting, several features distinguish Modena's hand from his grandson's. The cursive ligature of the two Hebrew letters, *alef lamed*, offers one of the most telling distinctions. While Modena's ligature typically slants far to the left, Levi's typically stands erect.[84] The handwriting of the copyist of the Moscow manuscript bears close resemblance to other known samples of Levi's handwriting, particularly his copy of *Magen va-Herev*. In the Moscow manuscript, the ligature *alef lamed* usually stands erect rather than slanting to the left. The signatures used by both Modena and Levi in the manuscripts they copied may offer another clue. Levi used a symbol similar to an ampersand that often appears immediately above the catchword at the bottom of the page.[85] Modena used an elaborate circular curl on manuscripts written in his own hand.[86] On sixteen out of the first nineteen folios of the Moscow manuscript of *Ari Nohem* as well as another folio later in the manuscript, Levi's signature appears above the catchword.[87] On the penultimate page of the Moscow manuscript of *Ari Nohem*, a circular curl similar to Modena's signature appears immediately above a one-line colophon. This circular curl might constitute Modena's authorization.

This copy of *Ari Nohem* has been corrected. While it is impossible to identify the scribe who has corrected it, these corrections and revisions generally take one of three forms: correction of errors such as rewriting passages with awkward syntax or replacing a missing word;[88] addition of

---

[84] Cohen, "Who Wrote," 292.

[85] For example, Levi's copy of *Magen va-Herev*. See *Autobiography*, 291.

[86] See ibid., 71.

[87] The evidence from the ligature of the *alef lamed* and the signature marks is not absolute. While the ligature usually stands erect in MS A, there are numerous instances where it does not. See Cohen, "Who Wrote," 292.

[88] For example, in MS A 25A, line 2, he adds the word "as he wrote" before a citation from Maimonides. In 25A, line 15, he corrects the word order of a passage that cites a biblical verse (Isa. 28:8) to describe the writings of Meir ibn Gabbai. The verse in Isaiah reads, "All the tables are covered with vomit and filth." The crossed-out version of Modena's text reads, "All the tables filled with the vomit of his chapters." The revised version reads, "All the tables of his chapters are filled with vomit and filth."

bibliographic data and references to other sources to support a particular argument;[89] or mitigation of the critique to soften the harshness of the rhetoric. The two most substantial additions to the Moscow manuscript offer telling examples of the latter two types of revisions and provide an important clue that Modena himself was probably the scribe who corrected the text. One addition appears on the final page of the manuscript and the other appears at the end of the first chapter.

The note on the final page of the Moscow manuscript was probably in the same hand that composed the circular curl and the one-line colophon on the previous page: "Not through my mind[90] alone, I would not have undertaken this task in its entirety[91] to speak against this Kabbalah, had I not seen in writing and heard in speech the giants of the world who were of this opinion. These are the names of those mentioned here in my treatise and there are many more like them."[92] This note and list were almost certainly composed in Modena's own hand. The *alef lamed* ligature, which appears no fewer than seven times, slants far to the left on each occasion, as it does in other manuscripts in Modena's hand. Furthermore, a similar list of scholars opposed to Kabbalah appears in Modena's notebook from the same period.[93] The list presents sixteen medieval and early modern Jewish authors who had ostensibly expressed opposition to Kabbalah. It also offers a bibliography of the writers Modena cited throughout *Ari Nohem*. Saadya Gaon, Solomon ibn Adret, and Moses Isserles, who appear in the list, had written works that Modena drew upon in order to make various arguments. In some instances, such as Samuel Zarza and Elijah Mizrahi, Modena provided specific passages in their writings where they opposed Kabbalah.[94]

As much as this list functioned as a seventeenth-century version of an author and passage index, it also represented a bibliographic fantasy. Modena included several authors who were hardly opponents of Kabbalah: Saadya Gaon died in 942, several centuries before the emergence of Kabbalah, according to Modena's account elsewhere in *Ari Nohem*. While Saadya may

---

[89] For example, in MS A 6B, 8, he directs the reader to Moses Cordovero's *Or Ne'erav* for a further discussion of Cordovero's insistence on the imperative to believe in the *sefirot*.

[90] Cf. Num. 16:28.

[91] BT *Berakhot*, 64A, and Rashi's explanation.

[92] MS A 48B, 1–3.

[93] Richler, "Unknown Writings," 171, n. 114. The list appears in Ancona, Communità Israelitica, MS 7, 13B. Each includes an identical list of scholars, but there are minor variations. For example, in MS A the first person on the list, Saadia Gaon, is followed by the phrase "of blessed memory," whereas in the Ancona MS the phrase does not appear.

[94] Samuel ibn Zarza, *Sefer Mekor Hayim* (Mantua, 1559), 118B, Commentary on *Ki Teze*; Elijah Mizrahi, *Teshuvot She'elot* (Constantinople, 1559), 2A–3A, responsum no. 1. On Mizrahi, see Rachel Elior, "The Dispute over the Status of Kabbalah in the Sixteenth Century" (Hebrew), *JSJT* 1 (1981): 177–90.

have opposed the transmigration of souls, an idea attacked in *Ari Nohem* and *Ben David*, he could hardly be construed as an opponent of something that emerged centuries after his death.[95] Solomon ibn Adret, an important student of the Spanish Kabbalist Nahmanides, may have objected to the public teaching of esoteric wisdom and engaged in a protracted dispute over the status of philosophy in early fourteenth century, but he was hardly opposed to Kabbalah.[96] This list provides the clearest distillation of Modena's attempt to create an intellectual lineage out of the annals of medieval and early modern Jewish thought, a theme that runs throughout *Ari Nohem*. In emphasizing that he was not the first to criticize Kabbalah, Modena sought to soften potential opposition to his claims.

A series of shorter notes revise the text in such a way as to blunt the sharpness of the polemic. In the beginning of the second chapter, Modena recounted his own experience reading kabbalistic books:

> But each and every time I took within my hands a given volume from the books of Kabbalah and I attempted to study it deeply, with knowledge and discernment, I was not satisfied; and although lofty mountains towered above me,[97] they were closed to me and I could not enter inside; I would close the book and turn to books of Torah and the commandments. But as I grew older, and this happened to me countless number of times, my thoughts brought me to the point where I considered and reflected that not only was this neither wisdom nor tradition nor true knowledge, rather it is [close to being] a stone of stumbling and a rock of obstruction.[98]

Ari Nohem offered copious evidence that Modena's account of his own reading failed to capture how deeply he had immersed himself in kabbalistic literature. The corrector of the Moscow manuscript softened the critique by adding "close to being" as an interlinear note before the phrase a "stone of stumbling."

A similar instance occurred when Modena described kabbalists as ignorant of the legal intricacies of the Talmud. A scribe inserted three interlinear notes to change the sentence from a blanket critique of all kabbalists to an attack on the majority: "**The majority** [each and every one] of them who number among them and call themselves a kabbalist by their own

---

[95] See Saadia Gaon, *The Book of Beliefs and Opinions*, trans. Samuel Rosenblatt (New Haven: Yale University Press, 1948), treatise 6; Haggai Ben-Shammai, "The Transmigration of Souls in Jewish Thought in the East in the Tenth Century" (Hebrew), *Sefunot* 5, 20 (1991): 117–36.

[96] Moshe Idel, "Rabbi Solomon ibn Adret and Abraham Abulafia: History of a Submerged Controversy about Kabbalah" (Hebrew), in *Atarah le-Hayim: mehkarim ba-sifrut ha-Talmudit veha–rabanit–li-khevod Profesor Hayim Zalman Dimitrovksi*, ed. Daniel Boyarin et al., 235–51 (Jerusalem: Magnes Press, 2000).

[97] Cf. Gen. 7:19.

[98] Cf. Isa. 8:14. MS A 9B, 4–9.

knowledge.... there exists **very few** [not a single one] sharp and learned Talmudists among them. For the **majority** lack the clarity of mind."[99] In this case, Modena repeated a common criticism delivered against kabbalists by rabbis throughout the early modern period: kabbalists lacked the requisite knowledge of Jewish law and pursued the study of Kabbalah before mastering the Talmud.[100]

A final piece of evidence that may reflect Modena's involvement with the Moscow manuscript appears in the colophon. This colophon is immediately below a circular curl of Modena's signature mark and may have been written in the same hand. The one-line note reads, "the completion of this treatise or this letter was in the month of *Kislev* (5)399," which corresponds to the month of November–December 1638.[101] This records the date of the completion of the treatise rather than the date of the copying of the manuscript.[102]

Another manuscript of *Ari Nohem* currently in Warsaw bears a close relationship to the Moscow manuscript.[103] The copyist of the Warsaw manuscript has not been identified, although several factors indicate that he was close to Levi or Modena. First, the Warsaw manuscript has an almost

---

[99] The revisions in the interlinear notes are in bold. The text that is crossed out is between brackets. MS A 10A, 7–10.

[100] See Joseph Solomon Delmedigo, *Sefer Mazref le-Hokhmah*, in *Sefer Ta'alumot Hokhmah* (Hanau, 1629–1631), 21A. *Sefer Ta'alumot Hokhmah* contains several works within it. On the bibliographic problems posed by this book, see below. See also a similar comment by Jacob Emden quoted in Moshe Idel, "Perceptions of Kabbalah in the Second Half of the 18th Century," *JJTP* 1 (1991): 57.

[101] MS A 48A.

[102] The colophons to MS A and MS B (discussed below) state that the treatise was completed in Kislev (5)399 (November–December 1638). This date poses something of a chronological puzzle in light of the other evidence in the text itself and in Modena's other writings. In *Ari Nohem*, Modena stated that he was sixty-eight years old at the time of its composition. MS A 9A, 7–8; ed. Libowitz, 7. If he was born in April 1571, as indicated in his autobiography, Modena turned sixty-eight in April 1639. This is corroborated by the note about *Ari Nohem* in the autobiography written in late spring 1640: "About six months earlier I had completed a treatise against Kabbalah. I entitled it *Ari Nohem*." *Autobiography*, 153. The passage begins, "At the beginning of the month of Sivan [began May 22, 1640] I was in Padua." If so, six months earlier would have been Kislev (5)400 (November–December 1639), not Kislev (5)399 (November–December 1638). This would date the completion of *Ari Nohem* to November–December 1639, not 1638. Without attempting to definitively reconcile this discrepancy, several possibilities might account for it: First, the autobiography and the internal evidence of the work are correct, and Modena completed the work in November–December 1639. The year contained in the colophons is a mistake. Although the autobiography and the colophon differ on the year, they agree on the time of year. Second, both dates are correct. Modena completed a draft in 1638, continually revised it for a year and finished his revisions in 1639. I have followed the internal evidence in *Ari Nohem* and the autobiography in referring to 1639 as the date of composition.

[103] Richler, "Unknown Writings," 169–71.

identical colophon to the Moscow one: "the completion of this treatise was in the month of *Kislev* (5)399."[104] Apart from a slight variation in the definition of *Ari Nohem*—"this treatise or this letter" in the Moscow colophon as opposed to "this treatise" in the Warsaw colophon—the two colophons contain the same text and appear to be in the same hand. While the signature mark immediately above the colophon in the Moscow manuscript does not appear in the Warsaw one, other factors point to a close relationship. Levi's signature mark appears on two pages of the Warsaw manuscript.[105] The extensive interlinear note at the end of chapter 1 in the Moscow manuscript appears as an interlinear note in the identical place in the Warsaw manuscript. Furthermore, several other marginal and interlinear notes in the Moscow manuscript appear as marginal and interlinear notes in the Warsaw one. However, the Warsaw manuscript does not contain all the additions and revisions in the Moscow manuscript. For example, the list of writers opposed to Kabbalah found at the conclusion of the Moscow manuscript does not appear in the Warsaw one.[106]

Some evidence suggests that Modena nourished hopes of printing *Ari Nohem*. In addition to the wistful remark in the autobiography, the Moscow manuscript contains a short note beneath the owner's mark:[107] "Remember to call the three sections, First Roar, Second Roar, and Third Roar; and the chapters, First Voice, Second Voice, and so too with the remainder of them [the chapters]. And this is because the name of the work is the Roaring Lion." *Ari Nohem* is, in fact, divided into three different sections, each of which contains multiple chapters. This note may constitute Modena's instructions to a printer for titles of the sections and chapters of the book.[108] In the Moscow manuscript, the first section does not have a title and the second and third sections are simply referred to as "Second Part" and "Third Part," rather than "Second Roar" and "Third Roar." The chapters are referred to as "Chapter One," "Chapter Two," rather than "First Voice," or "Second Voice." After having certified this copy of the manuscript, Modena may have written this note to the printers about the titles of each section. However, given that Levi's signature mark appears next to this note, it seems more likely that Levi rather than Modena wrote it.

[104] MS B 31B. Consulted on microform reel F 12001 at the JNUL.
[105] 1B, 4B.
[106] Richler, "Unknown Writings," 170.
[107] The owner's mark reads, "'The earth is the Lord's and the fullness thereof' (Ps. 24:1) Solomon son of the esteemed eminence and master Jacob Menahem Treves." Solomon's father may be the same Jacob Treves who purchased twenty-two Hebrew manuscripts in Venice along with Isaac Treves. A list of their manuscripts appears on the flyleaf of London, Montefiore Collection, MS 517. Among these manuscripts were Modena's *Hayyei Yehudah*, *Magen va-Herev*, and *Magen ve-Zinah*, which appear as manuscripts 4, 5, and 6. The flyleaf is attached to a manuscript copy of Levi's *Medaber Tahpukhot*. Consulted on microfiche at the Library of Congress.
[108] Richler, "Unknown Writings," 170.

54 • Chapter One

In addition to this note, a letter written by Samuel Aboab to Moses Zacut in the summer of 1646 further suggests that Modena had hoped to print *Ari Nohem*. Zacut, who was planning to write a refutation of an unnamed rabbi who had recently denied the transmigration of souls, had written to Aboab to request reading recommendations.[109] Aboab's response to Zacut mentioned a rabbinic scholar in northern Italy who had criticized Kabbalah and hoped to print his work. Although neither Modena's name nor the title of his work appeared in this letter, a range of puns and allusions indicate that Aboab was referring to Modena and *Ari Nohem*.[110] Aboab wrote "he wanted to make us abhorrent[111] in print in the eyes of the gentiles. I declare about him, if he does this, the sin of Judah will be written with an iron stylus."[112] Further on, he wrote, "the lion roared to publish these words." The "sin of Judah" and "the lion roared" almost certainly refer to Modena. In his responses, Aboab asked him to beseech the scholar in question not to make "his roars[113] heard in public." Presumably he advised Zacut, at the time around twenty-five years old, to implore Modena not to print *Ari Nohem*.

Given the current state of evidence, hypotheses about efforts to publish *Ari Nohem* in print or in manuscript in the seventeenth century cannot be proven with absolute certainty. Neither of the extant manuscripts with the colophon in Modena's hand offers any indication as to the date it was copied. Assuming that the signature mark above the colophon in the Moscow manuscript as well as the two extensive revisions to the same manuscript are in Modena's own hand, this copy must have been produced before his death in 1648. Furthermore, assuming that Modena himself wrote the one-line colophon to the Warsaw manuscript, this copy must have also been produced before 1648.

The following hypothetical reconstruction attempts to account for the collaborative nature of Modena's writing and the conditions of publication in Modena's Venice: Modena wrote and completed a draft of *Ari Nohem* most likely around November–December 1639. Levi produced a scribal copy of this draft that is currently in Moscow. Another scribe produced a copy of *Ari Nohem*, either from Levi's copy or from Modena's draft. Modena edited Levi's copy in the form of revisions and interlinear notes and signed these revisions with his signature mark above the colophon. Modena may

---

[109] Zacut did not compose his treatise about the transmigration of souls until some years later. See Meir Benayahu, "The Positions of Rabbi Moses Zacut and Rabbi Samuel Aboab on the Controversies about Conversos from Portugal Who Returned to Judaism" (Hebrew), in *Shlomo Simonsohn Jubilee Volume*, ed. Daniel Carpi, 29–44 (Tel Aviv: Tel Aviv University Press, 1993).

[110] Ibid., 41–42.

[111] Cf. Ex. 5:21.

[112] Cf. Jer. 17:1.

[113] *Nehamotav*, another reference to *Ari Nohem*.

have made these revisions, many of which soften his criticisms, with an eye toward printing *Ari Nohem*. The scribe of the Warsaw copy checked his work against the Moscow copy and copied Modena's revisions in the form of interlinear notes and additions from the Moscow manuscript. Modena signed the Warsaw copy with its revisions in the form of a one-line colophon. Levi's copy remained in Modena's possession, and at a later date he added a list of anti-kabbalist writers on the final page of the manuscript. It is entirely possible that Levi's scribal copy with Modena's revisions was meant to appear in print. Levi may have signed the note with instructions about the titles of the sections and chapters under Modena's instructions. Modena may have wanted to print the work during the final decade of his life but failed to do so for a variety of reasons: fear of publishing such a polemical work in print, lack of funds, or inability to find a publisher. Alternatively, Levi may have attempted to print *Ari Nohem* in the years after Modena's death and affixed a note of instruction to the printers at the top of the manuscript with his own signature. This effort, like his attempt to print *Ziknei Yehudah*, ended in failure. Modena's colophon to both manuscripts might have constituted a form of publication in the scribal medium. Whether or not he was hoping to have his work printed at some point in the final decade of his life, Modena intended for the work to circulate among Venetian Jews. He may have wanted the text to circulate only with his permission or supervision. Such manuscripts often had colophons similar to the copies of *Ari Nohem* described above.

Print and Manuscript in *Ari Nohem*

The distinction between print and manuscript not only figured prominently in Modena's working environment, it was also one of the themes of his criticism. On numerous occasions, Modena paid careful attention to the material form of a given text. In particular, he lamented the effects of printing on two areas of Jewish knowledge, law and Kabbalah. In a brief but revealing comment about Joseph Karo's *Shulhan Arukh*, which existed in no fewer than eighteen printed editions when he composed *Ari Nohem*,[114] Modena wrote: "After the printing of the book *Shulhan Arukh*, my ears heard from an ignoramus, someone beloved to me, peace be upon him, who used to say: When I have the *Shulhan Arukh* underneath the joints of my arms[115] I do not need a single one of you rabbis."[116] For Modena

---

[114] See Naftali Ben-Menahem, "Early Printed Editions of the *Shulhan Arukh*" (Hebrew), in *Rabi Yosef Karo*, ed. Isaac Refael (Jerusalem: Mossad ha-Rav Kook, 1969), 101; Raz-Krakotzkin, "From Safed to Venice."

[115] Ez. 13:18.

[116] MS A 29B, 18–20; ed. Libowitz, 51.

the publication of knowledge in the form of a printed book had led the uneducated to suppose that living legal authorities were no longer necessary. Modena's beloved ignoramus, who could presumably read Karo's legal digest without any assistance, insisted that he had no need for a rabbi to decide the law. By consulting Karo's decision in any of the printed editions, he could simply determine it for himself.[117]

Modena's comment about the printing of Karo's *Shulhan Arukh* and its impact upon Jewish law appeared in passing. He sought to draw an analogy between the printing of legal books and kabbalistic books and in doing so made a revealing comment about the impact of printing on another realm of knowledge. In contrast, Modena's discussion of the printing of kabbalistic books occupied a central position in his polemic. He devoted an entire chapter to the appearance of Kabbalah in print in the middle of the sixteenth century. According to Modena, the printing of a range of kabbalistic texts such as the *Zohar* and *Sefer Yetzirah* had effected a radical rupture in the transmission of kabbalistic knowledge.[118] Before the appearance of these books in print, Kabbalah had remained an esoteric set of doctrines transmitted from master to disciple orally and through the supervised copying of handwritten manuscripts. In emphasizing the esoteric nature of Kabbalah before the advent of printing, Modena set out to counter a series of arguments made by the supporters of the early printed editions of the *Zohar*. The printing of the *Zohar* had generated an intense struggle among the Italian Jewish elite in the 1550s. Apart from those Jewish thinkers opposed to Kabbalah outright, some kabbalists themselves objected to the printing of the *Zohar* on the grounds that it would constitute the public revelation of esoteric secrets. Proponents of printing the *Zohar* sought to counter this argument by minimizing the impact it would have on the dissemination of esoteric knowledge.[119]

In an explicit rejection of these positions, Modena argued that Kabbalah had remained an esoteric doctrine throughout the Middle Ages but the appearance of kabbalistic books in print had altered this status. The eighty years between the publication of the *Zohar* in print and the composition of *Ari Nohem* had disproved their attempt to minimize the difference between

---

[117] Modena's comment has found an echo in contemporary scholarship. See Elchanan Reiner, "The Ashkenazi Elite at the Beginning of the Modern Era: Manuscript versus Printed Book," *Polin* 10 (1997): 85–98; Joseph Davis, "The Reception of the *Shulhan Arukh* and the Formation of Ashkenazic Jewish Identity," *AJS Review* 26 (2002): 251–76. In his section on Karo and the *Shulhan Arukh* in his bibliophilic compendium for Zalman Schocken, S. Y. Agnon took note of this passage. See his posthumously printed *Sefer, Sofer ve-Sipur* (Jerusalem and Tel Aviv: Schocken, 1978), 305. The passage does not appear in the same section in the first edition. See *Sefer, Sofer ve-Sipur* (Jerusalem and Tel Aviv: Schocken, 1937), 71–73.

[118] MS A 45A, 11–14; ed. Libowitz, 90.

[119] See chapter 2.

print and manuscript. Whatever problems Kabbalah may have posed on the theological level, and Modena described them in detail elsewhere in *Ari Nohem*, it had never affected large numbers of people. In the latter half of the sixteenth century, however, Kabbalah had spread to the masses.

Considerable evidence supports Modena's argument about the impact of printing on the dissemination of Kabbalah. In addition to the rival editions of the *Zohar* and *Ma'arekhet ha-Elohut* mentioned in *Ari Nohem*, a range of other important kabbalistic texts appeared in print for the first time in the second half of the sixteenth century: *Sefer Yetzirah*, Joseph Gikatilla's *Sha'arei Orah*, Shem Tov ibn Shem Tov's *Sefer ha-Emunot*, a series of works by Meir ibn Gabbai including *Avodat ha-Kodesh* and *Derekh ha-Emunah*, and Moses Cordovero's *Pardes Rimonim*. Contemporary Jewish kabbalists who resided and taught in cities throughout northern Italy also printed their own books. Menahem Azariah da Fano, a leading rabbinic authority in northern Italy, printed several of his own works of Kabbalah at Hebrew presses in Venice. Aaron Berekhya of Modena printed the first kabbalistic treatment of death in the early seventeenth century. Joseph Hamiz, Modena's student, printed a finding aid to the *Zohar* several years after Modena had addressed his polemic to him. Beyond these theological treatises, exegetical works, and reference aids, Kabbalah appeared in print in the form of liturgical pamphlets and manuals of confraternal piety. In the early decades of the seventeenth century, hagiographic narratives about recently deceased kabbalists such as Isaac Luria and Joseph Karo appeared in print for the first time. Christian Kabbalists such as Johannes Reuchlin, Guillaume Postel, and Cornelius Agrippa turned to the press to disseminate their works. While scholars continue to map the intersection of Kabbalah and printing throughout the early modern period, their accounts have tended to corroborate Modena's basic insight about the impact of printing on the dissemination of Kabbalah.[120]

Modena paid careful attention to the material forms that texts had taken over the course of several centuries, whether it was the spoken word, a manuscript book, or a printed book. He set out to counter the narrative of uninterrupted transmission that served as the foundation for claims to the antiquity of Kabbalah. He adamantly rejected the notion that Kabbalah had been orally transmitted for centuries along with the Oral Torah. Furthermore, he evaluated the shift in transmission that had occurred when Kabbalah began to appear in print. At the remove of eighty years, he argued that the printing of kabbalistic books in the middle decades of the sixteenth century had transformed a set of doctrines and practices previously

---

[120] On the printing of the *Zohar*, see chapter 2; on Christian Kabbalah, see chapter 5; on hagiographies of Luria, see chapter 4; on kabbalistic manuals of piety, see Gries, *Sifrut ha-hanhagot*.

available to a small circle of elites into a form of public knowledge accessible to anyone, Jew or Christian, with rudimentary Hebrew and limited funds.

At the most basic level, the difference between print and manuscript mattered. Modena's works that had appeared in print in his own lifetime, particularly his *Riti Hebraici* and his *Bet Yehudah*, had a wide readership throughout the seventeenth and eighteenth centuries. His works in manuscript, particularly his polemical writings, continued to circulate; however, they circulated within a much more limited audience. In the case of *Ari Nohem*, one can trace the copying and reading of the work in manuscript in nearly every generation between its composition and its first printing in 1840. These readers, however, generally read in isolation from one another. Yet the difference between print and manuscript not only mattered for the literary legacy of Modena in the centuries between his death and his supposed rediscovery in the nineteenth century. It mattered in the middle decades of the seventeenth century as well. As a document, *Ari Nohem* offers eloquent and biased evidence that the printing of kabbalistic books had played a crucial role in the spread of Kabbalah among Jews and Christians in the early modern period.

CHAPTER TWO

Early Modern Criticism of the *Zohar*

> But from whence will we bring to Jewish history its impartial Paolo Sarpi?
>
> —Leopold Zunz

> I have come to accept in substance the contention of [Heinrich] Graetz—itself only the most articulate expression of a whispered tradition of centuries—that the Spanish Kabbalist Moses de Leon must be regarded as the author of the *Zohar*.
>
> —Gershom Scholem

Figure 5 (previous page). Title page to the *Zohar*, Mantua, 1558.
Courtesy of the Library of the Jewish Theological Seminary.
One of the two editions of the *Zohar* that appeared in northern Italy in the 1550s.
The Mantua press printed a range of kabbalistic works such as *Sefer Yetzirah*,
Ma'arekhet ha-Elohut, and Joseph Gikatilla's *Sha'are Orah*.

Since its first printing in 1840, and to a certain degree in the prior two centuries, *Ari Nohem* has been known as a polemic against the *Zohar*.¹ A foundational work of Jewish mysticism that kabbalists attributed to the Mishnaic sage Simeon bar Yohai, the *Zohar* is an anthology of homilies and exegetical comments on the Bible. This chapter argues that Modena's criticism of the *Zohar*'s origins had little to do with its theological contents or with the ideas contained in its parables and narratives. It emerged as a reaction to the elevated status of the work among his Jewish contemporaries and immediate predecessors. The *Zohar*, once an esoteric corpus of texts, had become an exoteric book with a broad audience in the century prior to the composition of *Ari Nohem*. Jews had begun to treat it as a source of legal authority rather than a collection of stories and biblical glosses. Modena's critique constituted a denunciation of these larger trends in contemporary Jewish life rather than a rejection of the *Zohar* as a work of exegesis. In treating the *Zohar* as an ancient text, early modern Jewish readers had turned it into a foundational component of the Oral Torah. To refute this trend, Modena demonstrated the implausibility of its claims to antiquity. The sources he used to construct this case offer a telling portrait of the character of his criticism. In *Ari Nohem*, Modena very rarely quoted the *Zohar* itself. On some of the few occasions that he did, he quoted it via an intermediate and more recent source.² By contrast, he drew on a wealth of early modern works about the *Zohar*. Citations from legal responsa, historical chronicles, and philosophical treatises dominated his account. *Ari Nohem* offers a case study of how an early modern intellectual worked to prove that a text was pseudepigraphic. It also presents a wealth of information on attitudes toward the *Zohar* among Jews in Italy, Poland, and elsewhere. Modena rejected the status ascribed to the *Zohar* in contemporary Jewish life, denied the work's ostensible antiquity, and reflected on the deleterious impact of its packaging as a printed book. *Ari Nohem*, however, cannot be construed as a rejection of the *Zohar* as such.

The first section of this chapter outlines Modena's positive attitude toward the *Zohar* by juxtaposing his explicit appraisal of the work in *Ari*

---

¹ The title page identified it as "Streitschrift über die Echtheit des Sohar." See *Ari Nohem*, ed. Fürst, t.p.

² See, however, his discussion of biblical exegesis, where he quoted the *Zohar* directly. MS A 13B, 5–11; ed. Libowitz, 14.

Nohem with his other writings. The second section identifies the factors that impelled Modena to subject the *Zohar* to critical scrutiny and focuses on four causes: a series of conversations Modena held with prominent kabbalists in the early seventeenth century; the claims to antiquity made by kabbalists for a range of texts; the widespread dissemination of these same texts; and the use of the *Zohar* as a legal source. The third and final section analyzes the strategies Modena used to prove that the *Zohar* was not an ancient work. This included three components: the discrepancies between the *Zohar* and the Talmud as they related to legal practice and the figure of Simeon bar Yohai; the detection of anachronism as it applied to theories of authorship as well as to chronology, liturgy, and language; and the introduction of evidence that definitively assigned the authorship of the *Zohar* to Moses de Leon and his circle.

Modena's Attitude to the *Zohar*

When approaching Modena's scrutiny of the *Zohar*, one must first consider his explicit evaluation of the book. Modena framed his critical treatment of its recent origins with two comments that extolled its virtues.

> The book itself ... is beloved, dear, praiseworthy, and glorious to me in all its ways in the Torah, with its plain meaning, homiletical meaning, and allusive meaning, more than all of the compositions [that are] commentaries to the Torah. Such is its way: it is [constructed] in a full and beautiful order with elegant style; its weave of stories in and out of things cannot be paralleled. It wakens the sleeping, stirs the slumbering, and inflames the reader to the service of God.[3]

A similar evaluation appears later in *Ari Nohem*:

> He [the author of the *Zohar*] was very clever ... to mix within it easily intelligible explanations of verses, sweeter than honey, like the explanations of the sages of Castile.... Stories like those recounted in the collection of fables of the gentiles.[4] ... Truly they are pleasant to those who listen to them. How pleasant and how endearing! And that is why I praise and glorify the composition, the book of the *Zohar*, in exposition of its way, more than any other work composed among our nation in the past three hundred years.[5]

Modena specified three layers of meaning in the biblical exegesis of the *Zohar* that corresponded to the first three levels of biblical interpretation contained in the acronym *Pardes*, a term used to refer to four levels of biblical

---

[3] MS A 32B, 13–17; ed. Libowitz, 57

[4] It is unclear what collection of fables Modena meant. On his Hebrew translation of exempla about virtue and vice, see Joanna Weinberg, "Leon Modena and the *Fiore di Virtù*," in Malkiel, *The Lion Shall Roar*, 137–57.

[5] MS A 36B, 20–37A, 4; ed. Libowitz, 68–69.

interpretation.⁶ The biblical exegesis of the *Zohar*, in Modena's opinion, contained the plain sense, *peshat*, the allusive, *remez*, and the homiletical, *derash*. Modena pointedly excluded a fourth layer of meaning, the secret or mystical, *sod*. By omitting the mystical sense, Modena continued to affirm the importance of the other levels of exegesis in the *Zohar*. In these comments, Modena expressed his affection for both the exegetical and the narrative elements of the *Zohar*.⁷ He saw a salutary religious function to the *Zohar*'s homilies: they could serve as a goad to stir the catatonic and lethargic Jew to worship God.

Modena explicitly embraced the *Zohar* before and after he subjected it to critical scrutiny, finding religious utility in its exegesis and rhetorical value in its stories. While one might be tempted to dismiss these remarks as an effort to deflect potential criticism, his other writings corroborate these positive evaluations. In *Midbar Yehudah*, a volume of sermons printed in 1602, Modena drew on the *Zohar* as a work of exegesis explicitly and implicitly to amplify different points in his homilies.⁸ In one instance, he drew on a verse in the Psalms, "for I recognized my transgressions and am ever conscious of my sin,"⁹ as the basis for his discussion of repentance. To support his interpretation that the psalmist exhorted his listeners to be conscious of their sins before God, Modena cited the interpretation of this verse in the *Zohar*.¹⁰ In another sermon, Modena implicitly drew on the interpretation of the fifth chapter of Isaiah in the *Zohar* as a tool to explain a verse in Exodus. Moses asked God, "Is it not that you go with us,"¹¹ and, building on the *Zohar*, Modena interpreted this to mean that Moses sought to ensure the attachment of the people of Israel to the divine presence.¹²

---

⁶ See also MS A 13B, 5–11; ed. Libowitz, 14. On *Pardes*, see Wilhelm Bacher, "Das Merkwort PRDS in der jüdischen Bibelexegese," *Zeitschrift für die alttestamentliche Wissenschaft* 13 (1893): 294–305; Frank Talmage, "Apples of Gold: The Inner Meaning of Sacred Texts in Medieval Judaism," in *Jewish Spirituality: From the Bible through the Middle Ages*, ed. Arthur Green, 313–55 (New York: Crossroad, 1986); Idel, "PaRDeS." See also Boaz Huss, "NiSAN—The Wife of the Infinite: The Mystical Hermeneutics of Rabbi Isaac of Acre," *Kabbalah* 5 (2000): 155–81.

⁷ On exegesis, see Elliot R. Wolfson, "Beautiful Maiden without Eyes: *Peshat* and *Sod* in Zoharic Hermeneutics," in *The Midrashic Imagination: Jewish Exegesis, Thought, and History*, ed. Michael Fishbane, 155–203 (Albany: SUNY Press, 1993). On narrative, see Ronit Meroz, "Zoharic Narratives and Their Adaptations," *Hispania Judaica Bulletin* 3 (2000): 3–63.

⁸ For explicit citations, see Leon Modena, *Midbar Yehudah* (Venice: Zanetti, 1602), 16B, 22B, 26A, 90A. On 51A he implicitly cited the *Zohar*; as cited by Nehemiah Libowitz, *Rabi Yehudah Aryeh Modena: be-Komato ve-Tsivyono*, 2nd ed. (New York: Harry Hirsh, 1901), 76, n. 88. On Modena's sermons, see Rivkin, "The Sermons of Leon da Modena"; Israel Rosenzweig, *Hogeh yehudi mi-kez ha-Renesans: Yehudah Aryeh Modena ve-Sifro Midbar Yehudah* (Tel Aviv: Sifriyat Po'alim, 1972), 117; Joanna Weinberg, "Preaching in the Venetian Ghetto: The Sermons of Leon Modena," in Ruderman, *Preachers of the Italian Ghetto*.

⁹ Ps. 51:5.

¹⁰ Modena, *Midbar Yehudah*, 26A; as cited by Fishman, *Shaking the Pillars of Exile*, 5 n. 9.

¹¹ Ex. 33:16.

¹² Modena, *Midbar Yehudah*, 51B; as cited by Weinberg, "Preaching in the Venetian Ghetto," 117.

Several years after the publication of *Midbar Yehudah*, Modena came to the defense of David Farrar, a Portuguese Jew suspected by the Amsterdam rabbinate of heresy.¹³ In an Italian letter written to Farrar that has been dated to 1610, Modena responded to a series of theological inquiries. Farrar asked Modena about a verse in the book of Numbers that implies the idols in Egypt had suffered physical punishment. Drawing on the *Zohar*, Modena argued that the Egyptian deities had indeed received such punishment.

> The *Zohar* comments on the verse: "while the Egyptians were burying them that the Lord had smitten among them, even all of their first born upon their gods, also the Lord executed judgments."¹⁴ The *Zohar* says that the Egyptians buried the residue of the paschal lambs, the children of Israel having eaten the flesh and cast the bones into the street. Since the lambs were Egyptian deities, it is plain that the Egyptian deities suffered physical punishment. Cabalistically, of course the *Zohar* explains "executing judgment against all the gods" as referring to the Egyptian guardian angel in heaven or to the planet by which the Egyptians were influenced. At the same time, it cannot be gainsaid that punishment overtook the gods in a physical sense.¹⁵

Like his sermons printed several years earlier, Modena invoked the explanation of a biblical verse in the *Zohar* without apology.

In 1625 Modena printed *Bet Lehem Yehudah*, an annotated index to the rabbinic sayings in Jacob ibn Habib's *Ein Ya'akov* referred to in Italy as *Ein Yisrael*.¹⁶ Modena designed his index as a reference aid for preachers and students in using Ibn Habib's collection of nonlegal rabbinic passages from the Talmud.¹⁷ Ten years later, Modena compiled a list of Talmudic texts that had not been included in *Ein Ya'akov* and published this list with his own annotations under the title *Bet Yehudah*.¹⁸ Modena quoted the *Zohar* at several points in this later work.¹⁹ In one instance, he discussed the impor-

---

¹³ See Idel, "Differing Conceptions of Kabbalah in the Early 17th Century," 142–54; Fishman, *Shaking the Pillars of Exile*, 49, 64.

¹⁴ Num. 33:4.

¹⁵ Sonne, "Leon Modena and the Da Costa Circle in Amsterdam," 25. Translation by Sonne.

¹⁶ On the variation in title, see chapter 1. On Ibn Habib, see Joseph Hacker, "R. Jacob ibn Habib: Toward a Portrait of Jewish Leadership in Salonika in the Early Sixteenth Century" (Hebrew), *World Congress of Jewish Studies* 6, 2 (1976): 117–26; Marjorie Lehman, "The *Ein Ya'aqov*: A Collection of Aggadah in Transition," *Prooftexts* 19 (1999): 21–40.

¹⁷ Leon Modena, *Bet Lehem Yehudah* (Venice: Bragadin, 1625), 2B. Modena's work was included in several subsequent editions of *Ein Ya'akov*.

¹⁸ See Safran, "Leone da Modena's Historical Thinking," 392–98; *Autobiography*, 125, 237; Adelman, "Success and Failure," 714–22.

¹⁹ Modena, *Bet Yehudah*, 6B, 34A; as cited by Libowitz, *Rabi Yehudah Aryeh Modena*, 76, n. 88; Adelman, "Success and Failure," 792. Libowitz cited two other passages that contain allusions to works of Kabbalah or kabbalistic phrases. See *Bet Yehudah*, 8A, 9A. In the first Modena commented on a Talmudic passage about the blessing on creation in the morning liturgy (BT *Berakhot*, 52B). After discussing the argument he mentioned a potential kabbalistic

tance of a person not cursing against himself and cited a proof-text in order to indicate the severity of such a sin: "And in the book of the *Zohar*, they expounded upon this, in order to demonstrate that the danger of cursing oneself is so much greater than that of cursing others."[20]

There are almost certainly other allusions to the *Zohar* in Modena's writings, in print and in manuscript.[21] Although *Ari Nohem* articulated a largely negative vision of the work, Modena never disavowed the *Zohar*. No dramatic shift occurred in his attitude toward the *Zohar* between his earlier works and his later attack on Kabbalah.[22] He argued against its antiquity, its intrusion into the realm of Jewish law, and its unsupervised dissemination among a wider public. The two comments that frame his critical scrutiny outline his positive assessment of the book. Modena insisted upon its value as a hermeneutic key to quandaries of biblical interpretation or as an exhortative tool to improve the moral conduct of his listeners. His writings throughout his career, his early sermons collected in *Midbar Yehudah*, his letter to a questioning Jew in Amsterdam, and his short comments included in a reference work for preachers and students indicate that he used the work in precisely this fashion. From his youthful sermons up until his death, when the *Zohar* appeared in the inventory of his possessions, it remained a formative textual presence in Modena's intellectual landscape.[23]

THE CAUSES OF MODENA'S CRITICISM

Given Modena's positive evaluation of the *Zohar* as well as his continued engagement with it over several decades, one must interrogate the causes that led him to subject it to critical scrutiny. In *Ari Nohem* Modena provided several reasons for his criticism. His immediate social circumstances, particularly his familial and pedagogic relationships, offer an important

---

interpretation: "If I knew of a book from the wisdom of Kabbalah, it seems to me that I would make some allusion, one appropriate for those adept at hidden wisdom. Let he who understands, understand."

[20] Modena, *Bet Yehudah*, 34A.
[21] See *Magen va-Herev*, 12, n. 48.
[22] Weinberg, "Preaching in the Venetian Ghetto," 115–16. In one instance, however, Modena does appear to have revised a statement about the *Zohar*. In his sermon on circumcision, he described the importance of procreation and cited the *Zohar* about Eve in the Garden of Eden. He introduced his citation with the comment, "And this is what the holy Rabbi Simeon bar Yohai wrote, that this was the advice given by the snake to Eve to convince her to eat from the tree." A printed marginal note added "in the book of the *Zohar*." Modena explicitly invoked the *Zohar* as the writing of Simeon bar Yohai, a position he rejected in *Ari Nohem*. See *Midbar Yehudah*, 90A.
[23] Clemente E. Ancona, "L'inventario dei beni appartenenti a Leon da Modena," *Bollettino dell'Istituto di Storia della Società e dello Stato Veneziano* 4 (1962): 262, n. 23.

perspective. His son-in-law, Jacob Levi, and his prized student, Joseph Hamiz, both maintained that either Simeon bar Yohai or his students had composed the *Zohar* in antiquity. In a series of conversations in the early decades of the seventeenth century, Modena and Levi had argued about the origins of the *Zohar*. These discussions probably took place between 1613, when Levi married Modena's daughter, and 1629, the year of Levi's death. During this period, Levi composed his treatise *Nahalat Ya'akov*. In the opening of *Ari Nohem* Modena informed Hamiz about the origins of his son-in-law's work:

> The replies that you saw written in the introduction to his [Levi's] aforementioned work [*Nahalat Ya'akov*] attempt and endeavor to respond to someone who raises doubts about this Kabbalah, the author of the *Zohar*, its principles and foundation. [These replies] were directed at me and my words. For time after time, I posed difficult questions and spoke out against him. He sought to appease me with his replies and bring me into the traditional covenant held by those who cleave to it [Kabbalah]. But I would not hear of it, that is to say, it made no sense to me.[24]

Although *Nahalat Ya'akov* was not printed in the seventeenth century,[25] Hamiz had evidently seen a copy of the work in the 1630s. Modena's discussion of the *Zohar*'s authorship should be seen as his written response to his conversations with Levi and Hamiz as well as to Levi's written treatise.

Given that Modena had discussed the origins of the *Zohar* with Levi as early as the second decade of the seventeenth century, one should consider why he waited over twenty years to record his own response in writing. While it is possible that Modena had actually composed his criticism in an earlier form that has yet to be discovered,[26] *Ari Nohem* itself might offer a partial answer. Modena demonstrated a keen awareness of the unpopularity of his views not only with his close relative and prize student, but also among other Italian Jews. Invoking biblical imagery of a soldier about to embark upon a battle, Modena acknowledged that his critique would offend his contemporaries. He even recounted a story from his youth about the harmful fate that befell an earlier critic of the *Zohar*:

> One of those kabbalists told me that he had seen in the town of Pesaro a young woman who had within her the spirit of a man who said he was the spirit of a deceased Jewish man. They asked him why he had been punished in this way. He responded that when he was alive he had been audacious enough to say that

[24] MS A 6A, 3–8; ed. Libowitz, 2.

[25] Hallamish, "A Document Concerning a Controversy."

[26] As suggested by Fishman, *Shaking the Pillars of Exile*, 171. See also Huss, *Ke-zohar ha-rakia*, 301, n. 60. Modena's notebook from the 1630s does not contain a discussion of the *Zohar*'s origins. See Ancona, Communità Israelitica, MS 7.

the book of the *Zohar* was not composed by Rabbi Simeon bar Yohai, of blessed memory. Nevertheless, I shall not respond to the call of archers,[27] not one but many. Even my spirit within me[28] does not fear that after my death I shall be condemned for this sin.[29]

Although he immediately dismissed this story, Modena may have waited until the late 1630s to express his skepticism about the *Zohar*'s origins because of the unpopularity of his opinions.

Modena set out to counter a basic strategy employed by kabbalists to gain greater authority for their ideas and their texts. Kabbalists attempted to claim an antique origin for the *Zohar* as well as a range of other books, including *Sefer Yetzirah*, *Sefer ha-Bahir*, and *Ma'arekhet ha-Elohut*. Modena, however, declared that kabbalistic texts did not disclose the truth about their own origins. Referring to the subject of Kabbalah:

> It is obvious to me that of all the principal and fundamental books of this knowledge known to us today, not a single one of them informs us honestly and earnestly [about] the identity of its author, even according to those who uphold it. *Sefer Yetzirah* some say [was written] either by our father Abraham, peace be upon him, or by Rabbi Akiva; the *Zohar* some say [was written] either by Rabbi Simeon bar Yohai or by some of his students; *Sefer ha-Bahir* some say [was written] either by Rabbi Nehuniah ben ha-Kaneh or by one of the Geonim.[30]

Modena identified pseudepigraphy, the deliberate ascription of a text to a person other than the author, as a basic strategy employed by kabbalists in order to gain greater authority for their texts.[31] He sought to demonstrate, however, the recent origin of these works and noted that even kabbalists themselves did not agree about the specific authors of their works.

Drawing on Judah Hayyat, an Iberian kabbalist who lived at the turn of the sixteenth century and wrote a commentary entitled *Minhat Yehudah* to *Ma'arekhet ha-Elohut*,[32] Modena continued: "When he [Hayyat] mentions

---

[27] Jud. 5:11.
[28] Isa. 26:9.
[29] MS A 32B, 2–5; ed. Libowitz, 57.
[30] MS A 31A, 10–13; ed. Libowitz, 54.
[31] On forgery and pseudepigraphy, see Anthony Grafton, *Forgers and Critics: Creativity and Duplicity in Western Scholarship* (Princeton: Princeton University Press, 1990), 5–6. On medieval Jewish pseudepigraphy, see Elliot R. Wolfson, "Hai Gaon's Letter and Commentary on *Aleynu*: Further Evidence of Moses de León's Pseudepigraphic Activity," *JQR* 81 (1991): 365–409; Mark Verman, *The Books of Contemplation: Medieval Jewish Mystical Sources* (Albany: SUNY Press, 1992), 24–30; Joseph Dan, *The "Unique Cherub" Circle: A School of Mystics and Esoterics in Medieval Germany* (Tübingen: Mohr Siebeck, 1999), chap. 1.
[32] Gershom Scholem, "On the Problem of the Book *Ma'arekhet ha-Elohut* and Its Commentators" (Hebrew), in *Mehkere Kabalah*, ed. Yosef Ben-Shomo (Tel Aviv: Am Oved, 1998), 183. For further literature on *Ma'arekhet ha-Elohut*, see 188. For a different perspective on Hayyat, see Moshe Idel, *Messianic Mystics* (New Haven: Yale University Press, 1998), 136–38.

Sefer Yetzirah, he says 'attributed to Rabbi Akiva,' or *Sefer ha-Bahir*, [he says] 'attributed to Moses, our teacher, peace be upon him.' But even he [Hayyat] did not fill his heart with certainty to say that they composed them [these books]. Rather, [he said] 'attributed.' "[33] Hayyat's method of ascription indicated his uncertainty about the actual origins and genuine authors of kabbalistic books. This contrasts with the various apologies and self-justifications Modena offered for *Ari Nohem* itself. At the outset of the work and again at the beginning of his critique of the *Zohar*, Modena appeared determined to disclose the truth about the origins of his own work and the precise circumstances of its composition. His own writing on Kabbalah served as a clear counterexample to the way kabbalists wrote about their most important texts and ostensible authors.

Modena compared the pseudepigraphic character of the *Zohar* to *Sefer ha-Yashar*, a Hebrew work printed in Venice in the early seventeenth century.

> Behold, it [the *Zohar*] is like *Sefer ha-Yashar*, which they printed (without my knowledge and without the knowledge of the sages here in Venice, about twenty years ago).[34] Although I removed the fantasies and falsehoods from it, [e.g.,] that it is the *Sefer ha-Yashar* mentioned in Scripture, there are still those who claim that it was discovered during the time of the destruction [of the temple]. But who can stop those who imagine in their minds whatever they wish.[35]

As a member of the Venetian rabbinate who supervised the printing of Hebrew books in Venice, Modena had stopped the editors from identifying *Sefer ha-Yashar* with a work by the same name mentioned in the book of Joshua but had failed to prevent them from claiming it was discovered at the time of the destruction of the temple.[36] The editors of the printed edition seized upon stories about Titus and the Jews within *Sefer ha-Yashar* and claimed it was written in antiquity. Modena's explicit comparison between *Sefer ha-Yashar* and the *Zohar* reveals an important aspect of his attitude toward pseudepigraphic literary activity. When a group of experts lost control over a given pseudepigraphic text, they could no longer determine how people would conceive of it or its origins. With the *Zohar*, the text had taken on not only the veneer of authenticity but also the status of tradition.

---

[33] MS A 31A, 13–15; ed. Libowitz, 54

[34] *Sefer ha-Yashar* appeared in Venice in 1625. See Joseph Dan, ed., *Sefer ha-Yashar* (Jerusalem: Mossad Bialik, 1986).

[35] MS A 38A, 21–24; ed. Libowitz, 73–74.

[36] Joseph Dan, "R. Judah Aryeh Modena and *Sefer ha-Yashar*" (Hebrew), *Sinai* 78 (1976): 197–98; Dan, "Introduction," in *Sefer ha-Yashar*, 20; Meir Benayahu, *Haskamah u-reshut bi-defuse Venetsyah* (Jerusalem: Ben-Zvi Institute, 1971), 43–47, 270–74; Fishman, *Shaking the Pillars of Exile*, 60–62.

Modena emphasized that the issue of authorship plays a crucial role in the constitution of tradition: "If it is unknown who created these [works] and who formed them,[37] how can he be regarded as a kabbalist and his words the words of tradition (Heb. *Kabbalah*)?"[38] By appropriating the term Kabbalah, the word for tradition, and the title *mekubal*, the word for a recipient of tradition, adherents to the *Zohar* and similar texts presumed a continuous transmission over the course of generations. Modena argued that if one does not know the origin of a given book or set of books, then one cannot claim they constitute part of a tradition. In demonstrating the medieval origins of the *Zohar* and questioning the antiquity of a range of other texts, such as *Sefer ha-Bahir* and *Sefer Yetzirah*, Modena effectively invalidated any claim to continuity between these texts and genuine tradition, what he referred to elsewhere as Oral Torah.

Apart from *Sefer ha-Bahir*, all the works criticized in *Ari Nohem* as kabbalistic books of dubious authorship had been printed for the first time at Hebrew presses in northern Italy in the second half of the sixteenth century.[39] The widespread availability of kabbalistic texts in general and of the *Zohar* in particular was a third factor that drove Modena to subject the *Zohar* to critical scrutiny.[40] Between 1558 and 1560, rival editions of the *Zohar* were printed at Cremona and Mantua. The press in Mantua also printed an edition of *Tikkunei ha–Zohar* in a separate volume. In the same time period, rival editions of *Ma'arekhet ha-Elohut* appeared, one at Ferrara and one at Mantua. The first edition of *Sefer Yetzirah* appeared at Mantua in 1562. This flurry of printing in the middle of the sixteenth century was hardly coincidental. By and large, Jews had not initiated the printing of kabbalistic texts in the first half of the sixteenth century. In response to the printing of Kabbalah by gentiles and a ban on the printing of the Talmud, several members of the Italian rabbinate made a concerted effort to print kabbalistic classics.

The sixteenth-century editors of the *Zohar* reflected on the potential impact of their activity in various paratextual materials included in their editions. In his endorsement that appeared in the Mantua *Tikkunei ha–Zohar*,

---

[37] Cf. Isa. 40:26; 44:10.

[38] MS A 31A, 17–18; ed. Libowitz, 54.

[39] *Sefer ha-Bahir* was first printed in Amsterdam in 1651. Considerable portions of it had already appeared in the 1558 Cremona *Zohar*. For a facsimile of the first edition, see Daniel Abrams, ed., *Sefer ha-Bahir* (Los Angeles: Cherub Press, 1994), 263–86. For the *Bahir* in the Cremona *Zohar*, see 236–57.

[40] See Simha Assaf, "On the Controversy over the Printing of Kabbalistic Books" (Hebrew), *Sinai* 5 (1939): 360–68; Tishby, "The Controversy over the Book of the *Zohar* in Italy in the Sixteenth Century"; Ephraim Kupfer, "New Documents on the Controversy over the Printing of the *Zohar*" (Hebrew), *Michael* 1 (1972): 302–18; Joseph Hacker, "A New Letter about the Controversy on the Printing of the *Zohar* in Italy" (Hebrew), in Goldreich and Oron, *Masuot*, 120–30; Huss, *Ke-zohar ha-rakia*, 117–39.

the Italian rabbi Moses Provençal (1503–1575) minimized the difference between print and manuscript. He argued that Kabbalah had shifted from esoteric secrets to public knowledge as soon as it had been committed to writing. In terms of the disclosure of secrets, the printing of a book did not constitute a qualitatively different mechanism of transmission from the copying of a manuscript. Modena quoted Provençal's responsum in order to refute it.

> He [Provençal] too says that from the day these matters were committed to writing, they were thought to be well known so what would printing add, etc? He further said that manuscripts and print are the same to any who consider them. For this [printing] is like a manuscript; except that one [a manuscript] is purchased for the equivalent of several coins while the other one [a printed book], hewn with the tip of iron and lead,[41] goes out to the cheap market.[42]

For Provençal the only difference between print and manuscript was cost. By reducing this distinction to economics, Provençal sought to minimize the potential impact of printing on the status of esoteric wisdom. He claimed that the point of transition between esotericism and public knowledge had already occurred centuries earlier when Kabbalah had first been recorded in writing. Provençal may have adopted a minimalist perspective on the potential impact of the *Zohar* in print as a strategy to help the editors win approval for their project. Provençal's attitude toward any type of writing as a fundamental breach of the restrictions of esotericism had an antecedent among medieval kabbalists. In a celebrated letter to Nahmanides and Jonah Girondi, Isaac the Blind declared, "The written matter has no ark. For many times its author (Heb. *ba'alav*) will disappear or die and the books will fall into the hands of simpletons or scoffers and the name of heaven will be desecrated." Already in the thirteenth century, Isaac the Blind characterized a book as something beyond the control of its author.[43]

---

[41] Cf. Job 19:24. A phrase often used to refer to printing.

[42] MS A 45B, 8–11; ed. Libowitz, 92. See the approbation by Moses Provençal in *Tikkunei ha–Zohar* (Mantua, 1558), 2B–3A. For a similar argument, see the introduction by Emmanuel of Corfu to *Sefer ha–Zohar* (Mantua, 1558), 1A–3B. On Modena's confusion of Emmanuel Benveneto, editor of the *Tikkunei ha–Zohar*, with Emmanuel of Corfu, editor of the first volume of the Mantua *Zohar*, see Tishby, "The Controversy over the Book of the *Zohar* in Italy in the Sixteenth Century," 118, n. 136, and the letter from Scholem to Libowitz printed in *Ari Nohem*, ed. Libowitz, 157.

[43] Gershom Scholem, "A New Document about the History of the Beginnings of Kabbalah" (Hebrew), in *Mehkere Kabalah*, 9; Scholem, *Origins of the Kabbalah*, 394–403; Moshe Idel, "Nahmanides: *Kabbalah, Halakhah*, and Spiritual Leadership," in *Jewish Mystical Leaders and Leadership in the 13th Century*, ed. Moshe Idel and Mortimer Ostow, 15–96 (Northvale, NJ: Jason Aronson, 1998); Halbertal, *Concealment and Revelation*, 69–76. On esotericism in medieval Kabbalah, see Idel, "We Have No Kabbalistic Tradition on This"; Daniel Abrams, "Orality in the Kabbalistic School of Nahmanides: Preserving and Interpreting Esoteric Traditions

Modena claimed that Provençal misrepresented the popularity of Kabbalah before it appeared in print as well as underestimated the potential impact that the printing of the *Zohar* would have on Jewish life. For Modena, the printing of the *Zohar* had dramatically transformed the processes of kabbalistic transmission.

> "The punishment of the iniquity of my daughter is greater,"[44] and the breach has increased, particularly because books have emerged from the printing press, the *Zohar*, the *Tikkunim*, *Ma'arekhet ha-Elohut* and others like them. As long as they remained only written matters, very few people entered into them, and whoever had them in his possession would only hand them over to be copied down by one who was worthy, esteemed in his eyes, and deserving of it. In most cases, the first person would know [him] and teach him face to face, and only afterwards pursue the book.[45]

In this reconstruction, medieval Kabbalah had been transmitted in a social setting, involving a master and disciple. A social relationship accompanied by the verbal exchange of knowledge preceded the study of written texts. By granting permission only to worthy individuals to copy out from a manuscript, kabbalists maintained careful control over the circulation and dissemination of their texts.[46]

Modena contrasted this with conditions that prevailed since the printing of kabbalistic books:

> However, since their printing, whoever has coins or cash in his hands and knows how to read, whomever he may be or whatever or however it may be, purchases books, considers them, and imagines that he understands and knows them. The plague has spread[47] to countless individuals. For even if you say that these are the words of the living God and exalted wisdom, there is no doubt that abandonment, error, and heresy have increased among the masses.[48]

Kabbalah, according to Modena, had become all the rage, in no small part because of the availability of basic texts in print and a radical shift in the process of transmission. A free-for-all, where anyone with money and rudimentary knowledge of Hebrew could pick up a book of Kabbalah and fancy himself or herself an expert in divine wisdom, had replaced the

---

and Texts," *JSQ* 3 (1996): 85-102; Wolfson, "Beyond the Spoken Word"; Idel, "Transmission in Thirteenth-Century Kabbalah," in Elman and Gershoni, *Transmitting Jewish Traditions*, 138–65; Fishbane *As Light Before Dawn*, chaps. 3–4.

[44] Lam. 4:6.

[45] MS A 45A, 11–14; ed. Libowitz, 90.

[46] To the extent that current scholarship corroborates Modena's description, see the literature cited above.

[47] Lev. 13:5.

[48] MS A 45A, 14–18; ed. Libowitz, 90–91.

master–disciple relationship characteristic of the study of Kabbalah in prior centuries. In this account, Modena adopted a restrictive stance toward the spread of a particular form of knowledge. He argued that so long as Kabbalah had not become a form of public knowledge, it had had a limited impact on Jewish life. In the latter half of the sixteenth century, however, Kabbalah had spread. Even proponents of Kabbalah as an exalted wisdom would concede that this had debilitating consequences.

Provençal and Modena both agreed that the printing of kabbalistic books precipitated a change in scale. More copies of a given book were available at a cheaper price. Recent studies on sixteenth-century Italian printing confirm this argument at the quantitative level. Paul Grendler estimated that the average press run of a book printed in Venice with ordinary or modest sales potential was 1,000 copies.[49] The contract drawn up between Vincenzo Conti, the owner of the Cremona press, and Samuel ben Isaac of Verona and David ben Aharon Norliengen, two of the Jewish editors of the Cremona *Zohar*, stipulated that 675 copies of the *Zohar* would be printed.[50] If one posits a similar press run for the Mantua *Zohar*, then roughly 1,300 printed copies of the *Zohar* had appeared at Italian presses in the middle of the sixteenth century, augmenting the manuscript copies of the *Zohar* already circulating in Italy. A survey of private Jewish libraries in sixteenth-century Mantua, a midsize Italian town with a relatively large Jewish community, found that one-tenth of all libraries contained copies of the *Zohar*.[51] The printing of the *Zohar* led to a dramatic increase in the availability of the text.[52]

Modena stressed that the printing of the *Zohar* and other kabbalistic books was not limited to Italy. An edition of the *Zohar* printed in the Ottoman Empire had recently appeared in Venice:

> In my own time, right before my very own eyes, in the year 1602, a sage from the Levant, R. Naftali Ashkenazi, of blessed memory, arrived here [in Venice]. He used to study in our academy and died here. I delivered a eulogy for him, which is printed in my book of sermons, *Midbar Yehudah*. And this sage brought with

---

[49] *The Roman Inquisition and the Venetian Press*, 9.

[50] Shlomo Simonsohn, "A Contract for the Printing of Hebrew Books in Cremona" (Hebrew), in *Scritti in Memoria di Umberto Nahon*, ed. Robert Bonfil et al., 143-50 (Jerusalem: Sally Mayer Foundation, 1978).

[51] Shifra Baruchson, *Sefarim ve-korim: tarbut ha-keriah shel Yehude Italyah be-shilhe ha-Renesans* (Ramat Gan: Bar–Ilan University Press, 1993), 160.

[52] Huss, *Ke-zohar ha-rakia*, 102–27. Tishby and Bonfil have argued that there was a scarcity of *Zohar* manuscripts in Italy before it appeared in print. Penkower claimed that the number of *Zohar* manuscripts (some incomplete) in Italy was far from insubstantial. See Penkower, "A Renewed Inquiry," 48, n. 120. It stands to reason that Penkower would agree that the printing of the *Zohar* led to an increase in the number of available copies.

him a new portion of the *Zohar* and the *Midrash ha-Ne'elam*, which was printed in Salonika. . . . there are certainly some of them in Italy.[53]

Naftali Ashkenazi had left Safed around 1594 and intended to print his edition of the *Zohar Hadash* in Venice. Upon reaching Salonika, where he examined the literary remains of the kabbalist Judah Gedalya, he decided to print the *Zohar Hadash* in the Ottoman Empire and made ample use of Gedalya's annotations and his manuscripts in the possession of his son. Ashkenazi eventually reached Venice, where he printed his own collection of sermons, *Imre Shefer*, and worked on the publication of Hebrew books. Much to Modena's chagrin, he had also imported copies of his *Zohar Hadash* with him.[54]

Modena turned to Poland for corroboration of his polemic against the printing of Kabbalah. He drew on Moses Isserles (1520–1572), a central figure of sixteenth-century Polish Jewry, to justify his argument about a rupture in the transmission of Kabbalah. In *Torat ha-Olah*, a work printed less than a decade after the Cremona and Mantua editions of the *Zohar*, Isserles argued that the printing of kabbalistic books played a decisive role in the popularization of Kabbalah. Furthermore, he corroborated Modena's description of the transmission of Kabbalah before the advent of print:

> In his book *Torat ha-Olah*, part three, chapter four[55] [Isserles wrote], "Many people among the masses leap up to study this matter of Kabbalah because it is a delight to behold. This is especially in the words of the recent ones who explicitly revealed their matters in their books. All the more so in these times when the books of Kabbalah have been printed, the *Zohar*, Recanati,[56] and *Sha'arei*

---

[53] MSA 38A, 15–19; ed. Libowitz, 73.

[54] Modena composed a poem that appeared as an approbation to Ashkenazi's *Imre Shefer* (Venice: Zanetti, 1601). See Simon Bernstein, *The Divan of Leo de Modena* (Philadelphia: JPS, 1932), no. 27, 73–74. In his eulogy, Modena described Ashkenazi as a member of the yeshiva in Venice and listed his death as Nissan 5362 (March–April 1602). See *Midbar Yehudah*, 78A–80B. On Ashkenazi in Salonika and the library of Judah Gedalya, see Joseph Hacker, "The History of the Study of Kabbalah and Its Dissemination in Salonika in the 16th Century" (Hebrew), in *Creation and Re-Creation in Jewish Thought: Festschrift in Honor of Joseph Dan on the Occasion of His Seventieth Birthday*, ed. Rachel Elior and Peter Schäfer (Tübingen: Mohr Siebeck, 2005), 169.

[55] Isserles, *Sefer Torat Ha-Olah* (Prague, 1569), 72B. This passage from *Torat ha-Olah* was copied without ascription by Aaron Moses Altschuler, a native of Prague and rabbi of the Kromau community in Moravia, in the preface to *Sefer va-Yehal Moshe* (Prague, 1613). See Tishby, "General Introduction," in *The Wisdom of the Zohar: An Anthology of Texts* (Oxford: Littman Library, 1989) 1:38, n.182.

[56] Menahem Recanati was a fourteenth-century Italian kabbalist. His commentary on the Pentateuch was printed at Venice in 1523 and in 1545, and his *Sefer Ta'amei ha-Mizvot* at Constantinople 1543–1544 and Basel in 1581. See Moshe Idel, *Rabi Menahem Recanati ha-mekubal* (Jerusalem: Schocken 1998).

Orah,⁵⁷ which anyone can examine. Everything will be explained according to his understanding even though their words will not be understood by way of truth, since it is no longer transmitted from one recipient of the tradition to another. Not only this, that the enlightened ones should understand it, but even the common folk who do not know the difference between their right and their left, who walk in darkness,⁵⁸ who do not know how to explicate the weekly portion or the portion with Rashi's commentary, even they leap up to study Kabbalah."⁵⁹

Isserles offered an even more damning portrait than Modena of the new audience for kabbalistic books. These readers included not only "enlightened men," but also those who lacked knowledge of even the most basic of Jewish texts, the Pentateuch with Rashi's commentary.

While Modena accurately portrayed Isserles' criticism of the recent popularity of Kabbalah, he also cast him as an antikabbalistic writer who preceded him. Modena included Isserles as one of several scholars opposed to Kabbalah in a list that he appended to the manuscript of *Ari Nohem* copied by his amanuensis and cited the same passage in *Torat ha-Olah* as proof of Isserles' opposition to Kabbalah.⁶⁰ This was part of Modena's attempt to create an antikabbalist tradition among medieval and early modern Jews rather than an accurate description of Isserles' own position. Isserles was hardly an antikabbalist.⁶¹ While he may have decried the popularization of Kabbalah as a result of printing, he held positions that Modena rejected in no uncertain terms elsewhere in *Ari Nohem*. In the very passage from *Torat ha-Olah* adduced by Modena, Isserles alluded to a crucial distinction between genuine kabbalists and his contemporaries who considered themselves experts in esoteric wisdom: "Their words are not understood by way of truth, since it is no longer transmitted from one recipient of the tradition to another." The phrase "by way of truth" and the notion of an uninterrupted chain of transmission from one recipient to another allude quite pointedly to Nahmanides.⁶² In his biblical commentary, Nahmanides

---

⁵⁷ By Joseph Gikatilla, a thirteenth-century Castilian kabbalist. Printed in 1561 in Mantua.
⁵⁸ Ps. 82:5.
⁵⁹ MS A 45A, 18–24; ed. Libowitz, 91.
⁶⁰ For Isserles' name see MS A 48B, 11. See also MS A 27B, 6–7; ed. Libowitz, 45.
⁶¹ Yonah Ben-Sasson, *Mishnato ha-iyunit shel ha-Rema* (Jerusalem: Israel Academy of Sciences, 1984), 33–40, 47–59, 315–20; Jacob Elbaum, *Petihut ve-histagrut: Ha-yetsirah ha-ruhanit-ha-sifrutit be-Polin uve-artsot Ashkenaz be-shilhe ha-meah ha-shesh-esreh* (Jerusalem: Magnes Press, 1990), 286–92, 329–34. For Isserles' commentaries to the *Zohar* and *Ma'arekhet ha-Elohut*, see Pinchas Giller, *Reading the Zohar: The Sacred Text of the Kabbalah* (New York: Oxford University Press, 2001), 28, n. 194.
⁶² Moshe Halbertal, *Al derekh ha-emet: ha-Ramban vi-yetsiratah shel masoret* (Jerusalem: Mekhon Shalom Hartman, 2006); Haviva Pedaya, *Ha-Ramban: bit'alut, zeman mahzori ve-tekst kadosh* (Tel Aviv: Am Oved, 2003). On Nahmanides, see chapter 3.

repeatedly employed the phrase when offering a kabbalistic explanation of a given verse.[63] Nahmanides also refused to divulge divine secrets that he had received from a prior recipient of the esoteric tradition.[64] Isserles clearly valued the transmission of esoteric secrets by a master to his disciple. For him, the availability of kabbalistic texts in print had not obviated the need for personal instruction by a master authorized to transmit esoteric secrets. It had only enabled his contemporaries to delude themselves into thinking they were genuine masters of esoteric wisdom. Elsewhere in the same section of *Torat ha-Olah* adduced by Modena, Isserles cited with approval a statement by Moses Botarel on the similarities between Kabbalah and philosophy; in *Ari Nohem*, Modena went to great lengths to refute such a position.[65]

In contrast to Provençal, who supported the printing of the *Zohar*, Modena and Isserles emphasized the dramatic cultural change that had been introduced by the appearance of the *Zohar* as a printed book. Not all the proponents of the *Zohar*'s printing, however, took Provençal's minimalist stance in considering the potential effects of publication. Isaac de Lattes, a sixteenth-century Italian rabbi who wrote an approbation that appeared in the first volume of the Mantua *Zohar*, claimed that printing the *Zohar* would hasten the advent of the Messiah.[66] Modena countered this claim by simply observing: "But we have seen that it is approximately two hundred and fifty years since the revelation of the *Zohar* in writing and the Messiah has not come. And it is some seventy years since it has been printed and the Messiah has not come, and the land [still] lacks understanding!"[67] Modena's

---

[63] Wolfson, "By Way of Truth."

[64] Idel, "We Have No Kabbalistic Tradition on This."

[65] Isserles, *Sefer Torat Ha-Olah*, 75B. Botarel, a late medieval Provencal kabbalist, composed a commentary to *Sefer Yetzirah* that appeared in the 1562 Mantua edition. See Zipporah Brody, "R. Moses Botarel: His Commentary on *Sefer Yetzirah* and the Image of Abu Aharon" (Hebrew), in Dan, *Sefer zikaron le-Gershom Scholem bi-mlot esrim ve-hamesh shanim le-petirato*, 1:159–206. On Kabbalah and philosophy in *Ari Nohem*, see chapter 4.

[66] *Sefer ha-Zohar* (Mantua, 1558), 4A–6B. See Tishby, "The Controversy over the Printing of the *Zohar* in Italy," 99–106. On De Lattes, see Elliott Horowitz, "Speaking of the Dead: The Emergence of the Eulogy among Italian Jewry of the Sixteenth Century," in Ruderman, *Preachers of the Italian Ghetto*, 129–62; Saverio Campanini, "Anima in itinere: Un'orazione funebre di Avraham da Sant'Angelo," in *La cultura ebraica a Bologna tra medioevo e rinascimento*, ed. Mauro Perani, 129–68 (Florence: Giuntina, 2002); Bernard Dov Cooperman, "Political Discourse in a Kabbalistic Register: Isaac de Lattes' Plea for Stronger Communal Government," in *Be'erot Yitzhak: Studies in Memory of Isadore Twersky*, ed. Jay M. Harris, 47–68; 79–93 (Hebrew appendices) (Cambridge: Harvard University Press, 2005). On messianism and the *Zohar*, see Yehuda Liebes, "The Messiah of the *Zohar*: The Messianic Image of Simeon bar Yohai" (Hebrew), in *Ha-Ra'ayon ha-Meshihi be-Yisrael*, ed. Shmuel Reem, 87–236 (Jerusalem: Israel Academy of the Sciences, 1982).

[67] MS A 45B, 23–24; ed. Libowitz, 92.

sarcastic rebuttal cast kabbalists who linked the printing of the *Zohar* with the advent of the Messiah as delusional.

Modena directed his polemical ire not only at the supposedly ignorant masses who had recently started to read the text but also at the elite custodians of the Jewish tradition, contemporary rabbis who had begun to use the *Zohar* as an authoritative source of Jewish law. In the late Middle Ages, jurists had occasionally quoted the *Zohar* in adjudicating specific cases.[68] At the turn of the sixteenth century, this process increased due to the incorporation of rulings from the *Zohar* in the legal writings of scholars such as Jacob Landau, author of *Sefer Agur*,[69] and David ibn abi Zimra, a jurist in Egypt and Palestine.[70] By the middle of the sixteenth century this further accelerated with the work of Joseph Karo.[71] Karo's *Bet Yosef*, a commentary on the *Arba'ah Turim* of Jacob Ben Asher, and *Shulhan Arukh*, a précis of his *Bet Yosef*, became standard works of Jewish law. Karo's writings marked a different approach to the incorporation of the *Zohar* into the realm of Jewish law from his predecessors and contemporaries. In contrast to Landau and Ibn abi Zimra, who occasionally cited the *Zohar*, Karo quoted the *Zohar* explicitly or implicitly dozens of times in his legal writings.[72] In addition to these instances, Karo listed the *Zohar* in the introduction to his *Bet Yosef* as one of several authoritative texts taken into consideration when formulating his commentary. Karo had thus elevated the status of the *Zohar* into an authoritative source for the determination of the law.

Modena rejected the insertion of the *Zohar* into the realm of Jewish law and sought to extricate it from the legal sphere. At the level of theory, he dismissed the attempt by sixteenth-century rabbinic authorities to formulate a legal principle that incorporated the *Zohar* as a source of authority. According to their opinion, when a legal case was not explicit in the

---

[68] Ta-Shma, *Ha-Nigleh she-ba nistar*; Jacob Katz, *Halakha ve-Kabalah: Mehkarim be-toldot dat Yisrael al medoreha ve-zikatah ha-hevratit* (Jerusalem: Magnes Press, 1984).

[69] Written in Italy in the 1480s, *Sefer Agur* was printed in 1490, 1526, and 1546. For references to the *Zohar*, see paras. 36 and 84. Jacob Landau, *Sefer Agur* (Venice: Giustinian, 1546), 5B–6A, 8B; as cited in Jacob Katz, "Post-Zoharic Relations between Halakhah and Kabbalah," in Cooperman, *Jewish Thought in the Sixteenth Century*, 294, n. 40.

[70] The one volume of his responsa printed in the seventeenth century, Livorno 1652, appears as volume 4 in subsequent editions. Ibn abi Zimra quoted the *Zohar* or kabbalistic books in responsa, vol. 4, 55, and 80. See David ben Solomon ibn abi Zimra, *She'elot u-Teshuvot* (Livorno, 1652), 11A, 25B; as cited in Israel M. Goldman, *The Life and Times of Rabbi David Ibn Abi Zimra* (New York: Jewish Theological Seminary of America, 1970), 70–74, 245; Katz, "Post-Zoharic Relations," 289, n. 17.

[71] Moshe Hallamish, "Kabbalah in the Adjudication of Joseph Karo" (Hebrew), *Daat* 21 (1988): 85–102.

[72] See, for example, *Tur Orah Hayim*, para. 31, where Karo cites the *Zohar* in his commentary in conjunction with wearing phylacteries on the intermediate days of a festival. As cited by Katz, "Post-Zoharic Relations," 304, n. 89. Ta-Shma argued that Karo quoted the *Zohar* as many as a hundred times in his legal writings. *Ha-Nigleh she-ba nistar*, 88–104.

Talmud and subject to dispute among later legal authorities, the law should follow the *Zohar* if it had issued an explicit ruling. While Modena cited this principle in the name of Abraham Zacut and Gedalya ibn Yahya, authors of Jewish chronicles, Karo had also formulated and applied a similar type of argument.[73] Modena raised the following objection: "If the *Zohar* contains the words of Rabbi Simeon bar Yohai, and if when he argues with his colleagues in the Talmud, the law does not follow his opinion, then why should his opinion gain greater strength now? . . . Why should we decide the law in accordance with his opinion when the matter is subject to dispute?"[74] Modena posited that the *Zohar* should have no bearing on contemporary legal practice. He further objected to specific instances where early modern authorities had formulated Jewish law on the basis of the *Zohar*. In direct contradiction to several passages in the Talmud and the rulings of later legal authorities such as Maimonides and Jacob ben Asher, the *Zohar* had ruled that Jewish slaves owned by Jews were exempt from the fulfillment of the commandments. Drawing on his contemporary Joseph Solomon Delmedigo, Modena posited this as a flagrant contradiction between the *Zohar* and accepted legal norms.[75]

Modena drew another example from the laws concerning phylacteries. Following an opinion ascribed to Simeon bar Yohai in the *Zohar*, legal authorities had ruled that men should recite one blessing rather than two when donning them, that they should sit down while wrapping the straps bound around the arm, and that they should refrain from wearing them on the intermediate days of a festival.[76] In his treatment of this issue, Modena

---

[73] After citing the *Zohar* in his ruling about phylacteries on the intermediate days of a festival, Karo wrote in his *Bet Yosef*: "Since in our Talmud this issue is not explicitly determined, who would dare to transgress actively what Simeon bar Yohai has so emphatically proscribed." Cited and translated in Katz, "Post-Zoharic Relations," 304. For references to the sources cited by Modena, see Abraham Zacut, *Sefer Yuhasin* (Constantinople, 1566), 37A; Gedalya ibn Yahya, *Shalshelet ha-Kabalah* (Venice: Di Gara, 1587), 31B. David ibn abi Zimra formulated a similar principle with respect to "books of Kabbalah," but he did not specifically mention the *Zohar*, citing only "one of the more recent sages who wrote in the name of Rabbi Simeon bar Yohai, of blessed memory." See Goldman, *The Life and Times*, 71, n. 156. This is responsa 4, 36, and appears in Ibn Zimra, *She'elot u-Teshuvot*, 6A.

[74] MS A 35A, 24–35B, 1; ed. Libowitz, 65.

[75] MS A 35B, 1–8; ed. Libowitz, 65. Immediately following, Modena quoted two passages from the *Zohar*, neither of which had any direct bearing on Jewish law. He derived these citations from Joseph Solomon Delmedigo. See *Sefer Mazref le-Hokhmah* in *Sefer Ta'alumot Hokhmah*, 28A. Modena was apparently unaware of a contemporary work that collected the laws in the *Zohar* arranged according to the *Shulhan Arukh*. See Issachar Baer of Kremenitz, *Yesh Sakhar* (Prague, 1609). See also Tishby, "General Introduction," 26 n. 119; Jacob Katz, "Halakhic Statements in the Zohar," in *Divine Law in Human Hands: Case Studies in Halakhic Flexibility*, 11–12 (Jerusalem: Magnes Press, 1998).

[76] Ta-Shma, *Ha-Nigleh she-ba nistar*, 73–79. For Provençal on this issue, see Penkower, "A Renewed Inquiry," 58, n. 149.

turned to another luminary of sixteenth-century Polish Jewry, Solomon Luria.[77] A correspondent, relative, and occasional rival of Isserles, Luria had been asked by one Mordechai bar Tanhum for his opinion on the matter and responded with an extensive polemic against the use of the *Zohar* in Jewish law. Modena cited nearly the entirety of his responsum in *Ari Nohem*.[78] Luria's acidic rejection of Simeon bar Yohai epitomized Modena's opposition to the *Zohar* in the legal sphere:

> New ones who come but lately[79] wanted to be part of the sect of kabbalists and of the expounders of the invisible.[80] They are weak of vision and do not see in the light of the *Zohar* and do not know its origin or its source. Know, my beloved, that all my holy ancestors and teachers, who served the eminences of the world, I saw that they did not behave in such a way. Rather, [they followed] the words of the Talmud and those of the legal authorities. And if Rabbi Simeon bar Yohai were to stand screaming before you to change the custom that was practiced by the early ones, we would not pay any attention to him, because in most matters the law does not follow his opinion.[81]

Further on, Luria cited both Karo and Jacob Landau and argued that in this case the law should not follow either of their opinions. For Modena, Luria served as a well-respected legal authority who had rejected the intrusion of the *Zohar* into Jewish law in no uncertain terms.

Luria's text was hardly a matter of arcane legal inquiry to Modena's contemporaries. Menahem Azariah da Fano, a prominent kabbalist and sometime mentor to Modena, had read Luria's dismissal of the *Zohar* and vehemently opposed it: "his [Luria's] lips spoke boastfully and disdainfully against these discourses, and he was indeed impoverished at that moment, and all his words here are completely vain."[82] While Modena did not mention Menahem Azariah da Fano's reaction, he certainly knew of Joseph Solomon Delmedigo's citation of Luria in *Mazref le-Hokhmah*. Delmedigo, however, did not offer a refutation and cited Luria's ruling only as evidence of different practices between Ashkenazim and Sephardim. Modena, who could have known Luria's responsum on his own, appears to have cited it via Delmedigo's work.[83]

---

[77] See Simha Assaf, "A Contribution to the Biography of R. Solomon Luria" (Hebrew), in *Sefer ha-Yovel li-khevod Levi Ginsburg*, 45–63 (Philadelphia: JPS, 1946); Reiner, "The Ashkenazi Elite," 93, n. 22; Davis, "The Reception of the *Shulhan Arukh*," 261–62.

[78] Solomon Luria, *She'elot u-Teshuvot* (Lublin, 1599), no. 98, 68A.

[79] Deut. 32:17.

[80] Heb. *Midrash ha-Ne'elam*, an allusion to a section of the *Zohar*.

[81] MS A 34B, 6–11; ed. Libowitz, 63.

[82] Menahem Azariah da Fano, *Sefer Teshuvot* (Venice: Zanetti, 1600), no. 108, 111A; as cited by Tishby, "General Introduction," 27. For secondary literature on this figure, see chapter 4.

[83] Delmedigo appears to have taken Luria's responsum from the 1599 edition and cited it in its entirety. *Sefer Mazref le-Hokhmah* in *Sefer Ta'alumot Hokhmah*, 25A–25B. In two instances,

In sum, kabbalists such as Hamiz and Levi had attributed the origins of the *Zohar* to antiquity and argued that the book had been composed either by Simeon bar Yohai or by his students. The printing of the *Zohar* had enabled many more people to gain access to the esoteric knowledge contained within the *Zohar* without the oversight of known experts. At the same time, rabbinic scholars had elevated the *Zohar* to a legal authority and relied on it to adjudicate specific cases. Modena objected to the packaging of the *Zohar* as a printed book available for purchase and perusal as well as to its use as a legal authority by leading rabbinic jurists.

MODENA AND EARLIER *ZOHAR* CRITICISM

Scholars have traced the whispered traditions of *Zohar* criticism between the appearance of the *Zohar* in Castile in the late thirteenth century and the composition of *Ari Nohem* in Venice in the early seventeenth. Christians and Jews repeatedly questioned the authenticity of the *Zohar* as an ancient work.[84] Elijah Delmedigo's *Behinat ha-Dat*, a treatise composed in Crete in 1490–1491, contained several critical comments on the *Zohar*.[85] In the first half of the sixteenth century, Elijah Levita's grammatical works included an implicit critique of the *Zohar*'s antiquity.[86] Because of its recent origin, the *Zohar* could not serve him as a source for the history of biblical vocalization. In the 1550s, during the controversy over the printing of the *Zohar*, several rabbinic opponents of publication included questions about the work's antiquity in their arguments. Their doubts survive largely in the

---

Modena's spelling of a Hebrew word—*tzavah* with two *vav* (34B, line 9) and *ke'ilu hem* (34B, line 17) — follows Delmedigo rather than the 1599 edition, which reads *tzavah* with one *vav* and *ke'ilu hen*. Modena knew of Solomon Luria's responsa independently. In his responsum on head covering in public, he cited Luria. The citation appears at the end of the responsum preceded by the following note: "Several years after I had already written the aforementioned remarks, a responsum came into my possession, [written by] our master and teacher, Solomon Luria, author of *Hokhmat Shlomo* and *Yam Shlomo*, a great an awesome man among all the people of Poland and Germany." Modena, *Ziknei Yehudah*, no. 21, 37. It is unclear whether he appended this note before or after writing *Ari Nohem*. On this responsum, see Isaac Rivkind, "A Responsum of Leo da Modena on Uncovering the Head" (Hebrew), in *Sefer ha-Yovel li-khevod Levi Ginsburg*, 401–23 (Philadelphia: JPS, 1946).

[84] Tishby, "General Introduction, " 30–87; Zviah Rubin, "The Zoharic Works of R. Moses Hayim Luzatto and His Messianic Attitude" (Hebrew), *JSJT* 8 (1989): 407, n. 74; Huss, *Ke-zohar ha-rakia*, 284–358.

[85] Tishby, "General Introduction," 30–32; Ross, Introduction to *Sefer Behinat ha-Dat*, 38–43; Kalman P. Bland, "Elijah Del Medigo's Averroist Response to the Kabbalahs of Fifteenth-Century Jewry and Pico Della Mirandola," *JJTP* 1 (1991): 23–53; Harvey J. Hames, "Elia Del Medigo: An Archetype of the Halachic Man?" *Traditio* 56 (2001): 213–27.

[86] Penkower, "A Renewed Inquiry," 35.

responses to their claims written by proponents of publication.[87] At the turn of the seventeenth century, humanists such as Joseph Scaliger asserted that the *Zohar* postdated the composition of the Talmud.[88] While Modena drew on *Behinat ha-Dat* and on arguments included in early editions of the *Zohar*, he only alluded to Levita's and never mentioned the doubts expressed by Scaliger.

Modena correctly identified Moses de Leon as the primary author of the *Zohar*.[89] The accuracy of his claim may have contributed to a scholarly consensus that casts *Ari Nohem* as a rejection of the *Zohar*.[90] While Julius Fürst described *Ari Nohem* as a polemic about the authenticity of the *Zohar*, Modena himself characterized it as a defense against those "authors who call themselves kabbalists and criticize the Great Eagle, Maimonides."[91] If modern scholars have thought of *Ari Nohem* as a debunking of a late-medieval pseudepigraphic work, Modena himself cast this unmasking within a much larger critical treatment of Kabbalah. While Modena made scattered references to the *Zohar* throughout the work, he devoted less than a third, chapters 16–22, to the antiquity of the *Zohar*.

Modena's intensive efforts to debunk the antiquity of the *Zohar* and demonstrate its pseudepigraphic character should be seen as only one aspect of his larger emphasis on the recent origins of Kabbalah. He attempted to demonstrate that the multiple forms of Kabbalah did not possess an antique heritage and were of recent origin. His estimates varied between 250 and 350 years, which would place the origins of Kabbalah

---

[87] See above.

[88] François Secret, *Le Zôhar chez les kabbalistes chrétiens de la Renaissance* (Paris: Mouton, 1964), 99–102. Secret raises the possibility that Jean Morin (1591–1659) may have known *Ari Nohem*. In a letter to Johann Buxtorf dated to 1613, the Hebraist Johannes Drusius discussed the lateness of the *Zohar* and pointed to the importance of *Sefer Yuhasin* by Zacut. See Anthony Grafton and Joanna Weinberg, *"I have always loved the Holy Tongue": Isaac Casaubon, the Jews, and a Forgotten Chapter in Renaissance Scholarship* (Cambridge: Harvard University Press, 2011), 325, n. 62.

[89] Scholars debate whether Moses de Leon was the sole author of the *Zohar*. Yehuda Liebes posited that De Leon worked within a circle of collaborators in Castile, including Joseph Gikatilla and Bahya ben Asher. Nevertheless, Liebes continued to ascribe a central role to Moses de Leon. See his "How the *Zohar* Was Written" (Hebrew), *JSJT* 8 (1989): 1–71; Liebes, "*Sefer Sheqel ha-Qodesh* of R. Moses de Leon" (Hebrew), *Kabbalah* 2 (1997): 271–85; Charles Mopsik, "Moïse de Léon, le *Sheqel ha-Qodesh* et la rédaction du *Zohar*: Une réponse à Yehuda Liebes," *Kabbalah* 3 (1998): 177–218; Elliot R. Wolfson, *Luminal Darkness: Imaginal Gleanings from Zoharic Literature* (Oxford: Oneworld, 2007), xiii–xiv.

[90] While this characterization appears repeatedly, the most radical formulation is Tishby's: "His [Modena's] most powerful ammunition was reserved for his criticism of the *Zohar*." And a later comment: "If [Jacob] Emden had been a man like Modena, a not-too serious freethinker who was not wholeheartedly committed to Judaism anyway and was positively antagonistic to Kabbalah . . . ." See Tishby, "General Introduction," 35, 40.

[91] MS A 5A, 11–12; ed. Libowitz, 1.

between 1288 and 1388.⁹² For him, Kabbalah constituted neither a part of the Oral Torah transmitted to Moses at Sinai nor a component of esoteric secrets that existed in antiquity. He pointedly rejected the theory that Kabbalah was an ancient body of knowledge that had been committed to writing in the Middle Ages. At the outset of the second part of *Ari Nohem*, Modena emphasized the recent origin of Kabbalah in conjunction with the *Zohar* and in contrast to ancient Jewish esoteric secrets that had been irrevocably lost:

> Either as a result of the diminishing of the hearts or as a result of the many misfortunes, persecutions, and exiles, the transmission of those secrets did not continue until today.... Nor [did the transmission continue] until the [secrets] began to be called by the name of the *Zohar* and the [other] books which they have possessed for around three hundred years. The knowledge that they call by the name of Kabbalah, as if it had been received from the prophets, is not it—[those secrets] in any way.⁹³

Modena explicitly embraced the notion that esoteric secrets had once existed among the Jews; however, due to the exigencies of history, they could no longer be recovered.⁹⁴ He sought to distinguish between those secrets and what his contemporaries referred to as Kabbalah. Elsewhere in *Ari Nohem*, he contested the very application of the Hebrew words *Kabbalah* (Tradition) or *Hokhmah* (wisdom or knowledge) to this set of doctrines and insisted on referring to it as *Yediah* (a lesser form of knowledge). This distinction between ancient esoteric secrets and the doctrines referred to as Kabbalah lay at the very heart of *Ari Nohem*.⁹⁵ Modena's critical scrutiny of the *Zohar* constituted only one element of a larger polemic against Kabbalah as a recent invention.

The adoption of the *Zohar* as a legal source served as a stimulus for Modena's critical analysis, which, in turn, highlighted an argument against its antiquity. Expanding upon an observation first made by Elijah Delmedigo, Modena pointed to the discrepancy between the legal opinions attributed to Simeon bar Yohai in Tanaitic writings and accepted legal norms in the Jewish tradition.⁹⁶ Modena reasoned that if the *Zohar* were such an extraordinary work and dated from antiquity, then it should have had an impact on the formulation of classical Jewish law. The fact that it did not could be explained in one of two ways: either it was not an extraordinary

---

⁹² Modern scholarship tends to date it a century earlier. See Scholem, *Origins of the Kabbalah*; Pedaya, *Ha-Shem veha-mikdash*.
⁹³ MS A 21B, 13–16; ed. Libowitz, 33
⁹⁴ For Maimonidean character of this argument see chapter 3.
⁹⁵ For another measure of its centrality, see the discussion in chapter 1 of the marginal note at the end of the first chapter in the two manuscripts of *Ari Nohem* that Modena authorized.
⁹⁶ *Sefer Behinat ha-Dat*, ed. Ross, 90–91.

work, a notion that he was unwilling to entertain, or it was not an ancient one. While Delmedigo's account of the *Zohar* consisted of a few comments, Modena's spanned several chapters. Furthermore, Delmedigo did not deliver his criticism in his own voice. Before each of his remarks on the *Zohar*'s antiquity, he employed the phrase "they further say," invoking the comments of unnamed Talmudists and philosophers who opposed kabbalists. By contrast, not only did Modena compose his attack in the first person, but personal relationships served as a central stimulus to it. In the century and a half between the composition of *Behinat ha-Dat* and *Ari Nohem*, the *Zohar* had come to play an increasingly prominent role in the formulation of Jewish law. Furthermore, several authors had formulated responses to Delmedigo's objections, either mentioning him by name or implicitly confronting his argument.

A descendant of Elijah Delmedigo, Joseph Solomon Delmedigo (1591–1655) treated his ancestor's arguments at length. The younger Delmedigo printed *Behinat ha-Dat* for the first time along with his own reflections on Kabbalah, entitled *Mazref le-Hokhmah*, in *Ta'alumot Hokhmah*. This collection of works, whose title page advertised it as a book printed in Basel, actually appeared in Hanau.[97] The frontispiece of Delmedigo's book was hardly the only aspect of his life and work to confound later scholars. *Ta'alumot Hokhmah* purports to have been edited by Samuel Ashkenazi, a figure who may have been a literary fiction invented by Delmedigo.[98] At various points in *Ta'alumot Hokhmah*, Delmedigo declared himself a supporter and proponent of Kabbalah, and he claimed to offer a defense of Kabbalah in *Mazref le-Hokhmah*.[99] However, Delmedigo also furnished nearly as many arguments and references to sources that oppose Kabbalah as he did to those that support it. He further advised his readers not to trust written sources as an accurate depiction of what an author thought. His other writings

---

[97] See Joseph Prijs, *Die Basler Hebräischen Drucke (1492–1866)*, ed. Bernhard Prijs (Olten: Urs-Graf Verlag, 1964), 475–79. Gershom Scholem, *Avraham Kohen Herera: Ba'al Sha'ar ha-Shamayim"* (Jerusalem: Mossad Bialik, 1978), 26; Alexander Altmann, "Lurianic Kabbalah in a Platonic Key: Abraham Cohen Herrera's *Puerta del Cielo*," in Twersky and Septimus, *Jewish Thought in the Seventeenth Century*, 8, n. 46.

[98] As argued by Senior Sachs. For the citation to Sachs and an attempt to refute it, see Isaac Barzilay, *Yoseph Shlomo Delmedigo (Yashar of Candia): His Life, Works, and Times* (Leiden: Brill, 1974), 116–21. On Delmedigo and Kabbalah, see also Geiger, *Melo Chofnajim*; Scholem, *Origins of the Kabbalah*, 102, n. 88, 213–14, n. 24; Tishby, "General Introduction," 32; Zev Harari, "On the Problem of Joseph Solomon Delmedigo's Relationship to Kabbalah" (Hebrew), M.A. thesis, Hebrew University, 1980; Joseph Levi, "A Jewish Academy for Sciences in the Early Seventeenth Century: The Effort of Joseph Solomon Delmedigo" (Hebrew), *Proceedings of the Eleventh World Congress of Jewish Studies* B:1 (1994), 169–76; Ruderman, *Jewish Thought and Scientific Discovery*, 128–52.

[99] Delmedigo, *Sefer Mazref le-Hokhmah* in *Sefer Ta'alumot Hokhmah*, 20A–20B; cited in Barzilay, *Yoseph Shlomo Delmedigo*, 242.

offer little assistance in deciphering his actual opinion. While a partial version of his letter that appeared at the opening of *Ma'ayan Ganim* in the 1629 edition of *Sefer Elim* included little that was critical of Kabbalah, the version printed in the nineteenth century articulated a full-scale assault on Kabbalah as well as doubts about Simeon bar Yohai's authorship of the *Zohar*.[100] Earlier doubts about this version of the *Ahuz* letter as a possible fabrication by nineteenth-century scholars may have recently been laid to rest by the discovery of an eighteenth-century copy.[101] The search for a coherent stance toward Kabbalah in Delmedigo's work may betray a late modern desire for consistency rather than an empirical reality of early modern intellectual life.

In *Ari Nohem* Modena repeatedly drew upon *Ta'alumot Hokhmah*, at times explicitly mentioning his source and at other times, as with Solomon Luria's responsum, simply citing a text that appeared in *Mazref le-Hokhmah* without mentioning it. Modena held Delmedigo in high esteem and had met him when he had passed through Venice at several points during his travels throughout Europe and the Ottoman Empire. In addition to composing an approbation for Delmedigo's *Sefer Elim*, Modena called him a sage and referred to him with the Hebrew acronym "a master and a teacher" on two occasions in *Ari Nohem*.[102] Elsewhere in the work, Modena left no doubt about his own opinion on Delmedigo's stance toward Kabbalah: "he fashions himself as defending the wisdom of Kabbalah and praising it, but his intention is to degrade it and denigrate it with all his might. Truly, he was a cunning sage."[103]

While Modena may have considered Delmedigo an opponent of Kabbalah, he took his arguments against his ancestor Elijah quite seriously. In *Mazref le-Hokhmah*, Delmedigo responded to the argument in *Behinat ha-Dat* about the discrepancy between the opinions contained within the *Zohar* and the actual rulings of Jewish law. In an artful display of his cunningness, Delmedigo basically sidestepped the objections raised about the *Zohar* and Jewish law by positing two separate spheres of knowledge: Jewish law and Kabbalah.

> One should not say that the author [of the *Zohar*] was an ignoramus[104] like most of the kabbalists who are not learned in the Talmud and legal authorities, for they spend all their days dealing with the internal and do not know the external.

---

[100] Geiger, *Melo Chofnajim*, 1–28 (Hebrew section).
[101] Penkower, "S. D. Luzzato, Vowels and Accents," 128.
[102] MS A 10A, 11; 11A, 1; ed. Libowitz, 8, 10. On Modena's approbation to *Sefer Elim*, see Fishman, *Shaking the Pillars of Exile*, 170.
[103] MS A 39B, 24–40A, 2; ed. Libowitz, 78.
[104] Aramaic for "to cut reeds in the meadow" and used to refer to an ignoramus. See BT *Sanhedrin*, 33A.

Because how many explanations more valuable than fine gold, and how many precious things are [in] its [the *Zohar*'s] storehouses. Even contrary opponents agree that whoever composed them was a great man.[105]

Modena posited that Delmedigo had conceded a basic point of his argument: kabbalists lacked requisite knowledge of Jewish law.[106]

While Delmedigo may have been disingenuous in arguing that the *Zohar* and Jewish law were two separate spheres of knowledge, Modena's son-in-law Jacob Levi was certainly not. In *Nahalat Ya'akov*, Levi adopted a similar strategy in his attempt to refute doubts about the legal authority of Simeon bar Yohai.[107] But Levi appears to have been unaware of *Behinat ha-Dat*, which had not been printed when he wrote *Nahalat Ya'akov*, he was aware of other challenges to Simeon bar Yohai's legal authority, such as an opinion mentioned in Jacob Gozalo's colophon to the first edition of *Tikkunei ha–Zohar*.[108] Seeking to refute this skeptic, Levi offered several counterarguments that Modena cited in *Ari Nohem*.

> Whoever had composed the book from the beginning, should, according to this, have attributed the *Zohar* to Rabbi Hanina ben Dosa, or Honi the circle-maker, or Rabbi Pinhas ben Jair, or Jonathan ben Uziel, or Rabbi Akiva, or Rabbah bar Nathan, or Rabbi Johanan, (and he gave a reason for the greatness of each one of them), but not to Rabbi Simeon bar Yohai. Then, in their opinion, the book of the *Zohar* would be of even greater importance. Rather, [given that this was not the case,] it certainly must be true that Rabbi Simeon bar Yohai, peace be upon him, composed it.[109]

Levi formulated several other responses that amplify but do not fundamentally alter the tenor of this earlier claim. He argued that while the Talmud did not portray Simeon bar Yohai as a legal authority, its narratives indicated that he possessed the Secrets of the Torah and their deeper meaning.

Modena rejected this line of reasoning and posited that if Simeon bar Yohai had indeed possessed knowledge of esoteric secrets, then it should have had a corresponding effect on the practice of Jewish law. Levi's arguments betrayed a flaw in historical reasoning. Only at the remove of ten centuries did the distinction between Kabbalah and Jewish law contain any validity. In the Talmudic period, when legal scholarship was still in

---

[105] MS A 33B, 14–18; ed. Libowitz, 61. See *Sefer Mazref le-Hokhmah* in *Sefer Ta'alumot Hokhmah*, 21B.

[106] For similar comments by Jacob Emden a century later, see chapter 1.

[107] Hallamish, "A Document Concerning a Controversy."

[108] Ibid., 184.

[109] MS A 33A, 22–24; ed. Libowitz, 60. A paraphrase of *Nahalat Ya'akov*. See Hallamish, "A Document Concerning a Controversy," 194.

its formative stages, a text of the *Zohar*'s caliber would have affected practice. This claim appears with greatest clarity in Modena's treatment of the *Shofar*.[110]

> For instance if Rabbi Simeon bar Yohai had differed from his colleagues about the sounding of the *Shofar* . . . and the law does not follow his opinion, did he or did he not know the secret and the proper intention? One cannot avoid one of two conclusions: either all of Israel acts foolishly in [performance] of the laws because they did not want to accept the opinion of the person who knew their essence, and thus we are all like straying sheep;[111] Or, Rabbi Simeon bar Yohai did not know anything about their mystery. How could it be said that he did not have a great portion in the Mishnah but that he had his portion in the mysteries of the Torah, if the mysteries of the Torah are at the root of the commandments! How could one who knows about the roots be so foolish about the branches?[112]

Modena implicitly drew on the argument made by Levi about the figure of Simeon bar Yohai in the Talmud. If these claims were true, Modena reasoned, Simeon bar Yohai's knowledge should have had an impact on the actual practice of Jewish law.

Modena further contested the way that Levi and Delmedigo interpreted Talmudic sources and argued that Simeon bar Yohai as he appeared in the Talmud did not possess any significance as a kabbalistic figure.

> I say that one cannot plough through either the Mishnah or the Talmud and the many statements attributed to him [Simeon bar Yohai] and discover this method [Kabbalah]. . . . Behold you will see in the first chapter of [tractate] *Berakhot* several statements, and they are all just like other statements of the rabbis, of blessed memory.[113] And the greatest of these is one that speaks about the names of the Holy One, blessed be He, "Rabbi Johanan said in the name of Rabbi Simeon bar Yohai: From the day that the Holy One, blessed be He, created the world, no man called the Holy One, blessed be He, 'Master' until Abraham came and called him 'Master,' as it says, 'O Lord God how shall I know that I am to possess it.' "[114] And it is plainly obvious that he means to say that it is a name that indicates that

---

[110] Modena's discussion of the *Shofar* emerged in response to a claim made by Moses Basola in his responsum in support of the printing of the *Zohar*. Basola, a leading legal authority of sixteenth-century Italian Jewry, initially supported the printing of the *Zohar* and argued that kabbalists understood the reasons for the commandments such as the *Shofar*. See *Tikkunei ha-Zohar*, 1B—2A. Basola later reversed his support for the printing of the *Zohar*, but Modena does not seem to have been aware of this change. See Tishby, "The Controversy over the Book of the *Zohar* in Italy in the Sixteenth Century," 106–13.

[111] Isa. 53:6.
[112] MS A 34A, 19–25; ed. Libowitz, 62.
[113] BT *Berakhot*, 7B.
[114] Gen. 15:8.

the Holy One is the master of the universe, and that our father Abraham, peace be upon him, was the first to make Him known among the nations as Master.[115]

In other words, claimed Modena, Simeon bar Yohai's exegesis of a verse in Genesis was wholly consistent with the rabbinic understanding of God and exhibited no trace of the kabbalistic claim that the description of God as "Master" referred to *Malkhut* (Kingship), one of the sefirot kabbalists associated with the divine attributes.

Equally important, noted Modena, none of the Talmudic commentators interpreted these statements in a kabbalistic fashion. He singled out two commentaries, the glosses by sages from medieval France known collectively as the Tosafists and the novellae of the Iberian scholar Solomon Ibn Adret.[116] Modena's choice of these commentaries was hardly accidental. In his *Ein Ya'akov*, Jacob ibn Habib cited both of them on this passage, and Modena presumably knew of their comments via Ibn Habib.[117] The Tosafists discussed Simeon bar Yohai's statement about Abraham in the context of other passages in Genesis where people who lived prior to Abraham called out to God. Ibn Adret dealt with the same question as well as with Abraham's astrological inquiries about the potential birth of a son. When Abram discovered via astrology that he would not have a son, he complained to God; God corrected him and informed him that while Abram would not have a son, Abraham would. As a result Abraham called out in the name of God and recognized his dominion over the world. Like the Tosafists, Ibn Adret did not mention any kabbalistic allusion in this passage.[118] While Ibn Adret's appearance in Ibn Habib may have directed Modena's attention to his comment, Modena may also have mentioned Ibn Adret because of his connection to the school of Nahmanides.[119] If Ibn Adret, a scholar who had vast knowledge of Kabbalah and had been a student of one of the most important kabbalists of the Middle Ages, did not offer a kabbalistic interpretation of this passage or the figure of Simeon bar Yohai, then contemporary kabbalists such as Levi had little precedent to do so.

---

[115] MS A 33A, 4–12; ed. Libowitz, 59.

[116] On the Tosafists, see Ephraim E. Urbach, *Ba'ale ha-Tosafot* (Jerusalem: Mossad Bialik, 1980). On Solomon ibn Adret's Talmudic novellae, see Israel M. Ta-Shma, *Ha-Sifrut ha–parshanit la-Talmud be-Europah uvi-Tsefon Afrikah: 1200–1400* (Jerusalem: Magnes Press, 2000), 2:55–66.

[117] Jacob ibn Habib, *Ein Yisrael* (Venice, 1566), 13A–13B.

[118] The passage quoted by Ibn Habib appeared in Ibn Adret's commentary to the narrative portions of the Talmud, *Perush ha-Hagadot*, not his novellae to the Talmud. Ibn Adret's *Perush ha-Haggadot* first appeared in print as citations embedded within *Ein Ya'akov*, a work printed repeatedly in the sixteenth century.

[119] On Ibn Adret and Kabbalah, see Idel, "Rabbi Solomon ibn Adret and Abraham Abulafia"; Halbertal, *Al derekh ha-emet*, 321–24.

Anachronism and the *Zohar*

Modena identified several anachronistic features of the *Zohar* as proof of its recent origin. He exhibited a keen sense of anachronism in a variety of his writings. In a responsum written to defend the practice of Jewish males baring their heads in public, he rejected the attempt made by rabbinic authorities to apply Talmudic statements to the contemporary Italian context.[120] Modena reasoned that when the Talmud referred to a bare head as arrogant and defiant of God, it described a different time and place from seventeenth-century Italy, where the removal of one's hat demonstrated respect.[121] In *Kol Sakhal* the author attempted to discredit particular laws, such as the phylacteries, by offering evidence of their late incorporation into Jewish practice.[122] Modena devoted much of *Ben David* to a demonstration that Jews had only recently begun to believe in the transmigration of souls. And in *Magen va-Herev* Modena depicted Jesus as a faithful adherent of Jewish law and described him as a sectarian Jew who professed one of the multiple forms of Judaism practiced in the Second Temple period.[123] Sensitivity to historical change combined with a focus on anachronism functioned as critical weapons for Modena in a wide range of polemical contexts.

Modena focused particularly on the theory of Simeon bar Yohai's authorship of the *Zohar*. He treated the foundation narratives for the authorship of kabbalistic texts as historically implausible, arguing that the very Talmudic passage repeatedly invoked by kabbalists about Simeon bar Yohai and the writing of the *Zohar* did not support their claim. Concerning the story about Simeon bar Yohai spending many years with his son in a cave and performing numerous miracles upon returning to the world, Modena wrote:[124]

> It is not to be believed that Rabbi Simeon bar Yohai composed and wrote any of the Secrets of the Torah, and certainly not anything else, during the thirteen years that they were in the cave. It was only by way of miracle that they had carob to eat and a spring from which to drink. There was no paper, nor ink, nor pen with which to write. And even if they had such [writing implements] they would not have been able to do so. For the rabbis, of blessed memory, recounted that they were sitting in sand, naked up to their necks. . . . If so, they certainly did not write.[125]

To Modena this cave narrative could not provide an adequate identification of authorship for any book, much less a book of putative esoteric wisdom

---

[120] Rivkind, "A Responsum of Leo da Modena on Uncovering the Head."
[121] BT *Kiddushin* 31A; as cited by Simonsohn in *Ziknei Yehudah*, no. 21, 35; Safran, "Leone da Modena's Historical Thinking," 383.
[122] Fishman, *Shaking the Pillars of Exile*, 45–47.
[123] Fishman, "Changing Early Modern Jewish Discourse about Christianity," 166.
[124] BT *Shabbat* 33B.
[125] MS A 32B, 22–33A, 1; ed. Libowitz, 59.

as complicated as the *Zohar*. Kabbalists who identified it as such had inadequate notions of authorship and appealed to a story that was manifestly absurd.

Though the preceding comment suggested that Modena was aware of the impossibility of the tale, he attempted to assure his reader that his rejection of Simeon bar Yohai's authorship of the *Zohar* did not involve disrespect for the Talmudic sage:

> I do not intend to shame or impugn the glory of the one thought to be the author [of this book] or the splendor of this book, heaven forbid. Precisely the opposite.... A great man of the Tanaim like him, one learned in miracles. Heaven forbid, [that I should touch] even a hairsbreadth! Let me be made into a mattress beneath his feet, lapping up the dust of his tread,[126] which I am not fit to recall without prostrating and bowing down. For if I say what it is impossible to avoid, and prove that he did not compose this book, this proof, I believe, will not diminish his glory but will, on this account increase, exalt, and raise it.[127]

Modena's analysis of the passage in tractate Shabbat was entirely in keeping with this reverential attitude toward Simeon bar Yohai. He did not question the veracity of the story or the plausibility of the miracles performed for Simeon bar Yohai and his son. He focused his criticism on the inadequacy of kabbalistic notions of authorship.

Modena pursued a similar strategy in discussing *Sefer Yetzirah* and its ostensible authors. While this early text of Jewish mysticism that dealt with the creation of the world was usually attributed to Abraham,[128] Modena contested the very possibility that Abraham could have composed the work.

> There are those who ascribe it [*Sefer Yetzirah*] to our father Abraham, peace be upon him.... These things are astonishing: that in those days a man of the Lord [Abraham], traveling and preparing for his journey from the Negev to Beth El, should write in his own hand with ink upon parchment, skin, or the bark of a tree in order to instruct? For whom? And why? Not for the people of his own generation, for among them, there was not a single man with whom it was even worth speaking, let alone giving a written document. If it were for his son Isaac, speech alone would have been sufficient. As he certainly handed over to him such secrets of prophecies and divinity, he would have instructed him face to face in knowledge and the way of wisdom.[129]

In arguing that Abraham could not have composed *Sefer Yetzirah*, Modena never rejected the possibility that Abraham possessed divine secrets or the keys to prophecy. Rather, as in his treatment of the Simeon bar Yohai,

---

[126] Isa. 49:23.
[127] MS A 32B, 6–13; ed. Libowitz, 57.
[128] For further discussion of *Sefer Yetzirah*, see chapter 4.
[129] MS A 31A, 21–31B line 3; ed. Libowitz 55.

Modena emphasized the historical implausibility of writing in such a case and indicated that writing played a determining role in the ascription of authorship. Simeon bar Yohai may have been the beneficiary of numerous miracles while living in a cave, but he certainly could not have written esoteric secrets in the form of a book known as the *Zohar*. Even if Simeon bar Yohai had the necessary implements for writing, he would not have been able to do so while submerged in sand up to his neck. Abraham may have possessed divine secrets and may have even transmitted them to his son Isaac, but he could not have written them down in the form of a book known as *Sefer Yetzirah*.

Modena also dismissed the possibility that Rabbi Akiva, a second-century Tanna, wrote *Sefer Yetzirah*:

> But others slightly improved their words in saying that Rabbi Akiva taught it [*Sefer Yetzirah*] from a tradition dating from our father Abraham, peace be upon him, and that these are ancient matters taken from the correct thought. As if those things from the Oral Torah, which they would not write down at that time, were actually appropriate for everyone, young and old, and they would inscribe the deepest secrets upon a book for people far and near?[130]

Inscribing esoteric secrets in written form would have made them accessible to a much wider public, something Rabbi Akiva would never have wanted to do.

In addition to criticizing implausible theories of authorship, Modena claimed that the *Zohar* itself contained several anachronistic features. Expanding on a point discussed by Elijah Delmedigo and Azariah de' Rossi, Modena observed that numerous figures mentioned in the *Zohar* flourished after the death of Simeon bar Yohai.[131]

> Most of the people mentioned in the book of the *Zohar* were *Amoraim* who lived many years after Rabbi Simeon bar Yohai and the sages of the Mishnah, as the author of the book *Meor Enayim* wrote.... "And I was amazed to find that the *Midrash ha-Ne'elam* adduced in the *Zohar* on the pericope Toledot Yitzhak, on

---

[130] MS A 31B, 6–8; ed. Libowitz, 55.

[131] Delmedigo, *Sefer Behinat ha-Dat*, ed. Ross, 91; Azariah de' Rossi, *Meor Enayim* (Mantua, 1573–1575), 86B; de' Rossi, *The Light of the Eyes*, trans. Joanna Weinberg (New Haven: Yale University Press, 2001), 329. Modena's *Meor Enayim* with his annotations is extant in the Palatine Library, Parma, St. De Rossi, 983. See Giovanni Bernardo de' Rossi, *Dizonario storico degli autori ebrei e delle loro opere* (Parma: Reale Stamperia, 1802), 2:7–8. On the importance of *Meor Enayim* for Modena's treatment of Zacut's *Sefer Yuhasin*, see below. In the margin of chapter 19, the sole passage of *Meor Enayim* quoted in *Ari Nohem*, there are two notes, possibly in different hands. The first note appears next to de' Rossi's citation of the *Zohar* on pericope Toledot and reads: "In the *Zohar*, sages after Rabbi Simeon bar Yohai." The second note appears next to de' Rossi's mention of Avtalion of Modena later in the chapter: "This was my uncle and he said this. He died on the ninth of Ab 5371 [1611] at the age of eight-two in Ferrara, may his resting be an honor." See *Autobiography*, 190. Modena also quoted *Meor Enayim* in his responsa, *Ziknei Yehudah*, no. 16, 30, and in *Magen va-Herev*, 26.

the verse, 'Once when Jacob was cooking a stew'[132] contained quotations from Rav Nahman, Rabbah, and Rav Joseph that they all said.[133] And it is not as ancient as we thought." If so, how is it possible that the *Zohar* was written by Rabbi Simeon bar Yohai or in his time?[134]

Although Modena quoted this claim via de' Rossi, it had been in circulation for some time.

Abraham Zacut's *Sefer Yuhasin*, a work completed in the early sixteenth century and printed in 1566, contained a response to this argument. To resolve such chronological contradictions, Zacut, like other defenders of the *Zohar*'s antiquity, adduced the notion of collective authorship, arguing that students of Simeon bar Yohai compiled the wisdom of their teacher after his death.[135] Modena refuted this possibility by pointing to elements of the *Zohar* that contradicted any attempt to cast it as the product of ancient rabbis: "But even this does not make sense to a thinking person: because one can find in the stories they recounted and in matters uttered in Rabbi Simeon bar Yohai's presence the names of the sages who lived a long time after his death."[136] Modena noted that references to figures who lived many years after Simeon bar Yohai's death invalidated any attempt to attribute the *Zohar* to him or even to his students.

Furthermore, Modena pointed to references to liturgical customs that were not shaped until hundreds of years after Simeon bar Yohai's lifetime. "Because one can even see liturgical customs that were formed eight hundred years after him [Simeon bar Yohai], such as *Nishmat Kol Hai*, *Keter Yitenu Lekha*, and others."[137] In *Nahalat Ya'akov*, Levi had pointed to people who questioned Simeon bar Yohai's authorship of the *Zohar* given that it mentioned *Nishmat Kol Hai* and *Keter Yitenu Lekha*. In response to this argument, which may have been made by Modena in one of their conversations, Levi posited that these prayers were early compositions that had been rediscovered at a later date.[138] Modena clearly disagreed and characterized his son-in-law's argument as "empty words." Whether or not Modena was correct in his argument about these liturgical rites, he offered few clues as to how he arrived at his conclusions.[139]

---

[132] Gen. 25:29.

[133] *Sefer ha-Zohar al ha-Torah* (Mantua, 1558), 139A. De' Rossi included the pagination for the *Zohar* citation in parentheses. This is another instance where Modena cited the *Zohar* via an intermediary source.

[134] MS A 36A, 13–17; ed. Libowitz, 67.

[135] Zacut, *Sefer Yuhasin*, 41B–42A; Tishby, "General Introduction," 86–87.

[136] MS A 36A, 20–21; ed. Libowitz, 67.

[137] Ibid., 21–22.

[138] Hallamish, "A Document Concerning a Controversy," 198.

[139] With regard to *Nishmat Kol Hai*, the first three words of the prayer appeared in BT *Pesahim* 118A. Scholars have argued that the language of this prayer, which is by and large identical

In Modena's account the language of the *Zohar*, more than any other aspect of the work, revealed it as a late composition. Had the sages of antiquity wished to restrict access to the secrets of the *Zohar*, why would they have written the work in Aramaic, the vernacular language of the rabbis?

> If Rabbi Simeon bar Yohai or his students were composing the book of the *Zohar* and the *Tikkunim* and had come to the point of writing down oral matters and Secrets of the Torah, they certainly would have only written them in the holy language [Hebrew]. Whether because of the holiness contained in them [the secrets], it would only be fitting to speak them in the holy language and not in the contemptible and disgraceful Aramaic language, for which the ministering angels have no use; or because of the appropriate concealment, because the secret of the Lord is for those who fear him,[140] and it would be fitting for it to be in a language intelligible only to the select few who are called by God,[141] and not in a language intelligible to women and ignoramuses. For it is known to all that Aramaic in those days was the language spoken by the masses.[142]

It was clear to Modena that the work was written for a small circle of elites and that language played a key role in determining the limits of its readership.[143] In committing esoteric secrets to writing, the ostensible rabbinic authors of the *Zohar* would have chosen Hebrew, a holy language, rather than Aramaic, a vulgar one. The choice of Aramaic, a vernacular language in the Talmudic period and a language understood only by the elite in the Middle Ages, further demonstrated the recent origin of the *Zohar*.

Modena drew two analogies to his claims about language, secrecy, and writing, one contemporary and the other historical. He reasoned that any contemporary author who wanted to write a book about Kabbalah would choose Hebrew rather than a vernacular language such as Spanish or German. In contrast to such vernaculars, which he referred to as "Christian language," Hebrew would allow a writer to conceal the content of his secrets. He also invoked a historical analogy to the language of Maimonides'

---

in different communal rites, points to its antiquity. See Ismar Elbogen, *Jewish Liturgy: A Comprehensive History*, trans. Raymond P. Scheindlin (Philadelphia and New York: JPS and Jewish Theological Seminary of America, 1993), 96, n. 3. As for *Keter Yitenu lekha*, Modena may have been correct in detecting mystical influence. Elbogen identified a prayer called *Keter*—not *Keter Yitenu Lekha*—in several early rites and concluded that it may have originated in mystical circles in Babylonia. See ibid., 57, n. 14.

[140] Ps. 25:14.
[141] Joel 3:5.
[142] MS A 36B, 3–7; ed. Libowitz, 68.
[143] Tishby, "General Introduction," 64. On the Aramaic of the *Zohar*, see Ada Rapoport-Albert and Theodore Kwasman, "Late Aramaic: The Literary and Linguistic Context of the Zohar," *Aramaic Studies* 4 (2006): 5–19; Yehuda Liebes, "Hebrew and Aramaic as Languages of the Zohar," *Aramaic Studies* 4 (2006): 35–52; Charles Mopsik, "Late-Judeo Aramaic: The Language of Theosophic Kabbalah," *Aramaic Studies* 4 (2006): 21–33.

Guide of the Perplexed, a work composed in Judeo-Arabic. According to Moses Provençal, Simeon bar Yohai and his students had followed a strategy employed by Maimonides and deliberately concealed the meaning of their words.[144] Modena neither denied the elitist character of the *Guide of the Perplexed* nor raised any objection to the notion that Simeon bar Yohai and his students copied a strategy from Maimonides. Instead, he focused on the relationship between language and esotericism: "But do not respond to me with the following: that Maimonides, of blessed memory, composed his book, *The Guide*, [in] Arabic; because he intended to delude[145] many and foreign nations as it is revealed in his treatise and to respond to several of those from our nation philosophizing in his time, to restore them to the true philosophy."[146] Modena argued that the authors of the *Zohar* had an elitist agenda similar to that of Maimonides:

> But Rabbi Simeon bar Yohai or his students, who only had to direct their words to the giants of their generation of Israel, if they were the actual writers [of the *Zohar*], the language of their writing would have only been the holiest of the holy and in allusion, and only the knowledgeable would understand.[147] Rather this certainly points the finger[148] and reveals the truth that one of the later sages composed it, for in his time, Aramaic was intelligible only to scholars.[149]

Modena's analysis focused exclusively on the choice of language and its relationship to its intended audience. As elsewhere in his criticism, he did not engage specific linguistic usage of individual passages. He never pointed to the prevalence of medieval philosophical Hebrew terms or to Arabic and Spanish words in the *Zohar* that later critics would use as proof of its medieval origins.[150]

Given Modena's focus on anachronism, his failure to emphasize discussions of biblical vocalization in the *Zohar* is striking.[151] The issue had been

---

[144] *Tikkunei Zohar*, 2B–3A.

[145] Libowitz emends this to "le-horot," to instruct. However, MS A clearly gives "le-hazot." At the end of the introduction to the first part of the *Guide of the Perplexed*, Samuel ibn Tibbon employed the verb "hazaya" twice in the same sentence, to which Modena alluded. Modena's citations from the *Guide* clearly indicate that he used Ibn Tibbon's translation. Both Hebrew editions of the *Guide of the Perplexed* printed in the sixteenth century were of Ibn Tibbon's translation, which has the word "*hazaya*." See Moses Maimonides, *Moreh Nevukhim* (Venice: Bragadin, 1551), 5B; Maimonides, *Moreh Nevukhim* (Sabbioneta: Cornelius Adelkind, 1553), 5B. For the English translation of this word as "fantasy," see Maimonides, *The Guide of the Perplexed*, trans. Shlomo Pines (Chicago: University of Chicago Press, 1963), introduction, 14.

[146] MS A 36B, 11–14; ed. Libowitz, 68.

[147] Cf. Dan. 12:10.

[148] Prov. 6:13.

[149] MS A 36B, 14–17; ed. Libowitz, 68.

[150] Tishby, "General Introduction," 64–68. Modena was apparently unaware of an anthology of Zohar texts in Hebrew translation. See Issachar Baer of Kremenitz, *Mekor Hokhmah* (Prague, 1611). See Boaz Huss, "Zohar Translations" (Hebrew), *Teuda* 21–22 (2007): 39–40.

[151] Adelman, "Success and Failure," 813–15.

the focus of Christian-Jewish polemic in the Middle Ages. Raymond Martin (1220–1287) and others alleged that Jews had fabricated the vowel points in order to change the meaning of the biblical text when it validated Christianity.[152] Early moderns such as the Catholic Johannes Reuchlin (1455–1522) and the Protestant Conrad Pellicanus (1478–1556) considered the vowel points and cantillation marks in the Hebrew Bible as later additions to the biblical text.[153] In the early sixteenth century, Elijah Levita, a Jewish grammarian who had served as a Hebrew tutor to Cardinal Egidius of Viterbo, concluded that even Jewish sources indicated the vowel points had postdated the Talmud. In contrast to his Christian predecessors and interlocutors who viewed the vowel points as a corruption of the biblical text, Levita claimed that the vowel points reflected an ancient oral tradition that had not been written down until the Middle Ages. In *Massoret ha-Massoret*, a discussion of the technical terms of the *Masorah* first printed in Venice in 1538, Levita alluded to sections of the *Zohar* and *Bahir* that discussed the vowel points and cantillation marks as the product of more recent kabbalists.[154]

Levita's allusions to the *Zohar* escaped his later readers, particularly de' Rossi.[155] In the fifty-ninth chapter of his *Meor Enayim*, de' Rossi posited that had Levita read the *Zohar* and other kabbalistic works that contained numerous references to the vowel points and were attributed to the sages of the second century, he would have argued for an early date for the vowel points.[156] De' Rossi attributed Levita's ostensible ignorance of the *Zohar*, *Bahir*, and *Ma'arekhet ha-Elohut* to the fact that these works had not appeared in print when he composed *Massoret ha-Massoret*: "Thus Bahur's [Levita's] view is patently undermined since we have intimations to prove that the different kinds of vowels and accents were in existence not only before the close of the Gemara, but even before the composition of the Mishnah. And if he were with us today, he would certainly submit to our view."[157] In a marginal note to his copy of *Meor Enayim*, Modena annotated this passage: "If he were with us today, I am sure that to someone who would want to prove to him the antiquity of the vowels and accents from the kabbalistic books which appeared in our times, he too would reply to him and say: it is easier for me to believe that all these books are a recent invention that have come but lately[158] than for me to believe that the vowels

---

[152] On Martin, see Jeremy Cohen, *Living Letters of the Law: Ideas of the Jew in Medieval Christianity* (Berkeley: University of California Press, 1999), 342–58.

[153] Penkower, "A Renewed Inquiry," 17–24.

[154] Ibid., 33–36.

[155] Ibid., 50. On the reverberations of the discussion between Levita and de' Rossi in the seventeenth century, see Burnett, *From Christian Hebraism to Jewish Studies*, 203–39.

[156] De' Rossi, *Meor Enayim*, 178B–81A; *The Light of the Eyes*, 699–709.

[157] De' Rossi, *Meor Enayim*, 179B. English translation by Weinberg in *The Light of the Eyes*, 703.

[158] Deut. 32:17.

Figure 6: Title page to Azariah de' Rossi *Meor Enayim*, Mantua, 1573-1575. Parma, Biblioteca Palatina, St. De Rossi, 983.
Reproduced by permission of the Ministero per i Beni e le Attività Culturali. Modena's owner mark to this copy of *Meor Enayim* appears in the upper left corner.

and accents are earlier than these books."[159] In short, as scholars have demonstrated, Modena was well aware of the arguments against the antiquity of the vowel points.[160] Nonetheless, in *Ari Nohem* itself, Modena was noncommittal: "Several opinions are found among recent scholars whether or not the vowel points and accent marks were before Ezra or not. And there are those who maintain that they [vowels and accents marks] are much later than him [Ezra]."[161] Given Modena's awareness of contemporary opin-

---

[159] De' Rossi, *Meor Enayim*, 179B. See above. A full translation of this note appears in Adelman, "Success and Failure," 573. A partial translation appears in Adelman, "Rabbi Leon Modena and the Christian Kabbalists," in *Renaissance Rereadings*, ed. Maryanne Cline Horowitz (Urbana: University of Illinois Press, 1988), 276. I have slightly modified Adelman's translation to reflect Weinberg's translation of the passage in de' Rossi and to echo Modena's allusion to a biblical verse that appeared in Solomon Luria's responsum discussed above.

[160] Adelman, "Success and Failure," 813; Penkower, "S. D. Luzzatto, Vowels and Accents," 127.

[161] MS A 21A, 5–7; ed. Libowitz, 31.

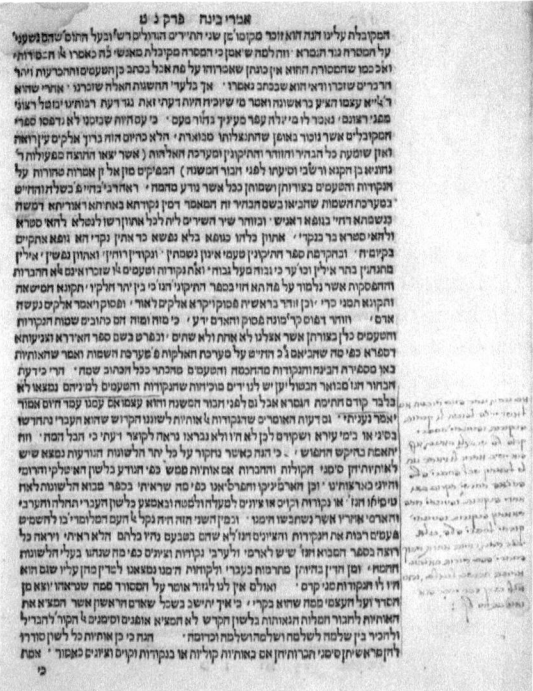

Figure 7. Azariah de' Rossi *Meor Enayim*, Mantua, 1573-1575, 179b.
Parma, Biblioteca Palatina, St. De Rossi, 983.
Reproduced by permission of the Ministero per i Beni e le Attività Culturali.
Modena's response to Azariah de' Rossi's discussion of biblical vocalization in the *Zohar* appears in the marginal annotation.

ions about the lateness of the vowel points, his failure to reject their antiquity in *Ari Nohem* was a deliberate choice. Modena may not have wanted to provide polemical ammunition either to Christians or to Jewish apostates who might point to the lateness of the vowels as an argument against rabbinic Judaism.[162]

New Evidence: The Testimony of Isaac of Acre

In addition to identifying the anachronisms that pointed to the *Zohar* as a product of antiquity, Modena introduced a piece of evidence that positively identified its author as Moses de Leon. He gleaned this from the account of

---

[162] Adelman, "Success and Failure," 813–15.

Isaac of Acre preserved in the work of Abraham Zacut.[163] *Sefer Yuhasin*, literally "the book of genealogy," recorded evidence about rabbinic scholars in a chronological order.[164] When Zacut discussed the generation of Simeon bar Yohai in his account of rabbinic scholars, he wrote that the *Zohar* had been composed by the students of Simeon bar Yohai but had not been revealed until after the generation of Nahmanides (d. 1270).[165] When he reached the generation of Isaac ibn Sahula and Isaac of Corbeil, two scholars who lived in the second half of the thirteenth century, he recorded an account of the *Zohar* that modern scholarship would use to establish Moses de Leon as the author of the work.[166] Invoking Zacut, Modena wrote: "O Israel, observe and listen with attentive, clean, and balanced ears[167] to what the author of the *Sefer Yuhasin* wrote in the Constantinople edition of his book, because in the Krakow edition the passage was omitted, perhaps to satisfy the desire of one of those belonging to the sect of the kabbalists, lest the truth be revealed to the world."[168]

Modena was not the first early modern scholar to point to the importance of *Sefer Yuhasin* for the history of the *Zohar*, as de' Rossi, Drusius, and Joseph Solomon Delmedigo had preceded him. While Modena was apparently unaware of de' Rossi's treatment[169] and almost certainly had

---

[163] Adolf Neubauer, "The Bahir and the Zohar," *JQR* 4 (1892): 361–68; Tishby, "General Introduction," 13–20.

[164] On Zacut, see Yerushalmi, *Zakhor*, 57, n. 2; Ram Ben-Shalom, *Mul tarbut Notsrit: toda'ah historit ve-dimuye avar bi-kerav Yehude Sefarad ve-Provens bi-Yeme ha-Benayim* (Jerusalem: Ben-Zvi Institute, 2006), 28.

[165] Zacut, *Sefer Yuhasin*, 41B–42A.

[166] Ibid., 142B–43A. Isaac ibn Sahula (1244–ca. 1284) wrote the collection of Hebrew fables *Meshal haqadmoni*. For an account of his life, see Raphael Loewe, "Introduction," in *Meshal Haqadmoni: Fables from the Distant Past*, (Oxford: Littman Library, 2004). On his attitude toward Kabbalah, see Hartley Lachter, "Spreading Secrets: Kabbalah and Esotericism in Isaac ibn Sahula's *Meshal ha-kadmoni*," *JQR* 100 (2010): 111–38. Isaac of Corbeil was a French Tosafist best known for his *Sefer Mitzvot Katan*, an abridgment of Moses of Coucy's *Sefer Mitzvot Gadol*. See Urbach, *Ba'ale ha-Tosafot*, 2:571–75.

[167] II Chr. 7:15.

[168] MS A 37A, 17–19; ed. Libowitz, 70. *Sefer Yuhasin* appeared in Constantinople in 1566 and Krakow in 1581.

[169] In chapter 19 of *Meor Enayim* quoted by Modena, de' Rossi mentioned *Sefer Yuhasin*. While de' Rossi conceded that certain passages of the *Zohar* appeared to have been written after Simeon bar Yohai, he rejected Isaac of Acre's testimony. *Meor Enayim* appeared in print in multiple stages, and Modena's copy did not include this passage on *Sefer Yuhasin*. On the printing of *Meor Enayim*, see Israel Mehlman, "Concerning the Book *Meor Enayim* by Azariah de' Rossi in Italy" (Hebrew), in *Genuzot Sefarim*, 21–39 (Jerusalem: JNUL Press, 1976); Robert Bonfil, "Some Reflections on the Place of Azariah de Rossi's *Meor Enayim* in the Cultural Milieu of Italian Renaissance Jewry," in Cooperman, *Jewish Thought in the Sixteenth Century*, 25–31; Meir Benayahu, "The Controversy concerning the *Meor Enayim* of Azariah de' Rossi" (Hebrew), *Asufot* 5 (1991): 213–65; Weinberg, "Translator's Introduction," in *The Light of the Eyes*, xlii–xliv.

no knowledge of Drusius's letter, he may have compared the two editions as a result of Delmedigo's *Mazref le-Hokhmah*. At two points, Delmedigo compared editions of Zacut's work and observed the discrepancy in their accounts of the *Zohar*, although he did not attribute the editing of the Krakow edition to the schemes of a knowing kabbalist.[170] Modena, however, accepted Isaac of Acre's testimony and identified Moses de Leon as the author of the *Zohar*. In presenting his account, Zacut had simply remarked, "The story circulated in that time period. In order that it be recounted to a later generation, I shall inform you what I have found written there." The printer of *Sefer Yuhasin* in Constantinople, Samuel Shullam, even included a note dismissing it as "useless and of no benefit."[171]

In the account Isaac of Acre, a kabbalist from Palestine and author of *Meirat Enayim*, had traveled to Spain in the early fourteenth century to ascertain the origins of a book containing "extraordinary things."[172] Isaac had received conflicting responses to his inquiries about the book's origins. Some claimed that Nahmanides had sent it to Spain from Palestine but that it had ended up in De Leon's possession. Others posited that De Leon had written it himself but had ascribed it to Simeon bar Yohai in order increase its value. In Valladolid Isaac met Moses de Leon, who swore that he had an ancient book written by Simeon bar Yohai at his home in Avila. De Leon's sudden death, however, prevented Isaac from examining this book. He continued to make inquiries among a number of people, including De Leon's widow, who remained nameless throughout the story. She claimed that her husband had written the book himself, and that he had confessed to her that he attributed the work to earlier scholars in order to increase its value.[173]

In *Ari Nohem*, Modena transcribed nearly verbatim Isaac of Acre's testimony from the Constantinople *Sefer Yuhasin*, omitting only the disparaging remark by Shullam. After citing the testimony, Modena addressed his reader, presumably Hamiz: "Now do not become angry, and do not become red in the cheeks. Respond to me with words of substance, not words of emptiness. Neither you, nor anyone in the world can tell me truly and honestly from whose womb this terrible ice came forth or who gave birth to the frost of heaven[174] that is this book [the *Zohar*]."[175] Modena's personal appeal at the close of his treatment of the *Zohar* serves as a reminder that

---

[170] Delmedigo, *Sefer Mazref le-Hokhmah* in *Sefer Ta'alumot Hokhmah*, 5B, 21B.

[171] Zacut, *Sefer Yuhasin*, 142B–143A.

[172] On Isaac of Acre, see Amos Goldreich, *Sefer Meirat Enayim le-R. Yitshak de-min Ako: Mahudarah madait* (Jerusalem: Hebrew University, 1981); Huss, "NiSAN—The Wife of the Inifinite"; Fishbane, *As Light Before Dawn*.

[173] Tishby, "General Introduction," 16–20.

[174] Job 38:29.

[175] MS 38A, 3–5; ed. Libowitz, 72

one of the primary causes of his criticism was to offer a response to his student and to his son-in-law. Chronology, bibliography, and Jewish law may have dominated his account, but the personal relationships and intense conversations about the authorship of the *Zohar* were never far from his mind.

Modena summarized the evidence and demonstrated his own absolute clarity on the issue of the *Zohar*'s authorship: "But I recount to you the words of the sage and pietists [Isaac] from Acre, who was deeply involved with this matter.... If so I have discovered the identity of the author while you people know nothing about him."[176] He invoked a legal principle from the Talmud that ruled in favor of a certain claim against an uncertain claim: "Against your will, [in a case of] the certain versus the uncertain, the certain is preferred.[177] Given the several plausible reasons[178] and sound theories that have been truthfully spoken, we should believe that Rabbi Simeon bar Yohai and his colleagues never even saw in a dream or night vision[179] the book of the *Zohar* or the *Tikkunim*."[180] Modena had made his case and come to a definitive conclusion. Simeon bar Yohai and his students had nothing to do with the composition of the *Zohar*.

Modena's use of evidence from *Sefer Yuhasin* reveals his critical reading habits and points to one of the basic features that distinguished his criticism of the *Zohar* from prior treatments. Earlier discussions, including *Behinat ha-Dat*, had raised doubts about a given issue or a range of issues, such as the *Zohar* and Jewish law or the figure of Simeon bar Yohai in the Talmud, but did not present a coherent theory about the origins of the book. In his criticism, Modena employed a range of arguments, many of them explicitly drawn from prior comments. He pointed to the contradictions between the *Zohar* and accepted legal norms, argued that Simeon bar Yohai's ostensible knowledge of divine secrets should have had an impact on Jewish law, and detected several anachronistic elements in the *Zohar*. Modena not only gathered doubts culled from various authorities, he used his sources to present a coherent theory about the origins of the *Zohar* in medieval Castile. While he may have bemoaned the destructive impact that printing had on the transmission of Kabbalah and the vastly expanded field of kabbalistic readers, printing was a value-neutral medium. The printing of Hebrew books, specifically historical chronicles, responsa, and philosophical treatises, enabled Modena to have access to a wide range of sources with which formulate his criticism.

---

[176] MS 38A, 5–13; ed. Libowitz, 72–73.

[177] BT *Ketubot* 12B.

[178] *Amatla* is a Talmudic term that indicates a plausible reason for retracting evidence. BT *Ketubot* 22A.

[179] Job 33:15.

[180] MS A 38A, 13–15; ed. Libowitz, 73.

To an extent, Modena's use of critical methods and historical reasoning to uncover the origins of a medieval book commonly assumed to be the product of an ancient author was typical of European intellectuals at the turn of the seventeenth century. When the Dutch scholar Daniel Heinsius demonstrated that Aristotle had not composed the cosmological treatise *De Mundo*, he pointed to the fact that Aristotle did not mention the treatise in his other works.[181] Modena made an analogous claim when he called attention to the absence of allusions or citations to the *Zohar* in rabbinic literature from antiquity. Historicist criticism had a similar function for Modena as it did for contemporary Christian intellectuals. The Protestant Isaac Casaubon exposed the *Corpus Hermeticum* as a forgery as part of a larger polemic against Cardinal Baronius, a Catholic theologian.[182] Like Casaubon, who used criticism to prove the *Corpus Hermeticum* was a late forgery, Modena demolished the pretensions to antiquity of another crucial pillar of Renaissance ancient theology, the *Zohar*. Throughout this period, criticism functioned as a handmaiden to religious polemic, whether among Christians, among Jews, or between Christians and Jews.[183] The dynamic between forgery and criticism in this period has also been the subject of considerable attention.[184] Like many of his near contemporaries, Modena not only unmasked an ancient text as a later pseudepigraphic work, he also dabbled in literary concealment. *Kol Sakhal*, a work Modena may have composed, offered a criticism of rabbinic culture through the pseudepigraphic mask of a fictional character.[185]

Any comparison between Modena and his contemporaries has limits. In contrast to Casaubon, who drew on close philological analysis in order to expose the *Corpus Heremticum*, Modena restricted himself largely to historical reasoning and relied primarily on external evidence to expose the *Zohar* as a pseudepigraphic work. While he paid close attention to the language of the *Zohar*, Aramaic as opposed to Hebrew, he never offered philological analysis of individual passages or specific words. Furthermore, he did not reject the *Zohar* at the level of ideas or raise philosophical objections to the contents of the work. This stands in marked contrast to his treatment of Cordovero's *Pardes Rimonim*, which offers a sustained analysis of individual chapters and a complete rejection of his ideas about the

---

[181] Jill Kraye, "Daniel Heinsius and the Author of *De Mundo*," in *Classical Traditions in Renaissance Philosophy* (Aldershot: Ashgate, 2002).

[182] Grafton, *Defenders of the Text*, 150.

[183] Jonathan Sheehan, "Thinking about Idols in Early Modern Europe," *JHI* 67 (2006): 568–69.

[184] See William McCuaig, *Carlo Sigonio: The Changing World of the Late Renaissance* (Princeton: Princeton University Press, 1989); Grafton, *Forgers and Critics*; Ingrid D. Rowland, *The Scarith of Scornello: A Tale of Renaissance Forgery* (Chicago: University of Chicago Press, 2004).

[185] Fishman, *Shaking the Pillars of Exile*, 60–66.

sefirot. Throughout his criticism, Modena emphasized that he never opposed the *Zohar* as such. In *Ari Nohem* he articulated his opposition to the confusion of epistemological categories by early modern readers of the *Zohar*. Not only did the ignorant masses have access to the text, the learned elite had also begun to read the book in entirely new ways. Late medieval readers had turned to the *Zohar* as a collection of homilies and as a reserve of esoteric secrets. Early modern readers looked to the *Zohar* as a source of legal authority and as a text constitutive of the Jewish tradition. This shift in orientation, anchored in claims of the antiquity of the *Zohar*, propelled Modena to identify it as a medieval pseudepigraphon. He employed a range of sources to argue that tradition has a history. Texts that identify themselves or are identified by their adherents as part of tradition required more than rhetorical insistence or implausible scenarios of authorship.

CHAPTER THREE

Guiding the Perplexed

> About six months earlier I had completed a treatise against the Kabbalah. I entitled it *Ari Nohem* because of my great anger at one of those [kabbalists] who had spoken wrongly in his books against the great luminaries of Israel, especially "the eagle" Maimonides, of blessed memory.
> —Leon Modena

Figure 8 (previous page). Title page to Maimonides *Guide of the Perplexed*, Venice, 1551. Courtesy of the Library of the Jewish Theological Seminary.
One of two editions of the *Guide of the Perplexed* that appeared in northern Italy in the 1550s. Modena held up Maimonides' *Guide of the Perplexed* as a model of the spiritual use of reason.

MODENA'S OBJECTION to the elevated status of the *Zohar* in contemporary Jewish life, combined with his concerted effort to historicize its medieval origins, formed a crucial part of his engagement with the Jewish past in *Ari Nohem*. But it was only a part. In the same decade that the *Zohar* appeared in print, another classic of medieval Judaism was also printed in rival editions: Maimonides' *Guide of the Perplexed*.[1] Much of the intellectual energy that animated Modena in *Ari Nohem* involved the demolition of claims to antiquity by proponents of the *Zohar*; yet he was equally stirred to defend his own version of Judaism, one that he identified with Maimonides' *Guide of the Perplexed*. Modena's reading of these two medieval works—the *Zohar* and the *Guide of the Perplexed*—structured his engagement with contemporary Kabbalah in Venice. The previous chapter traced Modena's attempt to historicize the *Zohar*; the present one takes Modena's short statement in his autobiography quoted as the epigraph and explores the role of Maimonides in *Ari Nohem*.

The first part of this chapter identifies the numerous critics of Maimonides who appeared in the pages of *Ari Nohem* and examines the various strategies Modena used to defend "the great eagle." Modena was only half-correct in this description of *Ari Nohem*. While his anger certainly was great, he directed it at more than one of Maimonides' critics. The second part focuses on Modena's study of the *Guide of the Perplexed*, repeatedly mentioned in *Ari Nohem*, and offers a profile of the passages in the *Guide* that Modena advised Hamiz to study and reflect upon. The third part connects Modena's discussion of two crucial issues in his criticism of Kabbalah to his reading of Maimonides: the history of esoteric secrets and the distinction between Kabbalah and philosophic knowledge. Scholars have long noticed the presence of Maimonides in *Ari Nohem* in particular and in

---

An earlier version of this chapter appeared as "Maimonideanism in Leon Modena's *Ari Nohem*," in *The Cultures of Maimonideanism: New Approaches to the History of Jewish Thought*, James T. Robinson, ed., 211–44 (Leiden: Brill, 2009). Reprinted by permission of the publisher.

[1] Venice (1551) and Sabionetta (1553). See Jacob I. Dienstag, "Maimonides' *Guide for the Perplexed*: A Bibliography of Editions and Translations," in *Occident and Orient: A Tribute to the Memory of Alexander Scheiber*, ed. Robert Dán, 97–98 (Budapest and Leiden: Akadémiai Kiadó and Brill, 1988). An earlier edition had appeared in Rome in the late fifteenth century.

Modena's writings in general.² Modena's Maimonideanism, a philosophical position and cultural posture that had clear manifestations in some of his earlier writings, including his letters and his mnemonic treatise, *Lev ha-Aryeh*, attained its clearest and most sustained articulation in his late work, *Ari Nohem*.³ This discussion reopens the question of Maimonides in *Ari Nohem* by placing him at the center of Modena's polemic rather than the periphery.⁴

Modena began *Ari Nohem* with an explicit evocation of Maimonides: "Concerning the cause that impelled the author to compose this treatise for his beloved student,⁵ bold in his speech, who examined those compositions that call themselves kabbalistic and open their mouths wide⁶ against the great eagle, Maimonides, of blessed memory."⁷ The very first lines of *Ari Nohem* addressed Hamiz as a reader of kabbalistic books openly critical of Maimonides. Here, as opposed to in his autobiography, Modena mentioned multiple books critical of Maimonides rather than a single work. Modena quoted, paraphrased, defended, or alluded to Maimonides on nearly every page of *Ari Nohem*. He mentioned Maimonides explicitly on more than forty occasions in a treatise that consisted of thirty chapters; in addition, he often cited Maimonides without mentioning his name and engaged Maimonides' critics at great length.⁸

A précis of the different ways late medieval and early modern kabbalists read Maimonides and his *Guide*, as reflected in *Ari Nohem*, helps explicate Modena's own reading of Maimonides. This is neither a synopsis of

---

² Adelman, "Success and Failure," 795; Ruderman, *Jewish Thought and Scientific Discovery*, 119–20; Fishman, *Shaking the Pillars of Exile*, 32–33; Idel, "Differing Conceptions of Kabbalah in the Early 17th Century," 154, 74.

³ On Modena's letters, see below. *Lev ha-Aryeh* appeared in Venice in 1612, twenty-seven years before Modena wrote *Ari Nohem*. This short work concludes with a listing of the 613 commandments according to Maimonides compiled by Nathan Ottolenghi. On *Lev ha-Aryeh*, see David Margalit, "On Memory: Concerning *Lev ha-Aryeh* by Rabbi Judah Aryeh Modena," (Hebrew) *Korot* 5 (1972): 759–72; Giuseppe Sermoneta, "Aspetti del Pensiero Moderno nell'Ebraismo Italiano tra Rinascimento e Età Barocca," in *Italia Judaica Gli Ebrei in Italia tra Rinascimento ed Età Barocca*, 17–35 (Rome, 1986); Gerrit Bos, "Jewish Traditions on Strengthening Memory and Leone Modena's Evaluation," *JSQ* 2 (1995): 39–58; Kalman P. Bland, "A Jewish Theory of Jewish Visual Culture: Leon Modena's Concept of Images and Their Effect on Locative Memory," *Ars Judaica* 5 (2009): 59–66.

⁴ For a different perspective, see Adelman and Ravid: "Modena defended Maimonides in several ways, including reference to the favorable view of him by Nahmanides, himself a kabbalist (*Ari Nohem*, chaps. 6 and 21). In context, however, this point was a minor aspect of this important book." *Autobiography*, 261.

⁵ S. of S. 4:3.

⁶ Job 29: 23.

⁷ MS A 5A, 9–12; ed. Libowitz, 1.

⁸ In his discussion of Abraham's faith, Modena quoted "The Laws of Idolatry" from Maimonides' *Sefer ha-Mada*. See MS A 14B, 19–22; ed. Libowitz, 17. In his history of the Oral Torah, Modena explicitly drew on Maimonides' introductions to his code of law and commentary on the Mishnah. See MS A 22B, 2–7; ed. Libowitz, 35.

Maimonidean interpretation in the four and a half centuries that transpired between the writing of the *Guide* and the composition of *Ari Nohem*[9] nor an exhaustive discussion of Maimonides and Kabbalah.[10] It does, however, offer a menu of some of the ways of engaging Maimonides available to a Jewish intellectual in seventeenth-century Venice. Modena demonstrated a keen awareness of three different approaches adopted by kabbalists over the previous centuries to Maimonides and his *Guide*. Some kabbalists engaged in outright criticism of Maimonides and his work; others engaged in a defense of Maimonides and his *Guide*; and still others appropriated Maimonides' thought. This appropriation took one of two forms, as will emerge below.

KABBALISTIC CRITICISM OF MAIMONIDES

Modena began with "authors who call themselves kabbalist and open their mouths wide against the Great Eagle." Two figures in particular, whom Modena subsequently accused of "mouthing empty words,"[11] appeared repeatedly throughout *Ari Nohem*: Shem Tov ibn Shem Tov (d. 1429) and Meir ibn Gabbai (ca. 1480—ca. 1540). Although they were separated by over a century, these two Iberian kabbalists frequently appeared together.[12] If Shem Tov and Ibn Gabbai displayed no compunction in criticizing Maimonides, Modena minced few words in his response. At one point Modena

---

[9] Thus the esotericism of Samuel ibn Tibbon, who translated the *Guide of the Perplexed* into Hebrew and composed his own philosophical works, does not appear in *Ari Nohem*. See Aviezer Ravitzky, "Samuel Ibn Tibbon and the Esoteric Character of the *Guide of the Perplexed*," *AJS Review* 6 (1981): 87–123; James T. Robinson, *Samuel Ibn Tibbon's Commentary on Ecclesiastes: The Book of the Soul of Man* (Tübingen: Mohr Siebeck, 2007); Carlos Fraenkel, *Min ha-Rambam li-Shmuel Ibn Tibbon* (Jerusalem: Magnes Press, 2007). Modena was deeply indebted to Maimonides himself on the issue of ancient esotericism. See below.

[10] Gershom Scholem, "From a Scholar to a Kabbalist: Kabbalistic Stories about Maimonides" (Hebrew), in *Mehkere Kabalah*, 189–200; Alexander Altmann, "Maimonides's Attitude toward Jewish Mysticism," in *Studies in Jewish Thought: An Anthology of German Jewish Scholarship*, ed. Alfred Jospe, 200–219 (Detroit: Wayne State University Press, 1981); Elliot R. Wolfson, *The Book of the Pomegranate: Moses de Leon's Sefer Ha-Rimmon* (Atlanta: Scholars Press, 1988), 27–34; Moshe Idel, "Maimonides and Kabbalah," in *Studies in Maimonides*, ed. Isadore Twersky, 31–81 (Cambridge: Harvard University Press, 1990); Gil Anidjar, *"Our Place in al-Andalus": Kabbalah, Philosophy, Literature in Arab Jewish Letters* (Stanford: Stanford University Press, 2002); Elliot R. Wolfson, "Beneath the Wings of the Great Eagle: Maimonides and Thirteenth-Century Kabbalah," in *Moses Maimonides (1138–1204): His Religious, Scientific, and Philosophic Wirkungsgeschichte in Different Cultural Contexts*, ed. Görge K. Hasselhoff and Otfried Fraisse, 209–237 (Würzburg: Ergon Verlag, 2004); Eli Gurfinkel, "Maimonides and Kabbalah: An Annotated Bibliography" (Hebrew), *Daat* 64–66 (2009): 417–85.

[11] MS A 23B, 11; ed. Libowitz, 37. See Job 35:16.

[12] MS A 23B, 12; 24B, 12; 30A, 24; 42B, 9; ed. Libowitz, 37, 39, 52, 84.

referred to Ibn Gabbai's reliance on Shem Tov to prove the authenticity of kabbalistic transmission as "the blind leading the blind"; in another instance he referred to the two of them as "foolish ones of the people."[13] In one of the manuscripts of *Ari Nohem* corrected by Modena, Shem Tov's *Sefer ha-Emunot* (Heb. *The Book of Beliefs*) appeared on two separate occasions as *Sefer ha-Dimyonot* (Heb. *The Book of Fantasies*) and Ibn Gabbai was referred to as "the one who reproaches and curses."[14]

Although Shem Tov and Ibn Gabbai each wrote several works, Modena focused on Shem Tov's *Sefer ha-Emunot* and Ibn Gabbai's *Avodat ha-Kodesh* and, to a considerably lesser extent, his *Tola'at Ya'akov*. *Sefer ha-Emunot*, printed for the first time at Ferrara in 1556, was Shem Tov's only work to appear in print before the twentieth century, and it appeared among the Hebrew books in the inventory of Modena's possessions drawn up after his death.[15] While none of Ibn Gabbai's works appeared in the same inventory, Modena demonstrated a thorough familiarity with *Avodat ha-Kodesh* and *Tola'at Ya'akov*,[16] both printed twice during the sixteenth century. *Tola'at Ya'akov* appeared in Constantinople in 1560 and again in Krakow in 1581. *Avodat ha-Kodesh* appeared in Venice under the title *Marot Elohim* in 1567 and a second time in Krakow, under the title *Avodat ha-Kodesh*, in 1576.[17] Modena

---

[13] For the first reference, see MS A 22A, 18–19; ed. Libowitz, 34. For the second, see MS A 24B, 12; ed. Libowitz, 39.

[14] For *Sefer ha-Dimyonot*, see MS A 7A, 17; 8A, 4. For Ibn Gabbai, see MS A 14A, 6–7; ed. Libowitz, 15. See Ps. 44:17.

[15] Ancona, "L'inventario dei beni appartenenti a Leon da Modena," 263, n. 40. On Shem Tov, see Meir Benayahu, "*Sefer ha-Emunot* by Rabbi Shem Tov ibn Shem Tov: Its Concealment and Revelation" (Hebrew), *Molad* 5 (1973): 658–62; Ephraim Gottlieb, "Shem Tov ibn Shem Tov's Path to Kabbalah" (Hebrew), in *Mehkarim be-Sifrut ha-Kabalah*, ed. Joseph Hacker, 347–56 (Tel Aviv: Tel Aviv University Press, 1976); David S. Ariel, "Shem Tob ibn Shem Tob's Kabbalistic Critique of Jewish Philosophy in the 'Commentary on the Sefirot,' " Ph.D. diss., Brandeis University, 1981; Roland Goetschel, "Providence et destinées de l'âme dans le Sefer ha-Emunot de Shem Tob Ibn Shem Tob (1380–1441)," in *Mehkere Misgav Yerushalayim be-Sifruyot am Yisrael*, ed. Ephraim Hazan, 53–71 (Jerusalem: Misgav Jerusalem 1987); Charles Mopsik, *Les Grands Textes de la Cabale: Les rites qui font Dieu* (Lagrasse: Verdier, 1993), 254–65; Erez Peleg, "Between Philosophy and Kabbalah: The Criticism of Jewish Philosophy in the Thought of Rabbi Shem Tov ben Shem Tov" (Hebrew), Ph.D. diss., Haifa University, 2002.

[16] On Ibn Gabbai, see Gershom Scholem, "Revelation and Tradition as Religious Categories in Judaism," in *The Messianic Idea in Judaism*, 298–300; Roland Goetschel, *Meir ibn Gabbay: le discours de la Kabbale espagnole* (Leuven: Peeters, 1981) ; Elliot K. Ginsburg, *Sod ha-Shabbat, the Mystery of the Sabbath: From the Tola'at Ya'aqov of Meir Ibn Gabbai* (Albany: SUNY Press, 1989); Mopsik, *Les grands textes de la Cabale*, 364–83.

[17] Although Modena referred to the book exclusively as *Avodat ha-Kodesh*, as the title appears in the Krakow edition, and never once used the title of the Venetian edition, *Marot Elohim*, his citations indicate that he did use the Venetian edition. The first time he cited Ibn Gabbai, he quoted from the opening chapter of the first section of *Avodat ha-Kodesh*: "The fulfillment of the soul and its success cannot possibly be imagined in any way if the secrets of the scholars of this knowledge, that is to say the true Kabbalah, are not transmitted to the worshiper." "The secrets

never quoted from Ibn Gabbai's *Derekh Emunah*, printed at Padua in the year 1562, although he was clearly familiar with it.[18] The multiple works of Ibn Gabbai—five editions in three different regions: the Ottoman Empire, northern Italy, and the Polish-Lithuanian Commonwealth—printed in the course of the second half of the sixteenth century suggest a wide audience and high demand for the work of this recently deceased kabbalist.

A number of Jewish thinkers in the sixteenth and seventeenth centuries read and cited Shem Tov's *Sefer ha-Emunot*.[19] Many of these authors, specifically Ibn Gabbai, Moses Cordovero, Menahem Azariah da Fano, Judah Moscato, and Samuel Uceda, were mentioned in *Ari Nohem*.[20] Modena also cited three scholars who have been identified as readers of Ibn Gabbai: Elijah de Vidas, Aaron Berekhya of Modena, and Joseph Solomon Delmedigo. Furthermore, Jacques Gaffarel, in his preface to the first edition of Modena's *Historia de gli Riti Hebraici*, published in Paris in 1637, cited a passage from Ibn Gabbai's *Derekh Emunah*, the one work of Ibn Gabbai printed in the sixteenth century that did not appear in *Ari Nohem*.[21]

The works of Ibn Gabbai and Shem Tov were the primary anti-Maimonidean writings in print prior to the composition of *Ari Nohem*. With the exception of the polemics surrounding Maimonides in the responsa of Solomon ibn Adret, written in the early fourteenth century and printed several times during the sixteenth century, medieval and early modern anti-Maimonidean writing circulated largely in manuscript.[22] Modena never actually engaged

---

of the scholars," or "me-sodot ha-hakhamim," follows the Venice edition; by contrast, the Krakow edition has "the traditions of the scholars," or "mesorot ha-hakhamim." The citation from *Ari Nohem* appears in Libowitz, 3. Libowitz has the following text: "Me-sodot ha-hokhmah ha-zot." In MS A 6B, 9-11, the text reads: "me-sodot ha-hakhamim shel ha-da'at ha-zot." See Meir ibn Gabbai, *Marot Elohim* (Venice, 1567), 9A; and *Avodat ha-Kodesh* (Krakow, 1576), 9A.

[18] See below.

[19] Peleg, "Between Philosophy and Kabbalah," 326–27.

[20] For Cordovero, Da Fano, and Moscato in *Ari Nohem*, see chapter 4. For Uceda, see MS A 40A, 22; ed. Libowitz, 79.

[21] Goetschel, *Meïr ibn Gabbay*, 485–99. Modena cited Elijah de Vidas in MS A 10A, 5–6; ed. Libowitz, 8; and Aaron Berekhya of Modena in MS A 5B, 5; ed. Libowitz 1. On Gaffarel, see chapter 5.

[22] Ibn Adret's responsa appeared in Bologna in 1539 and Venice in 1545–46. See Steinschneider, *Catalogus Librorum Hebraeorum in Bibliotheca Bodleiana*, 2272–74. Modena was apparently unaware of one of the most virulent anti-Maimonidean texts of the sixteenth century, a polemic by Joseph Ashkenazi that circulated in manuscript. Had Modena read Ashkenazi's claim that the printing of the *Guide* caused the burning of the Talmud, he almost certainly would have responded. See Gershom Scholem, "New Information on Joseph Ashkenazi, the Tanna of Safed" (Hebrew), *Tarbiz* 28 (1959): 71. Ashkenazi's rival Abraham Horowitz first attributed this claim to Ashkenazi's father-in-law, Aaron Land, in his summary of a sermon preached by Land in Posen in 1559. See Phillip Bloch, "Der Streit um den Moreh des Maimonides in der Gemeinde Posen um die Mitte des 16. Jahrhundert," *MGWJ* 47 (1903): 153–69, 263–79, 346–56. According to Scholem, Ashkenazi repeated this claim at the end of chapter 50 of his polemic, written in the mid 1560s while he was in northern Italy. This section does not appear

with Ibn Adret's criticism of Maimonides; for him, Ibn Adret functioned only as an opponent of Kabbalah, more specifically as a well-respected medieval authority who denied the transmigration of souls.[23] When Modena mentioned the second Maimonidean controversy in fourteenth-century Provence and Catalonia, he omitted any reference to actual criticism of Maimonides by Ibn Adret or his colleagues. Modena the polemicist ignored the main controversy and its anti-Maimonidean elements and drafted Ibn Adret into his own argument as a critic of a given kabbalistic doctrine.

Modena engaged both Shem Tov and Ibn Gabbai with great intensity, mentioning the former on fourteen occasions and the latter on twenty-four. He focused on Ibn Gabbai to a much greater extent than on Shem Tov, and his reading of Ibn Gabbai was far more intensive.[24] Rather than recapitulate the range of criticisms leveled by Modena against the claims made by these kabbalists, such as the authenticity of the transmission of Kabbalah, the nature of the sefirot, the transmigration of souls, and the theurgic power of prayer, I explore these themes through the specific defenses of Maimonides offered in *Ari Nohem*.

In his introduction to the second part of *Ari Nohem*, Modena discussed the transmission of kabbalistic secrets, an issue of vital importance to his criticism of Kabbalah.[25] After citing the opening paragraph of Maimonides' *Guide*, I, 71, which described how the transmission of "Secrets of the Torah" among the people of Israel had diminished over the course of generations, Modena turned to critics of Maimonides and, in particular, to Shem Tov.

> But please listen to how the stupid ones thought to respond to these words spoken by Moses [Maimonides], the Rabbi, of blessed memory. Rabbi Shem Tov, in Gate One, Chapter One, said:[26] "But I ask the rabbi [Maimonides]: either indi-

---

in the excerpts published by Scholem. See also the response to Ashkenazi written by an unknown author in Ephraim Kupfer, "Strictures of a Scholar on the Writings of R. Joseph Ashkenazi" (Hebrew), *Kovez Al Yad* 21 (1985): 213–88; as cited and discussed in Elchanan Reiner, "The Attitude of Ashkenazi Society to the New Science in the Sixteenth Century," *Science in Context* 10 (1997): 589–603.

[23] MS A 26B, 6; 27B, 4; ed. Libowitz, 43, 44. In the list of antikabbalistic writers that Modena appended to the end of MS A 48B, 6, he included Ibn Adret. On the second Maimonidean controversy, see A. S. Halkin, "Yedaiah Bedershi's Apology," in *Jewish Medieval and Renaissance Studies*, ed. Alexander Altmann, 165–84 (Cambridge: Harvard University Press, 1967); Gregg Stern, "What Divided the Moderate Maimonidean Scholars of Southern France in 1305?" in Harris, *Be'erot Yitzhak*, 347–76.

[24] He quoted ten passages from Ibn Gabbai's writings, nine from *Avodat ha-Kodesh* and one from *Tola'at Ya'akov*; by contrast, he quoted only two or three passages from Shem Tov's *Sefer ha-Emunot*. One of the instances where Modena claimed to cite from Gate 1, chapter 1, of *Sefer ha-Emunot*, he actually cited from Gate 2, chapter 1. See below.

[25] MS A 21B–23A; ed. Libowitz, 33–36. In Libowitz's edition this section appears as chapter 11. The citation from Shem Tov appears on 22A, 5–10.

[26] Actually Gate 2, chapter 1. Shem Tov ibn Shem Tov, *Sefer Ha-Emunot* (Ferrara: Usque, 1556), 12B. Modena was probably misled by an error at the page header which lists it, as he did, as Gate 1, chapter 1.

viduals had a tradition in the secrets of the Torah and or they did not have this tradition at all. [If you say they had no tradition at all,][27] then you deny that there was any tradition in the Torah, and you deny the entire Oral Torah. For how is it possible that Moses our teacher, peace be upon him, did not receive Account of Creation and the Account of the Chariot, and did not hand it over to the sages and Joshua son of Nun?"[28]

Shem Tov's question to Maimonides rested upon a basic assumption that Modena simply would not grant: the identification of the Secrets of the Torah with the Oral Torah. A basic concept in rabbinic Judaism, the Oral Torah referred to precepts that had been transmitted to Moses at Sinai along with the written Torah and had been passed down from generation to generation.[29] Some kabbalists, particularly those associated with the school of Nahmanides, maintained that the Secrets of the Torah had been transmitted along with the Oral Torah in an uninterrupted chain that stretched all the way back to antiquity.[30]

A few lines later, Modena offered the following retort that relied implicitly on Maimonides:

> As if we were incapable of distinguishing in terms of continuity between the transmission of the Oral Torah and the Secrets of the Torah, and specifically to respond to his claims, that yes, it is certainly so, it is a truth and belief of all Israel that Moses our teacher, of blessed memory, received from Sinai such and such, and handed it down to Joshua, etc. But the transmission of the Oral Torah was handed down continually to this day through basic principles. While certain doubts may have occurred about specific subsections, they were clarified and rectified over the generations to the extent that they are well known, and necessary at each point in time to all men, women, and ignoramuses. But the Secrets of the Torah that were bequeathed exclusively to extraordinary individuals of each generation, as the number of these individuals declined and we became subject to the dominion of other nations, the transmission ceased to be in their hands.[31]

Modena posited a basic distinction between the Oral Torah and the Secrets of the Torah, and he refused to accept the claim made by Shem Tov and Ibn

---

[27] Modena omitted this phrase in Shem Tov's text.

[28] MS A 22A, 5–10; ed. Libowitz, 34.

[29] Martin S. Jaffee, *Torah in the Mouth: Writing and Oral Tradition in Palestinian Judaism, 200 BCE—400 CE* (New York: Oxford University Press, 2001).

[30] Nahmanides, Introduction to Biblical Commentary. For an English translation, see Nahmanides, *Commentary on the Torah*, trans. Charles B. Chavel (New York: Shilo, 1971); Moses de Leon, *Sefer Sheqel ha-Qodesh*, ed. Charles Mopsik (Los Angeles: Cherub Press, 1996), 17–18; Fishbane, *As Light Before Dawn*, 58–59. According to Rivka Shatz, the claim of continuous oral transmission was made by the kabbalists associated with Nahmanides in Catalonia. By contrast, kabbalists in the circle of Isaac the Blind in Provence claimed to have received divine revelation. See "Kabbalah: Tradition or Innovation," 448.

[31] MS A 22, 12–18; ed. Libowitz, 34.

Gabbai that the transmission of the Oral Torah over generations included within it the Secrets of the Torah.[32]

Elsewhere in *Ari Nohem*, Modena expanded his argument about the rupture in the transmission of secrets. He rejected the attempt by kabbalists to appropriate the term "Kabbalah" to refer to their teachings. "Kabbalah," he argued, meant tradition, and kabbalists only had inventions.[33] Though he was not opposed to esotericism in principle, Modena criticized kabbalists for claiming that their inventions constituted ancient esoteric secrets. Modena suggested that the secrets considered Kabbalah were different from an ancient esoteric tradition. In his refutation of Shem Tov, he indicated that "Secrets of the Torah" existed as part of an esoteric tradition. In addition to Shem Tov and Ibn Gabbai, other early modern kabbalists had argued that Kabbalah constituted an oral tradition passed from Moses to the sages of antiquity to the early modern period.[34] While Modena never mentioned these figures in this context, his argument about the rupture of transmission may have been an attempt to refute a similar claim.[35]

Modena's engagement with Ibn Gabbai can be profitably examined in light of another central theme of *Ari Nohem*, one that is related but not identical to his argument about Maimonides and the transmission of kabbalistic secrets. He turned to Ibn Gabbai and his criticism of Maimonides at the conclusion of a discussion of biblical interpretation. Modena mentioned four levels of biblical interpretation known by the acronym *Pardes*, which he defined as "*litterale, allegorico, tropologico, enigmatico* or *mistico,*" using the Italian terms rather than their Hebrew equivalents in medieval rabbinic literature.[36] When discussing the fourth level, *sod*, defined as "*enigmatico o*

---

[32] A citation to Ibn Gabbai appears shortly after the discussion of Shem Tov.

[33] The word "invention" reflects Modena's use of *hamza'ah* to refer to the emergence of Kabbalah. See Idel, "Differing Conceptions of Kabbalah in the Early 17th Century," 162, n. 125.

[34] Both Pico della Mirandola and Abraham Cohen de Herrera stressed the unbroken continuity in the oral character of kabbalistic transmission. See Altmann, "Lurianic Kabbalah in a Platonic Key," 4–8. Altmann pointed to the possibility of a polemical anti-Christian stance in Herrera's notion of oral tradition.

[35] The same year they issued *Sefer ha-Emunot*, the Usque press printed a set of glosses by Moses Alashkar defending Maimonides against the attacks of Shem Tov. On one occasion, in what appears to have been no more than an afterthought, Modena cited this work: "In his glosses against him [Shem Tov], Rabbi Alashkar, of blessed memory, justifiably said that he was surprised that those who saw his book had not ordered it burned on the day of atonment." MS A 8A, interlinear note at 11. For the citation to Alashkar, see *Hasagot she-hisig he-Hakham Moshe Alashkar* (Ferrara: Usque, 1556), 9B. Modena hardly used Alashkar's criticism in his treatment of *Sefer ha-Emunot*. Two factors might account for this: First, Modena focused on only a few passages in the work that interested him. Second, for all his criticism of Shem Tov and defense of Maimonides, Alashkar remained a committed kabbalist. See Moshe Idel, Introduction, in Yosef ben Moshe Alashkar, *Sefer Tsafnat Paneah* (Jerusalem: Misgav Jerusalem, 1991).

[36] MS A 13B, 14–15; ed. Libowitz, 15. On *Pardes*, see chapter 2.

mistico," Modena summarized the claim made by several kabbalists that only this type of interpretation could yield the meaning of the biblical text. Kabbalists argued that they possessed a monopoly over the interpretation of the Bible and that only their mystical interpretation could offer a correct interpretation of God's word. Responding to this claim, Modena paraphrased Maimonides' introduction to the *Guide*: "The Rabbi, the Guide, of blessed memory, has already written pure utterances for us about the verse, 'apples of gold encased in silver.'[37] In the Torah there exists the revealed as well as the concealed, but the revealed is not a mere husk, as those cited above contend. It, too, is good and precious, even though the concealed is more important than it, just like gold is more valuable than silver."[38] Modena praised a multiplicity of interpretive modes and rejected the attempt by the kabbalists to acquire hegemony over biblical hermeneutics: "And so, thank God, the earlier and later commentaries increase and continue to increase,[39] those that explain the Torah to us through the allusive manner, in addition to the rabbis, of blessed memory, who preceded and explicated it in a homiletic manner. Who would [dare] say that you people [kabbalists] know the secret sense in your wisdom, but we do not know [it]?"[40] Kabbalists denigrated other levels of interpretation, such as the plain sense of the text, known as *peshat*, the allusive sense of the text, known as *remez*, and the homiletic sense, known as *derash*. Modena stressed the importance of other ways of interpreting the Bible apart from the mystical one.

Modena connected this discussion of biblical interpretation to Ibn Gabbai's critique of Maimonides:

> But the Gabbai continues to curse and revile the Rabbi, The Guide, of blessed memory. In [the third section of] his work, *Helek ha-Takhlit*,[41] chapter 16, he wrote: "the intellect is precluded from grasping the Secrets of the Torah and even the intellect of Moses our teacher, peace be upon him, could not grasp it until the Ancient of Days Himself revealed them." As if to say that everything that they [i.e. the kabbalists] utter about these matters, [they say because] the spirit of the Lord speaks to them, as it did to Moses.[42]

Over and above the claims that kabbalists made about the exclusive importance of their mystical interpretation of the Bible, they posited that it could

---

[37] Prov. 25:11; Maimonides, *Guide of the Perplexed*, introduction, 11.
[38] Following Ibn Tibbon, Modena used the terms *nigleh* and *nistar*, translated, respectively, as "revealed" and "concealed." Pines used the "internal" and "external" for the equivalent passage. Ibid., 12.
[39] Zech. 10:8.
[40] MS A 14A, 1–6; ed. Libowitz, 15.
[41] The third of four sections of *Avodat ha-Kodesh*.
[42] MS A 14A, 6–9; ed. Libowitz, 15. Modena quoted this passage without citation elsewhere, see MS A 17A, 11; ed. Libowitz, 22.

not be derived through intellectual inquiry; one must either have had an oral tradition that stretched back to Moses at Sinai or received divine revelation. Given that Kabbalah had not been transmitted continuously from the divine revelation at Sinai, the only remaining option was that each and every kabbalist had received divine revelation like Moses. Modena saw this as an expression of hubris and concluded his discussion with a stinging rebuke.

While Modena portrayed Ibn Gabbai as a harsh critic of Maimonides, the boundaries between different kabbalistic readings of Maimonides were by no means hard and fast. In Ibn Gabbai's case, they were explicitly crossed, if not in Modena's reading of him, then certainly in Ibn Gabbai's work. Modena cast Ibn Gabbai solely as a critic of Maimonides, a curser and reviler, yet he ignored the fact that at various points in *Avodat ha-Kodesh*, Ibn Gabbai softened his polemic against Maimonides and attempted to turn him into a kabbalist.[43] Ibn Gabbai was hardly the only kabbalist to treat Maimonides in such a fashion, as will emerge below. For Modena's polemical purposes, however, Ibn Gabbai appeared only as a Maimonidean critic.

Modena delivered these criticisms of both Shem Tov and Ibn Gabbai only after having quoted from Maimonides; in these two instances he quoted from the *Guide*, while elsewhere in *Ari Nohem* he quoted from the introduction to the commentary on the Mishnah and the Code, specifically the introduction and *Sefer ha-Mada*. To a certain extent, Maimonides functioned as a shield behind which Modena could hide as he delivered his criticism of learned and well-respected kabbalists. Maimonides and the *Guide* served as an anchor within Jewish tradition for Modena's polemic, and he invoked both the man and his work as part of a rhetorical strategy in his attack on kabbalists. One might question whether Modena was as committed to hero-worship as the kabbalists he criticized. Kabbalists impugned the authority of Maimonides, and what was more, their work had repeatedly appeared in print. This affront required a vigilant response on the part of a champion of Maimonides.

KABBALISTS WHO DEFENDED MAIMONIDES

According to Modena, Ibn Gabbai derived his argument that Kabbalah was beyond intellectual inquiry from Nahmanides.[44] In particular, Modena associated this position with a certain phrase whose origin he assigned to Nahmanides: "investigation of it [Kabbalah] is foolishness."[45] Yet Modena

[43] Scholem, "From a Scholar to a Kabbalist," 198.
[44] For the connection between Ibn Gabbai and Nahmanides on this point, see MS A 12A, 19–12B, 8; ed. Libowitz, 12.
[45] MS 12A, 20–21; ed. Libowitz, 12. "[But] this type of investigation and speculation is forbidden, from the words of Nahmanides, of blessed memory.... The first among them who said: investigation of it is foolishness. Many of them took this from him and said the same." For other instances, see MS A 12B, 1; 14B, 7; 42A, 1; ed. Libowitz, 13, 16, 82. Nahmanides used

never denounced Nahmanides as he did Ibn Gabbai; his attitude toward Nahmanides was far more nuanced. Although he criticized Nahmanides' claim that Kabbalah was beyond intellectual inquiry, Modena invoked him as a model particularly regarding his attitude toward Maimonides. For Modena, Nahmanides served as the foremost kabbalist to have defended Maimonides and the *Guide*. A thinker of intellectual and spiritual stature who functioned as a counterweight to Shem Tov and Ibn Gabbai, Nahmanides defended Maimonides and his philosophical work. If Modena repeatedly returned to Ibn Gabbai and Shem Tov throughout *Ari Nohem*, he mentioned Nahmanides considerably fewer times, and when he did, his name most frequently occurs embedded within the citation of another text. On two occasions Modena cited Nahmanides' letter in defense of Maimonides addressed to the sages of northern France in the 1230s during the first Maimonidean controversy.[46]

Although written over four centuries before Modena's polemic, Nahmanides' letter was of more than casual interest to a Jewish intellectual in Venice in the 1630s. The letter had appeared in print for the first time as part of Joseph Solomon Delmedigo's *Ta'alumot Hokhmah*.[47] Nahmanides' actual defense of Maimonides' *Guide* was quite limited: he merely called for revocation of the ban by the French sages on the private study of the *Guide* but upheld their ban on group study of the text.[48] In describing Nahmanides' letter as "long and blessed, bound and attached, in defense of the book, the *Guide*,"[49] Modena was apparently influenced by the presentation of the

---

this phrase at the conclusion of his introduction to his biblical commentary. See Halbertal, *Al Derekh ha-Emet*, 311.

[46] On the first Maimonidean controversy, see Daniel J. Silver, *Maimonidean Criticism and the Maimonidean Controversy, 1180–1240* (Leiden: Brill, 1965); Joseph Shatzmiller, "Toward a Portrait of the First Controversy over the Writings of Maimonides" (Hebrew), *Zion* 34 (1969): 126–44; Azriel Shohat, "Clarifications on the Episode of the First Controversy over the Books of Maimonides" (Hebrew), *Zion* 36 (1971): 27–60; Bernard Septimus, *Hispano-Jewish Culture in Transition: The Career and Controversies of Ramah* (Cambridge: Harvard University Press, 1982). For Nahmanides' role, see David Berger, "How Did Nahmanides Propose to Resolve the Maimonidean Controversy?" in *Me'ah She'arim: Studies in Medieval Jewish Spiritual Life in Memory of Isadore Twersky*, ed. Gerald Blidstein et al., 135–46 (Jerusalem: Magnes Press, 2001); Nina Caputo, *Nahmanides in Medieval Catalonia: History, Community, and Messianism* (Notre Dame: University of Notre Dame Press, 2007), chap. 1. On Nahmanides' attitude toward Maimonides, see Bernard Septimus, "'Open Rebuke and Concealed Love': Nahmanides and the Andalusian Tradition," in Twersky, *Rabbi Moses Nahmanides*, 11–34; Jacob I. Dienstag, "Maimonides and Nahmanides: A Bibliography," *Daat* 27 (1991): 125–39; Halbertal, *Al Derekh ha-Emet*.

[47] On Delmedigo and Modena, see above. For the textual history of Nahmanides' letter, see Mauro Perani, "Mistica e Filosofia: la mediazone di Nahmanide nella polemica sugli scritti di Maimonide," in *Nahmanide: Esegetica e cabbalista*, ed. Moshe Idel and Mauro Perani (Florence: Giuntina, 1998), 115, n. 34.

[48] Berger, "How Did Nahmanides Propose to Resolve the Maimonidean Controversy?," 145.

[49] See MS A 7B, 1–20, 24B, 14; ed. Libowitz, 4, 39.

letter in Delmedigo's *Ta'alumot Hokhmah*, where it appears under the title "Nahmanides' Epistle in Defense of the Book of the *Guide*."[50]

For Modena, Nahmanides' letter emphasized two vitally important points: the personal piety of Maimonides and the role of the *Guide* in preventing the apostasy of numerous Jews. Quoting Nahmanides about the *Guide*, Modena asked, "How many of those displaced from the faith did he gather up? To how many epicureans did he respond? ... The Rabbi [Maimonides] placed his books as crowns in the face of tribulation, as a shield to the arrows of the bows of the Greeks, those who write out evil writs."[51] Dismissing Shem Tov's attempt to rebut Nahmanides' letter as a "perversion," Modena noted that Nahmanides was never "satiated as he wrote to praise, laud, glorify, and exalt his [Maimonides'] wisdom and piety." At the conclusion of his account, Modena further asked, "How will they [the kabbalists] respond to Nahmanides, of blessed memory, first in this Kabbalah, who praises him [Maimonides] and glorifies him?"

Nahmanides played a complicated role in *Ari Nohem*. Although Modena used Nahmanides' reputation as a kabbalist to criticize others for daring to attack Maimonides, he rejected his attempt to claim Kabbalah as beyond intellectual inquiry. But he restrained himself from denouncing Nahmanides in the same manner as Ibn Gabbai and Shem Tov and only indirectly criticized his engagement with Kabbalah. Throughout *Ari Nohem*, Modena repeatedly discussed Isaac bar Sheshet's responsum on the study of Kabbalah and at one point quoted Bar Sheshet on Nahmanides: "Rabbenu Nissim, of blessed memory, told me in private that Nahmanides became far too absorbed in his belief of this Kabbalah."[52] Modena rarely shirked from criticizing those figures, living or dead, with whom he disagreed; his treatment of Nahmanides as a kabbalist seems doubly significant in this respect. Despite his utility as a defender of Maimonides, Nahmanides and his study of Kab-

[50] Delmedigo, *Sefer Ta'alumot Hokhmah*, 85A–89B.

[51] Isa. 10:1; MS A 7B, 6–11; ed. Libowitz, 4.

[52] MS A 27A, 10; ed. Libowitz, 44. Other instances of this responsum in *Ari Nohem* include MS A 18A, 13; 26B, 25; 28B, 18; 43B, 13; ed. Libowitz, 25, 43, 47, 87. Bar Sheshet also appeared in the list of writers against Kabbalah at the end of MS A 48B, 10. Ibn Gabbai responded to this passage of Bar Sheshet's responsum with Rabbenu Nissim's critique of Nahmanides. See *Avodat ha-Kodesh*, 2:13. Modena cited this passage in Ibn Gabbai on at least one occasion. See MS A 18A, 12–13; ed. Libowitz, 25. Bar Sheshet's responsum was also quoted in Delmedigo, *Sefer Mazref Le-Hokhmah* in *Sefer Ta'alumot Hokhmah*, 13A. On Bar Sheshet, see Yitzhak Baer, *A History of the Jews in Christian Spain* (Philadelphia: JPS, 1992), 2:73–83; Halbertal, *Al Derekh ha-Emet*, 11. Penkower pointed to the discrepancy between the text in Libowitz's edition, responsum 156, and the actual responsum where the phrase appears, 157. See Penkower, "S. D. Luzzatto, Vowels and Accents," 104, n. 82. In the manuscript authorized by Modena the reference is to responsa 157. Two editions of these responsa had appeared before *Ari Nohem*. For responsum 157, see Isaac bar Sheshet, *Teshuvot Ha-Rav* (Constantinople, 1546), n.p.; and *She'elot U-Teshuvot* (Riva di Trento, 1559), 88A–89A. For the possibility that Modena owned a copy, see Ancona, "L'inventario dei beni appartenenti a Leon da Modena," 261, n. 5.

balah required some form of rebuttal. Modena offered this criticism only through the voices of the past: Isaac bar Sheshet quoting Rabbenu Nissim.

KABBALISTIC APPROPRIATION OF MAIMONIDES

While some kabbalists criticized Maimonides and others defended him, still others appropriated his thought. One line of thinking was found in a legend about Maimonides' embrace of Kabbalah at the end of his life. According to this conversion story, Maimonides embraced the study of Kabbalah right before his death, recanting his rationalism and expressing regret for his philosophical writings, and particularly for the *Guide*.[53] The second kabbalistic mode of appropriating Maimonides was to interpret the *Guide* itself in kabbalistic terms.

In discussing Maimonides' alleged conversion to Kabbalah, Modena posed a rhetorical question: if Kabbalah were a tradition from Moses and the prophets, how was it possible that Maimonides had not studied it with his teachers, among whom Modena mistakenly included Isaac Alfasi (ca. 1013–ca. 1103)?[54] Rather, argued Modena, Maimonides had knowledge of certain kabbalistic practices or protokabbalistic practices, including traditions about the theurgic usage of the divine names and the composition of amulets.[55] And he condemned them in no uncertain terms. A sentence later, Modena alluded to the legend about Maimonides' conversion to Kabbalah before his death:

> But when those unhappy people saw this ... they sought for themselves this refuge of falsehood, saying that it has been found written in the name of the Rabbi. These are the words of R. Elijah son of Hayim from Genazzano ... in *Iggeret*

---

[53] Scholem, "From a Scholar to a Kabbalist"; Michael A. Shmidman, "On Maimonides' 'Conversion' to Kabbalah," in *Studies in Medieval Jewish History and Literature II*, ed. Isadore Twersky, 375–86 (Cambridge: Harvard University Press, 1984); Louis Jacobs, "Attitudes of the Kabbalists and Hasidim Towards Maimonides," *The Solomon Goldman Lectures* 5 (1990): 45–55; Abraham Melamed, "Conversion Myths: Maimonides and Aristotle" (Hebrew), *Daat* 64–66 (2009): 166–93. Traditions about a philosopher's deathbed repentance circulated about numerous figures in the Middle Ages. Modena quoted a similar tradition about Aristotle recanting his philosophy and believing in the true God. See MS A 25B, 1–11; ed. Libowitz, 40–41. This tradition had been translated into Hebrew and printed as part of *Sefer ha-Tapuah* (Riva di Trento, 1562).

[54] MS A 24B, 9–16; ed. Libowitz, 39. A legal authority from North Africa, Alfasi was not actually a teacher of Maimonides. On Maimonides' education, see Herbert A. Davidson, *Moses Maimonides: The Man and His Works* (New York: Oxford University Press, 2005), 75–121. On Alfasi, see Ta-Shma, *Ha-Sifrut ha-parshanit la-Talmud be-Europah uvi-Tsefon Afrikah: 1000–1200* (Jerusalem: Magnes Press, 1999), 1:145–54.

[55] On the term "protokabbalistic" in this context, see Menachem Kellner, *Maimonides' Confrontation with Mysticism* (Oxford: Littman Library, 2006), 18–31.

ha-Hamudot which I shall certainly mention[56] for opprobrium in the chapter after this one. This was brought in his name in *Shalshelet ha-Kabala* of [Gedalya ibn] Yahya, of blessed memory. In addition, the Gabbai in his *Avodah*,[57] Gate ____ Chapter___ expanded and insisted upon saying all of the above in the name of several writers[58] after all the tables of his chapters were filled with vomit and filth[59] against the Rabbi, of blessed memory, and his pure teachings.[60]

In this passage Modena merely alluded to the conversion story noting its popularity and its citation by three different figures, Elijah of Genazzano, Meir ibn Gabbai, and Gedalya ibn Yahya.[61]

A page later, Modena cited the story in its entirety and connected it to his criticism about the antiquity of Kabbalah:

> They invented in his [Maimonides'] name these words: upon hearing about Kabbalah at the end of his life, he retracted and regretted what he had written. But who would believe this rumor, who would believe this, who is it that testifies that these words ever originated from the Rabbi, of blessed memory, and not from them, and the masses? Moreover, the lie is self-evident and entirely unfounded. If it [Kabbalah] had been a tradition from the prophets like the Oral Torah, the Rabbi, of blessed memory, would already have known about it from his youth. And his teachers who had taught him the one would have taught him the other, as I said earlier. Certainly they would have considered him a student worthy of receiving the Secrets of the Torah and he would never have dared write against it, heaven forefend.[62]

For Modena, the story about Maimonides, much like Kabbalah in general, was an invention lacking any factual basis. Once the kabbalists realized that the *Guide* condemned many of the beliefs and practices central to their worldview, such as the combinations of letters, the use of numerology, and the theurgic invocation of the names of God, they needed to appropriate Maimonides but abandon his *Guide*. Modena exploded in anger about this legend; for him, the kabbalization of Maimonides was worse than Kabbalah itself.

---

[56] Jer. 31:19.

[57] There is a gap in the manuscript as to the location of the citation in Ibn Gabbai's *Avodat ha-Kodesh*. In his edition of *Ari Nohem*, Libowitz lists the citation as *Avodat ha-Kodesh*, 2:13 and 3:18.

[58] Presumably Isaac Abravanel in *Nahalat Avot*, cited by Ibn Gabbai in *Avodat ha-Kodesh*, 2:13.

[59] Isa. 28:8.

[60] MS 25A, 10–16; ed. Libowitz, 40.

[61] See Eliyyah Hayyim ben Binyamin da Genazzano, *La lettera preziosa*, ed. Fabrizio Lelli (Florence: Giuntina, 2002), 129–30; Ibn Gabbai, *Marot Elohim*, 33A; Ibn Yahya, *Shalshelet ha-Kabalah*, 44A–44B; Ibn Yahya quoted Genazzano. See also Delmedigo, *Sefer Mazref le-Hokhmah* in *Sefer Ta'alumot Hokhmah*, 15B–16A.

[62] MS A 25B, 16–22; ed. Libowitz, 41.

Describing another strategy used by kabbalists to appropriate Maimonides, Modena continued: "There are some of them who strove to explain with all their might his words, and one of these commentaries on his book the *Guide of the Perplexed* [even explains] it in accord with their Kabbalah."[63] Only a page later, Modena returned to this approach: "Among them, there was also one who chose a different path to defend this [legend of Maimonides the kabbalist], and he explicated his esteemed book, the *Guide of the Perplexed*, in terms of their Kabbalah. And it is in your possession."[64] The addressee of this passage and owner of a kabbalistic commentary on the *Guide* was clearly Hamiz, the addressee of *Ari Nohem*. While several kabbalistic commentaries on the *Guide* were composed in the Middle Ages, the one in Hamiz's possession was almost certainly by Abraham Abulafia.[65] Hamiz collected Abulafia's writings over the course of his life and had access to writings by Abulafia that have not survived.[66] Given that Modena did not shirk from criticizing his opponents by name, his unflattering reference to an unnamed kabbalistic commentator on the *Guide* may indicate that he did not know the author's identity. The only works of Abulafia to have appeared in print before the composition of *Ari Nohem* appeared anonymously, and Abulafia's name did not appear anywhere in *Ari Nohem*.[67]

Modena posed a rhetorical question that offers a revealing insight into the different approaches taken by kabbalists to Maimonides and the *Guide*: "Who shall explain to me how to reconcile the insult and spittle[68] that they scattered on every place of his aforementioned book—Gabbai and Shem Tov—with the commentary of this man?"[69] Modena juxtaposed the kabbalistic critics of Maimonides, Shem Tov and Ibn Gabbai, with the kabbalistic commentator to the *Guide*, Abraham Abulafia, and pointed to the fundamental discrepancy between their approaches. The former criticized Maimonides; the latter appropriated him by writing kabbalistic commentary

---

[63] MS A 24B, 22–23; ed. Libowitz, 39.

[64] MS A 25A, 16–18; ed. Libowitz, 40.

[65] See Isaac Reggio's unpublished notes to his working edition of *Ari Nohem*, MS L, 41B. On medieval kabbalistic commentaries to the *Guide*, see Idel, "Maimonides' *Guide of the Perplexed* and the Kabbalah."

[66] See Idel, "Abraham Abulafia's Work and Doctrine" (Hebrew), Ph.D. diss., Hebrew University, 1976; Idel, "Rabbi Solomon ibn Adret and Abraham Abulafia," 249, n. 89. Hamiz used the phrase "Ari Nohem" in the opening of his polemic against Solomon ibn Adret in defense of Abraham Abulafia. See the text identified by Moshe Idel in Jerusalem, JNUL, MS 3009 8°, 1A.

[67] Excerpts from Abulafia's works appeared in Avraham ben Yehudah Almalikh, *Likute Shikhehah u-Feah* (Ferrara: Usque, 1556). However, Abulafia was mentioned in *Sefer Mazref le-Hokhmah* in *Sefer Ta'alumot Hokhmah*, 13B.

[68] Isa. 50:6.

[69] MS 25A, 18–19; ed. Libowitz, 40.

on the *Guide*. Modena was keenly aware of the incompatibility between the criticism leveled at Maimonides by Ibn Gabbai and Shem Tov and the appropriation of Maimonides by the *Guide*'s kabbalistic commentators.[70]

THE STUDY OF THE *GUIDE* IN SEVENTEENTH-CENTURY VENICE

Modena and Hamiz studied Maimonides' *Guide* together, and this joint undertaking provided them with the opportunity to debate central theological issues. By reading over their shoulders, one can isolate both the specific passages they examined and the primary concerns of their study. In *Ari Nohem* Modena explicitly drew on the *Guide*, as well other writings by Maimonides, to construct arguments about prayer, the nature of heresy, the biblical figure of Abraham, the reasons for the commandments, and the transmission of the Oral Torah. On at least one occasion, Modena juxtaposed rabbinic dicta in ways very similar to Maimonides without explicitly mentioning the *Guide*.[71] Modena referred to his joint reading of the *Guide* with Hamiz on several occasions, and two of these passages, which appear toward the end of the treatise, merit close attention. Modena outlined what he expected his student to derive from his reading of Maimonides. In chapter 27, Modena discussed the requirements, both personal and intellectual, that one must fulfill before engaging in the study of divine wisdom, or metaphysics. Citing the parable of the palace in chapter 51 of the third section of the *Guide*, Modena compared kabbalists to "those who have turned their backs upon the ruler's habitation, their faces being turned another away. The more these people walk, thinking they are coming close, the greater is their distance, because their paths lack a solid foundation and a trustworthy place."[72]

The *Guide* functioned as an authoritative source, in some sense the authoritative source, for the requirements that had to be fulfilled before engaging in the study of metaphysics. Shortly thereafter Modena addressed Hamiz directly:

> But you know how much the Rabbi, the *Guide*, of blessed memory, in his esteemed book, doubled and tripled his warning that any person who enters

---

[70] Christian kabbalists such as Johannes Reuchlin also read Maimonides' *Guide* as a kabbalistic text. See Moshe Idel, "Introduction to the Bison Book Edition," in Johann Reuchlin, *On the Art of the Kabbalah: De Arte Cabalistica* (Lincoln: University of Nebraska Press, 1993), xvi, n. 43; Elliot R. Wolfson, "Language, Secrecy and the Mysteries of Law: Theurgy and the Christian Kabbalah of Johannes Reuchlin," *Kabbalah* 13 (2005): 24, n. 49; Brian P. Copenhaver, "Maimonides, Abulafia and Pico: A Secret Aristotle for the Renaissance," *Rinascimento* 46 (2006): 23–51. Modena did not connect his criticism of Christian Kabbalah to the kabbalistic appropriation of Maimonides.

[71] MS A 17A, 15; ed. Libowitz, 22. See Maimonides, *Guide of the Perplexed*, 3:26, 508.

[72] MS A 44B, 12–14; ed. Libowitz, 89. See Maimonides, *Guide of the Perplexed*, 3:51, 619.

into metaphysics to which he alludes in that treatise, if he has not first acquired [the prerequisites] of knowledge of wisdom, a purification of his attributes, and [if] the days of his temptation have not preceded him.... He speaks about this in the fifth chapter of the first part, and in the thirty-first of it, as well as in the thirty-second, and thirty-third, as well as in other places. Examine them.[73]

Modena stipulated knowledge of wisdom, a purification of moral attributes, and the overcoming of temptation. In the continuation of this passage, he added two other prerequisites: humility and twenty years of age. These last two were drawn not from the *Guide*, but from writings by the kabbalists themselves, notably Moses Cordovero and the work of his own son-in-law.[74] While this may simply be part of Modena's polemical strategy—he employed whatever source he could to make his point as effectively as possible—he used the comments about the requirements of age in Cordovero and Levi as a means of expanding upon a concept in the *Guide*. Maimonides had described the importance of "overcoming temptation" before beginning the study of metaphysics. Cordovero and Levi offered a specific age and added humility. Modena not only cited the relevant passages from the *Guide* but also directed Hamiz to examine these same passages on his own in greater detail.

At the outset of the third section of *Ari Nohem*, Modena addressed Hamiz and referred to a passage in the *Guide* they had studied: "I am certain that you have not forgotten what we read together in his book, there is no limit to its praise, *The Guide of the Perplexed*, part 1, chapter 61."[75] Modena cited this passage in *Ari Nohem* more than any other passage from the *Guide*. He emphasized this chapter, along with those that immediately preceded and succeeded it, in order to reinforce his criticism of the kabbalistic notions about the names of God and the kabbalistic doctrine of the sefirot. As in other cases, Modena invoked Maimonides in order to anchor his own claims:

> However, if you envisage His essence as it is when divested and stripped of all actions, He no longer has a derived name in any respect . . . but that which they call names and which they think that they necessitate holiness and purity and perform miracles. All these are stories that it is not seemly for a perfect man to hear, much less believe. Here end his [Maimonides'] words. From this it appears that in the time of the great rabbi, of blessed memory, this vanity also existed,

---

[73] MS A 44B, 16–19; ed. Libowitz, 89.

[74] MS A 44B, 20–26; 45A, 1–4; ed. Libowitz, 89–90. On Cordovero's rejection of a requirement to reach age forty before studying Kabbalah, see Moshe Idel, "On the History of the Prohibition to Study Kabbalah before Age 40" (Hebrew), *AJS Review* 5 (1980): 13.

[75] MS A 39A, 8–10; ed. Libowitz, 75–76.

and he knew about it and distanced himself from it as the pursuit of wind[76] and contrary words, as I wrote earlier in chapter 11.[77]

Elsewhere in *Ari Nohem*, Modena decried the notion that kabbalists knew the names of God and could use them to effect change in heaven and on earth, and he attributed a similar stance to Maimonides.[78] In Modena's reconstruction of the *Guide*, contemporaries of Maimonides claimed to have secrets and traditions about the divine name, something he dismissed offhand as "this vanity." Maimonides had rejected these ideas in no uncertain terms. Modena saw his own argument against contemporary kabbalists who claimed to be able to perform miracles using divine names as entirely within this Maimonidean tradition and, in fact, as a continuation of Maimonides' own program. Furthermore, he rejected kabbalistic attempts to interpret this passage of the *Guide* as evidence that Maimonides himself knew of these same traditions about the divine name.[79]

Modena also objected to the kabbalistic notion of sefirot, criticizing this doctrine as one that led to a concept of divinity that was plural in nature. To emphasize the essential unity of God, Modena invoked the very same passage in the *Guide*. He posed this question about the sefirot: "Which is simpler to visualize in the human mind and [which is] the greater expression of God's unity, a greater safeguard against erring: thinking that He is one, singular and unique through a denial of plurality in Him, or imagining in one's thoughts the proliferation of sefirot, channels, and lights?"[80] Railing against the belief in sefirot, Modena asserted that the primary method of combating such a belief was to adopt the Maimonidean notion of the negative attributes of God. Modena's rejection of sefirot was hardly new in the history of Jewish thought, and he himself was keenly aware that numerous figures before him refused to accept their validity. To take only one example: on at least four occasions Modena cited with approval a comment quoted in Isaac bar Sheshet's responsum about belief in the ten sefirot: "The Christians believe in the trinity and they [the kabbalists] believe in the decad."[81] Like the unnamed philosopher quoted by Isaac bar Sheshet, Modena saw belief in the sefirot as akin to belief in the multiplicity of God.

---

[76] Ecc. 1:14.

[77] MS A 39A, 10–14; ed. Libowitz, 76. The text in Libowitz's edition differs slightly from MS A.

[78] MS A 24B, 18–25A, 7; ed. Libowitz, 39–40.

[79] MS A 25A, 3–4; ed. Libowitz, 40. For an echo of Modena's position in Maimonidean scholarship, see Kellner, *Maimonides' Confrontation with Mysticism*.

[80] MS A 16A, 18–20; ed. Libowitz, 20.

[81] MS A 27A, 7–9; 27A, 20–21 [not in the Libowitz edition], 43B, 13–14; 46A, 24; ed. Libowitz, 44, 87, 94; Idel, "Differing Conceptions of Kabbalah in the Early 17th Century," 175, n. 181. On Modena's criticism of the *sefirot* and his reading of Cordovero, see chapter 4.

The sense of urgency that one detects in Modena's polemic against the sefirot overlaps with his appeal to Hamiz regarding their joint study of the *Guide*. Hamiz, by contrast, read Maimonides with kabbalistic commentaries and discovered an interpretation of Maimonides that validated kabbalistic traditions about the divine names as well as a justification of the sefirot. Maimonides had prescribed the *Guide* as a type of therapeutic cure for the spiritual ailments of his own student, Joseph ibn Shimon, whom he described as a confused reader of philosophical and theological works: "As I also saw, you had already acquired some smattering of this subject from people other than myself; you were perplexed, as stupefaction had come over you.... Your absence moved me to compose this Treatise, which I have composed for you and those like you, however few they are." Similarly, Modena wrote *Ari Nohem* in order to prescribe the *Guide* as a cure for Hamiz's kabbalistic tendencies.[82]

Modena's Maimonideanism

Maimonides' discussion of the relationship between writing and esotericism had an enormous impact on Modena. According to some kabbalists, particular individuals had been compelled to record esoteric secrets in writing at periodic moments of crisis in order to prevent their disappearance. This explanation accounted for the inscription of the *Zohar* in writing in late medieval Castile and for its printing in sixteenth-century Italy. Only by the public revelation of esoteric doctrine had they managed to avert a complete rupture in the transmission of their secrets. Modena's response to this theory drew heavily on Maimonides—both the history of the Oral Torah presented in the introduction to his code of law and the notion of ancient esoteric secrets outlined in the *Guide of the Perplexed*. The kabbalistic narrative itself echoed Maimonides' history of the Oral Torah sketched in the introduction to his code of law. In Maimonides' rendering, Judah the Prince recorded the Mishnah in writing as a response to a crisis in the transmission of tradition.[83] While the Mishnah had succeeded in preventing the loss of the Oral Torah, Maimonides argued elsewhere that ancient esoteric secrets had actually been lost. In the *Guide of the Perplexed*,

---

[82] Maimonides, *Guide of the Perplexed*, introduction, 4. On the addressee of the *Guide*, see Sarah Stroumsa, *Reshito shel Pulmus ha-Rambam ba-Mizrah: Igeret ha-Hashtakah al Odot Tehiyat ha-Metim le-Yosef Ibn Shimon* (Jerusalem: Ben-Zvi Institute, 1999). Nearly half a century earlier, in a series of letters to Gershon Cohen written in 1593, Modena had advised his correspondent to examine Maimonides' *Guide* for the account of creation and account of the chariot. See *Letters*, 60–67.

[83] Moshe Halbertal, "What Is the *Mishneh Torah*? On Codification and Ambivalence," in Harris, *Maimonides after 800 Years*, 81–111.

Maimonides emphasized that a set of esoteric secrets given to Moses had not survived the vagaries of history. Only through the power of his own intellect had Maimonides himself been able to recover these secrets.[84]

As a committed Maimonidean, Modena posited that ancient esoteric secrets had been irrevocably lost. An extensive marginal note at the conclusion of the first chapter addressed to Hamiz in the second person indicates that Maimonides' claim about the loss of esoteric secrets was central to Modena's criticism: "Not only did I know, but all my life I taught to the multitudes that Moses our teacher, of blessed memory, and the prophets had in their dominion secrets and mysteries about every stroke in our Torah; but as a result of the persecutions and exiles of Israel, these pathways ceased, as Maimonides, of blessed memory, wrote."[85] Modena violently opposed the attempt by late medieval and contemporary kabbalists to associate the set of ideas and practices referred to as Kabbalah with the ancient esoteric secrets possessed by Moses. After an explicit invocation of Maimonides and his theory of esoteric secrets, Modena posited a basic disjuncture between what his contemporaries referred to as Kabbalah and the ancient esoteric secrets given to Moses at Sinai:

> But those who nowadays refer to the Secrets of the Torah and the wisdom of truth, this is all an invention of the last three hundred and fifty years, and was not received from the prophets. And of all that is opposed to Kabbalah in this treatise of mine, my intention is not against those Secrets of the Torah, heaven forefend, but against that which they refer to in our time as Kabbalah. As for the true secrets, the blessed Lord shall return and reveal them during the redemption of Israel; about this it is said, for the land shall be filled with devotion to the Lord,[86] and all your children shall be disciples of the Lord,[87] and the like.[88]

Only with the redemption of Israel would knowledge of these secrets be revealed. But this redemption was hardly at the forefront of Modena's mind. In *Ari Nohem* he had dismissed those who had supported the printing of the *Zohar* as hastening the advent of the Messiah with a sarcastic quip; in *Magen va-Herev*, written a few years later and perhaps at the same time that he composed this note, Modena went even further. Drawing on Isaac Arama (ca.1420–1494), whose biblical commentary *Akedat Yitzhak* was frequently printed in the sixteenth century, Modena argued that belief in the Messiah was not as central a doctrine in Judaism as it was in Christianity. He concluded: "I frequently say that I believe in the Messiah because I am

---

[84] Maimonides, *Guide of the Perplexed*, 1:71, 175–84.
[85] MS A 8B, between lines 15 and 16. A transcription of the note appears in Richler, "Unknown Writings," 170–71.
[86] Isa. 11:9.
[87] Isa. 54:13.
[88] MS A 8B, between lines 15 and 16.

a Jew but I am not a Jew because I believe in the Messiah."[89] The messianic redemption and its attendant restoration of esoteric secrets was clearly not an imminent concern for Modena. Far more pressing was the spread of kabbalistic theology.

For Modena, many of the most distressing problems generated by the spread of Kabbalah resulted from a series of category errors made by its devotees. The previous chapter examined how kabbalists had elevated the *Zohar* into a foundational text of Judaism and used it as a normative source of the law; this chapter examines another such error: the confusion of kabbalistic theology with philosophic wisdom. Modena rejected the argument that Kabbalah was *Hokhmah*, a medieval Hebrew philosophical term used to denote knowledge, science, or wisdom. Modena's position on this issue appears to have been influenced by the discussion of the term *Hokhmah* in the final chapter of Maimonides' *Guide*.[90] Although he never explicitly cited this chapter, his rejection of the identification of Kabbalah with *Hokhmah* has a distinctly Maimonidean character. In the final chapter of the *Guide*, Maimonides outlined four different senses of the word *Hokhmah*. His distinction between knowledge derived from tradition and knowledge derived from philosophical speculation is especially relevant to Modena's discussion of Kabbalah and *Hokhmah*.

> One who knows the whole of the Law in its true reality is called *wise* in two respects: in respect of the rational virtues comprised in the Law and in respect of the moral virtues included in it. But since the rational matter in the Law is received through tradition and is not demonstrated by methods of speculation, the knowledge of the Law came to be set up in the books of the prophets and the sayings of the *Sages* as one separate species, and wisdom, in an unrestricted sense, as another species. It is through this wisdom, in an unrestricted sense, that the rational matter that we receive from the Law through tradition is demonstrated.[91]

Adopting this understanding of *Hokhmah*, Modena pointed to Nahmanides and Ibn Gabbai, who had declared that Kabbalah was beyond rational inquiry. For these kabbalists, Kabbalah was a closed set of doctrines and not an area where one could advance through rational inquiry. This being the case, reasoned Modena, Kabbalah could not possibly be defined as *Hokhmah* because philosophical knowledge was necessarily the product of speculation and inquiry.

The distinction between Kabbalah and *Hokhmah* functioned as a leitmotif throughout *Ari Nohem*. The clearest formulation appears in chapter

---

[89] *Magen va-Herev*, 64.
[90] Maimonides, *Guide of the Perplexed*, 3:54, 632–38.
[91] Ibid., 633.

4: "It [Kabbalah] is not knowledge. Because knowledge entails understanding a thing in its causes, and the derivation of secondary principles from primary principles by means of inquiry and analysis as we have said. But in this instance [Kabbalah], inquiry and analysis are forbidden, as in the words of Nahmanides, of blessed memory . . . who said investigation of it is foolishness."[92] Modena proceeded to cite Ibn Gabbai to similar effect. He explicitly invoked Maimonides' discussion of esoteric secrets in the *Guide* and appears to have drawn on the work in his distinction between Kabbalah and *Hokhmah*. He did not, however, use Maimonides to construct an independent and coherent theological or philosophical system; rather, the *Guide* served as a source of authority, an integral part of a rhetorical strategy, a polemical resource, and a common point of reference with Hamiz. Modena's defense of Maimonides against his kabbalistic critics involved the adoption of particular Maimonidean positions on a host of issues, ranging from the nature of God, the intellectual requirements that must be fulfilled before studying metaphysics, and the transmission of the oral Torah to the relationship between writing and esotericism.[93]

In the early seventeenth century, numerous other readers, Christian as well as Jewish, turned to the writings of Maimonides in order to make a range of philosophical and theological points. While Modena may have read the *Guide* in Ibn Tibbon's Hebrew translation, contemporary readers of Latin had access to the *Guide* in Johannes Buxtorf's translation, printed in Basel in 1629. Modena's use of the *Guide* and the *Code* against Jewish kabbalists coincided with the interest in Maimonides by the Dutch translators of the *Code* in Amsterdam and English students of the *Guide*, such as John Selden and John Spencer.[94] While one cannot point to a direct connection between Modena's Maimonideanism and these contemporary

---

[92] MS A 12A, 18–21; ed. Libowitz, 12.

[93] Idel, "Differing Conceptions of Kabbalah in the Early 17th Century," 174.

[94] On the Dutch translators of the *Code*, see Aaron L. Katchen, *Christian Hebraists and Dutch Rabbis: Seventeenth Century Apologetics and the Study of Maimonides' "Mishneh Torah"* (Cambridge: Harvard University Press, 1984). On Spencer, see Guy G. Stroumsa, "John Spencer and the Roots of Idolatry," *History of Religions* 41 (2001): 14. On Selden, see Jason P. Rosenblatt, *Renaissance England's Chief Rabbi: John Selden* (Oxford: Oxford University Press, 2006). See also Amos Funkenstein, *Theology and the Scientific Imagination from the Middle Ages to the Seventeenth Century* (Princeton: Princeton University Press, 1986), 241; Richard H. Popkin, "Some Further Comments on Newton and Maimonides," in *Essays on the Context, Nature, and Influence of Isaac Newton's Theology*, ed. James E. Force and Richard H. Popkin (Dordrecht: Kluwer Academic Publishers, 1990), 2; Jonathan Sheehan, "Sacred and Profane: Idolatry, Antiquarianism and the Polemics of Distinction in the Seventeenth Century," *Past and Present* 192 (2006): 54; Martin Mulsow, "Idolatry and Science: Against Nature Worship from Boyle to Rüdiger, 1680–1720," *JHI* 67 (2006): 702.

Protestant readers of Maimonides, Modena felt enormous pride in having been quoted in one of Selden's works and had served as an adviser to the Jews of Amsterdam on a range of issues.[95]

In the postscript to *Ari Nohem*, Modena addressed Hamiz directly. In a similar fashion to the opening of the treatise, he invited Hamiz to respond should he disagree with him.[96]

> But if you would like to labor to deliver a response to my words, respond to those anxious of heart,[97] lovers of simplicity,[98] to strengthen them in it, lest they hear the justice of these words of mine and return from this folly; but in order to have me renounce my belief in this, at the end of my days, in order that they may say about me what they imagined and invented about Maimonides, of blessed memory, do not belabor yourself, have the sense to desist[99] because . . . you shall not move me from my opinion.[100]

Hamiz remained a committed kabbalist well after Modena's death.[101] Not only was *Ari Nohem* unsuccessful in its attempt to convince its primary addressee of the folly of Kabbalah, later readers, despite Modena's best intentions, made what they would of the text and its author. Readers of *Ari Nohem* at the turn of the nineteenth century offer an ironic postscript about Modena and Maimonides. One of the later manuscripts of *Ari Nohem* included an asterisk next to the passage where Modena informed Hamiz that he had written *Ari Nohem* in old age to ensure that no one would invent stories about him akin to those invented about Maimonides. A short note near the asterisk reads: "Examine what I have cited at the end of the treatise."[102] On the next page, the colophon reads:

> Solomon said: "Many designs are in a man's mind, but it is the Lord's plan that is accomplished."[103] That which happened to Maimonides happened to him [Modena]. For at the end of his life, in his book *The Life of Judah*, extant in manuscript, he wrote that he saw a six-month-old baby boy who was about to die open its eyes and utter "Hear O Israel etc." And from that day on he believed

---

[95] On Modena and Selden, see Cecil Roth, "Leone da Modena and his English Correspondents," *Transactions of the Jewish Historical Society of England* 17 (1951–1952); *Autobiography*, 170–73. On Amsterdam, see Sonne, "Leon Modena and the Da Costa Circle"; Fishman, *Shaking the Pillars of Exile*, 49.
[96] MS 8B, 8–10; ed. Libowitz, 6.
[97] Isa. 35:4.
[98] Prov. 1:22.
[99] Prov. 23:4.
[100] MS 48A, 3–8; ed. Libowitz, 98.
[101] See epilogue.
[102] MS K, 40A.
[103] Pr. 19:21.

in the transmigration of souls. Examine *Shem ha-Gedolim*, part II, section *Yod*, paragraph 79, page 43, column four.[104]

Which manuscript of *The Life of Judah* the copyist referred to in his colophon remains obscure. This much is clear: the manuscript was copied at some point in the late eighteenth or early nineteenth century, as established by the reference to the second volume of Hayim Joseph David Azulai's *Shem ha-Gedolim*, printed in Livorno in 1786. This story dates from at least eight years earlier. In his travel diaries, *Ma'agal Tov*, Azulai mentioned in an entry recorded in the winter of 1777 that Modena recanted his denial of the transmigration of souls when he saw a dying baby recite the *Shema*.[105] The story of the philosopher's deathbed repentance, so prevalent in the Middle Ages, resurfaced in northern Italy about a Venetian rabbi intent on defending the legacy of Maimonides.

---

[104] MS K, 40B.

[105] *Ma'agal Tov ha-shalem*, ed. Aron Freimann (Jerusalem: Mekize Nirdamim, 1934), 113. Azulai also mentioned *Ari Nohem* on an account of his journey in the 1750s. See ibid., 9. Neither Azulai nor the scribe of MS K mentioned Modena's *Ben David*, which circulated in manuscript until 1854. Isaac Reggio argued that even if Modena were to have recanted his denial of *gilgul*, this would not have necessitated a recantation of his other criticisms of Kabbalah. See *Ari Nohem* MS L 48B–50A. On Reggio and Modena, see Howard Adelman, "New Light on the Life and Writings of Leon Modena," in *Approaches to Judaism in Medieval Times II*, ed. David R. Blumenthal, 109–22 (Chico: Scholars Press, 1984), and chapter 7.

CHAPTER FOUR

Safed in Venice

> After nearly fifteen hundred years of living in exile and persecution, he (God) remembered unto his people his covenant with their fathers, and brought them back from their captivity, one of a city and two of a family, from the corners of the earth to the land of glory, and they settled in the city of Safed, the desire of all lands.
>
> —Joseph Karo

Figure 9 (previous page). Title page to Moses Cordovero *Pardes Rimonim*, Krakow, 1592. Courtesy of the Library of the Jewish Theological Seminary.
Pardes Rimonim was one of the most important works of mystical theology composed in sixteenth-century Safed. It was assiduously studied by members of Modena's circle in Venice and elsewhere in northern Italy.

THE EXPLOSION of cultural creativity in sixteenth-century Safed took many forms: law, liturgy, exegesis, and Kabbalah. Karo's *Shulhan Arukh* became the basic Jewish law code for Jewish communities throughout Europe and the Mediterranean. The poems and prayers composed by Solomon Alkabetz and Israel Najara, preachers who lived in Safed for extended periods, came to occupy an integral place in many Jewish prayer books.[1] The myths and doctrines developed by Moses Cordovero and Isaac Luria had a lasting impact on many Jewish thinkers. Scholars have long demonstrated the centrality of Italy in general and Venice in particular for the circulation and dissemination of Kabbalah and law from Safed to Jewish communities in Europe and beyond.[2] While they continue to debate the processes and extent to which Kabbalah from Safed affected various regions of the Jewish world over the course of the early modern period,[3] opposition to Kabbalah from Safed has received far less attention. *Ari Nohem* not only documented the spread of Kabbalah from Safed, it offered a stinging rebuke of its encroachment upon Venetian Jewish life. This chapter argues that the presence of Kabbalah from Safed in Venice formed a central target of Modena's polemical ire.[4] Although written in 1639, *Ari Nohem* constitutes an important source for the reception of Kabbalah from Safed in Venice at the turn of the seventeenth century.

---

[1] On Karo, see below. On Alkabetz's celebrated hymn *Lekhah dodi*, see Reuven Kimelman, *Lekhah dodi ve-kabalat Shabat: ha-mashma'ut ha-mistit* (Jerusalem: Magnes Press, 2003). On Najara, see Meir Benayahu, "Rabbi Israel Najara" (Hebrew), *Asufot* 4 (1990): 203–84; Israel Najara, *Mikveh Yisrael*, ed. Shaul Regev (Ramat-Gan: Bar-Ilan University Press, 2004).

[2] Tishby, "The Conflict between Lurianic Kabbalah and Cordoverian Kabbalah"; Avivi, "The Writings of the Ari in Italy Up to the Year 1620"; Avivi, "The Writings of R. Menahem Azariah da Fano on the Wisdom of Kabbalah"; Avivi, *Kabalat ha-Ari*, vol. 1, pt. 3; Moshe Idel, "On Mobility, Individuals and Groups: Prolegomenon for a Sociological Approach to Sixteenth-Century Kabbalah," *Kabbalah* 3 (1998): 145–73; Idel, "Italy in Safed, Safed in Italy"; Raz-Krakotzkin, "From Safed to Venice."

[3] For Safed Kabbalah elsewhere in Italy, see the studies cited above. For Salonika at the turn of the seventeenth century, see Hacker, "The History of the Study of Kabbalah." For Prague, see Elchanan Reiner, "A Biography of an Agent of Culture: Eleazar Altschul of Prague and His Literary Activity," in *Schöpferische Momente des europäischen Judentums in der frühen Neuzeit*, ed. Michael Graetz (Heidelberg: C. Winter, 2000), 232.

[4] Adelman, "Rabbi Leon Modena and the Christian Kabbalists," 274, n. 19.

The three sections of this chapter trace different components of Modena's response to Safed Kabbalah. The first part charts Modena's rejection of stories about the magical and theurgic powers of Isaac Luria and other kabbalists from Safed that circulated in Venice. Emissaries and preachers who had lived in Safed and traveled through Venice recounted these tales to Modena and to other Venetian Jews. Additionally a set of hagiographic narratives about Luria and Karo were printed in the early seventeenth century. These stories, in print and as spoken word, constituted a crucial dimension of a growing myth about Safed in general and Luria in particular. The second section concentrates on Modena's attempt to dissociate Kabbalah from philosophy, a response to and rejection of the thought of Israel Saruq. While the relationship between Kabbalah and philosophy had a long prehistory, Modena's polemic against the identification of Kabbalah with philosophy focused largely on Saruq, one of the most important kabbalists to travel from Safed to Venice in the late sixteenth century.[5] The third section traces Modena's response to Cordovero's *Pardes Rimonim*, a work that systematically examined a central doctrine of theosophical Kabbalah, the sefirot or the ten hypostases of the divine being. The chapter concludes with an attempt to explain Modena's focus on *Pardes Rimonim* as the primary target for his criticism of the sefirot.

STORIES ABOUT SAFED

In the last decade of the sixteenth century, famine, economic depression, and excessive taxation had combined to precipitate a steep decline in the fortunes of Safed and its Jewish residents.[6] In the decades after the central figures of the Safed renaissance had died, stories began to circulate about the extraordinary powers of numerous kabbalists and rabbis who had lived in Safed in the third quarter of the sixteenth century. These stories formed the beginnings of a myth about Safed as a town teeming with kabbalists of great piety and wondrous abilities.[7] Solomon Shlomel Dresnitz, a Jew from Moravia who had left his family to emigrate to Safed in the early seventeenth century, emerged as one of the most important propagators of this myth. At the moment when the economic and cultural fortunes of the town and its Jewish community had reached their lowest point in over half a cen-

---

[5] See below. On the spelling of his name as Saruq rather than Sarug, see Ronit Meroz, "Contrasting Opinions among the Founders of R. Israel Saruq's School," in Fenton and Goetschel, *Expérience et écriture Mystiques dans les Religions du Livre*, 191.

[6] Mordechai Pachter, "*Hazut Kasha* of Rabbi Moses Alsheikh" (Hebrew), *Shalem* 1 (1974): 166.

[7] Eli Yassif, "The Conflict over the Myth of Safed: Then and Now" (Hebrew), *Mikan* 4 (2005): 42–79.

tury, he wrote a series of open letters that described the extraordinary powers of figures who had once lived in Safed, such as Karo and Luria. Given that Dresnitz arrived in Safed in the early seventeenth century and that Luria had died in 1572 and Karo in 1575, he had never met either figure.

Dresnitz's letters might have remained entirely unknown to Modena had they not appeared in print. Less than a decade before Modena wrote *Ari Nohem*, they were included as part of *Ta'alumot Hokhmah*.[8] Modena devoted most of the third chapter of *Ari Nohem* to the stories about Karo in Dresnitz's letters. He quoted an extended passage about Karo while attempting to explain to Hamiz why he had never been drawn to the study of Kabbalah. Dresnitz described Karo's strategy for inducing the presence of his *maggid*, a celestial mentor whom he identified as the hypostasis of the Mishnah.[9]

> Every time he [Karo] recited the Mishnah by heart, the *maggid* appeared to him and people would hear his voice through the door or at the back of the house saying: "Peace be upon thee, Rabbi Joseph Karo. I am the Mishnah which thou has studied. I came to teach thee understanding. . . . I the Mishnah have seen the place that is prepared for thee in Paradise. . . . And now I have come to reveal the following kabbalistic mystery. . . . And all the revelations of the *maggid* he collected in a book entitled *The Book of the Maggid*—and yet they are like unto nothing when compared with the wisdom of the *Ari*. He [Karo] wanted to study with him the mysteries of the Torah, but the *Ari* refused to teach him, saying that his [Karo's] soul was unfit to receive higher wisdom than that of Cordovero.[10]

Modena proceeded to address Dresnitz's claim that Karo was not deemed worthy to grasp Luria's teachings and had to suffice with those of Cordovero.[11] Focusing on the hierarchy of kabbalistic scholars in Dresnitz's account, Modena found it absurd that a legal scholar with a reputation for piety such as Karo would not have been fit to study with Luria.

To the extent that it appears at all, Modena's criticism of Karo's *maggid* surfaced in a parenthetical remark in the midst of a rhetorical question: "Who would be worthy and who would be fitting [to study Luria's

---

[8] Delmedigo, *Sefer Ta'alumot Hokhmah*, 37A–50B.

[9] For editions of *Maggid Mesharim*, Karo's diary of his relationship with his *Maggid*, see Werblowsky, *Joseph Karo*, 308. It was first printed in Lublin 1646. See also Rachel Elior, "Joseph Karo and Israel Ba'al Shem Tov" (Hebrew), *Tarbiz* 65 (1996): 671–709.

[10] MS A 11A, 1–12; ed. Libowitz, 10; Delmedigo, *Sefer Ta'alumot Hokhmah*, 47A. Translation by Werblowsky, *Joseph Karo*, 17. See also Desplanches, "Le monde de la Kabbale," 175–76.

[11] Karo (1488–1575) was eighty-two when the thirty-six-year-old Luria (1534–1572) arrived in Safed in 1570. Elsewhere in *Ari Nohem*, Modena quoted a passage from *Pardes Rimonim* that indicated that Cordovero (1522–1570) was Karo's disciple, not vice versa. See MS A 28B, 6; ed. Libowitz, 47; Moses Cordovero, *Pardes Rimonim* (Krakow, 1592), 31B. On Cordovero and Karo, see Bracha Sack, *Be-Sha'are ha-Kabalah shel Rabi Moshe Cordovero* (Beer Sheva: Ben-Gurion University of the Negev Press, 1995), 11.

teachings], if not a great man, who (they say) received the revelations of a *maggid* . . . but if a man like this was unworthy, will anyone born of woman be worthy, even someone lofty and elevated, all the more so a miserable wretch like me today."[12] By including the phrase "they say" in parenthesis, Modena inserted a hint of skepticism about the existence of Karo's celestial mentor. While this passage constitutes one of the first critical reactions to the accounts of Karo's *maggid*, Modena's primary target was Luria rather than Karo and his celestial mentor. Modena's criticism of Karo focused on the printed *Shulhan Arukh* as obviating the need for rabbinic authority, not on Karo's *maggid*.[13] The remainder of *Ari Nohem* corroborates the importance of Luria rather than Karo as the subject of a growing number of hagiographic accounts.

Modena devoted a later chapter to the stories about Luria in Dresnitz's letters. These stories formed the basis of *Shivhei ha-Ari* (Heb. "In Praise of Isaac Luria"), a collection of hagiographic narratives that helped establish Luria's reputation and enjoyed enormous popularity in the early modern period.[14] Modena began with an attenuated summary of the opening pages of Dresnitz's letters and offered a sketch of several stories about Luria. He recounted a story about presence of the biblical prophet Elijah at Luria's circumcision. With cutting sarcasm, Modena remarked that apart from Luria's father no one had noticed the biblical prophet.[15] He then turned to Luria's study in the heavenly academies as a young man:

> Every night legions of angels would come to him [Luria] and bring him into the heavenly academies. And sometimes he would choose the academy of Rabbi Simeon bar Yohai and others times the academy of Rabbi Akiva. . . . On the Sabbath [whose weekly reading was] the pericope of Balak, Rabbi Eliezer[16] ha-Levi appeared to him while he was sleeping, and he [Luria] woke up. And Luria said to him that he had been brought by the angels before Metatron . . . and that he had studied the Secrets of the Torah. And Rabbi Eliezer told him to reveal what he had studied that time. He responded: Heaven and earth can testify before me, "Were I to explicate for eighty years, without exaggeration, I would not be able

---

[12] MS A 11B, 4–9; ed. Libowitz, 11.

[13] See chapter 1.

[14] See Meir Benayahu, *Sefer Toldot ha-Ari* (Jerusalem: Ben-Zvi Institute, 1967); David Tamar, *Mehkarim be-Toldot ha-Yehudim be-Erets Yisrael uve-Italyah* (Jerusalem: Rubin Mass, 1970), 166–93; Tishby, "The Conflict between Lurianic Kabbalah and Cordoverian Kabbalah," 180–82; Fine, *Physician of the Soul, Healer of the Cosmos*, 84–87; Eli Yassif, "In the Fields and in the Open Spaces: On Space and Its Meaning in Stories about Safed" (Hebrew), *Katedra* 116 (2005): 67–102.

[15] Delmedigo, *Sefer Ta'alumot Hokhmah*, 37A; *Ari Nohem*, MS 40A, 4–6; ed. Libowitz, 78.

[16] The text of *Ari Nohem* reads "Eliezer." However, in Dresnitz's letter the name appears as Abraham. See Delmedigo, *Sefer Ta'alumot Hokhmah*, 37B. Libowitz's edition gives Abraham.

to recount what I had learned about Balaam and the Ass."[17] He further said to the sages of France: if all the seas were ink, all the skies parchment, and all the reeds quills, it would not be sufficient to write all of my wisdom.[18]

Dresnitz boasted of Luria's prowess and his knowledge of the Secrets of the Torah, and Modena vigorously contested the claim of kabbalists who identified contemporary Kabbalah with ancient esoteric secrets.

After summarizing Luria's heavenly journey and his acquisition of esoteric wisdom, Modena turned to Dresnitz's account of Luria's magical and theurgic powers.

> For he [Luria] used to go to the graves of sages and prophets and prostrate himself upon them by spreading his hands and feet and placing mouth upon mouth like Elisha and Habakuk[19] and direct his mind. . . . In this way the dry bones lying in the grave were revived and the soul of that righteous person would descend into the bones and he would actually come alive, just as a man speaks to his neighbor. And he [the deceased righteous man] would reveal to him [Luria] all the Secrets of the Torah.[20]

In addition to his ability to revive the dead, Luria's extraordinary powers among the living were conveyed by one of his most important disciples, Hayim Vital (ca. 1542–1620), referred to here as Hayim Calabrese: "For the sage, [Hayim] Calabrese, of blessed memory, wrote that his teacher [Luria] hinted to him several times that he was Messiah son of Joseph . . . that through metoposcopy he used to tell a person every sin he had committed since childhood, and whose soul had been transmigrated into him. He knew the wicked ones who had transmigrated into animals, birds, trees, and stones; he heard and understood the chirping of the birds."[21] According to Vital, Luria was deeply knowledgeable about esoteric secrets and capable of performing extraordinary marvels.

---

[17] Balaam and the Ass (Numbers 22) appears in the pericope Balak referred to earlier in the story.

[18] MS A 40A, 7–13; ed. Libowitz, 78. Modena abridged the story as it appears in Delmedigo, *Sefer Ta'alumot Hokhmah*, 37B.

[19] See 2 Kings 4:34. For the identification of the son of the Shunammite, who Elisha restored to life, with the prophet Habakuk, see *Zohar* 1:7B; as cited in *The Zohar*, trans. Daniel C. Matt (Stanford: Stanford University Press, 2004), 1:47.

[20] MS A 40A, 13–17; ed. Libowitz, 78. Delmedigo, *Sefer Ta'alumot Hokhmah*, 38A. See Lawrence Fine, "Benevolent Spirit Possession in Sixteenth-Century Safed," in *Spirit Possession in Judaism: Cases and Context from the Middle Ages to the Present*, ed. Matt Goldish, 113 (Detroit: Wayne State University Press, 2003).

[21] MS A 40A, 17–20; ed. Libowitz, 78–79; Delmedigo, *Sefer Ta'alumot Hokhmah*, 38A–38B. See also Lawrence Fine, "The Art of Metoposcopy: A Study in Isaac Luria's Charismatic Knowledge," *AJS Review* 11 (1986): 79–101.

Though Modena rejected these claims, he did not subject each story to a point-by-point criticism. Instead, he recounted a range of stories culled from the first several pages of Dresnitz's letters and included deeply skeptical comments at the beginning and end of his account. Modena's skepticism was bound up with his discussion of Joseph Solomon Delmedigo's stance toward Kabbalah. After citing these stories about Luria embedded within *Ta'alumot Hokhmah*, Modena suggested that Delmedigo himself was dissimulating: "He [Delmedigo] fashions himself as defending the wisdom of Kabbalah and praises it, but his intention is to degrade it and denigrate it with all his might ... his intention was that any intellectual person who would read their exaggerations would judge that they do not contain any truth."[22] Modena expressed his disbelief concerning the stories recounted about Luria with a reference to "their exaggerations."

Modena also responded to legends about Luria that circulated in Venice in the form of kabbalistic raconteurs. He described several incidents when kabbalists from Safed traveling through Venice recounted stories about Luria's wondrous abilities. Several decades before writing *Ari Nohem*, Modena witnessed an exchange between Yedidiah Galante and Elijah Montalto that appears to have taken place around 1612.[23] Galante, a kabbalist who had lived in Palestine, had traveled to Venice to raise funds for the Jewish communities of Palestine. While in Venice, he encountered Elijah Montalto, a Converso physician who had taken refuge there. With palpable glee Modena recounted an exchange between an ailing Montalto on his sickbed and a well-meaning Galante who had come to visit him:

> While we were there, Galante began to recount the miraculous and wondrous deeds of the *Ari*, of blessed memory.... After most of his words, the doctor [Montalto], of blessed memory, became stronger and sat up in his bed. And he began to scream in a very loud voice. We had no idea what happened to him and we thought that perhaps he had been gripped by some pain from his sickness. While screaming he said in Spanish, "I can no longer keep silent and suffer this: may the truth live! This is all lies and falsehood! I have not seen proofs, for there is no longer any prophet or anyone among us who knows for how long.[24]

---

[22] MS A 39B, 25—40A, 4; ed. Libowitz, 78.

[23] Modena dated the exchange to "over twenty-five years ago," thus before 1614. For evidence that Galante was an emissary in northern Italy between 1607 and 1614, see Abraham Yaari, *Sheluhe Erets Yisrael* (Jerusalem: Mossad ha-Rav Kook, 1997), 1:247. For evidence that Montalto was in Venice in the spring of 1612, see Cecil Roth, "Quatre lettres d'Elie de Montalte: contribution à l'histoire des Marranes," *REJ* 87 (1929): 137–65. On this encounter, see Bernard Cooperman, "Eliahu Montalto's 'Suitable and Incontrovertible Propositions,' a Seventeenth-Century Anti-Christian Polemic," in Twersky and Septimus, *Jewish Thought in the Seventeenth Century*, 490; Ruderman, *Jewish Thought and Scientific Discovery*, 122–23.

[24] Cf. Ps. 74:9.

Either he [Luria] was a sorcerer or this is all lies. Do not continue speaking to me about this."[25]

Modena did not mention the specific stories about Luria that Galante told Montalto but indicated that they were similar to those recounted in Dresnitz's letters. He clearly identified with Montalto's skepticism, and his narration of the story was designed to convince his reader that he was not alone in his doubts about Luria's supernatural abilities.

Modena turned directly to Hamiz and attempted to marshal skepticism about these stories from the ranks of the kabbalists themselves.

> [Concerning] a great and pious sage from our academy, whose name I shall not write but I shall tell you face to face, for he is well known and important to you. On the night of the fourth of Kislev in the year 5397 [1 December 1636] he was in the midst of recounting the wonders of the *Ari*, of blessed memory, before we had begun studying. He said that several times, the rabbi and sage Jacob Abulafia,[26] of blessed memory, who was like a friend and brother to the *Ari*, of blessed memory, said to him that these things, these wonders of his [Luria's] that had been recounted, had never occurred. That even the *Ari* used to say that the things they said about him were not true. Lest you say that he said this out of modesty, [this] is impossible; if he [Jacob Abulafia] were so close with him [Isaac Luria], he would have at least conceded partially.[27]

Throughout *Ari Nohem* Modena framed his discussion of Luria's abilities with skepticism. He cited doubts about Luria's magical and theurgic powers allegedly expressed by a kabbalist, even if only hearsay in the name of Jacob Abulafia, in order to convince his student Hamiz to abandon Kabbalah. Modena's refusal to identify the sage who expressed skepticism about Luria's miraculous abilities is revealing on several accounts. In a passage explicitly addressed to Hamiz in the second person, Modena called attention to his own reticence to express in writing what he would reveal in conversation. This discretion offers further evidence that he envisioned readers of *Ari Nohem* beyond Hamiz. Modena's tact may have stemmed from his own recognition of the unpopularity of his views about Luria. Not wishing to jeopardize the reputation of a colleague by imputing a similar skepticism about Luria, he remained silent. Furthermore, the date of the exchange indicates that Venetian Jews continued to talk about Luria over half a century after his death and decades after the collapse of Safed as a cultural center. Luria was a recurring presence in Venetian Jewish culture. Modena recounted discussions about Luria in three different

---

[25] MS A 40B, 20–25; ed. Libowitz, 80.
[26] On Jacob Abulafia, see Tishby, "The Conflict between Lurianic Kabbalah and Cordoverian Kabbalah," 202, n. 84; Yassif, "The Conflict over the Myth of Safed," 54–59.
[27] MS A 41A, 1–6; ed. Libowitz, 80.

decades—the 1590s, 1610s, and 1630s—over and above the references in printed texts.

At the very conclusion of his criticism of the stories about Luria, Modena tied his skepticism about these miracles to his larger criticism of Kabbalah. He refused to believe that "this Kabbalah," an epithet that betrayed his contempt here and elsewhere in *Ari Nohem*, could enable a sage, no matter how holy and learned, to perform miracles: "Nevertheless, do not let my words, heaven forbid, defame the sage, the *Ari*, of blessed memory, because I believe that he was wise and pious. But the signs and miracles, the prophecy and the resurrection of the dead, and the like—with due pardon to his pure bones—this I cannot believe. For it cannot enter my understanding that one could be able to do this with this Kabbalah."[28] Modena extended his skepticism to the wondrous tales told of Hayim Vital and reminded Hamiz of another conversation held with an unnamed kabbalist:

> So they say about his most celebrated student, Rabbi Hayim Calabrese, may he rest in Eden and may his honor rest in place. I might think that he was wise and pious, but I do not believe the miraculous stories and divine inspiration attributed to him. Certainly you have not forgotten, before the year had ended a sage had arrived here, one of his students, humble and modest. You and I spoke to him about this, but he did not expound about these wonders. Specifically, in your presence, I asked him if what Joseph Solomon Delmedigo had adduced in his book were true. For they said that he [Vital] did not see light for three hours a day. And he [the anonymous student] said that it was not true, that the light of his [Vital's] eyes was with him the entire day and the entire night.[29]

If Modena's own skepticism about the stories in Delmedigo's anthology was insufficient, Hamiz should have at least trusted the unnamed kabbalist who had been Vital's student and had conceded the implausibility of the stories in Dresnitz's letters.

The most prominent kabbalist from Safed with whom Modena had prolonged personal contact was Israel Saruq, a figure who traveled from Palestine to Italy in the late sixteenth century and claimed to have been a student of Luria's in Safed.[30] While doubts have been raised about his discipleship given the absence of any mention of Saruq in Vital's writings, more recent scholarship suggests that Saruq numbered among Luria's first students after his arrival in Safed in 1570.[31] Modena himself undoubtedly

---

[28] MS A 41A, 9–12; ed. Libowitz, 80.

[29] MS A 41A, 12–18; ed. Libowitz, 80–81.

[30] For Saruq in *Ari Nohem*, see Scholem, "Israel Sarug, a Student of the *Ari*?," 220–21; MS A 11B, 1–3; 26A, 22–26B, 1; 30B, 6–8; 41A, 17–20; 42B, 21–24; ed. Libowitz, 11, 42, 53, 81, 85. A sixth passage occurs at MS A 29A, 19; ed. Libowitz, 49.

[31] For skepticism, see Scholem. For arguments in favor, see Ronit Meroz, "R. Israel Saruq, Student of the *Ari*, a Renewed Inquiry into the Issue" (Hebrew), *Daat* 28 (1992): 41–51;

believed Saruq's claim and even referred to him at one point as Luria's "most eminent student."[32] Saruq visited Venice several times over a six-year period between 1592 and 1598.[33] Modena reported to Hamiz with apparent envy that forty years earlier Saruq had succeeded in ingratiating himself with the wealthy and learned Jews of northern Italy.[34]

> And the sage, Rabbi Israel Saruq, of blessed memory, who was one of his [Luria's] greatest students, was with us here, standing, coming and going for more than six years. They used to say about him that he performed frightening things with the Names [of God]. How can I describe to you how I attempted to verify this with numerous people,[35] people whom he owed because of favors they did for him, but they could not find [proof for] even the slightest of his actions that he had been speaking about.[36]

Modena implied that Saruq used magical or theurgic techniques to procure some type of advancement with members of the Venetian Jewish community.

In another instance, Modena accused Saruq of pandering to wealthy Venetian Jews and of customizing his kabbalistic teachings for the individual benefit of a given member of the community: "I was with him [Saruq] and spoke with him countless times when he was here in Venice. And his entire glory consisted in recognizing the soul of such-and-such a person and who it had once been. I shall not let my lips utter the names that I heard from him, especially since he used to assign the names according to the wealth or importance of a given person."[37] Saruq's activities appear to have infuriated Modena even more than the stories recounted about Luria. Luria and his disciples had performed their magical feats half a world away in Safed. Saruq had encroached upon Modena's home territory at a period in his life when he was struggling to establish himself among the rabbinic elders of Venice.

Another cryptic story about Saruq indicates that Modena's antipathy toward him was deeply personal. After a long discourse about the importance of humility, Modena expounded:

> And what happened to me with him [Saruq] at the feast of circumcision, as a result of his arrogance that reached the heavens.... He almost threw an entire

---

Meroz, "Faithful Transmission versus Innovation: Luria and His Disciples," in *Gershom Scholem's Major Trends in Jewish Mysticism 50 Years After*, ed. Peter Schäfer and Joseph Dan, 257–74 (Tübingen: Mohr Siebeck, 1993).

[32] MS A 30B, 7; ed. Libowitz, 53.
[33] Scholem, "Israel Sarug, a Student of the *Ari*?", 222.
[34] Adelman, "Rabbi Leon Modena and the Christian Kabbalists," 274.
[35] Ex. 20:5.
[36] MS A 41A, 17–21; ed. Libowitz, 81.
[37] MS A 26A, 22–26B, 2; ed. Libowitz, 42.

loaf of bread from the table, for no reason or cause.... Finally, he asked for my forgiveness. But I shall put an end to this matter. Because I know that it is not appropriate to chastise someone about a dispute for the sake of heaven, especially for someone like me, who has accustomed his tongue only to speak about the honor of the sages, even those from the nations of the world, and all the more so, the sages of Israel, whoever it may be.[38]

The nature of this confrontation between Modena and Saruq remains obscure. In any case, Modena emphasized that Saruq had apologized to him and pointedly informed his reader that he would remain silent about Saruq.

Saruq not only performed kabbalistic techniques for members of the Jewish community in Venice, he also instructed one of the leading rabbinic authorities in northern Italy, Menahem Azariah da Fano, in Lurianic Kabbalah.[39] Modena repeatedly emphasized Saruq's hold over Menahem Azariah da Fano. At one point he wrote that Saruq "was thought to be a second Rabbi Simeon bar Yohai by Rabbi Menahem Azariah da Fano, of blessed memory, and [by] all of Italy."[40] Expanding upon this comment, he noted:

And the Rabbi, Rabbi Menahem Azariah da Fano, wrote in the introduction to his *Pelah ha-Rimon*,[41] these are his words: Just as the pathways of the *Pardes* [*Rimonim* by Moses Cordovero] are higher than Kimhi,[42] so too the pathways of the *Ari*, of blessed memory, ascended higher than the pathways of this book [*Pardes Rimonim*]. And exactly these words were said to me in person by the aforementioned Rabbi Menahem Azariah da Fano, when I was in Reggio thirty-two years ago. He continued to say ... "When the sage, Rabbi Israel Saruq, came to me and taught me the Kabbalah of the *Ari*, of blessed memory, I realized that up until that point I had been like an unknowing dolt[43] in that wisdom."[44]

Modena cited both written and oral testimony to highlight the priority of Lurianic Kabbalah over Cordoverian Kabbalah in Saruq's teaching and

---

[38] MS A 42B, 23–43A, 2; ed. Libowitz, 85.

[39] See Robert Bonfil, "New Information on the Life of Menahem Azariah da Fano and His Time Period" (Hebrew), in *Perakim Be-Toledot ha-Hevrah ha-Yehudit be-Yeme ha-Benayim u-ba'et ha-Hadasha: mukdashim li-Profesor Yakov Katz*, ed. Yosef Salmon and Immanuel Etkes, 98–135 (Jerusalem: Magnes Press, 1980); Bonfil, "Halakhah, Kabbalah, and Society: Some Insights into Rabbi Menahem Azariah da Fano's Inner World," in Twersky and Septimus, *Jewish Thought in the Seventeenth Century*, 39–61; Bonfil, "Cultura e mistica a Venezia nel Cinquecento," in *Gli Ebrei e Venezia: secoli XIV–XVIII*, ed. Gaetano Cozzi, 487–92 (Milan: Edizioni Communità, 1987); Avivi, "The Writings of the Ari in Italy Up to the Year 1620"; Avivi, "The Writings of R. Menahem Azariah da Fano on the Wisdom of Kabbalah"; Avivi, *Kabalat ha-Ari*, vol. 1, pt. 3.

[40] MS A 42B, 22–23; ed. Libowitz, 85.

[41] *Pelah ha-Rimon* (Venice, 1600), 4A.

[42] David Kimhi (1160–1235), a biblical exegete. See Frank Talmage, *David Kimhi: The Man and the Commentaries* (Cambridge: Harvard University Press, 1975).

[43] Cf. Ps. 73:22.

[44] MS A 29A, 16–19; ed. Libowitz, 48–49.

relayed Menahem Azariah da Fano's own account of his abandonment of Cordoverian Kabbalah and conversion to Lurianic Kabbalah. Menahem Azariah da Fano had performed Modena's circumcision, a fact Modena mentioned both in his autobiography and in *Ari Nohem*.[45] Like Modena, Menahem Azariah da Fano clearly believed that Saruq had been a student of Luria's and was instructing him in Lurianic Kabbalah.

KABBALAH AND PHILOSOPHY

Saruq was not only a propagandist for Lurianic Kabbalah and a foreigner who pandered to the Venetian Jewish establishment, he was also one of the principal figures who identified Kabbalah with philosophy. Modena recounted: "I too heard from the mouth of the sage, Israel Saruq, the most eminent student of the *Ari*, of blessed memory, who used to say that there was no difference between philosophy and Kabbalah. Everything he learned from Kabbalah, he would explain in a philosophical manner."[46] A long line of thinkers from the Middle Ages through the early modern period attempted to clarify the relationship between Kabbalah and philosophy. Positions on this subject, which often depended on the definitions of the terms themselves, varied from a total identification of Kabbalah with philosophy to an insistence on an absolute distinction between the two modes of thought.[47]

In *Ari Nohem* Modena presented both positions before offering his own opinion. Some kabbalists sought to differentiate between Kabbalah and philosophy. In this group, he included his son-in-law Jacob Levi as well as Ibn Gabbai and Shem Tov. Others, like Joseph Solomon Delmedigo, Jacob Nahmias, and Hamiz, posited that Kabbalah and philosophy were identical.[48] Modena argued that these thinkers understood philosophy as a form of Platonism or Neoplatonism.[49] Whether Saruq himself identified philosophy with Platonism,[50] Modena understood this to be his position.

---

[45] *Autobiography*, 82; MSA A, 10B, 10; ed. Libowitz, 9.

[46] MS A 30B, 6–8; ed. Libowitz, 53.

[47] Georges Vajda, *Recherches sur la philosophie et la kabbale dans la pensée juive du Moyen Age* (Paris: Mouton, 1962); Sara O. Heller Wilensky, "Isaac Ibn Latif—Philosopher or Kabbalist?," in Altmann, *Jewish Medieval and Renaissance Studies*, 185–223; Scholem, *Avraham Kohen Herera, Ba'al "Sha'ar Ha-Shamayim"*; Moshe Idel, "Kabbalah and Ancient Philosophy According to R. Isaac and R. Judah Abravanel" (Hebrew), in *Filosofiyat ha-Ahavah shel Yehudah Abravanel*, ed. Menahem Dorman and Zeev Levy, 73–112 (Tel Aviv: Ha-Kibutz ha-Meuhad, 1985); Altmann, "Lurianic Kabbalah in a Platonic Key"; Aviezer Ravitzky, *History and Faith: Studies in Jewish Philosophy* (Amsterdam: J. C. Gieben, 1996); Halbertal, *Concealment and Revelation*.

[48] Idel, "Differing Conceptions of Kabbalah in the Early 17th Century," 155–57.

[49] See also Luzzatto, *Ma'amar al Yehude Venetsyah*, 144–46.

[50] For arguments in favor, see Scholem, "Israel Sarug, a Student of the *Ari*?," 228–32; Scholem, *Avraham Kohen Herera, Ba'al "Sha'ar Ha-Shamayim*," 17. For arguments against, see Idel, "Differing Conceptions of Kabbalah in the Early 17th Century," 178–90.

One of the instances where Modena pointed to Saruq's identification of Kabbalah with philosophy appeared after his discussion of Jacob Nahmias's ideas about Kabbalah and Platonism and before his indication that Hamiz identified Kabbalah with Platonic philosophy.[51]

> The editor's introduction to *Mazref le-Hokhmah* recounts that while Rabbi Joseph Solomon Delmedigo was in Constantinople, the esteemed Rabbi Jacob ibn Nahmias showed him notebooks written by the *Ari*.[52] And he [Nahmias] was proud to demonstrate the wisdom of Kabbalah was close to the philosophy of Plato, whose beliefs are just. And he [Nahmias] wanted him [Delmedigo] to translate Greek commentaries on Plato, because he was composing a book that reconciled the two systems of thought.[53]

Modena specifically identified the author of the notebooks seen by Delmedigo in Constantinople as Luria. In his attempt to reconcile Platonic philosophy with Lurianic Kabbalah, Nahmias had sought the help of Joseph Solomon Delmedigo. In addition to Saruq, Modena understood Delmedigo and Nahmias as arguing for the identification of Kabbalah with philosophy.

Immediately following this passage, Modena mentioned Saruq's identification of Kabbalah with philosophy and turned to Hamiz: "And you too, just like one of them, gloated before me several times in demonstrating to me that Kabbalah contains only that which is present in philosophy. The parallel to the *idea* described by Plato is clear. And the transmigration of souls, which they support by claiming as the opinion of Pythagoras."[54] In his description of his conversations with Hamiz, Modena offered even greater detail about the relationship between Kabbalah and philosophy. The statement about the Platonic *idea* as parallel to a concept in Kabbalah may refer to the similarities between the emanations in Neoplatonic thought and the sefirot in theosophic Kabbalah. Kabbalists themselves pointed to the parallels between specific concepts, such as the belief in the transmigration of souls, and the thought of Pythagoras, a pre-Socratic philosopher who was known for his beliefs on metempsychosis. Elsewhere in *Ari Nohem*, Modena rejected the belief in the transmigration of souls as a recent development in Jewish thought.[55]

Modena argued that the parallels between Kabbalah and philosophy, in particular Platonic philosophy, were of relatively recent origin. Kabbalists in the late Middle Ages had searched for parallels to their ideas among the

[51] See MS A 30B, 1–10; ed. Libowitz, 53.
[52] Delmedigo, *Sefer Mazref le-Hokhmah* in *Sefer Ta'alumot Hokhmah*, 2A.
[53] MS A 30B, 3–6; ed. Libowitz, 53.
[54] Ibid., 8–10.
[55] See MS A 24A, 18–24B, 2; ed. Libowitz, 38–39. See also his *Ben David*.

writings of Platonic philosophers. Modena located the origin of this type of reasoning in late medieval Iberia and suggested that it occurred as a partial reaction to the emergence of Maimonides' thought. Saruq, Nahmias, and other kabbalists who argued for the identification of Kabbalah with philosophy had numerous predecessors. While Modena did not mention specific people, modern scholars have identified Isaac ibn Latif, Joseph ibn Wakar, Samuel ibn Motot, Hasdai Crescas, and Isaac Arama as late medieval Iberian thinkers who sought to combine Kabbalah and philosophy in some form.[56]

> It certainly appears that in recent times (and in my opinion, in Spain) several of the sages who flourished shortly after the great rabbi Maimonides, of blessed memory, focused on studying philosophy ... especially the wisdom of Plato, which of all his colleagues, is truly the closest in its principles to the principles of the sages, of blessed memory. His riddles are like their homilies. From these distinctions and discoveries, they arranged them according to the method of the *Sefer Yetzirah*, which was not written for such a purpose as I mentioned earlier. They spun, wove and stretched the fine cloth of this teaching and called it the knowledge of Kabbalah hanging their words on the great authority of Rabbi Simeon bar Yohai, peace be upon him, in such a manner that they came to teach that this was a prophetic tradition.[57]

Modena's identification of Maimonides as a stimulus to attempts to identify Kabbalah with philosophy has found an echo in modern scholarship that has described the publication of the *Guide of the Perplexed* as a principal cause of the emergence of Kabbalah.[58] When kabbalists learned about the esoteric secrets in the *Guide*, they decided to commit a body of knowledge to writing that had hitherto been transmitted orally.

---

[56] See the literature cited in note 47 above. In spite of a mutual acquaintance with Saruq, Modena does not appear to have been aware of Abraham Cohen de Herrera (d. 1635). For the intersection of Kabbalah and philosophy in Herrera, Saruq's student who eventually settled in Amsterdam, see Scholem and Altmann, cited in note 47, as well as Nissim Yosha, *Mitos u-Metaforah: Ha-Parshanut ha-Filosofit shel R. Avraham Kohen Hererah le-Kabalat ha-Ari* (Jerusalem: Magnes Press and Ben-Zvi Institute, 1994); Gerold Necker, "Circle, Point and Line: A Lurianic Myth in the *Puerta del Cielo*," in Elior and Schäfer, *Creation and Re-Creation in Jewish Thought*, 193–207. Written in Spanish, Herrera's *Puerta del Cielo* appeared in print in a Hebrew translation by Isaac Aboab de Fonseca. See Abraham Cohen de Herrera, *Sefer Bet Elohim*, trans. Isaac Aboab (Amsterdam: Benvenisti, 1655). For recent editions, see *Puerta del Cielo*, ed. Kenneth Krabbenhoft (Madrid: Fundación Universitaria Española, 1987); *Gate of Heaven*, trans. Kenneth Krabbenhoft (Leiden: Brill, 2002); *Bet Elohim Sha'ar ha-Shamayim*, trans. Nissim Yosha (Jerusalem: Ben-Zvi Institute, 2002).

[57] MS A 30B, 23–31A, 4; ed. Libowitz, 53–54.

[58] Idel, "Maimonides and Kabbalah," 31–54.

Modena's passing comment about *Sefer Yetzirah*, an early esoteric work attributed to Abraham, implicitly attacked kabbalists for interpreting ancient texts in a kabbalistic manner. Modena contested the necessity of reading *Sefer Yetzirah* as a kabbalistic book and drew upon earlier Jewish thinkers to bolster his position. By the seventeenth century, a long line of commentators had argued for a philosophical rather than kabbalistic approach to *Sefer Yetzirah*.[59] Though Modena was apparently unaware of the medieval philosophical commentaries by Saadya Gaon, Dunash ibn Tamim, Shabbetai Donnolo, and others,[60] he drew upon Judah ha-Levi's *Kuzari*, which mentioned *Sefer Yetzirah* in the context of a dialogue between the king of the Khazars and the *Haver*, a representative of Judaism.

> He [Judah Halevi] stated in the name of the Khazar: "Now I want you to show me some of the remains of the natural sciences that you said had once been found among your people." And the *Haver* responded to him: "Among them is *Sefer Yetzirah* and it is [attributed] to our father Abraham, peace be upon him. It is deep and its explanation lengthy. It teaches about His [God's] divinity and His [God's] unity etc." And he continued to explain to him several things contained in that book in a manner that coincided with reason and upright Torah-like philosophy.[61]

For Modena the interpretive crux of this passage hinged on whether or not Halevi interpreted *Sefer Yetzirah* in a philosophical fashion.[62]

Modena invoked a passage from *Kol Yehudah*, a commentary to the Kuzari by Judah Moscato (1530–1593) printed in the 1594 edition of the work, a volume that Modena appears to have owned:[63] "And thus wrote the commentator, the erudite scholar Rabbi Judah Moscato, of blessed memory, on that passage. These are his words: Specifically, may the explanation of the

---

[59] The *Sefer Yetzirah* printed in Mantua in 1562 included only kabbalistic commentaries. On Moses Botarel's commentary, see chapter 2. On those attributed to Abraham ben David and Nahmanides, see Gershom Scholem, "The Actual Author of the Commentary to *Sefer Yetzirah* Attributed to Rabad and His Books," in Ben-Shlomo, *Mehkere Kabalah*, 112–36; Scholem, "The Actual Commentary of Nahmanides to *Sefer Yetzirah* and Other Kabbalah Attributed to Him," in ibid., 67–111. Although Modena argued for a philosophical approach to *Sefer Yetzirah* in *Ari Nohem*, he categorized it as a "kabbalistic book" in his notebook from the 1630s. See Ancona, Communità Israelitica, MS 7, 4B.

[60] By and large they had not appeared in print by the middle of the seventeenth century. Raphael Jospe, "Early Philosophical Commentaries on the *Sefer Yezirah*: Some Comments," *REJ* 149 (1990): 369–415.

[61] MS A 31B, 11–15; ed. Libowitz, 55.

[62] See Jospe, "Early Philosophical Commentaries on the *Sefer Yezirah*," 394–402.

[63] On Moscato and Kabbalah, see Idel, "Judah Moscato: A Late Renaissance Jewish Preacher," in Ruderman, *Preachers of the Italian Ghetto*, 41–66. On his *Kuzari* commentary, see Adam Shear, *The Kuzari and the Shaping of Jewish Identity, 1167–1900* (Cambridge: Cambridge University Press, 2008), chap. 4. On Modena's possible ownership of this volume, see Ancona, "L'inventario dei beni appartenenti a Leon da Modena," 262, n. 17.

words of *Sefer Yetzirah* that is brought here [in the *Kuzari*] spread.[64] When I send it before you, may it expel any idea you might have that it [the passage from Sefer Yetzirah] was explained by the *Haver* in a kabbalistic manner."[65] Although he did not develop this interpretation, Modena implied that *Sefer Yetzirah*, literally "the book of creation," should be conceived of as a work about nature. The book offered instruction on a human being's place in the world rather than the basis for a kabbalistic theology.[66] Modena turned to the title of the work to support his argument: "In addition the name of the book demonstrates that it will discuss the creations and the order of the world, that which appears, that which can be examined and known to man in nature."[67] In addition, Modena summoned the authority of the medieval biblical exegete Abraham Ibn Ezra (ca. 1092–1167), who had quoted *Sefer Yetzirah* in his commentary to Ecclesiastes without mentioning a kabbalistic interpretation.[68] In short, Modena contested the kabbalists' effort to coopt *Sefer Yetzirah* as a work of Kabbalah, and he mobilized the authority of Halevi, Moscato, and Ibn Ezra to support his philosophical interpretation of the work. Saruq and others who equated Kabbalah with philosophy did so through discovering affinities between concepts and through the rereading of texts. Modena argued that the former was a relatively recent and intellectually dubious task while the latter constituted a misreading of sources.

Modena and Cordovero

Modena obtained his knowledge of Lurianic Kabbalah through a number of channels: travelers from Safed to Venice, printed hagiographies of Luria and Vital, and the kabbalistic theology of Saruq and Menahem Azariah da Fano. But Luria was not the sum total of Safed or even of Safed Kabbalah. Modena further contested Safed Kabbalah through his

---

[64] Modena paraphrased as the actual text in Moscato's commentary reads: "Before the explanation of the words of *Sefer Yetzirah* brought here [in the *Kuzari*] should become fixed, let me send my words to you." See Moscato's commentary in Judah ha-Levi, *Ha–Kuzari* (Venice: Di Gara, 1593), 227A.

[65] MS A 31B, 15–17; ed. Libowitz, 55.

[66] On *Sefer Yetzirah*, see Yehuda Liebes, *Torat ha-Yetsirah shel Sefer Yetsirah* (Jerusalem and Tel Aviv: Schocken, 2000); Steven M. Wasserstrom, "Further Thoughts on the Origins of *Sefer yesirah*," *Aleph* 2 (2002): 201–21; David Shulman, "Is There an Indian Connection to *Sefer yesirah*?," *Aleph* 2 (2002): 191–99; Elliot R. Wolfson, "Text, Context, and Pretext: Review Essay of Yehuda Liebes's *Ars Poetica* in *Sefer Yetsira*," *Studia Philonica Annual* 16 (2004): 218–28.

[67] MS A 32A, 10–11; ed. Libowitz, 56.

[68] Delmedigo appeared to conceive of *Sefer Yetzirah* as a kabbalistic book and appealed to different passages in Halevi, Moscato, and Ibn Ezra to support his argument. See Delmedigo, *Sefer Mazref le-Hokhmah* in *Sefer Ta'alumot Hokhmah*, 8A–8B.

criticism of Moses Cordovero (d. 1570), the kabbalist who loomed largest in Safed before Luria's arrival and who had written a systematic theology of Kabbalah.[69] Modena drew largely on Cordovero's *Pardes Rimonim*, a synthetic treatment of Kabbalah printed in Krakow in 1592.[70] Cordovero's *Pardes*, as Modena and other early modern readers frequently referred to it, appeared in *Ari Nohem* in conjunction with a variety of issues, such as the importance of humility in the study of metaphysics or the audacity of kabbalists who criticized Maimonides. However, Modena's criticism focused primarily on the nature of the sefirot and, to a lesser extent, on the definition of Kabbalah as *Hokhmah*.[71] Both the subject matter that Modena discussed in conjunction with Cordovero's *Pardes* as well as the frequency with which he referred to it offer some indication of the centrality of Cordovero and his theology to Modena's larger criticism of Kabbalah.

In the very first chapter of *Ari Nohem*, Modena cited a passage from *Pardes Rimonim* in which Cordovero argued that someone who was ignorant of the sefirot would live his entire life without wisdom.[72] Quoting Cordovero, Modena wrote: "Those people to whom the nature and the existence of the sefirot have already been revealed, but they contradict them because of their corrupted minds, for they frequent the external sciences and abound in the customs of strangers,[73] these people, if they are not deemed heretics and deniers because they still believe in all the theological concepts, nevertheless they should be deemed heretics because they deny an interpretation of the Oral Torah."[74] Cordovero not only argued that denial of the sefirot constituted heresy, he argued that belief in the sefirot constituted a fundamental part of the Oral Torah. In the continuation of this passage, Cordovero drew on the authority of Maimonides to establish his definition of a heretic as someone who denied an interpretation of the Oral Torah. Modena found this appalling. That a kabbalist should declare the doctrine of the sefirot a tenet of the Jewish faith was bad enough; that he used the authority of none other than Maimonides to justify the denial of this belief as heresy made it even worse.

---

[69] See Yosef Ben-Shlomo, *Torat ha-Elohut shel Rabi Moshe Cordovero* (Jerusalem: Mossad Bialik, 1965); Sack, *Be-Sha'are ha-Kabalah shel Rabi Moshe Cordovero*; Sack, ed., *Ma'ayan En Ya'akov le-Rabi Moshe Cordovero* (Beer Sheva: Ben-Gurion University of the Negev Press, 2009).

[70] He mentioned Cordovero's *Or Ne'erav*, an abridgement of *Pardes Rimonim* printed in Venice in 1587. See MS A 6B, 8; 42B, 13; ed. Libowitz, 84. The first instance is a marginal note that may not be in Modena's hand. On *Or Ne'erav*, see Ira Robinson, *Moses Cordovero's Introduction to Kabbalah: An Annotated Translation of his Or Ne'erav* (Hoboken: Ktav, 1994). Modena was apparently unaware of Cordovero's writings in manuscript.

[71] See chapter 3.

[72] *Pardes Rimonim* (Krakow, 1592), 10A.

[73] Isa. 2:6.

[74] MS A 6B, 1–5; ed. Libowitz, 3.

Modena pointed to disagreement among kabbalists themselves about the nature of the sefirot as a proof that belief in them did not and could not constitute a fundamental aspect of the Oral Torah. One disagreement concerned the identity of one of the sefirot called *Keter* (Heb. Crown). According to Shem Tov, *Keter* functioned as an intermediate stage between existence and *ein sof*, a kabbalistic term that referred to the realm beyond existence. The crucial point for Shem Tov, and in turn for Modena, related to the numbering of the sefirot: inasmuch as *Keter* was beyond existence, it could not be counted as one of the ten sefirot.[75] Cordovero, by contrast, included *Keter* as one of the ten sefirot and vociferously opposed Shem Tov's theory.[76] Modena cast the disagreement between Shem Tov and Cordovero as characteristic of disagreement among kabbalists: "But so it is with every gate in the book [*Pardes Rimonim*]. Nothing is agreed upon. And where there is no dispute, he [Cordovero] says 'most of the kabbalists agree,' [or] 'this is the opinion of most kabbalists,' to the extent that there are very few things that they all actually agree upon."[77] If kabbalists disagreed on such fundamental issues as the nature of the sefirot, argued Modena, then Kabbalah could hardly be considered a tradition or a constituent element of the Oral Torah.

> That which has come through tradition to Israel, His people,[78] from Moses, our teacher, peace be upon him, ... there has been no dispute about it any way. No one adds to it saying, "thus it has been transmitted to me from Moses, our teacher, peace be upon him." As the exalted rabbi, Maimonides, of blessed memory, wrote in his introduction to his Commentary on the Mishnah. These are his words: "So it shall be entirely clear that if this knowledge, as stated by its possessors, were a tradition given to Moses, our teacher, peace be upon him, at Mount Sinai, it would not be fitting for there to be a dispute about it in any way." But behold we have found, we have seen, these people are not peaceable with us or among themselves,[79] and they differ about several fundamental issues. What I have seen, what my eyes have seen about two [issues] I will declare,[80] although I know that the different branches among them have proliferated.[81]

Modena continued to discuss a range of opinions about the sefirot held by various kabbalists, including Menahem Recanati, Shem Tov ibn Shem Tov,

---

[75] Ariel, "Shem Tob ibn Shem Tob's Kabbalistic Critique of Jewish Philosophy,'" 67–68. On *Keter*, see Arthur Green, *Keter: The Crown of God in Early Jewish Mysticism* (Princeton: Princeton University Press, 1997).

[76] Cordovero devoted the entirety of the third gate of *Pardes Rimonim*, entitled "Whether *Ein Sof* Is *Keter*," to a refutation of Shem Tov. See Ben-Shlomo, *Torat ha-Elohut shel Rabi Moshe Cordovero*, 44–67.

[77] MS A 28B, 10–13; ed. Libowitz, 47.

[78] Ps. 148:14.

[79] Gen. 34:21.

[80] Job 15:17.

[81] MS A 28A, 9–16; ed. Libowitz, 46.

and Elijah Genazzano.⁸² However, his entire discussion took place through a summary of their opinions, as cited in Cordovero's *Pardes Rimonim*.

Elsewhere Modena articulated his opposition to the sefirot as a fundamental principle of Jewish faith: "Whoever said, 'the Christians believe in the Trinity, but the kabbalists believe in the decad,' spoke justly. If they [the sefirot] are vessels, would he who assigns divinity to them differentiate the created being from the creator? In the explanation of Rabbi Cordovero, of blessed memory, they are like a body that has been given substance. I mean to say that He [God] is being assigned corporeality like the belief of the Christians."⁸³ By equating Cordovero's theology of the sefirot with the embodied God of Christianity, Modena contributed to a larger polemic about the parallels between kabbalistic theology and Christian dogma.

Given that Modena possessed vast knowledge of kabbalistic theology and had read a wide range of theosophic texts that outline a theology of the sefirot, including the *Zohar* and *Ma'arekhet ha-Elohut*, his choice to target Cordovero as the primary object of his polemic against the sefirot requires some explanation. The *Zohar*, as Modena had to have known, articulated a kabbalistic theology informed by the theory of the sefirot. Many of the other kabbalistic texts cited in *Ari Nohem* espouse a theosophic Kabbalah dependent on the sefirot. Part of the reason for Modena's focus on Cordovero may stem from the systematic and theoretical nature of *Pardes Rimonim*. In his introduction to the work, Cordovero himself described it as an attempt to systemize the Kabbalah of the *Zohar*, and this judgment has been confirmed by modern scholarship.⁸⁴ Beyond this, Cordovero's repeated invocation of Maimonides as well as his insistence that the sefirot were demonstrable through reason must have surely irked Modena. Finally, several figures central to Modena's thinking about Kabbalah assiduously studied Cordovero's *Pardes Rimonim* and drew upon it in their writings. Menahem Azariah da Fano, Aaron Berekhya of Modena, and Jacob Levi all composed abridgements to Cordovero's *Pardes*.⁸⁵ Some were meant

---

⁸² On Recanati, see Idel, *R. Menahem Recanati*. On Shem Tov, see chapter 3. On Genazzano, a fifteenth-century Italian kabbalist, see chapter 3 as well as Judah Rosenthal, "Elijah Hayim Genazzano's Disputation with a Franciscan Monk" (Hebrew), in *Meḥkarim u-mekorot* (Jerusalem: Rubin Mass, 1967), 1:431–56; Roland Goetschel, "Elie Hayim de Genazzano et la Kabbale," *REJ* 142 (1983): 91–107; Alexander Altmann, "On the Border of Philosophy: The Figure of the Kabbalist R. Elijah Hayim Genazzano" (Hebrew), *JSJT* 7 (1988): 61–101; Genazzano, *La lettera preziosa*; Eric Lawee, "Abravanel in Italy: The Critique of the Kabbalist Elijah Hayyim Genazzano," *Jewish History* 23 (2009): 223–53; Brian Ogren, *Renaissance and Rebirth: Reincarnation in Early Modern Italian Kabbalah* (Leiden: Brill, 2009), chap. 5.

⁸³ MS A 46A, 24–46B, 2; ed. Libowitz, 94.

⁸⁴ Scholem, *Major Trends in Jewish Mysticism*, 248–49; Ben-Shlomo, *Torat Ha-Elohut Shel Rabbi Moshe Cordovero*, 10–11; Sack, *Be-Sha'are ha-Kabalah shel Rabi Moshe Cordovero*, 23.

⁸⁵ *Pelah ha-Rimon* and *Nahalat Ya'akov* were primers to Cordovero's thought. Modena did not mention Aaron Berekhya of Modena's abridgment. See Tishby, "The Conflict between Lurianic Kabbalah and Cordoverian Kabbalah," 185, n. 17.

for circulation and publication; others, for private study. Menahem Azariah da Fano reportedly went so far as to offer Cordovero's widow a thousand gold coins in order to borrow and copy a manuscript of Cordovero's *Zohar* commentary. In *Pelah ha-Rimon* he mentioned that the communal elders in Venice implored him to teach a portion of *Pardes Rimonim* every day.[86] Italian kabbalists—even those who became devotees of Isaac Luria, such as Aaron Berekhya of Modena and Menahem Azariah da Fano—never adopted a derisive posture toward Cordovero and his teachings as did Vital, Luria's disciple who remained in the Ottoman Empire.[87] Cordovero was a crucially important figure in Italy at the turn of the seventeenth century.[88]

The Jewish renaissance in Safed in the middle of the sixteenth century had a dramatic impact on Judaism. Venice and its Jews served as a conduit and entryway for many of the ideas, stories, and texts that spread from Safed to other Jewish communities in Europe. As a witness to and a participant in Venetian Jewish life at the turn of the seventeenth century, Modena watched in horror as his colleagues and relatives embraced Safed Kabbalah. While Modena's reaction to Safed Kabbalah contained several elements, it coalesced around two central figures: Cordovero and Luria. Modena heard and read about Luria the miracle worker, the physician of the soul and the healer of the cosmos, in the academy and at a circumcision feast, and he rejected the stories as fantastic and groundless. He read the work of Cordovero and bristled at his invocation of Maimonides and his branding as heretics anyone who objected to the belief in the sefirot.

---

[86] Ben-Shlomo, *Torat Ha-Elohut Shel Rabbi Moshe Cordovero*, 10.

[87] Tishby, "The Conflict between Lurianic Kabbalah and Cordoverian Kabbalah," 250–51.

[88] For Cordovero's impact on Isaiah Horowitz and Nathan Shapira, see Bracha Sack, "The Influence of Cordovero on Seventeenth-Century Jewish Thought," in Twersky and Septimus, *Jewish Thought in the Seventeenth Century*, 365–79.

CHAPTER FIVE

A Jewish Response to Christian Kabbalah

> Kant says (Second Preface to his *Critique*): "*I have found it necessary to deny knowledge, in order to make room for faith.* The dogmatism of metaphysics, that is, the preconception that it is possible to make headway in metaphysics without a critique of pure reason, is the true source of all that unbelief which opposes morality and is always very dogmatic."
> Very important! He was driven by a cultural need!
> —Friedrich Nietzsche

Figure 10 (previous page). Hebrew title page to Joseph Solomon Delmedigo *Sefer Ta'alumot Hokhmah*, Hanau 1629-1631.
The Dorot Jewish Division, The New York Public Library, Astor, Lenox, and Tilden Foundations.
Modena drew extensively on this collection of writings for sources and arguments about the history of Kabbalah, including his response to the phenomenon of Christian Kabbalah.

MUCH OF *Ari Nohem* amounted to an attack on the Jews of early modern Venice. Modena chastised his contemporaries for abandoning Maimonides' *Guide*, turning the *Zohar* into a legal authority, and creating a cult of personality around Isaac Luria. To these ends, *Ari Nohem* was a work of cultural criticism aimed at the Venetian Jewish community and later Jewish readers. Another theme that appeared throughout the work reached its climax in the final chapter, Modena's attack on Christian Kabbalah.[1] Several problems plague an attempt to analyze Modena's account of Kabbalah and Christianity: the first is one of definitions. The second is the nature of his rejection. Modena never defined the concept of Christian Kabbalah in a coherent and succinct manner. In contrast to his criticism of the *Zohar* or Luria, where the objects of his attack were clearly delineated, his treatment of Christian Kabbalah involved an almost enigmatic rejection of Pico della Mirandola (1463–1494).[2] A learned aristocrat in Florence to whom no realm of knowledge was alien, Pico conceived of Kabbalah as a crucial element of his ancient theology. For Pico, a single truth united all periods and cultures and a harmony of religious insight existed among ancient pagan, Jewish, and Christian writers.[3] Modena's account of Pico entailed a series

---

[1] David B. Ruderman, *The World of a Renaissance Jew: The Life and Thought of Abraham ben Mordecai Farissol* (Cincinnati: HUC Press, 1981), 52; Desplanches, "Le monde de la Kabbale," 220–21; Idel, "Differing Conceptions of Kabbalah in the Early 17th Century," 164–68; Adelman, "Rabbi Leon Modena and the Christian Kabbalists," 278.

[2] On Pico and Kabbalah, see Frances A. Yates, *Giordano Bruno and the Hermetic Tradition* (Chicago: University of Chicago Press, 1964), 84–116; Bohdan Kieszkowski, "Les rapports entre Elie del Medigo et Pic de la Mirandole," *Rinascimento* 4 (1964): 41–91; Idel, "The Magical and Neoplatonic Interpretations of the Kabbalah in the Renaissance"; Wirszubski, *Pico della Mirandola's Encounter with Jewish Mysticism*; Wirszubski, *Ben ha-Shitin: Kabalah, Kabalah Notsrit, Shabtaut* (Jerusalem: Magnes Press, 1990), 13–117; Fabrizio Lelli, "*Prisca Philosophia* and *Docta Religio*: The Boundaries of Rational Knowledge in Jewish and Christian Humanist Thought," *JQR* 91 (2000): 53–99; Brian P. Copenhaver, "The Secret of Pico's *Oration*: Cabala and Renaissance Philosophy," *Midwest Studies in Philosophy* 26 (2002): 56–81.

[3] On ancient theology, see Charles B. Schmitt, "Perrennial Philosophy: From Agostino Steuco to Leibniz," *JHI* 27 (1966): 505–32; D. P. Walker, *The Ancient Theology: Studies in Christian Platonism from the Fifteenth to the Eighteenth Century* (Ithaca: Cornell University Press, 1972); David B. Ruderman, *Kabbalah, Magic, and Science: The Cultural Universe of a Sixteenth-Century Jewish Physician* (Cambridge: Harvard University Press, 1988), 139–60; Bruce Rosenstock, "Abraham Miguel Cardoso's Messianism: A Reappraisal," *AJS Review* 23 (1998): 80–92; Christopher S. Celenza, "The Search for Ancient Wisdom in Early Modern Europe: Reuchlin

of misreadings, possibly accidental but probably deliberate, that attempted to dissolve the very category of Christian Kabbalah.

To complicate matters even further, Modena's rejection of Christian Kabbalah contained both factual and logical inconsistencies. In terms of fact, Modena provided two different figures for the number of Pico's kabbalistic theses and offered conflicting accounts of Pico's kabbalistic manuscripts he had seen in Venice the year he wrote *Ari Nohem*. Furthermore, for all his historicist acumen in his treatment of the *Zohar*, Modena showed little awareness of recent historical developments within Christianity. He attacked the category of Christian Kabbalah as if European Christianity was a unified monolith and the Reformation had never happened. Modena's analysis of Christian Kabbalah offers little indication that he lived in a city teeming with heretics and evangelists and that the Christianity he criticized was anything but homogenous.[4] At the level of logic, Modena objected to Christian Kabbalah for a variety of reasons similar to his opposition to Jewish Kabbalah: it was a recent innovation, and the attempt to argue for its antiquity defied both reason and textual evidence. Kabbalists, Jewish and Christian, misconstrued basic theological concepts, such as the nature of God, and attempted to monopolize the interpretation of sacred texts, such as the Bible. In the very same passages, however, Modena objected to Christian Kabbalah for the simple fact that it was Christian. At times, he even seemed to describe Christian Kabbalah as the Christian appropriation of an exclusively Jewish domain of knowledge. In one particularly revealing instance, Modena approvingly cited one of his contemporaries who compared the instruction of Kabbalah to Christians with the teaching of Torah to gentiles. In criticizing Christian Kabbalah as a perversion of a specifically Jewish set of esoteric secrets, Modena adopted a protectionist and proprietary attitude toward a form of knowledge and set of practices he had spent considerable energy criticizing and had otherwise rejected.

For all its inconsistencies, however, *Ari Nohem* represents the most sustained response by a Jew to Christian Kabbalah. When Modena wrote *Ari Nohem*, Christian Kabbalah was hardly a new phenomenon. For the prior century and a half, Christians had been using Kabbalah in support of Christian dogma and interpreting kabbalistic texts in the interest of Christianity.[5] In the early stages, Jews were extensively involved in the

---

and the Late Ancient Esoteric Paradigm," *Journal of Religious History* 25 (2001): 115–33; Moshe Idel, "Prisca Theologia in Marsilio Ficino and in Some Jewish Treatments," in *Marsilio Ficino: His Theology, His Philosophy, His Legacy*, ed. Michael J. B. Allen and Valery Rees, 137–58 (Leiden: Brill, 2002).

[4] John Martin, *Venice's Hidden Enemies: Italian Heretics in a Renaissance City* (Berkeley: University of California Press, 1993).

[5] Gershom Scholem, "The Beginnings of the Christian Kabbalah," in Dan, *The Christian Kabbalah*, 17.

instruction of Kabbalah to Christians. Pico studied with Elijah Delmedigo and Yohanan Alemmano, Jews active in northern Italy in the late fifteenth century.⁶ He engaged Flavius Mithridates, a Jewish convert to Christianity, in an extensive translation project of kabbalistic texts.⁷ The critical remarks about Kabbalah in Delmedigo's *Behinat ha-Dat* have been interpreted as a veiled polemical response to Pico, his pupil in Hebrew and medieval Aristotelian thought.⁸ In the early sixteenth century, Egidius of Viterbo studied Hebrew with Elijah Levita and hired Baruch di Benveneto to copy and translate kabbalistic texts.⁹ In the middle of the sixteenth century, several kabbalists opposed printing the *Zohar* on the grounds that its appearance in print would grant Christians unfettered access to a basic work of Kabbalah.¹⁰ Apart from the short remarks in *Behinat ha-Dat* and the passing comments of a few kabbalists in the sixteenth century, however, hardly any works written by Jews prior to *Ari Nohem* offer a sustained critical reaction to Christian Kabbalah.¹¹

The first section of this chapter sketches a brief history of Christian Kabbalah with an aim toward understanding its place within the intellectual life of seventeenth-century Venice. It focuses on the specific channels through which Christian Kabbalah reached Modena. The second section treats Modena's reading of Pico, particularly the kabbalistic conclusions included in the nine hundred theses Pico had proposed for public debate in 1486 and the *Oration* that was meant to serve as a prologue to the occasion. The disputation was canceled when a commission appointed by Pope Innocent VIII condemned a number of Pico's theses, and Pico composed an

---

⁶ On Delmedigo, see Giulio Busi "'Who Does Not Wonder at This Chameleon?' The Kabbalistic Library of Giovanni Pico della Mirandola," in *Hebrew to Latin, Latin to Hebrew: the Mirroring of Two Cultures in the Age of Humanism*, ed. Giulio Busi, 167–96 (Turin: Nino Aragno, 2006), 180. On Alemanno, see Idel, "The Magical and Neoplatonic Interpretations of Kabbalah in the Renaissance"; Fabrizio Lelli, "Un collaboratore ebreo di Giovanni Pico della Mirandola: Yohanan Alemanno," in *Homo Vivens* 5 (1994), 401–30.

⁷ See Flavius Mithridates, *Sermo de passione domini*, ed. Chaim Wirszubski (Jerusalem: Israel Academy of Sciences and Humanities, 1963); Wirszubski, *Pico della Mirandola's Encounter with Jewish Mysticism*, 69–118. For the timing of Mithridates' translations, see Busi, "Who Does Not Wonder," 188. For editions of Mithridates' translations, see Giulo Busi, ed., *The Great Parchment* (Turin: Nino Aragno, 2004); Saverio Campanini, ed., *The Book of Bahir* (Turin: Nino Aragno, 2005).

⁸ See the references to Delmedigo in chapter 2.

⁹ Secret, *Les Kabbalistes Chrétiens*, 106–126.

¹⁰ Tishby, "The Controversy over the Book of the *Zohar* in Italy in the Sixteenth Century," 87.

¹¹ Cordovero specifically mentioned the Christian study of Kabbalah in Italy. See Sack, *Be-Sha'are ha-Kabalah shel Rabi Moshe Cordovero*, 37, n. 22. See also Abraham ben Eliezer ha-Levi's letter quoted in Moshe Idel, "Jewish Thinkers versus Christian Kabbalah," in *Christliche Kabbala*, ed. Wilhelm Schmidt-Biggemann (Ostfildern: Thorbecke, 2003), 54. Modena was apparently unaware of either source.

154 • Chapter Five

Apology on their behalf.¹² For Modena, Pico functioned metonymically for the entire phenomenon of Christian Kabbalah. Modena's reading of Pico offers the clearest way of grappling with his actual conception of Christian Kabbalah as a social phenomenon and as a constellation of ideas, even though he never defined Christian Kabbalah and misrepresented several facts about Pico's theses. The chapter concludes with a discussion of the two most pressing concerns for Modena in his attack on Christian Kabbalah: the publication of esotericism and the use of Kabbalah by Christian preachers to encourage the conversion of the Jews.

CHRISTIAN KABBALAH IN EARLY MODERN VENICE

Although Pico claimed to be the first Latin scholar to employ Kabbalah, Modena's focus on him to the virtual exclusion of all other Christian kabbalists requires some explanation.¹³ Pico had flourished in Florence nearly a century and a half before Modena wrote *Ari Nohem*, and while he may have been the most prominent Christian to employ Kabbalah in his theology, he was hardly the only one. Furthermore, considerable evidence from Modena's other writings indicates that Modena was well aware of other Christian kabbalists. A brief sketch of their writings and their place within his literary output offers a map of the possible choices available to Modena as targets for his attack on Christian Kabbalah. A series of encounters in Venice before the writing of *Ari Nohem* and Pico's importance as a theologian offer the most compelling reasons for Modena's exclusive focus on the Florentine aristocrat.

Kabbalah began to surface in the writings of Jewish converts to Christianity as early as the fourteenth century when it appeared in the writings of Abner of Burgos (ca. 1270—ca. 1347). Although Modena owned a manuscript of Abner's writings that incorporated Kabbalah, the polemic against Judaism *Sefer Teshuvot li-Meharef*, he did not draw on it in his treatment of

---

¹² The theses were first printed in Rome in 1486. The oration was not printed until after Pico's death, when it was included in Pico's works edited by his nephew Gian Francesco. Decades later it came to be referred to as the *Oration on the Dignity of Man*. For a widely cited sixteenth-century text of the theses, the *Oration*, and the *Apology*, see Giovanni Pico della Mirandola and Gian Francesco Pico, *Opera Omnia (1557–73)* (Hildesheim: Georg Olms, 1969), 1:63–240, 313–31; as cited by Brian P. Copenhaver, "Number, Shape, and Meaning in Pico's Christian Cabala," in *Natural Particulars: Nature and the Disciplines in Renaissance Europe*, ed. Anthony Grafton and Nancy Siraisi, 25, n. 1 (Cambridge: MIT Press, 1999). For an English translation and the Latin text, see S. A. Farmer, ed., *Syncretism in the West: Pico's 900 Theses (1486)* (Tempe, AZ: Medieval and Renaissance Texts and Studies, 1998).

¹³ See Wirszubski, "Introduction," in Mithridates, *Sermo de passione domini*, 27. For possible antecedents, see Scholem, "The Beginnings of the Christian Kabbalah," 21.

Christian Kabbalah.[14] This omission becomes all the more curious when one considers that Modena extensively annotated it, had read it in the years immediately preceding the composition of *Ari Nohem*, and composed an extensive preface to it.[15] Modena simply overlooked the kabbalistic elements of Abner's work.

Modena made passing reference to two prominent Christian kabbalists who wrote in the years following Pico's death, Johannes Reuchlin (1455–1522) and Pietro Galatino (c. 1460–1540). A learned Hebraist who had met Pico in Florence, Reuchlin wrote several kabbalistic works, including *De verbo mirifico*, a treatise that employed Kabbalah in conjunction with the Tetragrammaton.[16] Reuchlin argued that the four-letter name of God attained its meaning only with the addition of the letter *shin* when it produced a form of the name of Jesus. Reuchlin's interest in Kabbalah was one of several factors that precipitated his participation in the fierce debate over Hebrew books that erupted in the Holy Roman Empire.[17] In a series of pamphlets, Johannes Pfefferkorn, a Jewish convert to Christianity, had argued that all of postbiblical Jewish literature was deeply anti-Christian and should be banned. In his rebuttal in defense of Jewish books written in 1511, *Die Augenspiegel*, Reuchlin countered that one had to distinguish between various genres of Jewish literature and that very few Jewish books actually dealt with Christianity. Reuchlin's *Augenspiegel* included a telling characterization of kabbalistic books as "not only harmless, but also eminently useful for our Christian faith."[18] Six years later his kabbalis-

[14] On Abner, see Scholem, "The Beginnings of the Christian Kabbalah," 26–30; Fritz Baer, "Abner aus Burgos," in *Korrespondenzblatt des Vereins zur Gründung und Erhaltung einer Akademie für die Wissenschaft des Judentums* 10 (1929): 20-37; Yitzhak Baer, "Abner of Burgos' *Minhat Kenaoth* and Its Influence on Hasdai Crescas" (Hebrew), *Tarbiz* 11 (1940): 188–206; Baer, "Kabbalistic Doctrine in the Christological Teachings of Abner of Burgos" (Hebrew), *Tarbiz* 27 (1958): 278–89; Judah Rosenthal, "From the Hebrew Writings of the Apostate Abner of Burgos" (Hebrew), in *Mehkarim u-mekorot*, 1:324–67. Baer and Rosenthal both used Modena's copy of Abner of Burgos. See below.

[15] For his annotations, see Parma, Biblioteca Palatina, Codex de Rossi 533 (Parma MS 2440), 10B, 12A, 14A, 14B, 26A, 45A, 48A, 49A, 60A, 61B, 61A, 62A, 84A, 96B, 98A, 100A. Modena had acquired the work in 1611 but did not write his preface until 1634. For a partial transcription of the preface, see Reggio, ed., *Behinat ha-Kabalah*, xiii–xiv. See also the contemptuous reference to Abner in *Kol Sakhal*, where the epithet "may the impure one be pulverized" follows his name. See Fishman, *Shaking the Pillars of Exile*, 153, 11, 72.

[16] Basel, 1494. It was reprinted several times in the sixteenth century.

[17] James H. Overfield, "The Reuchlin Affair," in *Humanism and Scholasticism in Late Medieval Germany*, 247–97 (Princeton: Princeton University Press, 1984); Erika Rummel, *The Case against Johann Reuchlin: Religious and Social Controversy in Sixteenth-Century Germany* (Toronto: University of Toronto Press, 2002). David H. Price, *Johannes Reuchlin and the Campaign to Destroy Jewish Books* (New York: Oxford University Press, 2011).

[18] *Recommendation Whether to Confiscate, Destroy, and Burn All Jewish Books*, trans. Peter Wortsman (Mahwah, N.J.: Paulist Press, 2000), 66. A partial translation of *Augenspiegel* (Tübingen: Thomas Anselm, 1511).

tic masterpiece *De arte cabalistica* equated Kabbalah with Pythagoreanism in a series of fictitious conversations between Simon the Jew, Philolaus the Pythagorean, and Marranus the Muslim.[19] Modena was well aware of Reuchlin and mentioned him in *Ari Nohem* but never engaged him at any length.[20]

Reuchlin's Kabbalah served as an inspiration for Pietro Galatino in his *De arcanis catholicae veritatis*, an anti-Jewish polemic deeply indebted to *Pugio Fidei* by Raymond Martin (1220–1287).[21] Galatino has often been dismissed as a mere plagiarist of his medieval predecessor, yet he demonstrated a considerably greater knowledge of Hebrew sources and Jewish culture than his unacknowledged source. Like Reuchlin, Galatino wanted to use Kabbalah to reveal the secret powers of the divine name and claimed that the Tetragrammaton secretly contained an allusion to the Trinity. Modena was quite familiar with Galatino's work, as he referred to it briefly in *Ari Nohem* and devoted a considerable portion of *Magen va-Herev* to its refutation.[22] However, he did not focus on Galatino's Kabbalah. In *Ari Nohem* Modena also mentioned another prominent Christian kabbalist, Agrippa von Nettesheim (1486–1535).[23] Agrippa identified Kabbalah with magic and believed Kabbalah endowed its practitioner with supernatural powers.[24] A Hebrew summary of Agrippa's *De incertitudine et vanitate scientarium* in Modena's notebook indicates that he had a thorough knowledge of at least one of Agrippa's works.[25]

---

[19] Hagenau, 1517. See Johann Reuchlin, *On the Art of the Kabbalah: De Arte Cabalistica*, trans. Martin and Sarah Goodman (Lincoln: University of Nebraska Press, 1993). On Reuchlin and Pico, see Idel, "Introduction to the Bison Book Edition," in ibid., vii–viii. On Pythagoreanism and Kabbalah, see Celenza, "The Search for Ancient Wisdom," 120–24; Wolfson, "Language, Secrecy and the Mysteries of Law."

[20] MS A 10B, 10; 47B, 10; ed. Libowitz, 9, 96. The spelling of Reuchlin's name is garbled in Libowitz's edition.

[21] On the printing of Galatino, see chapter 1. On his debt to Raymond Martin, see François Secret, "Notes pour une historie du *Pugio Fidei* a la Renaissance," *Sefarad* 20 (1960): 401–7.

[22] MS A 10B, interlinear note between lines 10 and 11. See also Modena, *Magen va-Herev*, ed. Simonsohn, 11, 13, 51–54; and chapter 6 below. Galatino was read in a number of different contexts in the early seventeenth century. In addition to Modena, Isaac Casaubon drew on Galatino, whose work he thought was both untrustworthy and chaotic, in his discussion of the Hebrew Bible. See Grafton and Weinberg, *"I have always loved the Holy Tongue,"* chap. 2 and appendix 2. In addition, in a trial before the Inquisition in Valladolid in 1639, Lope de Vera, a Hebraist at Salamanca who was later burned for Judaizing, used a passage from rabbinic literature quoted in Galatino to argue the Messiah had not yet come. See Miriam Bodian, *Dying in the Law of Moses: Crypto-Jewish Martyrdom in the Iberian World* (Bloomington: Indiana University Press, 2007), 163.

[23] MS A 10B, interlinear note at line 10.

[24] *De occulta philosophia, libri tres* (Cologne, 1533).

[25] Cologne, 1531. The work appeared repeatedly throughout the sixteenth century. For Modena's summary, see Ancona, Communità Israelitica, MS 7, 1A. Jacob Zemah, a seventeenth-century Jewish kabbalist in Palestine, wrote a refutation of Agrippa's Christological Kabbalah.

Given Modena's firsthand knowledge of these Christian kabbalists, his omission of their work in his attack on Christian Kabbalah only heightens his focus on Pico. Modena's concentration on Pico becomes clear only when one considers the publication history of the *Riti* and his connection with the French Orientalist and priest Jacques Gaffarel (1601–1681).[26] In 1635 Modena had sent a copy of the *Riti* to Gaffarel with instructions to print it in Paris to avoid Venetian censorship. When Gaffarel informed him in April 1637 that the *Riti* had appeared in print, Modena feared retribution by the Venetian Inquisition and voluntarily submitted a copy to the Holy Office for examination.[27] A revised *Riti*, which did not include potentially offensive passages on the transmigration of souls and on Maimonides' thirteen articles of faith, was printed in Venice a year later.

In the *Riti* Modena summarized Jewish customs and ceremonies in an attempt to defend Judaism from the critical treatment it had received in *Synagoga Judaica* by Johannes Buxtorf, professor of Hebrew at the University of Basel.[28] Buxtorf had emphasized those Jewish practices he had deemed superstitious, such as *kapparot*, a penitential rite before the Jewish New Year, and the search for crumbs of leavened bread on the eve of Passover. In the *Riti* Modena presented a more palatable version of Judaism before contemporary Christian opinion. Gaffarel's edition included a preface that directly confronted Modena's attitude toward Kabbalah and challenged his presentation of Judaism with evidence drawn from kabbalistic texts.[29] Gaffarel objected to the lack of discussion of Jewish rituals, "which do not a little puzzle and perplex the most learned of us Christians," such as burial rites, *kapparot*, and the "mystical kindling of the Sabbath lights."[30] In

---

See Idel, "Jewish Thinkers versus Christian Kabbalah," 56–57. Modena ignored or was unaware of two Christian kabbalists associated with Venice, Francesco Zorzi (1467–1540) and Guillaume Postel (1510–1581). On Zorzi, see Giulio Busi, "Francesco Zorzi: A Methodical Dreamer," in Dan, *The Christian Kabbalah*, 97–125. On Postel, see Secret, *Les Kabbalistes Chrétiens*, 171–86.

[26] On the *Riti*, see Mark R. Cohen, "Leone da Modena's *Riti*: A Seventeenth-Century Plea for Social Toleration of Jews," in Ruderman, *Essential Papers on Jewish Culture in Renaissance and Baroque Italy*, 429–73; Adelman, "Success and Failure," 757–69; Jacques le Brun and Guy G. Stroumsa, "Introduction," in *Les Juifs présentés aux chrétiens par Léon de Modène traduit par Richard Simon* (Paris: Les Belles Lettres, 1998); Leon Modena, *Jüdische Riten, Sitten, und Gebräuche*, ed. and trans. Rafael Arnold (Wiesbaden: Marixverlag, 2007).

[27] Cecil Roth, "Léon de Modène, ses *Riti Ebraici* et le Saint-Office à Venise," *REJ* 87 (1929): 86–88.

[28] Cohen, "Leone da Modena's *Riti*"; Burnett, *From Christian Hebraism to Jewish Studies*, 86–89.

[29] Leon Modena, *Historia de gli riti hebraici* (Paris, 1637). In his response to Gaffarel's preface in the second edition, Modena attempted to deflect this criticism. See *Historia de' riti hebraici* (Venice, 1638), "Responsio."

[30] Leon Modena, *The History of the Rites, Customes, and Manner of Life of the Present Jews throughout the World*, trans. Edmund Chilmead (London: J. Martin and J. Ridley, 1650), 11A.

discussing these practices, Gaffarel quoted the *Zohar*, *Derekh Emunah*, and *Pardes Rimonim*. Concerning the Sabbath candles, Gaffarel chided Modena about the "ancient superstition ... you have, very discreetly, forborn to make any mention."[31] In the preface to the *Riti* printed two years before Modena wrote *Ari Nohem*, Gaffarel had upbraided Modena for presenting a version of Judaism purged of any reference to kabbalistic rituals.

Gaffarel put his interest in Kabbalah to material effect when he went to purchase books on behalf of Cardinal Richelieu.[32] He eventually published a catalogue of three kabbalistic manuscripts he had purchased and claimed had once belonged to Pico.[33] Two of these manuscripts contained Latin translations of kabbalistic texts—Recanati's biblical commentary and a collection by Eleazar of Worms—while the third contained a medieval Hebrew philosophical work. A reference to this purchase may appear in *Ari Nohem*:

> But even several members of the uncircumcised nations [studied Kabbalah], as is well known about Giov[anni] Pico, Count of Mirandola. Among the nine hundred theses he established and proposed at Rome, there were one hundred and sixteen that derived from this Kabbalah: forty-five from other authors and seventy-one of his own invention as I shall discuss later in chapter [thirty] of the third section, with the help of God. This very year I saw in the possession of a French gentile twelve manuscript books of Kabbalah in Hebrew, of the choicest and most prominent by the aforementioned count.[34]

Modena did not name the gentile in question and indicated that he saw twelve manuscripts rather than three, the number subsequently described in Gaffarel's catalogue. Nor did he characterize the contents of the manuscripts, simply indicating that they were kabbalistic books in Hebrew; Gaffarel's catalogue described Latin translations of Hebrew texts.

---

[31] Ibid., 15B.

[32] Secret, *Les Kabbalistes Chrétiens*, 26, n. 13. On Gaffarel's Kabbalah, see Saverio Campanini, "Eine späte Apologie der Kabbala: Die *Abdita divinae cabalae mysteria* des Jacques Gaffarel," in *Topik und Tradition: Prozesse der Neuordnung von Wissensüberlieferungen des 13. bis. 17 Jahrhunderts*, ed. Thomas Frank, Urusla Kocher, and Ulrike Tarnow, 293–320 (Gottingen: V & R Unipress, 2007).

[33] *Codicum cabalisticorum manuscriptorum, quibus est usus Joannes Picus comes Mirandulanus index* (Paris: Blageart, 1651). On the veracity of Gaffarel's claims, see below. On Pico's library, see Anthony Grafton, "Giovanni Pico della Mirandola: Trials and Triumphs of an Omnivore," in *Commerce with the Classics: Ancient Books and Renaissance Readers* (Ann Arbor: University of Michigan Press, 1997), 102. On Pico's Hebrew manuscripts, see Giuliano Tamani, "I libri ebraici di Pico della Mirandola," in *Giovanni Pico della Mirandola*, ed. Gian Carlo Garfagnini, 2:491–530 (Florence: L. S. Olschki, 1997). On Mithridates' kabbalistic translations, which probably did not follow the same itinerary as Pico's other books, see Busi, "Who Does Not Wonder," 194.

[34] MS A 10B, 4–8; ed. Libowitz, 9.

A Jewish Response to Christian Kabbalah • 159

In spite of these discrepancies, another passage suggests that Modena may have referred to Gaffarel: "It seems certain that what Count Pico della Mirandola wrote, that he saw ten kabbalistic books composed by Ezra the scribe in the great library in Rome and that he purchased three of them at a very high price, if this is true that he saw these books—and those that he purchased I myself saw as I wrote earlier in chapter [two] —then they were certainly the handiwork of someone more recent."[35] Modena explicitly cited the earlier passage in *Ari Nohem* about Pico's kabbalistic manuscripts he had seen in Venice yet gave two different numbers of manuscripts: three in this instance, ten earlier. He also identified the manuscripts owned by Pico that he had seen in Venice with the kabbalistic books attributed to Ezra the Scribe mentioned in Pico's *Oration* and *Apology*.[36] This mistaken attempt to connect the manuscripts that he had seen in Venice with manuscripts mentioned in a passage in Pico's writing quite possibly derived from a conversation with Gaffarel. In the introduction to his catalogue, Gaffarel claimed that Pico had sought to obtain the kabbalistic books translated for Sixtus IV mentioned in the *Oration* and *Apology*. Having failed to do so, Pico had these same books retranslated, and Gaffarel claimed to have purchased these copies.[37] Modena did not mention that Pico had purchased copies of the manuscripts translated for Sixtus IV rather than the actual manuscripts mentioned in the *Oration* and the *Apology*. His mistaken attempt to identify the manuscripts Pico supposedly owned with those mentioned in the *Oration* and *Apology* may have been his misunderstanding of information conveyed to him by Gaffarel or simply an error. A final complicating factor in identifying the unknown Frenchman with Gaffarel has to do with timing. Gaffarel has been located in Venice in 1633, six years before Modena wrote *Ari Nohem*.[38] Given Modena's emphasis on having seen the kabbalistic manuscripts "this very year," Gaffarel must have returned to Venice if he indeed was the gentile in question.

If Gaffarel claimed to have purchased Pico's kabbalistic manuscripts and Modena claimed to have seen them in Venice the same year he wrote *Ari Nohem*, Hamiz possessed Pico's kabbalistic writings. At the close of *Ari Nohem*, Modena indicated that his addressee had been reading Pico:

---

[35] MS A 27A, 11–14; ed. Libowitz, 44.
[36] See below.
[37] *Codicum cabalisticorum*, 13–16; as cited in Wirszubski, *Pico della Mirandola's Encounter*, 15, n. 15. As Wirszubski has demonstrated, only one of the manuscripts described by Gaffarel was actually owned by Pico: Mithridates' translation of Recanati's biblical commentary. The second manuscript was almost certainly a copy of a manuscript that had been in Pico's library. The third was not a kabbalistic book, and there is no evidence that it was translated for Pico. See Wirszubski, "Introduction," *Sermo de passione domini*, 59–65.
[38] See Nicolas-Claude Fabri de Peiresc, *Lettres à Claude Saumaise et à son entourage (1620–1637)*, ed. Agnès Bresson, 147, n. 78 (Florence: L. S. Olschki, 1992).

"Among your Christian books, it is known to me that you possess a book composed by the Count of Mirandola, who was the first of the Christians to inquire into this Kabbalah. For in his time, it [Kabbalah] had begun to be called by this name. I have already seen that among the theses that he supported at Rome, sixty-one of them are derived from Kabbalah."[39] Modena specified that Hamiz actually owned Pico's theses and included them within a category he called "Christian books." In the list of possessions drawn up after his death, Modena's library was divided into "Libri Hebraichi" and "Libri Vulgari," the former encompassing books in Hebrew and Aramaic and the latter Italian and Latin. The Libri Vulgari included a number of books Modena may have labeled "Christian," including the New Testament, the sermons of Savonarola, and the *Bibliotheca Sancta* of Sixtus of Sienna; however, at his death Modena did not possess any works that can be easily identified as Christian Kabbalah.[40]

MODENA AND CHRISTIAN KABBALAH

Given Pico's importance to Gaffarel and Hamiz and his prominence as a theologian, Modena's virtual indifference to more than a century of Christian Kabbalah he had read and annotated begins to make greater sense. Modena objected to two separate aspects of Pico's Kabbalah: the claims to its ostensible antiquity in the *Oration* and the *Apology* and its use in support of Christian doctrine in the theses.[41] In the second half of the *Oration*, Pico discussed the unity of truth and offered a brief survey of the sources for his theses, including Plato, Aristotle, Hermes Trismegistus, and Pythagoras. In the final paragraphs, Pico turned to Kabbalah: "I come now to the things I have elicited from the ancient mysteries of the Hebrews and have cited for the confirmation of the inviolable Catholic faith."[42] Pico's genealogy of Kabbalah contained two stages: divine revelation to Moses and transcription in writing by Ezra. He emphasized oral transmission in the first stage: "When the true interpretation of the Law according to the command of God, divinely handed down to Moses, was revealed, it was called the Cabala, a word which is the same among the Hebrews as 'reception' among ourselves; for this reason, of course, that one man from another, by a sort

---

[39] MS A 47A, 17–19; ed. Libowitz, 96.
[40] See Ancona, "L'inventario dei beni appartenenti a Leon da Modena," 264–67.
[41] Modena did not cite Pico's *Heptaplus*, a commentary on biblical creation. On Kabbalah in the *Heptaplus*, see Crofton Black, *Pico's Heptaplus and Biblical Hermeneutics* (Leiden: Brill, 2006), chap. 4.
[42] Pico della Mirandola, "Oration on the Dignity of Man," trans. Elizabeth Forbes, in Cassirer, Kristeller, and Randall, *The Renaissance Philosophy of Man*, 249.

of hereditary right, received that doctrine not through written records but through a regular succession of revelations."⁴³ Like medieval Jewish kabbalists such as Nahmanides and Moses de Leon, Pico maintained the antiquity of Kabbalah and its oral transmission from Moses at Sinai. He went to great lengths to emphasize its antiquity by placing this genealogy after his account of Hermes Trismegistus and before Orpheus and Zoroaster, other components of his ancient theology.

The second stage in the transmission of Kabbalah occurred with Esdras, the Greek name of the biblical scribe Ezra who played a pivotal role in Jewish history in the fourth century BCE. In Pico's account, Esdras transcribed in writing the ancient secrets that had been transmitted orally from the time of Moses:

> When he [Esdras] plainly recognized that, because of the exiles, the massacres, the flights, and the captivity of the children of Israel, the custom instituted by their forefathers of transmitting the doctrine from mouth to mouth could not be preserved, and that it would come to pass that the mysteries of the heavenly teachings divinely bestowed on them would be lost, since the memory of them could not long endure without the aid of written records, [Esdras] decided that those of the elders then surviving should be called together and that each one should impart to the gathering whatever he possessed by personal recollection concerning the mysteries of the Law and the scribes should be employed to collect them into seventy volumes.⁴⁴

Pico's account of a national crisis as the impetus to record an oral tradition lest it disappear had a striking resemblance to Maimonides' narrative of the Mishnah and its transcription by Judah the Prince discussed in the introduction to the *Mishneh Torah* or the stories about the composition of the *Zohar* by Simeon bar Yohai and his circle recounted by medieval kabbalists.

To support this genealogy, Pico mobilized a passage that described the dictation of lost books in 2 Esdras, the second apocryphal and pseudepigraphic book attributed to Ezra.⁴⁵ Just as God had given two laws to Moses at Sinai, a public one and a secret one, Ezra was given a similar set of teachings, one exoteric and the other esoteric. After receiving the dictation, Ezra was told to publish the first books but to keep the last seventy secret. Pico identified these seventy volumes as kabbalistic books: "Pope Sixtus IV . . . took the greatest pains and interest in seeing that these books should be translated into the Latin tongue for a public service to our faith and, when

---

⁴³ Ibid., 251. A similar passage appears in the *Apology*.
⁴⁴ Ibid.
⁴⁵ 2 Esdras 14:5–6, 45–47. See Alastair Hamilton, *The Apocryphal Apocalypse: The Reception of the Second Book of Esdras (4 Ezra) from the Renaissance to the Enlightenment* (Oxford: Clarendon Press, 1999), 2, 34–36.

he died, three of them had been done into Latin.... When I had purchased these books at no small cost to myself, when I had read them through with the greatest diligence and with unwearying toil, I saw in them (as God is my witness) not so much the Mosaic as the Christian religion."[46] Such a commission by Sixtus IV probably never took place, and Pico was probably misled on this account by Flavius Mithridates.[47] Nevertheless, Pico believed it had and used the kabbalistic books he was given by Mithridates to prove that Kabbalah had been transmitted by God to Moses and transcribed in written form by Ezra.

Modena objected to Pico's genealogy of Kabbalah as it appeared in the *Oration* and the *Apology*. He challenged his assertion that Ezra the Scribe had composed works of Kabbalah and argued that these books were pseudepigraphic ascriptions to Ezra by a later author: "It seems certain that what Count Pico della Mirandola wrote, that he saw ten kabbalistic books composed by Ezra the Scribe in the great library in Rome and he purchased them at a very high price ... that they were certainly the handiwork of someone more recent, who devised them after this knowledge [Kabbalah] had already been invented and attributed them to Ezra."[48] Modena specified that he was paraphrasing one of Pico's written works rather than offering a summary of Pico provided by an informant. The paraphrase bears a striking resemblance to the passages about Kabbalah in the *Oration* and the *Apology*. With respect to Pico's genealogy of Kabbalah, Modena's argument was no different from his rejection of similar claims made by Jewish kabbalists who used pseudepigraphy to maintain the ancient origins of *Sefer Yetzirah*, the *Zohar*, and *Sefer ha-Bahir*. The location of this passage within *Ari Nohem* further indicates that the Christian content of Pico's Kabbalah had little bearing in terms of Modena's rejection of this specific argument: it appeared in the middle of a chapter devoted to post-Maimonidean Jewish scholars who argued for the antiquity of Kabbalah or of particular kabbalistic doctrines.

Modena expressed disbelief at Pico's claim that the secret kabbalistic books written by Ezra could have escaped the attention of Jews in antiquity:

> For how is it possible that they [Ezra's kabbalistic writings] had not been disseminated among Israel throughout the period of the Second Temple and the Men of the Great Assembly, and among the sects mentioned in the first chapter of [Tractate] *Avot* who received it from them, all the more so if they were written

---

[46] Pico, "Oration on the Dignity of Man," 252.

[47] Scholem, "The Beginnings of the Christian Kabbalah," 23. Wirszubski, introduction to Mithridates, *Sermo de passione domini*, 66–69.

[48] MS A 27A, 11–14; ed. Libowitz, 44–45.

down in a book and brought to strangers in the city of Rome. Apart from the fact that Ezra was an expert scribe in the Torah of Moses and not a prophet.[49]

Here one begins to sense some of the protectionism that erupts in the final chapter. Modena corrected Pico for mistakes he had not made: Pico had described Ezra as "head of the church," rather than a prophet. Modena simply could not conceive that esoteric Hebrew texts were unknown to the Jewish sages of biblical and rabbinic antiquity, particularly those listed in the chain of tradition that appeared in the Mishnah *Avot*. In the century and a half between Pico's *Oration* and *Ari Nohem*, Ezra had become a touchstone for individuals and movements that dissented from established churches such as the Anabaptists, the spiritualists, and Calvinists, and Pico's appropriation of Ezra stood at the beginning of this early modern obsession.[50] Modena's reference to Ezra as a scribe referred to rabbinic traditions that assigned a unique role to Ezra in the transmission of the written Torah.[51] *Ari Nohem* thus attempted to reclaim Ezra as a fundamental link in the transmission of Judaism by pointedly rejecting Pico's portrayal of Ezra as the author of kabbalistic books.

Only in the final chapter of *Ari Nohem* did Modena confront and condemn the Christianity within Pico's Kabbalah. Opening with a marked change in tone, Modena addressed Hamiz in the second person. The shift from a discussion that had been by and large analytical, historical, and theological to one that was relational and personal hardly seems accidental. Although Christian Kabbalah had been mentioned earlier, the most sustained discussion began with a note from the author to his addressee that served largely as an exercise in politesse. Modena pointed to the sensitivity of the subject matter as a primary factor in his reticence to engage in a sustained treatment. In a remark that echoed Pico's in the *Apology*, Modena described him as the first Christian to inquire into Kabbalah.

> For in his time, it [Kabbalah] had begun to be called by its name. I have already seen that among the theses he proposed [to debate] in Rome, sixty-one of them were derived from Kabbalah. However, several of their principal sages opposed him, saying that this was *new theology* and belief in it was heresy. He expounded at length to demonstrate to them that its methods and principles were all a fundamental basis for their belief in the Trinity, the Incarnation, the Virgin mother,

---

[49] MS A 27A, 15–17; ed. Libowitz, 45.
[50] Hamilton, *The Apocryphal Apocalypse*.
[51] On Ezra in antiquity, see David Weiss Halivni, *Peshat and Derash: Plain and Applied Meaning in Rabbinic Exegesis* (Oxford: Oxford University Press, 1991), chap. 5. On Ezra in medieval and early modern rabbinic literature, including *Kol Sakhal*, see Fishman, *Shaking the Pillars*, 53–55, 103–9; Halivni as cited in Fishman, 55, n. 62.

the [Virgin] birth, the name of Jesus, the Original Sin of Adam, which caused the death of the soul, and the days of the Messiah.[52]

Although he did not quote a single passage from Pico's theses and misrepresented their actual number, Modena offered a fairly accurate description of Pico's Christian Kabbalah.

Pico's theses included two sets derived from Kabbalah: forty-seven from the writings of earlier kabbalists, largely Menahem Recanati, and seventy-two by Pico himself.[53] In his own theses Pico employed Kabbalah precisely as Modena described. Three short theses offer some sense of how Pico sought to use Kabbalah as the basis for Christian doctrine: his seventh thesis, "No Hebrew Cabalist can deny that the name Jesus, if we interpret it following the method and principles of the Cabala, signifies precisely all this and nothing else, that is: *God the Son of God and the Wisdom of the Father, united to human nature in the unity of the assumption through the third person of God, who is the most ardent fire of love*"[54]; his thirtieth: "Following their own principles, the Cabalists must necessarily concede that the true Messiah will be such that of him it is truly said that he is God and the Son of God"[55]; and his thirty-eighth: "The effects that followed the death of Christ should convince every Cabalist that Jesus of Nazareth was the true Messiah."[56] In these theses, Pico used Kabbalah as proof for key elements of Christian doctrine including Jesus as the Messiah or Jesus as the Son of God. Other theses invoked the ten sefirot and the importance of Kabbalah for the revelation of doctrines such as the Trinity and Incarnation.[57] Modena rejected Pico's use of Kabbalah as a method of reading and as a doctrinal prop for the fundamental tenets of Christianity. The very Christianity of Pico's Kabbalah offended Modena, and he even attempted to marshal support for his position by pointing to Christian contemporaries of Pico who

---

[52] MS A 47A, 18–23; ed. Libowitz 96. Libowitz corrected Modena's error about the number of Pico's kabbalistic theses. Many of these topics formed the section headings of *Magen va-Herev*: "On the Sin of Adam, the First Human," "On the Trinity," "On the Incarnation," "On the Birth and Mary's Virginity," and "On the Messiah and the Conditions of His Arrival." By and large, however, Modena did not discuss Christian Kabbalah in *Magen va-Herev*.

[53] For the first group, see Farmer, *Syncretism in the West*, 344–63. For Recanati as the dominant source, see Wirszubski, *Pico della Mirandola's Encounter*, 53–55. For the second group, see Farmer, *Syncretism in the West*, 516–53. The title of the final set of kabbalistic theses reads LXXI rather than LXXII even though the number of theses is seventy-two. According to Copenhaver, the discrepancy is probably a simple error. See "Number, Shape, and Meaning in Pico's Christian Cabala," 41, n. 46. Modena referred to the number of Pico's own theses alternatively as sixty-one or seventy-one but not as seventy-two.

[54] Thesis 11, 7; Farmer, *Syncretism in the West*, 523.

[55] Thesis, 11, 30; Farmer, *Syncretism in the West*, 533.

[56] Thesis, 11, 38; Farmer, *Syncretism in the West*, 537.

[57] For the ten sefirot, see thesis 11, 66; for the Incarnation and Trinity; see thesis 11, 34; Farmer, *Syncretism in the West*, 549, 535.

referred to his theses as "new theology." Presumably this referred to the papal commission established by Innocent VIII that declared several of Pico's theses heretical or to the condemnation of all nine hundred theses following the publication of Pico's *Apology*.

Modena may have unequivocally rejected the Christianity of Pico's Kabbalah, but he maintained that a whole range of concepts within Jewish Kabbalah had the potential to be interpreted in a Christological manner. In a litany of terms included immediately following his discussion of Pico's theses, Modena implicated Jewish kabbalists in this process of Christian appropriation. For example, he mentioned the terms *or yashar*, *or hozer*, and *sah mesuhsah*, literally, "righteous light," "returning light," and "radiant transparency," which referred to the kabbalistic concept of three primordial lights.[58] Modena implied that this provided an opening for a Christian thinker to use a kabbalistic concept as proof for basic theological doctrine without further elaboration. In a fourteenth-century polemic against Christianity, Profiat Duran had reported that the kabbalistic doctrine of the three primordial lights had given rise to the Christian error of the Trinity.[59] Modena did not use the same terms as Duran to refer to each of these three lights, but his inclusion of the doctrine of the three lights was apparently a reference to a parallel to the Trinity. Similarly Modena mentioned *Shiur Komah*, a set of texts and doctrines that describe the body of God, without alluding to the possible parallel between it and the Incarnation.[60] He concluded the list of these kabbalistic concepts with an exclamation: "For the sake of the Lord I shall not recall more than one out of every hundred [of these terms], which would cause a great sensation to the ears and hearts of the believers among the children of Israel, and all the more so, shall be pleasing to the clever people who hold this belief."[61] The list of terms that concluded Modena's criticism of Christian Kabbalah was highly compressed, and Modena refused to elaborate on the possible parallels between Kabbalah and Christian theology.

Modena's account of Pico's Kabbalah included overlapping but distinct claims. He objected to the antiquity of Kabbalah in a similar fashion to his objection to Jewish kabbalists who maintained the same argument. But he further rejected the Christian content of Pico's kabbalistic theses. As

---

[58] Scholem, *Origins of the Kabbalah*, 354; Moshe Idel, *Ben: Sonship and Jewish Mysticism* (New York: Continuum, 2007), 600–601.

[59] Duran wrote that an unnamed Ashkenazi rabbi informed him that the basic tenets of Christianity grew out of the erroneous interpretation of Kabbalah. He cited the parallel between the Trinity and the three primordial lights, *or kadmon*, *or sah*, and *or mesuhsah*. See Frank Talmage, ed., *Kitve Pulmus le-Profiat Duran* (Jerusalem: Zalman Shazar Center, 1981), 11–13.

[60] Gershom Scholem, "*Shiur Komah*: The Mystical Shape of the Godhead," in *On the Mystical Shape of the Godhead*, 15–55.

[61] MS A 47B, 7–8; ed. Libowitz, 96.

a corollary to this, he made clear to Hamiz that Jewish kabbalists bore responsibility for employing a range of concepts that Christians could employ as proof for the basic tenets of their theology. Yet he never cited a single of Pico's theses much less engaged with them at any length. He demonstrated no awareness that Kabbalah was only one of several components of Pico's ancient theology and ignored the relationship between Kabbalah and magic so crucial to Pico's thought. Taken as a whole, it appears that this functioned within a larger rhetorical strategy of feigned ignorance rather than genuine lack of knowledge. Modena never actually admitted the extent of his knowledge of Pico or any other works of Christian Kabbalah. He referred to a passage from the *Oration* and *Apology* and treated it at some length without explicitly mentioning either work. As a cultural phenomenon, Christian Kabbalah was important enough to merit a harsh denunciation; however, Modena did not deign to analyze it on its own terms.

The lack of citations to Pico's theses and the schematic list of parallels between tenets of Christian theology and basic concepts of Kabbalah may have also derived from Modena's fear of possible conversion by his Jewish readers. Modena may not have wanted to fully articulate the similarities between Kabbalah and Christian theology lest his Jewish readers jettison Judaism altogether and convert to Christianity. While his direct addressee Hamiz remained a Jew, his student Samuel Nahmias converted to Christianity in 1649, less than two years after Modena's death.[62] In *Ari Nohem* Modena connected the popularity of Kabbalah with the conversion of Jews to Christianity: "I have already told you what was said[63] by the apostate in Israel, Hananel da Foligno, the father of the *little Jew*, the great preacher to those appointed in Bologna, about the book of the *Zohar*, which had been printed in that year, and it is sufficient merely to mention it."[64] Modena referred to a sixteenth-century Jewish convert to Catholicism named Hananel da Foligno, who was baptized as Alessandro Farnese, the name of Paul III before he became pope, but used the name Alessandro Franceschi. While scholars had previously attributed Hananel da Foligno's conversion to the collapse of his loan bank and as part of an effort to rehabilitate himself financially, a more recent study suggests that his conversion was due to his interest in Kabbalah.[65] In the fourteen years between his conversion in 1542 and his death in 1556, Alessandro Franceschi took an active part in church policy concerning the Jews. He served as a Hebrew scribe in the Vatican library and compiled an index of its Hebrew manuscripts; he

---

[62] See chapter 6.

[63] The abbreviation *mem shin*, here taken to mean *mah she-amar*, "what was said," given the context of preaching later in the sentence; however, it could also refer to *mah she-katav*, "what was written."

[64] MS A 47B, 9–10; ed. Libowitz, 96.

[65] Yosef Adichai Cohen, "Hananel da Foligno, the Man and his Time: Italy, the First Half of the Sixteenth Century" (Hebrew), Ph.D. diss., Bar Ilan University, 2004.

operated as a censor of Hebrew books and played a significant role in the campaign against the Talmud in 1553; he falsely accused the Roman Jewish community of having killed a Christian child and orchestrated a blood libel in 1555; and he composed a number of polemical works against Judaism, some of which drew upon Kabbalah to prove the truth of Christian doctrine. In addition, he supported the printing of the *Zohar*, a process that had begun before his death in 1556 but was not completed until a few years later.[66] At the time of his conversion, Hananel da Foligno took his son from his wife, who had refused to convert, and had him baptized. The son Ottavio, who adopted the same name as his father, became a famous preacher as well as bishop of Forli. Modena's characterization "*aviv shel ha-zudieto*," rendered as "father of the *little Jew*," referred to Alessandro Franceschi the younger, who was called *zudieto* or *ebreni*, Venetian and Italian for "the little Jew" throughout his career.[67] The phenomenon of Jewish converts to Christianity drawing on Kabbalah to proselytize to their former coreligionists was not a theoretical abstraction for Modena; it was an urgent and pressing matter that had a vivid and recent history.

Modena not only called attention to the impact that the printing of works such as the *Zohar* had on missionary activities against Jews in the middle of the sixteenth century, he also mentioned that Christians themselves had begun to distribute their own works of Kabbalah: "Johannes Reuchlin and others wrote [works] of this Kabbalah, and it spread out among them as an abundant support for the beams of their faith."[68] Just as he had decried the effects of printing on the transmission of Kabbalah and the popularization of esoteric knowledge among Jews, Modena pointed to similar effects on Christians:

> It was quite easy to destroy the ascent to God once this speculation [Kabbalah] was written down, and all the more so after it had been printed. Anyone who wants to take the name [of God] for a silver coin, takes it and ascends, becomes entangled and yearns with the beliefs in his heart and in his mouth. He makes it appear as if he sees God sitting on his exalted throne like Isaiah, or the animals of his chariot like Ezekiel, or the ancient of days like Daniel . . . over and above the continual damage to the apostates[69] caused by the printing of these books.[70]

Printed Kabbalah had given apostates and Christians unfettered access to what they thought were the ancient esoteric secrets of the Jews.

---

[66] Ibid., 48–52.

[67] Ibid., 46–48. According to Cohen, Italian Catholics frequently used such terms to refer to the Jewish past of a convert, and this constituted an affectionate epithet rather than a slur.

[68] MS A 47B, 10–11, ed. Libowitz, 96.

[69] MS A has *shomdim* or possibly *shomrim*. In other instances of this word in *Ari Nohem*, Sonne posited that it should be read *meshumadim*. See his "Church Use of the Kabbalah," 63.

[70] MS A 46A, 1–5; ed. Libowitz, 92–93.

Part of Modena's refusal to fully engage with Pico and other Christian kabbalists may have resulted from his skepticism of the category itself. Modena seemed to argue that there was something inherently Jewish about Kabbalah and that the very concept of Christian Kabbalah was an oxymoron. Thus the final chapter of *Ari Nohem* concluded on a harsh polemical note that drew a parallel between the transmission of Secrets of the Torah to gentiles and the instruction of Kabbalah to Christians. With evident approval, Modena cited a letter by Isaiah of Prague:[71]

> These are his words: "Would that they had not publicized the matters of the wisdom of the Kabbalah of the earlier sages. Since then, they have begun to call out in the name of God among the gentiles. And the sages, of blessed memory, said in chapter *Ein Dorshin*,[72] 'the teachings of the Torah are not to be transmitted to a gentile,' all the more so the Secrets of the Torah."[73] All the more so because you know that they, that is to say, the Christians, build their fundamental [beliefs] merely on allusions and the pronunciations of words.[74]

The Isaiah of Prague in question was none other than Isaiah Horowitz (ca. 1570–1626), author of *Shene Luhot ha-Brit* and one of the most important Ashkenazi kabbalists of the early seventeenth century, who had emigrated to Palestine late in life.[75] Samuel ben Meshulam, a scholar in Przemsysl, had asked Horowitz for copies of the writings of Isaac Luria. In his reply, published as part of Delmedigo's *Novlot Hokhmah*, Horowitz argued that the restrictions about transmitting Torah to gentiles were even more severe when it came to Kabbalah, which he characterized as "Secrets of the Torah." Elsewhere in *Ari Nohem*, Modena vigorously contested the identification of Kabbalah with the Secrets of the Torah. Furthermore, Modena had little patience for Luria's work, the general subject of Horowitz's letter. Yet he cited Horowitz and his strictures about the dissemination of Kabbalah to gentiles with evident approval. Modena used any argument he could to oppose the category of Christian Kabbalah. In this case, it meant positing that Kabbalah was and should remain the esoteric secrets of the Jews, a position he found anathema elsewhere.

---

[71] Modena quoted the letter from Joseph Solomon Delmedigo, *Sefer Novlot Hokhmah* in *Sefer Ta'alumot Hokhmah* (Hanau: 1629–1631), 3B.

[72] BT *Hagigah* 13A. For a sixteenth-century responsum that validated the instruction of Hebrew to gentiles by Jews but objected to the revelation of Jewish secrets, see David Kaufmann, "Elia Menachem Chalfan on Jews Teaching Hebrew to Non-Jews," *JQR* 9 (1897): 500–508.

[73] Sonne, "Church Use of the Kabbalah," 64–65.

[74] MS A 47B, 13–16; ed. Libowitz, 96–97.

[75] See Avivi, *Kabalat ha-Ari*, 1:435–36, 467–87. On Horowitz, see Elliot Wolfson, "The Influence of Luria on the Shelah" (Hebrew), *JSJT* 10 (1992): 423–48; Isaiah Horowitz, *The Generations of Adam*, trans. Miles Krassen (New York: Paulist Press, 1996).

The turn to Kabbalah by prominent Christian intellectuals in the centuries before the composition of *Ari Nohem* and the use of Kabbalah by Jews who had converted to Christianity as part of their arsenal to persuade their former coreligionists to convert to Christianity had left Modena incensed. In *Ari Nohem*, he rejected both of these phenomena in no uncertain terms. For Modena, Christian Kabbalah was not an abstract entity dependent on the written word. His contemporaries Gaffarel and Hamiz owned books that had been written by Pico or that they claimed had been part of Pico's library. As he mentioned at the outset of *Ari Nohem*, Modena had studiously avoided the subject of Kabbalah in his debates with Jewish apostates throughout his life. In his most sustained treatment of Christianity, *Magen va-Herev*, he generally avoided Kabbalah, Jewish or Christian. Modena opposed not so much the specific content of Christian Kabbalah as its very existence. But his opposition was inconsistent at the most basic level. In his criticism Modena seemed to accept the argument that Kabbalah was and should always be a form of esoteric knowledge exclusive to the Jews. The juxtaposition of this argument with other positions in *Ari Nohem* points to a crucial aspect of the work: its generic constraints as a work of criticism. In his defense of Maimonides, this meant distinguishing between the esoteric secrets of the *Guide* and Kabbalah espoused by Nahmanides and Meir ibn Gabbai. In the case of Christian Kabbalah, this involved denying Christian theologians the very possibility of engaging in sustained study with a domain of knowledge he chose, for a brief moment, to refer to as exclusively Jewish.

CHAPTER SIX

The Afterlife of *Ari Nohem*

> As one Jew-hating Austrian politician put it: "Scholarship is simply what one Jew copies from another."
>
> —George Steiner

Figure 11 (previous page). Title page to Yair Hayim Bacharach *Havot Yair*, Frankfurt, 1699.
Courtesy of the Library of the Jewish Theological Seminary.
In one of his responsa in this collection, Yair Hayim Bacharach pointedly alluded to *Ari Nohem*.

"SEFER ARI NOHEM, together with other of his [Modena's] polemical writings, remained hidden in his archives and did not see the light of day during his lifetime," thus Isaiah Tishby.[1] More recently David Malkiel maintained that "Modena's writings were not disseminated: almost none of his Hebrew works were reprinted and neither were his manuscript works recopied."[2] These assertions reflect an inherent bias toward print as the sole determinant of whether or not a given text was read. This chapter traces the reception of *Ari Nohem* in manuscript and challenges regnant interpretations about the importance of Modena's work in the two centuries after his death.

A census of extant manuscripts of *Ari Nohem* indicates that scribes continued to copy and annotate the work for two centuries. Much as in Modena's Venice, print was not the only medium through which scholars in Italy and elsewhere obtained and disseminated knowledge in the seventeenth and eighteenth centuries. The manuscript transmission of *Ari Nohem* was typical rather than aberrant for texts written by early modern Jewish intellectuals on a variety of subjects: polemical writings on Christianity, esoteric kabbalistic treatises, and epistolary campaigns against the mystical messiah Sabbatai Zevi and his followers.[3] The evidence of these manuscripts, combined with repeated citation of and allusion to *Ari Nohem* in letters, diaries, treatises, responsa, and compendia composed between 1639 and 1840, indicate that Jews and Christians continued to read Modena's text in nearly every generation between the death of the author and the printing of his book. This chapter aims to recover the readings of Modena's work in a period in which he was supposedly lost to the learned world, and before he became a hobbyhorse of nineteenth-century Jewish scholarship. The first part of this chapter traces some of the salient features about the copying and circulation of *Ari Nohem*. The second part identifies the more prominent readers of *Ari Nohem* and points to the uses they made of Modena's text.

---

[1] "General Introduction," 36.

[2] David Malkiel, "Leon Modena and His World: Past, Present, and Future," in *The Lion Shall Roar*, 8. But see the evidence surveyed in his "Christian Hebraism in a Contemporary Key: The Search for Hebrew Epitaph Poetry in Seventeenth-Century Italy," *JQR* 96 (2006): 132, 139.

[3] To a degree, this marks a line of continuity with the scribal habits of medieval Jewish scribes. See Malachi Beit-Arié, "Publication and Reproduction of Literary Texts in Medieval Jewish Civilization: Jewish Scribality and Its Impact on the Texts Transmitted," in Elman and Gershoni, *Transmitting Jewish Traditions*, 225–47.

The readings of *Ari Nohem*, particularly by scholars a generation or two younger than Modena, offer invaluable evidence about Modena's life and the early contexts in which his opposition to Kabbalah functioned. The early reception of *Ari Nohem* thus bears directly on Modena, his family, and his students. As one gets further away from Venice in the middle of the seventeenth century, discussions of *Ari Nohem* provide less insight into Modena and his immediate world. Instead they offer a vantage point on three crucial issues in eighteenth-century Italian Jewish culture: the modes of writing in the transmission of knowledge, the role of Kabbalah in the mental world of Jewish intellectuals, and the organization of information by bibliographers and encyclopedists. To claim that the copying and reading of *Ari Nohem* was the sole or even determining factor in any of these areas would be foolish; yet to ignore it or to explain it away would be equally so. Readers of *Ari Nohem* responded implicitly and explicitly to Modena's claims about the *Zohar*, Maimonides, and the history of Kabbalah. Like Modena in *Ari Nohem*, they paid careful attention to the material forms of the given texts they read and produced.

Historians of Kabbalah in Italy in this period tend to focus on Sabbatianism and its aftermath. The history of Sabbatianism points to certain limits in the reception of Modena's work as *Ari Nohem* did not play a role in the Sabbatian controversies. Important as the Sabbatian controversies were in the cultural history of Jewish life in early modern Italy, they were not the only defining factor in Italian Kabbalah. The attempts by a trio of Jewish intellectuals—Aviad Sar Shalom Basilea, Moses Hayim Luzzatto, and Joseph Ergas—to mount philosophical defenses of Kabbalah in the early decades of the eighteenth century indicate that opposition to Kabbalah expressed by figures such as Modena posed a considerable intellectual threat to an array of kabbalists working in different contexts.[4] In *Ari Nohem* Modena had articulated several of the signature arguments in the ongoing discussion about Kabbalah in Italy at the turn of the eighteenth century, and all three of these apologists responded to him either explicitly or implicitly. Finally, the decision whether or not to include *Ari Nohem* and Modena's polemics in the composition of reference works such as bibliographies and encyclopedias enables one to reconstruct the resources that other scholars sought to make available to a broader public in the late eighteenth century.

THE CIRCULATION OF *ARI NOHEM* IN MANUSCRIPT

A census of known copies of *Ari Nohem* indicates that the work survives in fourteen manuscripts, either alone or as part of a larger codex that included

---

[4] Luzzatto's alleged Sabbatianism had little direct bearing on his response to Modena. See below.

other works.⁵ Of these fourteen witnesses, five date from after 1800, including one that contains only excerpts from the work.⁶ Of the remaining nine, two appear to have Modena's authentication in the form of a colophon identified in the first chapter.⁷ The other seven have been dated to the seventeenth or eighteenth century. Several points emerge when these witnesses are viewed in aggregate. First and foremost, the transmission of *Ari Nohem* as a complete and integral text was fairly stable over the course of two centuries. With only one exception, *Ari Nohem* was transmitted in its entirety rather than piecemeal, and all these witnesses contain a work divided into three separate parts. In turn, each section consists of multiple chapters. The witnesses differ on the numbering of chapters in one crucial respect. The two manuscripts authorized by Modena have a long section at the beginning of the second part that does not have a chapter heading. In many of the later manuscripts as well as in the two printed editions, this section has been turned into chapter 11, bringing the total number of chapters in the work to thirty-one. In the two manuscripts authorized by Modena, the total number of chapters is thirty, and this section does not constitute its own chapter. The transmission of *Ari Nohem* in its entirety contrasts with other early modern works on similar themes. Moses Hayim Luzzatto's *Hoqer u-Mekubal*, a philosophical defense of Kabbalah examined later in this chapter, survives in multiple witnesses, none of which contains the text in its entirety or in the order Luzzatto hoped it would appear in print.⁸ Joseph Solomon Delmedigo's *Ahuz* letter survives in multiple copies, in manuscript and in print, some which do not have the entire text.⁹

At an early stage Modena's work began to circulate under a variety of titles. One group of manuscripts circulated as *Ari Nohem*, as Modena referred to the work in his other writings and as it appeared in both authorized copies.¹⁰ A second group circulated as *Sha'agat Aryeh*, one of Modena's other works.¹¹ The similarity between the two Hebrew phrases—*Ari Nohem*, "A Roaring Lion," and *Sha'agat Aryeh*, "The Lion's Roar"—may have contributed to the confusion of early modern scribes. A third group has both *Ari*

---

⁵ Manuscripts A, B, G, L, and M contain *Ari Nohem*. The remaining manuscripts contain other texts in the codices.

⁶ Manuscripts D, E, F, H, L; MS F contains an excerpt.

⁷ Manuscripts A and B.

⁸ Joseph Avivi, "*Ma'amar ha-Vikuah* of Ramhal" (Hebrew), *Ha-ma'ayan* (1974): 49–54; Isaiah Tishby, *Messianic Mysticism: Moses Hayim Luzzatto and the Padua School* (Oxford: Littman Library, 2008), 49–57.

⁹ Penkower, "S. D. Luzzatto, Vowels, and Accents," 128.

¹⁰ Manuscripts A, B, D, and L are titled *Ari Nohem*. Modena's autobiography, responsa, and reading notes leave no doubt that the title was *Ari Nohem*. See above.

¹¹ Manuscripts I, J, and K have the title *Sha'agat Aryeh*. Manuscript G has it as well, but the title appears to have been written in a different hand from that of the scribe who copied the text. Modena wrote *Sha'agat Aryeh* in response to *Kol Sakhal*. See Fishman, *Shaking the Pillars of Exile*, 3–4.

Nohem and *Sha'agat Aryeh* in the title.[12] Finally, one witness has no title at all.[13] Here again, comparison with Luzzatto's work proves particularly instructive. Luzzatto's philosophical defense of Kabbalah circulated under two different titles, *Ma'amar ha-Vikuah* and *Hoqer u-Mekubal*; the former was the phrase he used for it in his correspondence, and the latter was the title as it appeared in some of the manuscripts and as a printed book decades after his death. In addition, another version of the work edited by his students appeared under the title *Milhemet Moshe*.[14]

One of the most revealing aspects of the manuscript circulation of *Ari Nohem* pertains to the other texts in the codices that contain the work. Scribes frequently copied other texts by Modena or by other authors on similar topics. Of the nine manuscripts where *Ari Nohem* or an excerpt of it is included as part of a series of texts, six also contain *Ben David*, Modena's polemic against the transmigration of souls.[15] The physical evidence in these codices corresponds to the textual evidence of reactions by readers in the seventeenth and eighteenth centuries. Moses Zacut and Isaac Lampronti responded to Modena's arguments in both *Ari Nohem* and *Ben David* at the same time. Another codex that included *Ari Nohem* also included a copy of Delmedigo's *Ahuz* letter. Codices with multiple works by the same author or multiple works on a similar theme appear to be early modern versions of copybooks or anthologies. Luzzatto's kabbalistic works circulated in a similar manner, as did those of several other authors.

Scribes who copied *Ari Nohem* as well as later readers of their manuscripts reacted in the margins. These annotations reflect different attitudes toward Modena's text and tend to fall into one of three categories: annotation, correction, or contestation. Some of these notes attempt to correct the given text of *Ari Nohem*, quite possibly against another copy of the work, in an effort to restore what Modena had written. For example, Modena described Delmedigo as someone "who fashions himself as defending the wisdom of Kabbalah and praises it; but his intention is to degrade it and denigrate it with all his might. Truly he is a cunning sage and master of all forms of knowledge."[16] In a later copy of the work a scribe omitted this passage. In an annotation in a different hand, another reader reinserted the phrase in the margin at the bottom of the page.[17] Other annotations indicate a much less respectful attitude toward Modena's text. Often a scribe or later reader interjected in the margins in attempt to rebut Modena's point. For example, in the first chapter Modena treated the attempt by various kabbalists to

---

[12] Manuscripts C, E, F, H, and N.
[13] Manuscript M.
[14] *Milhemet Moshe* (Warsaw: Unterhendler, 1889).
[15] Manuscripts C, E, H, I, J, and N.
[16] MS A 39B, 25–40A, 2; ed. Libowitz, 78.
[17] MS C, 20B.

argue that Kabbalah constitutes both tradition and knowledge. At the same time, he argued, kabbalists attempt to protect themselves from any form of counterargument by invoking the verse in the Psalms, "God protects the simple."[18] After pointing to the frequent invocation of this verse, Modena wrote that he would "heap great ridicule upon these sayings."[19] In one copy of *Ari Nohem* this phrase was underlined and a later reader wrote in the margin, "may the Lord have mercy on him."[20]

Some readers attempted to supplement Modena's account with other information. One instance, discussed earlier in chapter 3, relates to the closing epistle of the treatise. Modena had warned Hamiz and later readers not to fabricate stories about a deathbed embrace of Kabbalah. At least two later copyists pointed to evidence that disputed this point. They claimed to have discovered a text written in Modena's own hand that indicated he had come to believe in the transmigration of souls at the end of his life.[21] Here too, evidence from scribal copies coincides with the written responses to the work. In his travel diaries, Hayim Joseph David Azulai mentioned the story about Modena and his acceptance of the belief in the transmigration of souls.[22] In the centuries after his death, Modena had become a historical personage whom later readers sought to appropriate. The two scribes who recounted this story appealed to a document written in Modena's own hand. Were such a document to exist, it would necessarily mitigate the critique in the polemic that these scribes had just copied and read. The marginal and interlinear notes offer repeated indications that Modena's readers were hardly passive in accepting his criticisms of Kabbalah. They used the open spaces of their manuscript copies to contest his claims.

Ari Nohem in Early Modern Culture

Modena's polemical writings circulated in manuscript between the time of his death and their first appearance in print in the nineteenth century. New Christians returning to Judaism read and annotated his criticism of Christianity, *Magen va-Herev*, and may have even used it as a manual of theological orientation.[23] Saul Berlin, an eighteenth-century rabbi who forged a collection of medieval rabbinic responsa entitled *Besamim Rosh*,

---

[18] Ps. 116:6.
[19] MS A 6B, 11–16; ed. Libowitz, 3.
[20] MS B 2A, note at line 19.
[21] MS N 31B; MS K 40A.
[22] *Ma'agal Tov*, ed. Freimann, 113.
[23] Fishman, "Changing Early Modern Jewish Discourse about Christianity," 178–83.

may have read *Kol Sakhal*.²⁴ In addition, Modena's *Magen ve-Zinah* and *Ben David* survive in multiple manuscript copies. Of all his polemical writings, *Ari Nohem* circulated the most extensively over the course of the seventeenth and eighteenth centuries. More copies of the work survive, and a considerable number of writers, Jewish and Christian, referred or alluded to the work in their own writings.²⁵ In nearly every generation between its composition and its appearance in print, at least one and sometimes several scholars mentioned or engaged with *Ari Nohem*.

The evidence for the circulation of *Ari Nohem* in Italy in the immediate years after its composition is circumstantial; however, it bears directly on Modena and the impact his work had on his contemporaries. Six years after Modena had written his criticism, Samuel Aboab (ca.1610–1694) alluded to it in his correspondence with Moses Zacut (ca. 1620–1697) discussed briefly in chapter 1. Over the course of their careers that spanned almost the entirety of the second half of the seventeenth century, Aboab and Zacut occupied positions of considerable prominence in the northern Italian rabbinate and conducted a long correspondence.²⁶ Aboab served as the rabbi who heard the testimony of the prophet Nathan of Gaza when he testified before the Venetian rabbinate after the apostasy of Sabbatai Zevi.²⁷ In the years after Modena's death, Zacut collaborated with Hamiz on the publication of Hebrew books and composed some of the earliest dramatic works in Hebrew.²⁸

In the summer of 1646, Zacut, a young scholar who had recently moved to Venice, wrote to Aboab, who was living in Verona. Zacut's letter has not survived, but his essential request can be reconstructed from Aboab's response. Zacut had met a scholar in Venice who had opposed Kabbalah

---

²⁴ Fishman, *Shaking the Pillars of Exile*, 172–74. On Berlin, see Fishman, "Forging Jewish Memory: *Besamim Rosh* and the Invention of Pre-emancipation Jewish Culture," in Carlebach, Efron, and Myers, *Jewish History and Jewish Memory*, 70–88; Emile G. L. Schrijver, "Saul of Berlin's *Besamim Rosh*: The Maskilic Appreciation of Medieval Knowledge," in *Sepharad in Ashkenaz: Medieval Knowledge and Eighteenth-Century Enlightened Jewish Discourse*, ed. Resianne Fontaine, Andrea Schatz, and Irene Zwiep, 249–59 (Amsterdam: Koninklijke Nederlandse Akademie van Wetenschappen, 2007).

²⁵ Fishman identified four copies of *Kol Sakhal*. A survey of Modena's other polemical writings conducted with the catalogue of the Institute for Microfilmed Hebrew Manuscripts identified eight copies of *Magen va-Herev*, six of which postdate 1800; eight copies of *Ben David*, six of which are in codices that contain *Ari Nohem* and two of which postdate 1800; and six copies of *Magen ve-Zinah*, four of which postdate 1800.

²⁶ See Meir Benayahu, ed., *Dor Ehad ba'aretz: Igrot Rabi Shmuel Aboav ve-Rabi Moshe Zakut be-inyene Eretz Yisrae* (Jerusalem: Yad Harav Nissim, 1988).

²⁷ Scholem, *Sabbatai Sevi*, 764–70.

²⁸ On Zacut, see Robert Bonfil, "Rabbis, Jesuits, and Riddles: An Inquiry into the World of Moses Zacut" (Hebrew), *Italia* 13–15 (2001): 169–89. *Peamim* 96 (2003) includes a series of articles on Zacut. Moses Zacut, *Esa et Levavi: Shirim*, ed. Dvora Bregman (Jerusalem: Ben-Zvi Institute, 2009).

and had criticized the belief in the transmigration of souls. Incensed at the audacity of this unnamed scholar, the young Zacut planned to write a defense of the belief in the transmigration of souls and had written to Aboab to solicit reading suggestions. Although Aboab never explicitly mentioned *Ari Nohem* or Modena in his response, he pointedly alluded to the author and his book on several occasions:[29]

> Your precious letter brought news that forces the heart to tears and causes grief, about this would-be scholar of rabbinic lore, may God forgive him, for in his old age his old sickness has returned, and, as has been his custom for the past several years, he argues against doctrines and beliefs, the cornerstone of whose foundations he has never laid eyes upon. And what is more, he wants to befoul our air a second time by printing it in front of the gentiles. I protest against him, if he does such a thing, for the sin of Judah shall be hewn in writing with an iron tip.[30]

The doddering old man evidently had a reputation among the rabbinic elite in northern Italy for acerbic criticism and hoped it would appear in print.

Aboab counseled Zacut to refrain from writing and printing a defense of the transmigration of souls. The issue was quite complicated and not one that Zacut should engage with in a public forum. A slightly elder Aboab counseled the young and angry Zacut to avoid making a fool of himself in print by engaging complex theology at so young an age. As for the elderly rabbinic critic in Venice, Aboab advised Zacut to appeal to him in person: "But my heart tells me that if men of understanding who seek justice deferentially beseech the aforementioned sage not to make his roars heard in public, he will heed their calls, and say enough with our raging sorrows that have come from our sins in that city [Venice] and all around it."[31] Aboab further corroborated Zacut's account of the critic of Kabbalah in Venice and added a crucial bit of information:

> But I was already informed by one of the gentile officials of this town [Verona] that when he was in [Venice] the aforementioned sage revealed to him his opposition to the wisdom of Kabbalah. But he [the official] rebuked him [the scholar] with open contempt by saying to him that as far as he had heard and understood, these books [of Kabbalah] had deep and authentic roots and had been transmitted by the ancient sages. Woe upon the people for such an affront to the Torah!

---

[29] Aboab's letter appears in what was formerly London MS Montefiore 257–58, 11B. The manuscript has been sold, and I have examined it on microfiche at the Library of Congress. For editions of the letter, see Benayahu, "The Positions of Rabbi Moses Zacut and Rabbi Samuel Aboab"; Bezalel Divlitzki "The Hasid R. Samuel Aboab and His Letters" (Hebrew), in *Kovetz Etz Hayim* 2 (2008): 219–33. Tishby appears to have referred to this letter in "General Introduction," 35, n. 167.

[30] Benayahu, "The Positions of Rabbi Moses Zacut and Rabbi Samuel Aboab," 41.

[31] Ibid., 42.

And the lion roared to publish his opinions. Who shall not fear for the desecration of the Lord and his Torah.[32]

Aboab punned repeatedly on the title of Modena's work, using "*nehamotav*," his roars, to refer to the aged man's criticisms and "*Aryeh Sha'ag*," the lion roared, to refer to his desire for his work to appear in print. "The sin of Judah" was probably a reference to Modena's name. One would have to be tone deaf to miss such pointed references. In a postscript to the letter, Aboab included a list of rabbinic opponents to the transmigration of souls. The list mentioned six writers, four of whom—Joseph Albo, Saadya Gaon, Yedaiah Bedersi, and Samuel Zarza—had appeared in Modena's list of antikabbalistic writers at the end of his manuscript of *Ari Nohem*.[33]

Aboab refrained from explicitly mentioning either Modena or the title of his work. While the constant allusion, coupled with a refusal to name the object of discussion, may have been a performance of his own erudition for his younger colleague, Aboab may have been motivated by other concerns. Rabbinic correspondence in early modern Italy was frequently semipublic.[34] Aboab may not have wanted to criticize openly one of his senior colleagues, even one whose opinions he clearly thought anathema, in a letter whose circulation he could not control. Aboab's family had long-standing connections with the aged rabbi in question. Modena had received a salary from the Aboab family for his work in a yeshiva in Venice until their move to Verona in 1638.[35] In November 1647, just over a year after his exchange with Zacut, Aboab received a stinging letter from Modena himself. Modena's letter does not appear to have survived, but Aboab's response indicates that Modena was furious when he learned that the Hebrew press in Verona planned to print a new edition of Jacob ibn Habib's *Ein Ya'akov* that would compete directly with his own *Bet Yehudah*.[36] In his conciliatory response, Aboab denied that he or his family had any connection to the Hebrew press in Verona and promised to intervene on Modena's behalf. He concluded by imploring Modena to remember their prior affection for one another. Aboab's response to Modena displays none of the vitriol against an aged rabbi who had clung to his misguided opinions; to the contrary, he

---

[32] Ibid., 41.

[33] The list does not appear in Benayahu's edition. See Divlitzki, "The Hasid R. Samuel Aboab," 233.

[34] Several rabbinic controversies were conducted through the circulation of semipublic letters. For a later example, see Elisheva Carlebach, *The Pursuit of Heresy: Rabbi Moses Hagiz and the Sabbatian Controversies* (New York: Columbia University Press, 1990), 254. A selection of Zacut's letters later appeared in print. See Moses Zacut, *Igrot ha-Remez* (Livorno: 1780).

[35] *Autobiography*, 151, 259.

[36] Benayahu, "Sources Concerning the Printing and Distribution of Hebrew Books in Italy" (Hebrew), *Sinai* 34 (1954): 157–58, 186–87.

was respectful to the point of obsequiousness and expressed his allegedly sincere desire to hear Modena preach from the pulpit in the near future.

Aboab's correspondence with Zacut yields three crucial pieces of information about the immediate context of *Ari Nohem*. First, as discussed in the first chapter, Modena had hoped to print the work in his own lifetime. As late as the summer of 1646, less than two years before his death in the winter of 1648 and before his health began to fail in late 1647, he still nourished hopes of seeing it in print. Second, Modena's opinions were well known among the rabbinic elite of northern Italy in the years before his death. Zacut and Aboab may have met or corresponded with Modena, but they were hardly his close colleagues or students. In Amsterdam Aboab had studied with Saul Levi Morteira, a Venetian Jew of Ashkenazi descent presumed to have been Modena's student, and had come to Venice with the intention of continuing on to Palestine.[37] Aboab may have respected Modena as a senior colleague and counseled Zacut not to engage in open debate with him, but he hardly considered Modena his teacher. Third, Modena's opposition to Kabbalah was well known among contemporary Catholics. Aboab indicated that a city official from Verona had already given him a similar report of Modena's criticism of Kabbalah and had attempted to defend the antiquity of kabbalistic books to the aging rabbi.

This unnamed official was not the only Catholic in early modern Italy to learn of Modena's opposition to Kabbalah. Two other figures, Giulio Morosini (1612–1687) and Giulio Bartolocci (1613–1687), have been identified as possible readers of *Ari Nohem*.[38] Born Samuel Nahmias into a Sephardic family in Venice, Morosini had converted to Catholicism in 1649, the year after Modena's death. Prior to his conversion he had been a close student of Modena's, and his father David had funded the publication of Modena's *Bet Lehem Yehudah* in 1625.[39] In his *Via della fede*, Moro-

---

[37] On Morteira as a descendant of the Katznellenbogens, a distinguished Ashkenazi family in Venice, see Marc Saperstein, *Exile in Amsterdam: Saul Levi Morteira's Sermons to a Congregation of "New Jews"* (Cincinnati: HUC Press, 2005), 5. On his connection with Modena, who has repeatedly been described as his teacher, see p. 6. Saperstein characterizes their relationship as "cordial if occasionally strained." In a letter dated June 15, 1618, Modena chastised Morteira for criticizing the words of the sages and Kabbalah in public. See *Letters*, 162; as cited in Saperstein, *Exile in Amsterdam*, 166, n. 74.

[38] Sonne, "Church Use of the Kabbalah," 61.

[39] On Morosini and Modena, see D. Simonsen, "Giulio Morosinis Mitteilungen über seinen Lehrer Leon da Modena und seine jüdischen Zeitgenossen," *Festschrift zum Siebzigsten Geburstage A. Berliner's*, ed. Aron Freimann and Meir Hildesheimer, 337–44 (Frankfurt: J. Kauffmann, 1903); Benjamin Ravid, "*Contra Judaeos* in Seventeenth-Century Italy: Two Responses to the *Discorso* of Simone Luzzatto by Melchiore Palontrotti and Giulio Morosini," *AJS Review* 7 (1982): 328–51. I have not had access to J. M. Cohen, "Il ghetto di Venezia nella rivistazione polemica e nostaligica di Giulio Morosini già Samuel Nahmias (1612–1687)," tesi di laurea, University of Amsterdam, 1989; cited in Pier Cesare Ioly Zorattini, *Processi del S. Uffizio di Venezia contro ebrei e giudaizzanti (1642–1681)* (Florence: L. S. Olschki, 1993), 11:10.

sini recounted the process of his conversion to Catholicism and stressed Modena's praise for Jesus as "*uomo da bene*," as one of the factors that drew him to Christianity.[40] Throughout the work, he mentioned Modena and drew on his *Riti*.[41] Although he never explicitly cited *Ari Nohem*, Morosini adopted a fairly negative attitude to Kabbalah.[42] If he had not actually read *Ari Nohem*, he was apparently aware of his teacher's opposition to Kabbalah.

In contrast to Morosini, who had a close personal connection to Modena, Giulio Bartolocci does not seem to have known him. Bartolocci was professor of Hebrew at the Collegio dei Neofiti in Rome and a student of a Jewish convert to Catholicism Giovanni Battista. Between 1675 and his death, he edited and published the multivolume *Bibliotheca magna rabbinica*. The work contains an account of Jewish literature that would serve as one of the most important bibliographic guides to Hebrew and Jewish literatures in the coming centuries. At various points Bartolocci and Carlo Giuseppe Imbonati, his student who completed the fourth volume, which was published posthumously, drew on arguments made in *Ari Nohem*. In one instance, they repeat the claim that recent Jewish converts to Christianity were particularly attracted to Kabbalah.[43] The evidence of Jewish and Christian scholars in Italy reading *Ari Nohem* in the decades immediately after its composition amount to a combination of allusions to Modena's name and the title of his work as well as a repetition of similar arguments against and about Kabbalah. Four of the possible readers—Zacut, Aboab, Morosini, and the unnamed official from Verona—had a personal relationship or exchange with Modena about Kabbalah before his death. Even if these figures had not read *Ari Nohem*, they appear to have been aware of its content and its arguments.

Given the variety of contexts in which *Ari Nohem* was read or alluded to in the decades after its composition, it is all the more remarkable that the text and its arguments played no role in one of the central episodes of

---

[40] *Via della fede* (Rome, 1683), 105; as cited in Cecil Roth, "Leone da Modena and the Christian Hebraists of His Age," in *Jewish Studies in Memory of Israel Abrahams*, 384–401 (New York: Jewish Institute of Religion, 1927), 390–91. On *Via della fede*, see Pier Cesare Ioly Zorattini, "Derekh Teshuvah: La via del ritorno," in *L'identità dissimulata: giudaizzanti iberici nell'Europa cristiana dell'età moderna*, ed. Pier Cesare Ioly Zorattini, 195–248 (Florence: L. S. Olschki, 2000). On Modena's Jesus, see the literature on *Magen va-Herev* cited in chapter 1, n. 70.

[41] *Via della fede*, 104.

[42] Sonne, "Church Use of the Kabbalah," 61.

[43] Giulio Bartolocci, *Bibliotheca Magna Rabbinica* (Rome: Sacrae congregationis de propaganda fide, 1675–1694), 4:233, 422; as cited by Sonne, "Church Use of the Kabbalah," 61, n. 19. On Bartolocci and his bibliographic project, see Saverio Campanini, "Wege in die Stadt der Bücher. Ein Beitrag zur Geschichte der hebräischen Bibliographie: Die katholische bibliographische 'Dynastie' Iona-Bartolocci-Imbonati," in *Reuchlin und seine Erbern*, ed. Peter Schäfer and Irina Wandrey, 61–76 (Ostfildern: Thorbecke, 2005).

seventeenth-century Jewish history: the messianism of Sabbetai Zevi.[44] A charismatic kabbalist whose learning has been the subject of vigorous debate, Sabbetai Zevi and his prophet Nathan of Gaza founded a messianic movement among the Jews of Europe and the Mediterranean in the middle of the 1660s. When Sabbetai Zevi converted to Islam at the behest of the Ottoman Sultan, the movement lost much of its energy; however, his most avid supporters held to their beliefs, and Sabbatianism continued to be one of the most divisive and potent forces in the history of the Jews well into the eighteenth century.

The role of Kabbalah, particularly Lurianic Kabbalah, in Sabbatian messianism has been the subject of intense scholarly debate.[45] What is beyond dispute, however, is that Kabbalah in its various forms was bound up with the messianic movement. Sabbetai Zevi and his prophets drew on Kabbalah as a source of authority and pointed to kabbalistic texts and invoked kabbalistic hermeneutics to support their claims.[46] The believers, as they were known, were not without their critics both during Sabbetai Zevi's lifetime and after his death. Jacob Sasportas (1610–1698), an itinerant rabbi who settled for a time in Amsterdam, penned a series of scathing attacks at the height of the messianic fervor. In the eighteenth century, Moses Hagiz (1671–1751) and Jacob Emden (1697–1776) sought to root out any vestiges of Sabbatianism among the Jews of Europe. None of these outspoken critics ever sought to delegitimize Kabbalah along the lines of Modena's *Ari Nohem*. All three were committed kabbalists, and none of them ever engaged in a total assault of Kabbalah. They repeatedly argued that Sabbetai Zevi and his prophets perverted genuine kabbalistic theology rather than claiming that kabbalistic theology itself was inherently suspect.[47]

---

[44] See Scholem, *Sabbatai Sevi*; Matt Goldish, *The Sabbatean Prophets* (Cambridge: Harvard University Press, 2004); Jacob Barnai, *Shabtaut: Hebetim Hevratiyim* (Jerusalem: Zalman Shazar Center, 2000); Rachel Elior, ed., *Ha-Halom ve-Shivro: ha-tenuah ha-Shabtait u-sheluhoteha* (Jerusalem: Magnes Press, 2001).

[45] Scholem saw Sabbatianism as the dialectical outcome of the spread of Lurianic Kabbalah; Idel and others reversed this paradigm and saw the diffusion of Lurianic Kabbalah as the direct result of the Sabbatian movement. See Scholem, *Sabbatai Sevi*, 22–93; Idel, "'One from a Town, Two from a Clan'"; Gries, *Sifrut ha-hanhagot*, chap. 2.

[46] In addition to the literature cited above, see Avraham Elqayam, "The Sacred *Zohar* of Sabbetai Sevi" (Hebrew), *Kabbalah* 3 (1998): 345–87.

[47] On Sasportas, see *Zizat Novel Zvi*, ed. Isaiah Tishby (Jerusalem: Mossad Bialik, 1954); Goldish, *The Sabbatean Prophets*, chap. 5. On Hagiz, see Carlebach, *The Pursuit of Heresy*. On Emden, see Yehuda Liebes, "The Messianism of R. Jacob Emden and Its Relation to Sabbatianism," *Tarbiz* 49 (1980): 122–65; Jacob J. Schacter, "Rabbi Jacob Emden: Life and Major Works," Ph.D. diss., Harvard University, 1988. For evidence that Emden knew of Modena's work, see below. Emden's *Mitpahat Sefarim* (Altona, 1768) was one of the principal early modern discussions of the medieval origins of the *Zohar*. See Tishby, "General Introduction," 38–43; Huss, *Ke-zohar ha-rakia*, 313–23; and below.

A significant exception to this group of Sabbatian critics who were also kabbalists was the Italian Hebrew poet of Portuguese descent, Jacob Frances (1615–1667). A sensitive poet who wrote of loss and grief, Frances was also a biting critic of contemporary followers of Sabbetai Zevi. He used his verse to ridicule their beliefs, composing mock poems in honor of Sabbatai Zevi and parodying their faith in the prophet Nathan as a would-be Elijah.[48] Unlike his contemporary Sasportas or the eighteenth-century anti-Sabbatians Hagiz and Emden, Frances was also a critic of Kabbalah.[49] In a poem that was printed as a broadside in Mantua in 1660 or 1661, several years before the eruption of Sabbatian messianism, Frances ridiculed his contemporaries for clinging to Kabbalah. His poem repeated many of the arguments made in *Ari Nohem*, such as the attempt by the ignorant to seek out Kabbalah before acquainting themselves with the basic rudiments of Jewish law.[50] Frances's poem was not well received by the Mantuan rabbinate. In a poetic defense to his printed broadside, Frances drew on the same phrase from Proverbs that gave Modena's work its title.[51] However, he never explicitly mentioned *Ari Nohem*.

As one progresses further from Modena's Venice in time and space, one can trace the readers of *Ari Nohem* with both greater ease and greater difficulty. The explicit mention of Modena and his work by the majority of his readers in the eighteenth century facilitates their identification; however, a basic fact frequently remains unaccounted for: how they had access to a manuscript of the book. Zacut, Aboab, Morosini, and the unnamed official from Verona all lived in Venice or the Veneto, and one can assume that they read *Ari Nohem* or heard about it in Venice or a nearby town. By the turn of the eighteenth century, Modena's work had acquired a reputation among a small circle of learned scholars who quoted or alluded to it without indicating how they had come across it. These readers drew on *Ari Nohem*, responded to its criticisms, and grappled with the sources it quoted in their attempts to mount philosophical defenses of Kabbalah or place Kabbalah within the ideal Jewish curriculum. Kabbalah had become the object of intense scrutiny by a variety of figures, many of them committed kabbalists, and Modena's *Ari Nohem* served alternatively as a point of departure or a cartographic description of prior sources for their discussions.

One of the monumental figures of early modern Jewish culture, Yair Hayim Bacharach, alluded to *Ari Nohem* in one of his works. Born into a

---

[48] For a parody of praise of Sabbetai Zevi, see *Kol Shirei Ya'akov Frances*, ed. Peninah Naveh (Jerusalem: Mossad Bialik, 1969), 470–74; for comparison between Nathan and Elijah, see 440.

[49] For an attempt to minimize Frances' criticism of Kabbalah, see Naveh, Introduction to *Kol Shirei Ya'akov Frances*, 91–104. For a harsh rebuttal, see Ezra Fleischer, "Review of *Kol Shirei Ya'akov Frances*" (Hebrew), *KS* 45 (1970): 185–87.

[50] *Kol Shirei Ya'akov Frances*, 401–8.

[51] Ibid., 409, line 30.

distinguished rabbinic family, Bacharach lived in Prague as a child before moving to Worms, where his father Samson served as rabbi. Before his death, Samson attempted to arrange for his son to succeed him as rabbi of Worms. But when he died in 1670, his son was passed over and spent nearly three decades teaching and writing in the privacy of his own home. In 1699 Bacharach finally assumed the position of rabbi of Worms, only to die three years later at the age of fifty-six. Bacharach's intellectual world defies easy summary. He was a man of astonishing erudition and encyclopedic learning who wrote assiduously throughout his life. Of his voluminous writings, however, he printed only an edition of his father's responsa, *Hut ha-Shani*, and a volume of his own responsa, *Havot Yair*. He repeatedly reneged on plans to print *Mekor Hayim*, his commentary to the first volume of Karo's *Shulhan Arukh*, and it did not appear in print until the twentieth century. Over the course of his life, he filled a series of notebooks on a wide range of subjects, such as critical notes to a contemporary commentary on the Passover Haggadah, a lexicon of Talmudic terms, and novellae on tractates of the Talmud. While he destroyed many of his own writings, some of his notebooks have survived.[52]

In failing health at the end of his life, Bacharach enlisted several copyists to select a series of his responsa that appeared in 1699 as *Havot Yair*.[53] One responsum included an extensive discussion of the value of Kabbalah.[54] An unnamed correspondent had asked Bacharach whether he should embark upon the study of Kabbalah, having read various statements in the *Zohar* on the importance of Kabbalah for a true comprehension of God. Bacharach began his answer with an elaborate exercise in self-effacement that simultaneously constituted a virtuoso display of his own familiarity with Kabbalah. After a plethora of citations to kabbalistic books such as *Pardes Rimonim* and Judah Hayyat's *Minhat Yehudah* that he assumed were well known to his reader, he mentioned critics of Kabbalah such as Elijah Delmedigo: "Presumably you have in your possession the book *Behinot ha-Dat*[55] which sought to mislead many [people] on page 5B.[56] But Joseph Solomon Delmedigo stood up against him like a roaring lion [*ke-Ari Nohem*] in his work

[52] See David Kaufmann, "Jair Chaim Bacharach: A Biographical Sketch," *JQR* 3 (1891): 292–313, 485–536.

[53] Ibid., 528.

[54] Responsum no. 210. Yair Hayim Bacharach, *Havot Yair: Teshuvot* (Frankfurt, 1699), 197A–201B. See Isadore Twersky, "Law and Spirituality in the Seventeenth Century: A Case Study in R. Yair Hayyim Bacharach," in Twersky and Septimus, *Jewish Thought in the Seventeenth Century*, 447–67.

[55] The text clearly gives *Behinot*, not *Behinat*.

[56] Whether or not Bacharach's correspondent had a copy of *Ta'alumot Hokhmah*, which contained the edition of *Behinat ha–Dat* cited here, Bacharach himself had access to the work. For Kabbalah in Bacharach's responsa, see Jay Berkovitz, "Custom in the Legal Thought of Rabbi Yair Hayim Bacharach" (Hebrew), in *Mehkarim be-toldot Yehude Ashkenaz: Sefer Yovel*

Mazref le-Hokhmah."⁵⁷ While one cannot prove decisively that Bacharach had read Modena's work, it hardly seems accidental that he used the phrase *Ari Nohem* in the midst of his discussion of Elijah Delmedigo and Joseph Solomon Delmedigo on the value of Kabbalah.

Bacharach's discussion of Kabbalah contained several similarities to *Ari Nohem*. Both used Joseph Solomon Delmedigo's collection as a point of departure for their own analysis. Like Modena, Bacharach had encountered Delmedigo during his wanderings. As a young boy in Prague, Bacharach had observed Delmedigo, and he later met him in Worms in 1652.⁵⁸ Bacharach and Modena both doubted Delmedigo's ostensible defense of Kabbalah. Modena was fully aware of the enigmatic and inscrutable nature of Delmedigo's anthology, even as he plundered it for sources and references. He had concluded that his younger colleague was actually an opponent of Kabbalah, although it remains unclear if he arrived at such a judgment in order to buttress his own position. Bacharach took a similar if more nuanced position: "But he himself [Delmedigo] tainted all of his own opinions by virtue of what he wrote there [in *Mazref le-Hokhmah*] on page 20A: 'that it is impossible to decipher a person's true opinions from his books. Sometimes a person will write a book that erects an edifice in support of a particular form of knowledge even though his actual opinion inclines toward a different direction.'"⁵⁹ Bacharach pointed to the inherent contradiction at the core of Delmedigo's writing, and Delmedigo's own awareness of this contradiction, but never came to a definitive conclusion about his stance on Kabbalah.

Bacharach may have learned of Modena's criticism of Kabbalah from Delmedigo when he encountered him in Worms. Like Modena, Bacharach expressed doubts about the antiquity of Kabbalah as a set of esoteric secrets that had been transmitted from Moses at Sinai through the Middle Ages. He questioned the kabbalistic practice of interpreting works of rabbinic literature as if they were esoteric texts. "I say that the kabbalists ascribed secrets to the words of the Mishnah or the Talmud just as one ascribes words of rebuke to the *shofar* and other such matters; for it is not the case that the authorities of the Mishnah themselves intended to discuss these

---

li-khevod Yitzhak Zimmer, ed. Gershon Bacon, Daniel Sperber, and Aharon Gaimani, 32, n. 9 (Ramat Gan: Bar Ilan University Press, 2008).

⁵⁷ *Havot Yair*, 197A. Solomon Helm (ca. 1710–1781) and Isaac Reggio took note of this passage in Bacharach's responsum. See Solomon Helm, *Mirkevet ha-Mishneh* (Frankfurt, 1750), 6. Helm used the phrase *nohem ke-ari* in reference to Bacharach. Reggio's comment as cited by Libowitz in his notes to *Ari Nohem*, ed. Libowitz, 115; as cited by Twersky, "Law and Spirituality," 448, n. 3.

⁵⁸ *Havot Yair*, 270B, note to 206B. Bacharach contemplated writing a separate work on Delmedigo. See Kaufmann, "Jair Chaim Bacharach," 529–30.

⁵⁹ *Havot Yair*, 197A. The passage quoted from Delmedigo appears in *Sefer Mazref le-Hokhmah*, in *Sefer Ta'alumot Hokhmah*, 20A.

matters, all the more so the sages of the Talmud."⁶⁰ Kabbalists who used statements in rabbinic literature as points of departure for the explication of esoteric secrets were similar to preachers who pointed to the blowing of the *shofar* as a call to repentance. Like Modena, Bacharach opposed the totalizing claims of kabbalists, in this case treating rabbinic literature as if it were a preserve of esoteric secrets.

Bacharach agreed with Modena's portrait about the transmission of Kabbalah in the Middle Ages and the recent changes in this process wrought by printing. He lamented the fact that his contemporaries studied Kabbalah by reading newly printed books rather than through a combination of oral instruction by an acknowledged master and the supervised reading of a kabbalistic text. Bacharach went even further and decried printed editions of kabbalistic texts as filled with errors and unreliable.⁶¹ In an appendix to the responsum, he included a section of his father's work that had disparaged the recent popularity of Kabbalah and poked fun at people who studied Kabbalah and purchased kabbalistic texts. Samson Bacharach's complaint took the form of an elaborate prose poem whose every phrase contained a rhyme or an allusion to a kabbalistic work that had recently appeared in print. He also quoted the identical passage of Isserles' *Torat ha-Olah* that Modena had drawn upon in *Ari Nohem*.⁶²

Bacharach adopted an approach to kabbalistic exegesis similar but not identical to the one argued in *Ari Nohem*. After discussing various kabbalistic hermeneutical strategies, Bacharach warned his correspondent "they should say that this is a possible way [of interpreting the Bible] but should not compel the matter."⁶³ Bacharach did not reject the different forms of number and letter exegesis employed by kabbalists, but he did object to the notion that kabbalists had a monopoly on scriptural exegesis. Bacharach's reservations about Kabbalah did not take the form of Modena's strident cultural criticism; however, his conclusions in this responsum can hardly be construed as a ringing endorsement of Kabbalah. He recommended that his correspondent read kabbalistic books with extreme caution and that he should only accept kabbalistic claims that he could corroborate elsewhere in rabbinic literature; however, he should make no attempt to solve the doctrinal differences between various kabbalists. Throughout the responsum Bacharach pointedly objected to the hegemonic claims made by kabbalists for their theology, hermeneutics, and ritual. In this respect, the thrust of his objections was strikingly similar to *Ari Nohem*.

---

⁶⁰ *Havot Yair*, 197B.
⁶¹ Ibid., 199A–199B.
⁶² For the prose poem, see ibid., 200A; for the citation of Isserles, see 200B.
⁶³ Ibid., 199B.

The Defense of Kabbalah in Eighteenth-Century Italy

If Bacharach's position on Kabbalah contained certain filiations with Modena's, this was hardly the case with a number of northern Italian rabbis who mounted philosophical defenses of Kabbalah in the early eighteenth century. Aviad Sar Shalom Basilea (c. 1680–1743), Moses Hayim Luzzatto (1707–1746), and Joseph Ergas (1688–1730) all composed theological treatises in support of Kabbalah. These three scholars were hardly in agreement with one another: Luzzatto was repeatedly suspected of harboring Sabbatian sympathies, and Ergas even questioned his personal piety during the first campaign waged against him by Hagiz in 1729–1730.[64] By contrast, when controversy flared up four years later, Basilea came to Luzzatto's defense in the face of mounting criticism by the Venetian rabbinate. Basilea and Luzzatto undoubtedly knew of *Ari Nohem*. Luzzatto pointed to it as the chief reason for writing *Ma'amar ha-Vikuah*, composed between 1732 and 1734, and Basilea mentioned it in a letter written in 1734. It remains unclear whether Basilea knew of *Ari Nohem* when he wrote *Emunat Hakhamim*, his defense of Kabbalah printed in Mantua in 1730. Ergas may not have read *Ari Nohem*, but his posthumously printed *Shomer Emunim* engaged with several of the central issues in Modena's work.

A student of Moses Zacut and Judah Briel, Basilea served as a rabbi in Mantua in the early eighteenth century.[65] Although he defended Luzzatto against charges of heresy, no evidence suggests that he had Sabbatian sympathies himself. The title of Basilea's apologia, *Emunat Hakhamim*, referred to an almost technical term in early modern Jewish literature rendered either as "faith of the sages" or "faith in the sages."[66] Defenders of the rabbinic tradition in the seventeenth and eighteenth centuries such as Morteira, Hagiz, and Immanuel Aboab employed the term or its variations to refer to the sanctity of the Oral Torah and the rabbinic tradition.[67] Although these writers did not appear as central figures in Basilea's work,

---

[64] Carlebach, *The Pursuit of Heresy*, 206, 210–11; Elliott Horowitz, "The Early Eighteenth Century Confronts the Beard: Kabbalah and Jewish Self-Fashioning," *Jewish History* 8 (1994): 96; as cited in Francesca Trivellato, *The Familiarity of Strangers: The Sephardic Diaspora, Livorno, and Cross-Cultural Trade in the Early Modern Period* (New Haven: Yale University Press, 2009), 98, n. 171.

[65] Basilea, *Emunat Hakhamim* (Mantua, 1730), 2B; Shlomo Simonsohn, *History of the Jews in the Duchy of Mantua* (Jerusalem: Kiryath Sepher, 1977), 158, 696–97; Ruderman, *Jewish Thought and Scientific Discovery*, 213–28; Alessandro Guetta, "Cabale et rationalisme en Italie à l'époque baroque," in *Réceptions de la Cabale*, ed. Pierre Gisel and Lucie Kaennel, 109–26 (Paris: Eclat, 2007).

[66] Shalom Rosenberg, "Emunat Hakhamim," in Twersky and Septimus, *Jewish Thought in the Seventeenth Century*, 341. On Basilea's admiration for Hagiz, see 310, n. 77.

[67] Carlebach, *The Pursuit of Heresy*, 260–61.

he invoked this line of argumentation as he upheld rabbinic authorities as transmitters of Kabbalah.

To defend the authenticity of the kabbalistic tradition, Basilea had to respond to prior rabbinic critics of Kabbalah. Early in *Emunat Hakhamim* Basilea referred to those who "explicitly claim that all that these kabbalists say are new things lately come[68] that were unheard of by our forefathers, and that the book of the *Zohar* was not written by Rabbi Simeon bar Yohai; for if it had been, it would not have escaped the attention of our ancestors. These issues [Kabbalah] are not present in the Talmud or in Aggadic literature. Therefore it is not fitting for any thinking person to believe in them."[69] Basilea identified Isaac bar Sheshet and Solomon Luria as such critics and pointed to the identical passages in their responsa that Modena had quoted in *Ari Nohem*. Elsewhere Basilea drew on a range of sources quoted in *Ari Nohem*, including the introduction to *Pelah ha-Rimon* by Menahem Azariah da Fano, the historical chronicles of Ibn Yahya and Zacut, and the kabbalistic treatise of Ibn Gabbai.[70] The extensive overlap in sources between *Emunat Hakhamim* and *Ari Nohem* does not in and of itself indicate that Basilea had read or heard of Modena's work at this point; however, the absence of an explicit reference may function as part of a larger rhetorical strategy within *Emunat Hakhamim*. One of Basilea's primary polemical targets, Samson Morpurgo's *Esh ha-Dat*, also did not appear by name.[71] Basilea may have known of Modena's work from his teacher Zacut, who had discussed it with Samuel Aboab.

At least three issues discussed in *Emunat Hakhamim* appear to be an implicit response to criticism leveled by figures such as Modena: the ostensible antiquity of Kabbalah, the centrality of Maimonides, and the modes of kabbalistic transmission in the Middle Ages. Basilea's defense of the antiquity of Kabbalah did not take the form of a historical genealogy or even a chain of transmission employed by the historical chronicles he invoked as corroborating testimony. Instead he employed a form of logic that obviated the need for empirical evidence. Basilea reasoned that the Torah as it appeared in the Hebrew Bible contained numerous commandments whose purpose required an explanation. This explanation took the form of the Secrets of the Torah given to Moses at Sinai and transmitted to particular chosen individuals from Sinai onward.[72] He further attempted to defend the antiquity of the *Zohar* by applying Maimonides' account of the transmission of the Mishnah to Simeon bar Yohai. Just as Maimonides had pos-

---

[68] Deut. 32:17.
[69] Basilea, *Emunat Hakhamim*, 11A.
[70] For *Pelah ha-Rimon*, see ibid., 25A; for Ibn Yahya and Zacut, see 24B; for Ibn Gabbai, see 19B.
[71] Ruderman, *Jewish Thought and Scientific Discovery*, 216.
[72] Basilea, *Emunat Hakhamim*, 11B and 13A.

ited the Mishnah as the product of oral transmission until its inscription in writing by Judah the Prince, Basilea described the *Zohar* as a composition of Simeon bar Yohai transmitted orally until its inscription in writing by his students.[73] In response to the claim that Simeon bar Yohai as he appeared in the Talmud bore no relation to his portrayal in the *Zohar*, a point emphasized by Modena, Basilea developed an elaborate theory. He reasoned that rabbinic statements in antiquity were divided by genre: legal ones appeared in the Talmud; exegetical ones in the Midrash; and those about the Secrets of the Torah in the *Zohar*.[74] Unlike Bacharach or Modena, Basilea had no doubts that the rabbis of antiquity knew about the esoteric Secrets of Torah and that their texts should be treated as repositories of such knowledge.

Basilea even cited Galatino as evidence of a gentile who appropriately rebuked the Jews on this account:

> Because of our sins that have increased . . . the sages of the nations of the world have inveighed against those of little faith in our nation who contradict and scoff at the words of our sages. And especially one of their sages named Pietro Galatino, in his book, part 1, chapter seven, wrote these words exactly. The earlier masters of the Talmud studied and taught the secrets in their parables and riddles almost without limit etc. From this stems the mistake of the later Jews (that is to say, our contemporaries) who, because they don't understand the ways of their predecessors when they discuss matters of nature or theology, turn many of the secrets in the Talmud into mockery and scorn.[75]

Basilea not only cited with approval the primary target of Modena's polemic against Christianity, a theologian referred to in *Magen va-Herev* as "chief among those who write against the Jews,"[76] he drew on his work in order to castigate contemporary Jews for denying the esoteric content of rabbinic literature.

Concurrent with his attempt to shore up the antiquity of Kabbalah, Basilea grappled with Maimonides. Basilea repeated the story about Maimonides' conversion to Kabbalah but seemed to understand that even this legend could not neutralize his impact or import.[77] As such, he attempted to confront the *Guide of the Perplexed* on a number of levels. He reasoned that had Maimonides known the esoteric secrets of Kabbalah, he would have come up with entirely different reasons for the biblical commandments from the ones offered in the *Guide*.[78] Had he known about the kabbalistic Secrets of the Torah, Maimonides would never have espoused his

[73] Ibid., 47B.
[74] Ibid., 48A.
[75] Ibid., 38A; Pietro Galatino, *Opus de arcanis catholicae veritatis* (Soncino: Ortona, 1518), 21B.
[76] *Magen va-Herev*, ed. Simonsohn, 11.
[77] Basilea, *Emunat Hakhamim*, 14B–15A.
[78] Ibid., 13B.

theory of biblical sacrifice, which posited that sacrifice was too ingrained in the cultures of the ancient Near East to be entirely eliminated by the God of Israel.[79] At one point he confessed, "I am extremely unsure whether Maimonides believes many of the things that he wrote in the *Guide*."[80] No other figure loomed as large in his work, and Basilea's confrontation with him functioned within a wider framework of kabbalistic attempts to convert, explain, and appropriate Maimonides.

In *Ari Nohem* Modena had objected to the antiquity of Kabbalah on the grounds that kabbalistic classics had been attributed to biblical or rabbinic authors but had been entirely unknown until the end of the Middle Ages. Basilea attempted to counter this argument with a material explanation about the transmission of Kabbalah and the circulation of books in the period before print.

> Print had not yet appeared and manuscript books were extremely expensive, and they would only copy those books common to everyone; but copies of esoteric books, if they were in the possession of a chosen few, they would not be revealed; if they were in the possession of the rich and ignorant, they would not recognize their worth; and if they were in the possession of sages who were not expert in this field of wisdom, they would not study them. Know that for this reason we have lost or not known about manuscripts of [these] books.[81]

Lack of manuscript evidence accounted for the inability to identify and locate works cited by medieval scholars on a range of subjects, including grammar, philology, and chronology. But Basilea drew on the argument to account for the seemingly inexplicable gap between the ostensible composition of kabbalistic books and the first recorded references to them. For all their differences, Basilea, Modena, and Bacharach all understood the invention of print as the cause of a dramatic change in the transmission of esoteric literature.

Emunat Hakhamim appeared in between two phases of an extended controversy over the messianism of Moses Hayim Luzzatto, a kabbalist, poet, and dramatist nearly thirty years younger than Basilea who lived in Padua and led a mystical circle.[82] Luzzatto's creative genius was exceeded only by his sense of his own world historical import, a posture that aggravated his rabbinic elders in Amsterdam, Livorno, and Venice. The first controversy occurred between 1728 and 1730 and centered on the alleged revelations

---

[79] Ibid. See *Guide for the Perplexed*, 3:32; Davidson, *Moses Maimonides*, 382.
[80] Basilea, *Emunat Hakhamim*, 27A.
[81] Ibid., 48B.
[82] Meir Benayahu, *Kitve ha-Kabalah shela-Ramhal* (Jerusalem: Menachem Press, 1979); Tishby, *Messianic Mysticism*; Joëlle Hansel, *Moïse Hayyim Luzzatto (1707–1746): Kabbale et philosophie* (Paris: Cerf, 2004); Gadi Luzzatto Voghera and Mauro Perani, eds., *Ramhal: Pensiero ebraico e kabbalah tra Padova ed Eretz Israel* (Padua: Esedra, 2010).

Luzzatto had received from a *maggid*, a heavenly mentor, as well as his supposed Sabbatian tendencies.[83] Orchestrated by Hagiz, a rabbinic firebrand who had already waged several campaigns against Sabbatian sympathizers, the controversy came to a temporary halt when Luzzatto took an oath under the supervision of his teacher Isaiah Bassan not to publicize his teachings in the name of the *maggid*.

The second phase of the controversy erupted when Luzzatto requested permission from Bassan to print his kabbalistic treatise *Ma'amar ha-Vikuah*. In the revival of the controversy, Sabbatianism receded from the foreground as the debate shifted to Luzzatto's plans to publicize Kabbalah and whether this violated his original oath.[84] Luzzatto had submitted a manuscript to Bassan in December 1733 and wrote a series of letters over the next several months requesting his permission to print the work with an approbation.[85] Bassan's letter to Luzzatto left no doubt as to his hesitation:

> I received your letters, one after the other, which beseech me to do something against my will. For even if there is nothing incorrect in your treatise, there is also nothing salutary; for this is not something new, and the book *Mazref le-Hokhmah* by Rabbi Joseph Solomon Delmedigo of Candia, may his memory be a blessing, has long been available, filled to the brim with supportive and clever letters . . . and after it came our friend Aviad in his work newly printed. And what will your work add to this? . . . For those leaping to purchase books like this have not increased, but have decreased.[86]

After this lengthy rebuke that explicitly mentioned Delmedigo's *Mazref le-Hokhmah* and Basilea's *Emunat Hakhamim* accompanied by a warning about an oversaturated book market, Bassan appended a short and tepid approbation.

Undeterred by his teacher's lukewarm response, Luzzatto planned to travel from Padua to Amsterdam to supervise the printing of his work. When he stopped in Venice at the beginning of his journey, Luzzatto was detained by the Venetian rabbinate who were suspicious of his plans to print Kabbalah. The Venetian rabbinate wrote to Bassan for instructions on how to handle his celebrated and controversial pupil. Bassan's letter to the Venetian rabbinate differed markedly from his response to Luzzatto. He vouched for the contents of Luzzatto's treatise and wrote that he had given his permission for it to appear in print.[87] Meanwhile Luzzatto him-

---

[83] Carlebach, *The Pursuit of Heresy*, 195–230.

[84] Ibid., 232.

[85] Simon Ginzburg, *Rabi Moshe Hayim Luzzatto u-Vene-Doro: Osef Igrot u-Te'udot* (Tel Aviv: Dvir, 1937), 2:242–45; letter no. 90 (Dec. 11, 1733); no. 91 (Jan. 3, 1734); and no. 93 (June 18, 1734).

[86] Ibid., 245–46; letter no. 94.

[87] Ibid., 253; letter no. 98.

self had written again to Bassan recounting his travails in Venice, and, in attempt to impress upon him a sense of urgency, he added:

> And by the way I should inform your honor of some news, that today I received a long letter from Aquila Ficci, known to you from Vicenza, where he is a judge. He wrote to me with all sorts of entreaties that I should write to him my opinion about an argument held in front of the minister, where he fought with another town resident about our Kabbalah. He maintained it was a sacred wisdom, extremely rarefied, and the revelation of the true mysteries of the Torah. But this town resident contradicted him and told him it was vanity. He brought in support of his opinion the words of R. Judah Aryeh Modena and his book, which demonstrates that it [Kabbalah] has no basis and is all vanity of vanities. Your honor, you see how far the bitter fruit of this man has gone, that his venom has even spread among the gentiles.[88]

This was the first of several statements of *Ari Nohem*'s importance to Luzzatto's thinking about Kabbalah. His account of the judge in Vicenza who had encountered a reference to Modena's work in his argument with a resident about Kabbalah bears a striking resemblance to Samuel Aboab's story about a magistrate in Verona who had quoted *Ari Nohem* nearly a century earlier. It also offers further evidence of the continued circulation of *Ari Nohem* among non-Jewish readers into the eighteenth century.

Luzzatto's entreaties notwithstanding, the Venetian rabbinate sided against him and sought to prevent the publication of his treatise.[89] In an official letter, they enlisted the help of Luzzatto's earlier nemesis Hagiz. After informing him about Luzzatto's plans, they wrote: "But he claims that now he only wants to print a polemic that he composed between a scholar and a kabbalist, to inflame the hearts of the people to pursue Kabbalah. And he claims that it responds to the book *Sha'agat Aryeh* that was written by Rabbi Judah Aryeh Modena. But we do not believe him and we have not listened to his promises and oaths, for he is already taken for a heretic and one who swears falsely."[90] According to the Venetian rabbinate, Luzzatto himself had pointed to Modena's work, erroneously called *Sha'agat Aryeh*, as the primary target of his treatise.

As the campaign against Luzzatto grew in geographical scope to include rabbis as far as Frankfurt and Lublin, Bassan took the side of his pupil and

---

[88] Ibid., 255; letter no. 99.

[89] According to Mordecai Samuel Ghirondi of Padua (1799–1852), they refused to allow Luzzatto to criticize Modena in print out of defense for a native son of Venice. See letter no. 5, *KH* 2 (1838), 55–56. On Ghirondi, see chapter 7.

[90] Ginzburg, *Rabi Moshe Hayim Luzzatto*, 268, letter no. 103. In his collection of writings on Sabbatianism, Emden included a copy of this letter with the reference to Modena's work as *Sha'agat Aryeh*. See *Torat ha-Kenaot* (Jerusalem: Makor, 1970) (reprint of Amsterdam 1752), 54A. In his commentary to the documents concerning Luzzatto, Emden did not focus on Modena.

enlisted the support of his colleagues in Italy and beyond. In a letter from 1734 to one of his allies in central Europe, Barukh Kahana Rapoport of Fürth, Bassan wrote: "In these territories there is a manuscript book composed by the rabbi and teacher Judah Aryeh Modena, of blessed memory, (a righteous teacher in Venice). It is called *Sha'agat Aryeh* . . . and the holy eminence, my master and teacher, the esteemed rabbi Moses Zacut . . . used to call it *Kol Sakhal* (Voice of a Fool) because the whole work contradicts the wisdom of truth, and speaks disparagingly about those who study it [Kabbalah] . . . and all the insolent and evil doers rely upon it."[91] Bassan's letter left no doubt that the work in question was Modena's *Ari Nohem*. He specified that it contradicted the "wisdom of truth," a reference to Kabbalah and a term that Modena sought to contest throughout *Ari Nohem*. He corroborated the account in the letter by the Venetian rabbinate to Hagiz that Modena's work was circulating in early eighteenth-century Padua and Venice under the title *Sha'agat Aryeh*. Furthermore, he confirmed that his teacher Zacut knew of *Ari Nohem* and added an interesting detail: Zacut referred to it as *Kol Sakhal*, the title of a pseudepigraphic critique of rabbinic culture that Modena had allegedly written.

Bassan continued his account of Luzzatto's treatise in an effort to secure his colleague's help in protecting his student: "And the esteemed master and rabbi, Moses Hayim Luzzatto, may the Lord preserve him, in his zealousness for the Lord composed a book in the holy tongue that he called the polemical treatise (*ma'amar ha-vikuah*) in which [he used] correct and reliable statements to destroy and break all the claims in the aforementioned book [Modena's polemic], which became like chaff that the wind blows away."[92] Bassan recounted his own efforts on behalf of Luzzatto to print his response to *Ari Nohem*. He mentioned that he had circulated Luzzatto's work among his colleagues in northern Italy, including David Finzi and Aviad Sar Shalom Basilea. Bassan quoted from Basilea's letter about Luzzatto's work: "I have read [Luzzatto's] answers to *Ari Nohem*, (of R. Judah Aryeh of Modena) and we find his answers really valuable . . . and I did not expect so much passion to be shown for this evil and bitter work of the aforesaid roaring lion [*Ari Nohem*] who said that the *Zohar* was a book of lies and that the true wisdom [of Kabbalah] was completely worthless and deceitful."[93] Letters by the Venetian rabbinate, Bassan, and Luzzatto himself leave no doubt that the polemical treatise on Kabbalah Luzzatto hoped to print was a direct response to Modena's *Ari Nohem*. Luzzatto eventually made his way to Amsterdam, where he enjoyed the hospitality of the Sephardic community. The mystical circle he directed in Padua

[91] Ginzburg, *Rabi Moshe Hayim Luzzatto*, 352–53, letter no. 148.
[92] Ibid., 353. Cf. Ps.1:4.
[93] Ibid.

soon disbanded and the controversy over his work died down. He did not succeed, however, in printing his polemical treatise, which continued to circulate in manuscript under the titles *Ma'amar ha-Vikuah* and *Hoqer u-Mekubal*. It eventually appeared as *Hoqer u-Mekubal*, "A Scholar and a Kabbalist," a phrase used in the letter by the Venetian rabbinate to Hagiz.[94]

The printed editions of *Hoqer u-Mekubal* pose somewhat of a conundrum. The correspondence of Luzzatto and his circle repeatedly mention *Ari Nohem* as the primary target of his polemical treatise, yet neither Modena nor *Ari Nohem* appears by name in the text of *Hoqer u-Mekubal*.[95] On a range of subjects, however, Luzzatto appears to have been responding to *Ari Nohem*. In the introduction to *Ma'amar ha-Vikuah* he addressed several issues central to Modena's criticisms, such as the antiquity of Kabbalah and the importance of its proper transmission.[96] Luzzatto argued that Kabbalah was transmitted to the people of Israel at Sinai by God through Moses. Only with the passing of the Jewish nation into exile did knowledge of this wisdom disappear among the Jews.[97] In an argument with distinctly Maimonidean overtones, Luzzatto claimed that with the prolonged exile of the Jewish people, Kabbalah became a subterranean and esoteric tradition known only to those adepts who were properly instructed. He referred to recent critics of Kabbalah: "Others are even worse, for not only have they neglected it [Kabbalah] but they have criticized it.... They have even rejected its fundamentals, and denied that the holy *Zohar* was composed by Rabbi Simeon bar Yohai, of blessed memory, and his colleagues. All this because the words of this wisdom are foreign to them."[98] Given the evidence in his correspondence, it stands to reason that he was referring to Modena and *Ari Nohem*.

Luzzatto did not engage Modena's claims about the origins of the *Zohar* at any length, although he may have answered this challenge elsewhere.

---

[94] Ibid., 268. Editions of *Hoqer u-Mekubal* appeared at Shklov (1785), Lemberg (1800), and Königsberg (1840). On the bibliographic problems posed by this work, see Avivi, "*Ma'amar ha-Vikuah* of Ramhal"; Tishby, *Messianic Mysticism*, 49–57; Benayahu, *Kitve ha-Kabbalah shel Ramhal*, 149–58.

[95] For attempts to minimize Modena's impact on Luzzatto, see Tishby, "General Introduction," 36; Joëlle Hansel, Introduction, in Moïse Hayyim Luzzatto, *Le philosophe et le cabaliste* (Lagrasse: Verdier, 1991), 36–39; Huss, *Ke-zohar ha-rakia*, 310. Nineteenth-century readers of Luzzatto and Modena had a different view. See chapter 7.

[96] The introduction to *Ma'amar ha-Vikuah* did not appear in any of the early editions of *Hoqer u-Mekubal*. It first appeared in Moses Hayim Luzzatto, *Yalkut yediot ha'emet* (Tel Aviv: Ahava, 1965), 2:298–310. On this edition, see Tishby, *Messianic Mysticism*, 57, n. 174. It appeared subsequently in Hayim Friedlander, ed., *Sha'are Ramhal* (Bnei Brak, 1986), 29–39. Both editions are versions of a text in Oxford, Bodleian Library, MS Opp. Add. 8° 79 (Neubauer 2593), 108A–115A.

[97] *Sha'are Ramhal*, 31–33.

[98] Ibid., 37.

In *Adir ba-Marom*, a commentary to part of the *Zohar*, Luzzatto outlined a theory of its origins: "And Rabbi Simeon bar Yohai revealed the secrets of the Torah and his associates were listening to his voice ... each one responding with his portion. Just as the Mishnah was composed by the Tanaim, and our holy Rabbi [Judah the Prince] gathered all the ideas and made the book of the Mishnah out of them, so too Rabbi Simeon bar Yohai wanted a book to be composed that included all the statements by members of his academy."[99] Authorship of the *Zohar* was hardly a pedantic question for Luzzatto. He conceived of his own kabbalistic fellowship as a circle of illuminati who had gathered around him in order to redeem the world. He repeatedly emphasized two prior reenactments in the history of Kabbalah: Simeon bar Yohai in the *Zohar* and Isaac Luria in *Toledot Ari*.[100] He consistently identified aspects of his own biography with the hagiographic accounts of Bar Yohai and Luria. Given Luzzatto's self-perception as a redemptive figure directly in the mold of Bar Yohai and Luria, his opposition to a text that denied Bar Yohai's authorship of the *Zohar* and attacked the cult of Isaac Luria among early modern Jews should come as no surprise.

In the dialogue itself, the scholar questioned the relationship between the sefirot and the Trinity. In his response, the kabbalist rejected such a parallel as entirely without basis.[101] In *Ari Nohem* Modena had repeatedly quoted the medieval jurist Isaac bar Sheshet, who had compared the sefirot to the Trinity. Elsewhere Luzzatto argued that the doctrine of the sefirot had been transmitted from the biblical prophets to the sages of antiquity. Although Modena's argument against the antiquity of Kabbalah had not focused on the sefirot, his criticisms repeatedly questioned the authenticity of its transmission. When read alongside the evidence in his correspondence, the different components of Luzzatto's polemical writing about Kabbalah offer a resounding and completely ahistorical response to *Ari Nohem*. Luzzatto was genuinely unmoved by the temporal aspects of Modena's criticisms—that Kabbalah had a history, that its history was very different from the one claimed for it by kabbalists—and imagined himself in conversation with prior kabbalists, such as Bar Yohai and Luria.

Joseph Ergas, a Livornese rabbi who had joined forces with Hagiz in the first campaign against Luzzatto, wrote a philosophical defense of Kabbalah that was printed posthumously. Like *Hoqer u-Mekubal*, *Shomer Emunim* took the form of a series of dialogues between a skeptical but philosophically inclined novice and an experienced and learned kabbalist. *Shomer Emunim* covered a set of familiar themes: the authenticity of Kabbalah and

---

[99] Luzzatto, *Sefer Adir ba-Marom* (Warsaw: Y. Goldman, 1886), 18; as cited in Rubin, "The Zoharic works of R. Moses Hayim Luzzatto," 406–7.

[100] Carlebach, *The Pursuit of Heresy*, 199–201.

[101] Luzzatto, *Hoqer u-mekubal* (Königsberg: E. J. Dalkowski, 1840), 3.

its transmission, the importance of the sefirot and the imperative to believe in them, and the necessity of kabbalistic knowledge for a true understanding of the Bible. In his description of the work, Ergas emphasized that he sought to "bring several proofs about the authenticity of the transmission of the hidden knowledge, in spite of the simpletons who oppose it with an outstretched hand, and to demonstrate to them their mistake . . . and I shall recount the opinions of several of our nation who philosophize and how they mistake several aspects of our holy Torah."[102] Over the course of the two dialogues that constitute *Shomer Emunim*, Ergas never identified these opponents of Kabbalah and ventriloquized their opinions in the voice of the skeptical novice named Shealtiel.

Like a range of earlier kabbalists, Ergas confronted the legacy of Maimonides and dutifully repeated the legend about his conversion to Kabbalah before his death. Unlike his predecessors, Ergas was willing to dispense with him:

> But in the end, however it may be, we do not need the testimony of Maimonides about the authenticity of the wisdom of Kabbalah, because we have many reliable witnesses, sages and eminences just like him, who received it [Kabbalah], authenticated it, and transmitted it to us, one generation after another. After all, Abraham ben David, [Eleazar] the Perfumer, Nahmanides, Solomon ibn Adret, and Yom Tov Isbili all testified that the Kabbalah that we possess today has been faithfully transmitted to them from the time of Moses from the mouth of the Almighty, as it is written in their books.[103]

Unlike Basilea and other early modern kabbalists who refused to let go of Maimonides, Ergas pointed to a line of medieval kabbalists as sufficient for his belief in the authenticity of Kabbalah.[104]

Basilea and Luzzatto had emphasized the need for a teacher with knowledge of the Secrets of the Torah for instruction in the byways of Kabbalah. For all his skepticism, Bacharach had conceded that if one had a teacher who had knowledge of esoteric secrets, one might become well versed in Kabbalah. At the beginning of his second dialogue, Ergas repeated this emphasis on a living link to the oral tradition of Kabbalah.[105] Elsewhere, however, he emphasized the importance of reading books. After a discussion of *Shiur Komah*, the kabbalist declares: "All of this is written in greater detail in kabbalistic books, go and read them if you want to know this wisdom, because I cannot enlighten you about these matters upon one foot. One must have considerable time, diligence with [one's] books, and the

---

[102] Joseph Ergas, *Shomer Emunim* (Amsterdam, 1736), Introduction, 1B. On the Ergas family in Livorno see Trivellato, *The Familiarity of Strangers*.
[103] Ibid. First disputation, sec. 13, 5B.
[104] Isaac Reggio attacked Ergas on this account. See *Ari Nohem*, MS L 42A, n. 16.
[105] Ergas, *Shomer Emunim*, introduction to second dialogue, 25A.

198 • Chapter Six

assistance of heaven."[106] Ergas did not ignore the necessity of oral instruction by a kabbalistic master, but he focused on the study of written texts. The imperative to read suggested that this study would occur individually without the supervision of a learned master.

A basic question remains unanswered but must at least be posed. Why did a trio of rabbis in northern Italy in the early decades of the eighteenth century feel impelled to defend Kabbalah from philosophically inclined critics? Why were the claims at the core of *Ari Nohem* so urgent almost a century after the work had been composed? Luzzatto mentioned that Modena's work was circulating among Christians in Vicenza, but he used this to justify a work he had already written. Basilea referred to critics of Kabbalah such as Isaac bar Sheshet and Solomon Luria, who had lived centuries before him. Along with Basilea and Luzzatto, Ergas cited critics of Simeon bar Yohai's authorship of the *Zohar*. None of these issues, however, was new in the decade between 1725 and 1735. For all the importance of the aftershocks of Sabbatianism in the early eighteenth century, none of these works contained extensive discussion of Sabbatianism. The debate over Luzzatto's alleged Sabbatianism had already subsided by the time he wrote his polemical treatise, and the terrain of the controversy had shifted to his compliance with the rabbinic authority. None of these works mentions any form of radical enlightenment criticism or skepticism that circulated in the late seventeenth and early eighteenth century. While it might be convenient to see these defenses of Kabbalah as a response to early Enlightenment attacks on Kabbalah, the existing evidence does not support such an interpretation.

Ari Nohem in Eighteenth-Century Reference Works

If the intensive defense of Kabbalah in the early eighteenth century lacks an obvious explanation, references to Modena and his polemical writings later in the eighteenth century point to an emerging literature that only increased with importance: scholarly reference works. Isaac Lampronti, a rabbi in Ferrara in the early eighteenth century, composed a monumental encyclopedia of rabbinic literature entitled *Pahad Yitzhak* that began to appear in his lifetime and continued after his death.[107] Under the entry for *Gilgul*, Lampronti cited a series of texts on the transmigration of souls: "*Sefer Ben David* written by the esteemed Rabbi Judah Aryeh Modena,

---

[106] Ibid. First dialogue, para. 65, 21B.
[107] Ruderman, *Jewish Thought and Scientific Discovery*, 256–72; David Malkiel, "The Burden of the Past in the Eighteenth Century: Authority, Custom, and Innovation in the *Pahad Yitzhak*," *Jewish Law Annual* 16 (2006): 93–132.

of blessed memory, to his student the physician, Rabbi Joseph Hamiz, of blessed memory, against the belief in the transmigration of souls. There he sought to prove that the belief in the transmigration of souls is of recent origin among the Israelite nation and was not received either from Moses or from the prophets."[108] In the entry for Kabbalah, a reference to Bacharach's responsum appears immediately before a similar description of Modena's criticism of Kabbalah: "Whether one should come close or distance oneself from the study of Kabbalah, [see] *Havot Yair*, responsum 210, page 197A. And examine the book *Sha'agat Aryeh* against Kabbalah and kabbalists, it is thirty-one chapters composed by the universal sage, our esteemed Rabbi Judah Aryeh Modena, may his righteous memory be a blessing, to his student the physician, our esteemed Rabbi Joseph Hamiz, of blessed memory."[109] These entries in *Pahad Yitzhak* did not engage with the substantive argument of either work and simply identified the subject matter. Lampronti juxtaposed Modena's criticism to Bacharach's responsum and referred to the work as *Sha'agat Aryeh* rather than *Ari Nohem*. He incorrectly identified the addressee of *Ben David* as Hamiz; it was actually written at the request of David Finzi.[110]

As the author or director of an encyclopedic reference project, Lampronti adopted a catholic approach to knowledge and referred to works that criticized one another and that he himself may not have held in high esteem. The reaction of another great eighteenth-century encyclopedist to Modena's work could hardly be any different. Hayim Joseph David Azulai, an emissary from the Jewish communities of Palestine who made two journeys to Europe in order to raise charity, eventually settled in Livorno for the last several decades of his life. On his travels, Azulai practiced a form of bibliographic tourism and made extraordinary efforts to examine Hebrew manuscripts. He recorded his findings in a travel diary he later entitled *Ma'agal Tov*. On his first trip Azulai encountered *Ari Nohem* in Venice among a range of other works: "There [in Venice] I saw the glosses of Rabbenu Asher to tractate Shabbat and tractate Horayot[111] ... and in contrast to his light I also saw the book *Ari Nohem*, a pamphlet that proves that the *Zohar* was not by Rabbi Simeon bar Yohai and his colleagues, but written by someone else, etc. And his words, 'grew thick and they had become as

---

[108] Isaac Lampronti, *Pahad Yitzhak* (Venice: Bragadin, 1753), 2:56B. Entry for *Gilgul*.

[109] Isaac Lampronti, *Pahad Yitzhak* (Lyck: Mekize Nirdamim, 1874), 10:64A, entry for Kabbalah. This volume was published over a century after Lampronti's death in 1756. On the publication history of the *Pahad Yitzhak* and Lampronti's working methods, see Malkiel, "The Burden of the Past in the Eighteenth Century," 97–98.

[110] *Autobiography*, 143.

[111] Asher ben Yehiel (ca. 1259–1328), known as the Rosh, was a jurist and Talmudist who moved from Germany to Spain. See Judah Galinsky, "Ashkenazim in Sefarad: The Rosh and the Tur on the Codification of Jewish Law," *Jewish Law Annual* 16 (2006): 3–23.

though they had never been.'"[112] In contrast to many other eighteenth-century readers, Azulai correctly identified the title of *Ari Nohem*. Furthermore, his diary points to a manuscript of *Ari Nohem* in Venice in the winter of 1754, more than a century after Modena's death. While Modena's criticism had traveled as far as Worms, at least one copy was present in Venice in the middle of the eighteenth century.

In his bio-bibliographic reference guide composed during and after his travels, *Shem ha-Gedolim*, Azulai included an entry on Modena. After describing Modena as a preacher and including a description of his autobiography, which he had examined in manuscript, Azulai recounted the story about Modena recanting his denial of the transmigration of souls.[113] However, he did not include any discussion of *Ari Nohem*, a work he clearly knew from his travels. For all its encyclopedic ambitions, *Shem Ha-Gedolim* bore the traces of Azulai's idiosyncratic choices. In the case of *Ari Nohem*, he did not mention a work he clearly found objectionable.

Between its composition and its printing, *Ari Nohem* was read by a small circle of learned elites, mostly Jews, who were interested in the antiquity of Kabbalah. Modena's criticism set the agenda for a range of apologists for Kabbalah in the early eighteenth century, but it did not enter into the larger European republic of letters. By contrast, his *Riti* was read, translated, and owned by a number of European intellectuals. Edmund Chilmead produced an English translation shortly after Modena's death.[114] In the late seventeenth century, Richard Simon translated it into French and added an extensive supplement about Karaites and Samaritans.[115] Early modern Jews were largely uninterested in the *Riti*, which did not appear in Hebrew until well into the nineteenth century.[116]

---

[112] Obadiah 1:16; Azulai, *Ma'agal Tov*, 9.

[113] Azulai, *Shem ha-Gedolim Helek Sheni* (Livorno, 1786), 42B–43A.

[114] Modena, *The History of the Rites*.

[115] Leon Modena, *Ceremonies et coustumes qui s'observent aujourd'huy parmy les juifs*, trans. Richard Simon (Paris: Loüis Billaine, 1674). John Locke owned a copy this edition. See Oxford, Bodleian Library, Locke 7.439. A second edition appeared in 1681. On Simon's translation, see Stroumsa and Le Brun, eds., *Les Juifs présentés aux chrétiens par Léon de Modène traduit par Richard Simon*. Simon's translation appeared in English as *The History of the Present Jews throughout the World*, trans. Simon Ockley (London: E. Powell, 1707). A second edition of Ockley's translation appeared in 1711.

[116] Leon Modena, *Shulhan Arukh le-Yehudah Aryeh mi-Modena*, trans. Salomon Rubin (Vienna: Schlossberg, 1867).

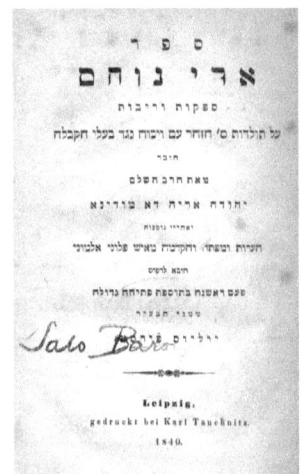

CHAPTER SEVEN

Kabbalah and Scholarship in the Nineteenth Century

> Where others had either disdained close acquaintance with the sources of what they frequently rejected and condemned, or erected some lofty edifice of speculation, I found myself constrained by circumstance and by inclination to perform the humble but necessary task of clearing the ground of much scattered debris and laying bare the outlines of a great and significant chapter in the history of Jewish religion.
>
> —Gershom Scholem, May 1941

Figure 12 (previous page). Hebrew Title page to *Ari Nohem*, Leipzig, 1840. Private collection.
This copy of the first printed edition of *Ari Nohem* was formerly owned by Salo W. Baron, the historian of the Jews who taught at Columbia University.

AT THE TURN OF THE NINETEENTH CENTURY, *Ari Nohem* circulated widely in manuscript. Four of fourteen witnesses date from the early decades of the century. Repeated references to the work appear in print, both in the correspondence of Jewish scholars published in newly founded periodicals and in reference works.[1] In the 1830s Isaac Reggio and Solomon Rosenthal both prepared editions of *Ari Nohem*. In an act of scholarly theft that infuriated them both, Julius Fürst printed Rosenthal's edition under his own name at Leipzig in 1840. Reggio, Rosenthal, and Fürst, as well as their better-known colleagues Solomon Judah Rapoport (*Shir*) and Samuel David Luzzatto (*Shadal*), all looked to Modena and his criticism of Kabbalah as a model for their own opposition to the contemporary mystical revival in Hasidism. In their correspondence, reviews, and annotations, nineteenth-century Jewish scholars associated with *Wissenschaft des Judentums* (Science of Judaism) and the *Haskalah* (Jewish Enlightenment) turned to *Ari Nohem* as part of their search for a usable past.[2] Rehabilitated by participants in the Jewish Enlightenment in the Habsburg Empire and elsewhere, *Ari Nohem* entered into a library of antikabbalistic texts that included Delmedigo's *Behinat ha-Dat*, Frances's poems, and Emden's *Mitpahat Sefarim*. In the century and a half after its composition, *Ari Nohem* circulated most extensively in Italy, with occasional readers elsewhere in Europe. At the turn of the nineteenth century, it began to travel farther as Jews in centers of the Habsburg Empire such as Prague and Pest as well as throughout Galicia assiduously sought manuscript and later printed copies.[3]

---

[1] Manuscripts D, F, H, and L. On references in print, see below. On Modena in the nineteenth century, see Umberto Cassuto, "Leon Modena e l'opera sua," *RMI* 8 (1933): 141–42; Adelman, "Success and Failure," 32–125. On *Ari Nohem*, see Libowitz, Introduction, in *Ari Nohem*, 23–31; Huss, *Ke-zohar ha-rakia*, 345–47, 354.

[2] On the science of Judaism, see Schorsch, *From Text to Context*. On the Jewish Enlightenment, see Feiner, *The Jewish Enlightenment*.

[3] On the Jews of the Habsburg Empire, see William O. McCagg Jr., *A History of Habsburg Jews, 1670–1918* (Bloomington: Indiana University Press, 1989). On Galicia, see Larry Wolff, *The Idea of Galicia: History and Fantasy in Habsburg Political Culture* (Stanford: Stanford University Press, 2010). On the Jews of Galicia, see Michael Stanislawski, *A Murder in Lemberg: Politics, Religion, and Violence in Modern Jewish History* (Princeton: Princeton University Press, 2007), chap. 1; Rachel Manekin, "Galicia," *The YIVO Encyclopedia of the Jews of in Eastern Europe*, ed. Gershon David Hundert (New Haven: Yale University Press, 2008, 1:560–67).

The printing of *Ari Nohem* left a deep impression on several Jewish thinkers whose positions on Kabbalah spanned from profound respect to unbridled hatred. A decade and a half after *Ari Nohem* was first printed, kabbalists Elijah Benamozegh and Isaac Haver Wildmann subjected it to searing criticism. Both tried to combat Modena's arguments against the antiquity of Kabbalah. A year later Abraham Geiger, one of the central figures of German-Jewish scholarship and a founder of Reform Judaism, wrote a short biography of Modena that included excerpts from his work. In contrast to Benamozegh and Wildmann, Geiger saw in Modena a model for his own efforts to combat the influence of Kabbalah and Hasidism. Geiger was not alone in his projection of his opposition to contemporary Hasidism onto *Ari Nohem*. As the century progressed, Jewish intellectuals further east, such as Isaac Baer Levinsohn, Abraham Baer Gottlober, and Moses Leib Lilienblum, continued to draw inspiration from *Ari Nohem*.

The nineteenth-century reception of *Ari Nohem*—its circulation in manuscript among scholars associated with the Science of Judaism and the Jewish Enlightenment, its appearance in print, and the reactions to the printed edition—complicates Scholem's claim that Kabbalah was ignored or forgotten by the early generations of modern Jewish scholars. Scholem's scholarly achievements were so significant that his foundational narrative of his own rediscovery of Jewish mysticism became a commonplace.[4] The empirical evidence, however, reveals a far more complicated story. Certain notable figures, such as Heinrich Graetz, may have abhorred Kabbalah, but few of them, Graetz included, ignored it altogether.[5] Many of those involved in the publication of *Ari Nohem*—Reggio, Fürst, and Rosenthal—identified with Modena's criticism of Kabbalah, but their polemical intent did not prevent them from arriving at insights into the history of Kabbalah. Furthermore, the responses to *Ari Nohem* by Benamozegh and Wildmann constituted forms of modern Kabbalah that had later analogues in the twentieth century.[6]

---

[4] On Scholem and his scholarly predecessors, see Biale, *Gershom Scholem*, 13–32; Idel, *Kabbalah*, 1–16; Peter Schäfer, "Gershom Scholem und die 'Wissenschaft des Judentums,'" in *Gershom Scholem: Zwischen den Disziplinen*, ed. Peter Schäfer and Gary Smith, 122–56 (Frankfurt: Suhrkamp Verlag, 1995).

[5] On Graetz, see Jonathan M. Elukin, "A New Essenism: Heinrich Graetz and Mysticism," *JHI* 59 (1998): 135–48; Peter Schäfer, "'Adversus cabbalam,' oder: Heinrich Graetz und die jüdische Mystik," in Schäfer and Wandrey, *Reuchlin und seine Erbern*, 189–210.

[6] For revisions to Scholem's thesis, see chapter 1, n. 2, as well as Moshe Idel, "On Adolf Jellinek and Kabbalah" (Hebrew), *Peamim* 100 (2004): 15–22; Roland Goetschel, "Samuel David Luzzatto et David H. Joël: Deux Regards sur la Kabbale," in Bonfil, Gottlieb, and Kasher, *Samuel David Luzzatto*, 35–54. See also Rivka Horwitz, "On Kabbala and Myth in 19th Century Germany: Isaac Bernays," *PAAJR* 59 (1993): 137–83; Eveline Goodman-Thau, "Meyer Heinrich Hirsch Landauer: Bible Scholar and Kabbalist," in *Mysticism, Magic, and Kabbalah in Ashkenazi Judaism*, ed. Karl Erich Grözinger and Joseph Dan, 275–94 (Berlin: Walter de

THE PUBLICATION OF *ARI NOHEM* IN PRINT

No modern figure looms larger for the study of Leon Modena than Isaac Samuel Reggio (1784–1855), a resident of Gorizia who adopted the Hebrew acronym *Yashar*.[7] A rabbi and an aspiring intellectual, Reggio combined his quest for communal authority with the pursuit of scholarship. Marriage to a woman of considerable wealth enabled him to accumulate a vast library that included an impressive collection of Hebrew manuscripts and afforded him the financial security to study in solitude. Until the unification of Italy in 1861, Gorizia, a small town northeast of Trieste, was under the domain of the Habsburg Empire. Although he felt a strong affinity for the intellectual heritage of Italian Jewry and translated the Pentateuch into Italian, Reggio's interests gravitated northward.[8] Many of his correspondents were colleagues in the urban centers of the Habsburg Empire, several of his books were printed in Vienna, and the targets of his arguments were other participants in the Jewish Enlightenment in Prague and Tarnopol rather than in Mantua and Florence. Reggio's life in Gorizia also points to another crucial aspect of his world. In spite of his vast library and relative proximity to Venice and Vienna, he was isolated from the cultural centers of European Jewish life. In his autobiography, which amounts to little more than an annotated listing of his publications, he lamented the absence of interlocutors in Gorizia.[9] What Reggio lacked in immediate social contacts, he compensated for with an extensive network of correspondents that included such luminaries of learning as Geiger and Luzzatto. Letters that circulated among participants in the Jewish Enlightenment were widely disseminated: much of Reggio's correspondence appeared in Hebrew periodicals that emerged and collapsed with astonishing frequency in the early nineteenth century.[10]

Gruyter, 1995); Boaz Huss, "Admiration and Disgust: The Ambivalent Re-Canonization of the *Zohar* in the Modern Period," in *Study and Knowledge in Jewish Thought*, ed. Howard Kreisel, 203–37 (Beer Sheva: Ben-Gurion University of the Negev Press, 2006).

[7] David Malkiel, "New Light on the Career of Isaac Samuel Reggio," in *The Jews of Italy: Memory and Identity*, ed. Bernard D. Cooperman and Barbara Garvin, 276–303 (Bethesda: University Press of Maryland, 2000); for references to prior literature on Reggio, see 277, n. 3.

[8] On Reggio's identification with Italy, see Lois C. Dubin, *The Port Jews of Habsburg Trieste: Absolutist Politics and Enlightenment Culture* (Stanford: Stanford University Press, 1999), 132.

[9] *Mazkeret Yashar* (Vienna: Franz von Schmid, 1849), 8–9; Shmuel Werses, "Patterns in the Autobiographical Literature of the Haskalah," in *Megamot ve-Zurot be-Sifrut ha-Haskalah* (Jerusalem: Magnes Press, 1990), 253.

[10] On epistolarity and the Jewish Enlightenment, see Moshe Pelli, "The Beginnings of the Epistolary Genre in Modern Hebrew Literature: Isaac Euchel and His Letters" (Hebrew), in *Bikoret u-Farshanut* 16 (1981): 85–101. On periodicals, see Bernhard Wachstein, *Die hebräische publizistik in Wien* (Vienna: Selbstverlag der Historischen Kommision, 1930); Menuha Gilboa, *Leksikon ha-Itonut ha-Ivrit ba-meot ha-shemoneh esreh ve-ha tesha-esreh*

Reggio's graphomania took forms other than frequent and lengthy letters. In 1821 he published an edition of the Bible self-consciously modeled on Moses Mendelssohn's *Biur* that included a newly edited text of the Hebrew Pentateuch, an Italian translation, and an extensive Hebrew commentary.[11] Six years later he attempted to reconcile philosophy with Judaism in a treatise called *Ha-Torah veha-filosofiya*. The book represented Reggio's part in a polemic about the newly founded modern rabbinical college in Padua.[12] When it appeared, *Ha-Torah veha-filosofiya* lacked a final chapter on Kabbalah that Reggio claimed he was not allowed to print. This chapter circulated in manuscript among Reggio's colleagues and, much to his own chagrin, would later resurface in print.

Reggio's opposition to Kabbalah and his valorization of *Ari Nohem* developed gradually. In 1816 he wrote a lengthy letter to Moses Kunitz (1774–1837), a rabbi in Pest who had written a defense of Simeon bar Yohai's authorship of the *Zohar*.[13] Reggio summarized the contents of *Ari Nohem*, expressed his bewilderment about Modena's skepticism of Kabbalah, and appealed to Kunitz for guidance.[14] In turn, Kunitz printed Reggio's praise, castigated Modena for his audacity, and repeated Azulai's claim about Modena's recantation late in life. In Kunitz's account, Modena had completely withdrawn his opposition to Kabbalah rather than only his denial of the transmigration of souls. But Kunitz admitted that he had never seen *Ari Nohem* and offered a handsome sum of money to anyone who would furnish him a copy.[15] Reggio in turn volunteered to send him one from Vienna, where he hoped to travel in the near future.[16]

(Jerusalem: Mossad Bialik, 1992). German periodicals did not constitute collection of letters. See Moshe Pelli, *Kerem Hemed: Hokhmat Yisrael bi Yavneh ha-Hadasha* (Jerusalem: Magnes Press, 2009), 26.

[11] Isaac Reggio, *Torat Elohim* (Vienna: Anton Strauss, 1821). On Mendelssohn's Bible, see Edward Breuer, *The Limits of Enlightenment: Jews, Germans, and the Eighteenth-Century Study of Scripture* (Cambridge: Harvard University Pres, 1996).

[12] *Ha-Torah veha-filosofiya* (Vienna: Anton von Schmid, 1827). On the polemic, see Maddalena del Bianco Cotrozzi, *Il Collegio rabbinico di Padova* (Florence: L. S. Olschki, 1995). On the purpose of *Ha-Torah veha-filosofiya*, see *Mazkeret Yashar*, 11.

[13] *Ben Yohai* (Vienna, 1815). On Kunitz, see Reuven Fahn, "Rabbi Moses Kunitz" (Hebrew), in *Pirke Haskalah: Kitvei Reuven Fahn II*, 70–99 (Stanisławów, 1937); Michael Silber, "The Historical Experience of German Jewry and Its Impact on Haskalah and Reform in Hungary," in Katz, *Toward Modernity*, 114.

[14] *Hamzaref* (Vienna: Anton Strauss, 1820), 1:41–47. I have followed the spelling of the title as it appears in Latin characters on the title page (and is frequently catalogued) rather than *Ha-Mezaref*. As cited and dated in David Malkiel, "The Reggios of Gorizia: Modernization in Micro," in *The Mediterranean and the Jews: Society, Culture, and Economy in Early Modern Times*, ed. Elliott Horowitz and Moises Orfali (Ramat Gan: Bar–Ilan University Press, 2002), 76–77.

[15] *Hamzaref*, 1:43.

[16] Ibid., 47.

Reggio evidently fulfilled his promise to Kunitz. A letter of his included in the first volume of *Kerem Hemed*, a journal published by the Galician *maskil* Samuel Goldenberg (1807–1846), demonstrates how the once fawning correspondent of Kunitz had changed over the course of a decade:

> The copy of *Sefer Ari Nohem* that is in the possession of Moses Kunitz from Ofen is mine. For I gave it to him personally when he was in Vienna several years ago so that he could make a copy for his own purposes before returning it. But I have waited in vain for several years now. I gave up and asked one of my acquaintances in the town of Mantua to send me a copy and he did. Behold this book is extremely precious to me. There is no other book like it that destroys the very foundations of Kabbalah.[17]

Reggio tellingly depicted the material conditions of scholarship in the early nineteenth century. He had waited so long for the manuscript he had loaned to Kunitz that he had to secure another copy. Reggio went on to describe his decision to withhold a planned edition of *Ari Nohem*, a text that had become extremely valuable to him: "But now our friend Samson Bloch has plans to publish it, I will pull back so as not to compete with him, heaven forefend. But if I see that his edition contains any aberrations not contained in my manuscript, I will rise up to purify it from any blemish and print a list of corrections in a future issue."[18] A Galician *maskil* and colleague of Goldenberg's, Bloch had written a work of geography in Hebrew and worked briefly as a typesetter for Reggio's Vienna publisher, Anton von Schmid.[19] He also contributed to *Kerem Hemed*, and the same volume contained his lengthy discussion of Kant.[20] In spite of Reggio's obvious desire to print *Ari Nohem*, his response to news of Bloch's rival edition was tempered by scholarly dispassion. He was determined not to compete with his colleague and indicated in his open letter that he would consign himself to a list of errata.

---

[17] Letter no. 24, *KH* 1 (Vienna: Anton von Schmid, 1833), 88. Dated 27 Tevet 5590 (22 January 1830). As cited and dated in Adelman, "Success and Failure," 39, n. 3. For the possibility that the colleague in Mantua was Samuel della Volta, see below. For Reggio's reflection on the change in his attitude toward Kabbalah, see his letter no. 21, *KH* 1, 79.

[18] Letter no. 24, *KH* 1, 88.

[19] On Bloch, see Shmuel Werses, "Hasidism and Sabbatianism in the Estimation of Galician Maskilim" (Hebrew), in *Haskalah ve-Shabtaut: Toldotav shel Ma'avak* (Jerusalem: Zalman Shazar Center, 1988), 114–15. On later tensions between Bloch and Reggio, see Werses, "An Unknown Satiric Work of Joseph Perl" (Hebrew), *Hasifrut* 1 (1968–1969): 215. On this printing house, which printed the first two volumes of *Kerem Hemed* as well as works by Reggio, see Raphael Julius, "Anton von Schmid: Royal Printer and Nobleman," *Jewish Book Annual* 51 (1993–1994): 195–202.

[20] Letter no. 34, *KH* 1, 109–22.

A letter Reggio received from Solomon Judah Rapoport (1790–1867), who was likewise deeply involved in the publication of *Kerem Hemed*, implied that Bloch had abandoned his edition.[21] Rapoport warned Reggio of possible problems with censorship:

> Concerning the book *Ari Nohem* I also think that permission will not be granted to print it. The apostate who is in charge of [censorship] is known to me as brutish and mean spirited. Every book is suspect in his eyes, especially if it contains excellent and upright ideas, and he would very quickly find reason to object to it. For example, [the sections] in *Ari Nohem* that mention Kabbalah, even if only to oppose it, he would question its necessity and say that it is forbidden to print secrets.[22]

Rapoport implied that Reggio himself was preparing the edition, although he did not indicate where he might want to print it or divulge the identity of the censor. Given that the first two volumes of *Kerem Hemed* as well as Reggio's edition of *Behinat ha-Dat* and a volume of his letters had all appeared in Vienna, it stands to reason that Reggio planned to print his edition there. Another alternative may have been Prague, the location of the Landau press, which published several of the later volumes of *Kerem Hemed*; however, Karl Fischer, the censor in Prague in the early 1830s, was a gentile from birth rather than the Jewish apostate described by Rapoport.[23] In the Habsburg Empire in the early nineteenth century, books that contained Hasidic and kabbalistic material were subject to a regime of censorship that became as celebrated for its incompetence as it was for its suspicion. Any book containing Kabbalah, even one that was critical of it, was subject to censorship.[24]

---

[21] For corroboration of Bloch's plans and their failure to come to fruition, see Meir Letteris, *Zikaron ha-sefer* (Vienna, 1869), 109; as cited in Huss, *Ke-zohar ha-rakia*, 354. On Letteris, who also worked as a Hebrew typesetter in Vienna, see Moseley, *Being for Myself Alone*, 77–80.

[22] Letter from S. Y. Rapoport to Isaac Reggio dated 29 Nissan 5591 (12 April 1831), in Abraham Berliner, "Causing the Lips of Those That Are Asleep to Speak" (Hebrew), in *Zikaron le-Avraham Eliyahu: Kevutsat ma'amarim be-hokhmat Yisrael li-khevod Avraham Eliyahu Harkabi*, ed. Baron D. V. Günzburg and I. Markon (St. Petersburg, 1908) (reprint Jerusalem, 1969), 487; cited and dated in Pelli, *Kerem Hemed*, 27, n. 54.

[23] Iveta Cermanová, "Karl Fischer (1757–1844), 1: The Life and Intellectual World of a Hebrew Censor," *Judaica Bohemiae* 42 (2006): 125–78; Cermanová, "Karl Fischer (1757–1844), 2: The Work of a Hebrew Censor," *Judaica Bohemiae* 43 (2007–2008): 5–63. On Rapoport's attempt to succeed Fischer, see 62–63.

[24] On Vienna, see Cermanová, "The Censorship of Hebrew Manuscripts in Vienna in the Early 19th Century: The Case of Abraham Trebitsch," in *Judaica Bohemiae* 39 (2003): 93–103; Raphael Mahler, *Hasidism and the Jewish Enlightenment* (Philadelphia: JPS, 1985), 105–19. Mahler discusses the censoring of Reggio's edition of *Behinat ha-Dat* on 107. On censorship in Galicia, see Rachel Manekin, "Joseph Perl on *Hok le-Yisrael* and the Spread of Hasidism" (Hebrew), in *Yashan mipnei Hadash: Shai le-Imanuel Etkes*, ed. David Assaf and Ada Rapoport-Albert, 2:345–54 (Jerusalem: Zalman Shazar Center, 2009).

In a letter to Samuel Goldenberg that appeared in the second volume of *Kerem Hemed*, Reggio again brought up a possible edition of *Ari Nohem*:

> I too yearn to see it printed in its entirety without anything missing, but I am still doubtful whether you and your colleague will succeed in printing it; for it is very difficult and for this reason I have guarded the copy that I obtained for myself with great effort and I have not sent it . . . but if you absolutely promise me to print it, listen to what I propose to do: Although my time is exceedingly precious, I will copy it out myself so that it should contain no mistakes due to the laziness of another copyist, and as I copy it out I shall add my annotations anywhere that I see fit. When I finish doing so, I shall send it to you on the condition that you do not delay its printing and that you send me thirty copies.[25]

Reggio thus volunteered to edit *Ari Nohem* on the condition that Goldenberg made a genuine effort to print it and agreed to compensate him.

At this point *Ari Nohem* was circulating quite widely among participants in the Jewish Enlightenment in Galicia and northern Italy, and repeated references to it were appearing in print.[26] An anonymous letter written later that year and included in the same volume of *Kerem Hemed* mounted a thorough assault on the antiquity of the *Zohar*: "Rabbi Judah Aryeh Modena . . . wrote an indictment of the *Zohar* and Kabbalah in a manuscript book called *Ari Nohem* (which has not yet appeared in print, but is concealed in the library of the doctor, Samuel della Volta of Mantua, and I copied it from him. I have no doubt that the author of *Kinat ha-Emet*[27] who mentioned it obtained it from him or from one of his compatriots)."[28] Immediately following was a list of the arguments that Modena had made against the antiquity of the *Zohar* as well as a separate list of those made by Emden in *Mitpahat Sefarim*. The letter cast doubt on the antiquity of Kabbalah through the time-honored strategy of demonstrating the lateness of the *Zohar*. The author of this anonymous letter was actually Samuel David

---

[25] Letter no. 20, *KH* 2 (Vienna: Anton von Schmid, 1836), 135, dated 28 Sivan 5591 (9 June 1831).

[26] See the bio-bibliographical entry on Modena, which mentions *Ari Nohem*, in Salomon Ephraim Blogg, *Aedificium Salomonis* (Hanover: E. A. Telgener, 1832), 105; as cited by Adelman, "Success and Failure," 36–37.

[27] For reference to *Ari Nohem* in this criticism of Kabbalah and Hasidism, see Judah Leib Mieses, *Kinat ha-Emet* (Vienna: Anton von Schmid, 1828), 135–36. Mieses did not draw extensively on *Ari Nohem*, and a letter he wrote on Maimonides and Kabbalah did not mention it. See *Bikurei ha-Itim* 11 (1831): 131–42; Moshe Pelli, *Bikurei ha-Itim: Bikure ha-Haskalah* (Jerusalem: Magnes Press, 2005), 243; the letter appears as an appendix to Melamed, "Conversion Myths." On Mieses, see Shmuel Werses, "Magic and Demonolgy as Reflected in the Satirical Literature of Galician *Masklim*" (Hebrew), in *Hakitzah Ami: Sifrut ha–Haskalah be–idan ha–modernizasyah*, 353–74 (Jerusalem: Magnes Press, 2000).

[28] Letter no. 25, 156, dated 16 Tammuz 5592 (14 July 1832); as cited and dated in Penkower, "S. D. Luzzatto, Vowels, and Accents," 120.

Luzzatto (1800–1865), who had composed a disputation against Kabbalah in 1825 that would not appear in print until 1852.[29] Many of the arguments Luzzatto made in this unsigned letter and in his longer polemic echoed or repeated arguments in *Ari Nohem*.

Shortly thereafter Reggio succeeded in printing an edition of *Behinat ha-Dat* accompanied by an extensive commentary.[30] In looking to Delmedigo for historical precedent in the defense of the religious value of philosophy, Reggio included lengthy excurses on contemporary philosophical issues. Two of these dealt with Delmedigo's opposition to Kabbalah, in which Reggio offered a summary of *Ari Nohem* that emphasized Modena's challenge to the antiquity of Kabbalah.[31] He also presented the entirety of the ninth chapter, which constituted the first appearance of a substantial portion of *Ari Nohem* in print. Elsewhere in his notes to *Behinat ha-Dat*, Reggio drew on his own working edition of *Ari Nohem*. When he dealt with the appearance of the *Zohar* in print, Reggio remarked on the absurd notions of sixteenth-century kabbalists who attached their approbations to a book that had ostensibly been written in the second century.[32] The following year the same press in Vienna issued the first of two volumes of Reggio's letters. These letters contained repeated references to Modena and included a description of *Ari Nohem* as having "destroyed, overturned, and uprooted in this short book of his more than the kabbalists built and planted in all of their large and many works."[33]

In between the appearance of *Behinat ha-Dat* and the first volume of his letters, Reggio had abandoned his plan to print *Ari Nohem*. His public appeal to Goldenberg in the pages of *Kerem Hemed* notwithstanding, Reggio had evidently been convinced by Rapoport's warning about censorship. In a letter from Gorizia to Solomon Rosenthal (1763–1845) of Pest, Reggio answered an inquiry about *Ari Nohem*:

> To respond briefly to your idea to print the book *Ari Nohem*: I am almost certain that the censor will not permit you to publish it, given that I know its contents.

---

[29] Following Wachstein, Pelli lists Hillel ha-Kohen della Torre as the author. See his *Kerem Hemed*, 306. However, Penkower proved it was Luzzatto by pointing to his acknowledgment on the Hebrew title page of *Vikuah al Hokhmat ha-Kabalah* (Gorizia, 1852) (photo offset edition, Jerusalem, 1968). See "S. D. Luzzatto, Vowels, and Accents," 120, n. 135.

[30] Reggio did not reedit the text but presented it as it appeared in *Ta'alumot Hokhmah*, which he claimed had become difficult to find. See Elijah Delmedigo, *Sefer Behinat ha-Dat*, ed. Isaac Reggio (Vienna: Anton von Schmid, 1833), i.

[31] Ibid., 103–7.

[32] Ibid., 108.

[33] *Igrot Yashar* (Vienna: Anton von Schmid, 1834), letter no. 6, 37. Further references to Modena appear in letter no. 13, 81–86, where he discussed *Ari Nohem* and letter no. 15, 95, where he discussed Modena's annotated copy of *Meor Enayim*.

But you may as well try, for maybe your good intentions will come to pass; but I have given up on it because of the impediments. And about what you have asked of me, to edit the text from the manuscript in my possession, here are edits to the passages to which you alluded, as I was able to understand from your letter.[34]

The grudging hope that Rosenthal might succeed where he had failed makes it hard to ignore the chilly tone of Reggio's letter. The letter concluded with four short notes to the text of *Ari Nohem* based on Reggio's working edition. Reggio's response, preserved in Rosenthal's correspondence, indicates that his fear of censorship was genuine enough for him to abandon a project in which he had invested considerable intellectual energy.

Although he may have given up on printing *Ari Nohem*, Reggio's edition survives.[35] Laid out as if it were a frontispiece to a printed book, the title page summarily announced "brought to the printing press now for the first time with new annotations."[36] Reggio's edition combined historical scholarship about *Ari Nohem* with a hagiographic portrait of it author and a sharp polemic against contemporary Kabbalah. As someone committed to the practice of scientific scholarship, Reggio furnished his edition with explanatory endnotes. When Modena mentioned Joseph Solomon Delmedigo, Reggio pointed to the difficulty in identifying Delmedigo's actual position on Kabbalah. He quoted the passage from *Mazref le-Hokhmah* adduced by Yair Hayim Bacharach in which Delmedigo argued that what authors wrote might not provide an accurate record of their beliefs.[37] In annotating a passage where Modena declared that he had regularly engaged in debates with Jewish converts to Christianity, Reggio pointed to a manuscript of *Magen va-Herev* in the de' Rossi collection.[38] At the mention of *Ben David*, Reggio confessed that he had not seen the work but indicated that it was mentioned in Lampronti's *Pahad Yitzhak* and in de' Rossi's catalogue of Hebrew manuscripts.[39] He later added to the same note that he had managed to secure a copy of the work for himself. Many of Reggio's annotations have been superseded by nearly two centuries of research, yet they offer invaluable insight into the state of historical scholarship in

---

[34] Warsaw, Jewish Historical Institute, MS 24; consulted on microform reel F 40157 at the JNUL. The manuscript is unpaginated. The letter is number 17. Signed by Reggio and dated 10 Heshvan 5594 (23 October 1833).

[35] Manuscript L.

[36] Ibid., i.

[37] Ibid., 40A, n. 7.

[38] Ibid., n. 8. He also cited a passage from Modena's introduction to *Sha'agat Aryeh* in the same collection. See ibid., 38B–39A, n. 6.

[39] Ibid., 41A, n. 13. On Lampronti, see chapter 6. On *Ben David* in de'Rossi's catalogue, see Cod. 85 in *MSS Codices Hebraici Biblioth. I. B. De-Rossi* (Parma, 1803), 1:53.

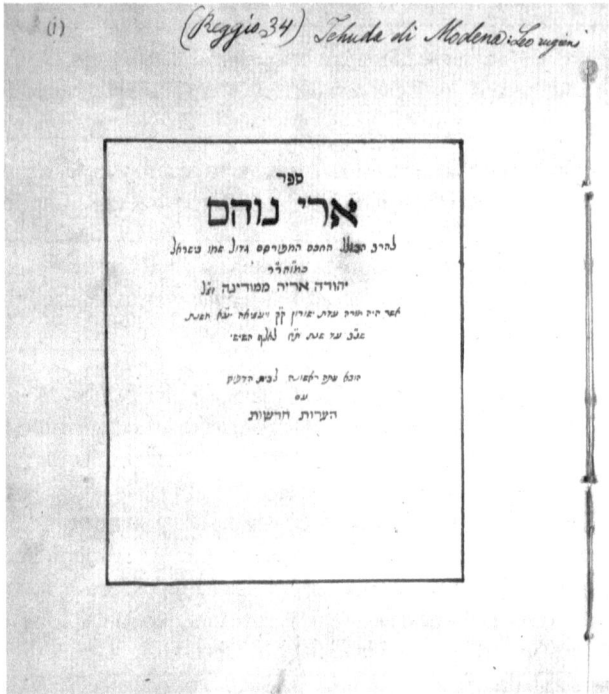

Figure 13. Title page to Isaac Reggio's working edition of *Ari Nohem*
Bodleian Library, University of Oxford, MS. Reggio 34, fol. 1r.
Reproduced by permission of the Bodleian Libraries, University of Oxford.
The title page to Reggio's abandoned edition of *Ari Nohem* declared: "Brought to press for the first time."

the early nineteenth century. Some even retain their critical value. For example, Reggio identified Modena's reference to a kabbalistic interpretation of Maimonides' *Guide* as an allusion to the commentary of Abraham Abulafia.[40]

For all of its bibliographic insight, Reggio's edition was hardly a model of scholarly dispassion. He depicted Modena as an exemplar of virtue and erudition. In his note to the description of Hamiz as prodigiously learned, Reggio asserted that "study of external sciences was so common during that period, even among the most celebrated rabbis of the generation, that this upright author who occupied the chair of instruction in the city of Venice for his entire life was proud of the fact that he himself had guided

[40] MS L, 41B, n. 15.

his student in the pathways of theology, astronomy, and natural science."[41] In addition to occupying a fictitious "chair," Reggio's Modena was fearless and judicious in his evaluation of Kabbalah:

> We see this complete scholar whose eyes beheld every splendor and who pursued knowledge his entire life ... engaging this subject with a balanced and careful mind for fifty years only to emerge with a true and just evaluation. He was not seduced or incited to flatter others or even himself, nor did he have any hope of glory or financial gain from the announcement of his views, for most of the sages of his generation were ardent devotees of the study of Kabbalah. His heart was like that of a lion, he was not afraid of anything and only desired to pursue the truth.[42]

Reggio's own opposition to Kabbalah led him to resist certain claims within *Ari Nohem*. Responding to Modena's characterization of the *Zohar* as an exegetical and homiletic source, Reggio wrote:

> He [Modena] exaggerates in the measure of his praises, for although it is possible that something can be found in this work [the *Zohar*] relevant to the ethical life or the performance of the commandments or the study of Torah, nevertheless it does not contain all of the positive attributes that this author [Modena] attributed to it, and especially not to the degree that he claims. And I will not enumerate all of the deficiencies contained in it, for I would have to compose an enormous work.[43]

Reggio saw his edition as the latest salvo in a battle against contemporary kabbalists. *Ari Nohem* was a crucial text in his own opposition to Kabbalah. But it was not the only one. His edition also included the antikabbalistic poetry of Jacob Frances, which had not appeared in print for over a century and which he hoped would serve a similar purpose to *Ari Nohem*.[44]

Reggio may have despaired of his edition, but *Ari Nohem* continued to circulate among the learned elites in the Habsburg Empire and northern Italy. In a letter to Mordecai Samuel Ghirondi in 1835, Rapoport chastised his correspondent: "You declared judgment on the book *Ari Nohem* by Rabbi Judah Modena, of blessed memory. And you said that he spoke deceitfully and tempestuously about the wisdom of truth. But I have read this extraordinary book from beginning to end and I have found that its author spoke with a pure heart, a proper spirit, and with the clarity appropriate to a scholar like him at his age.... His words penetrate the depths of

---

[41] Ibid., 38A, n. 1.
[42] Ibid., 38B, n. 5.
[43] Ibid., 42A, n. 18.
[44] Ibid., 36B–37B.

the heart. Who could oppose them?"⁴⁵ Rapoport also addressed Ghirdoni's argument about the reception of *Ari Nohem*:

> But you claimed that Moses Hayim Luzzatto, of blessed memory, destroyed and demolished all of his arguments, like chaff driven away by the wind.⁴⁶....
> I do not want to enter to deeply into these matters and express my thoughts about them, but I wanted to dispute with you as a beloved friend about that which you have hurriedly decided ... because if the book *Hoqer u-Mekubal* (which I have also seen several years ago) was intended to break the sharp teeth of the roaring lion [*Ari Nohem*], behold I say definitively that it did not accomplish its goal, and the lion continues to roar now as it did then, thundering in every ear.

A century after Luzzatto had written *Hoqer u-Mekubal*, participants in the Jewish Enlightenment continued to read it as a response to *Ari Nohem*. Rapoport harbored little affection for Kabbalah or Hasidism, but he was circumspect in his opposition. His critical glosses on Kunitz's *Ben Yohai*, a work he objected to in no uncertain terms, did not appear in his lifetime. *Ari Nohem* was part of a number of texts, including Emden's *Mitpahat Sefarim* and Delmedigo's *Behinat ha-Dat*, that he used to constitute a tradition of rabbinic antikabbalism that anticipated his own efforts.⁴⁷

For all the discussion among different scholars in both published and unpublished correspondence, and for all the editions that had been planned and even prepared, *Ari Nohem* had still not appeared in print. In the third volume of *Kerem Hemed*, Goldenberg confronted these repeated failures: "What shall we do with the book *Ari Nohem*? Has it been printed or not? ... The rabbi and sage Solomon Rosenthal of Pest was preparing to print this precious book but he was unsuccessful ... it appears that the fate of this beloved book will be like that of other old manuscripts that remain

---

⁴⁵ "Letter from Shlomo Yehuda Rapoport of Lvov to Mordecai Samuel Ghirondi of Padua" (Hebrew), in *Otzar Tov: Magazin für die Wissenschaft des Judenthums* (1891), 53, dated 9 Kislev 5596 (30 November 1835); cited by Adelman, "Success and Failure," 46, n. 22.

⁴⁶ Cf. Ps 1:4.

⁴⁷ See letter no. 29, *KH* 2, 172, which mentions *Ari Nohem* among other works critical of Kabbalah, including *Mitpahat Sefarim* and *Behinat ha-Dat*. The author describes critical glosses on Kunitz's *Ben Yohai*. On the difficulty of identifying the author of this letter, see Shmuel Werses, "The Dispute between Emden and Eibeschuetz in the Eyes of the Nineteenth-Century Maskilim" (Hebrew), in *Haskalah ve-Shabtaut*, 46. On the probability that the author of the glosses on Kunitz and owner of these books mentioned in the anonymous letter was Rapoport, see Fischel Lachover, "Revealed and Concealed in the Thought of Nachman Krochmal" (Hebrew), *Keneset* 6 (1941): 298, n. 8. Rapoport's response to Kunitz appeared posthumously as *Nahalat Yehudah* (Lvov, 1873). The unpaginated preface included an antikabbalistic poem by Jacob Frances. On Rapoport's later reevaluation of Modena after the appearance of *Kol Sakhal*, see letter no. 37 in *S. L. Rappoport's hebräische Briefe an S.D. Luzzatto (1833–1860)*, ed. Eisig Gräber (Przemysl, 1886), 208.

shut up and do not see the light of day."⁴⁸ In the continuation of the letter, Goldenberg described Reggio's plan to print an edition of *Ari Nohem* several years earlier and reproduced the short introduction to his abandoned edition.

The following year Rosenthal went ahead with his plans to print *Ari Nohem*. In a letter written to Goldenberg in February 1839, Rosenthal indicated that he would send him his completed edition in care of Moses Landau, whose press in Prague had published the third volume of *Kerem Hemed*: "I am sending you the book *Ari Nohem* . . . with my permission to print it along with the accompanying notes. But do not forget that you are bound to me by oath not to publish my name or that you received the notebook from me, although I already alluded to my involvement at the end of my introduction."⁴⁹ Rosenthal sought anonymity because he did not want to subject himself to the abuse that would befall whomever brought *Ari Nohem* to press. In his response from Prague written just over a week later, Goldenberg confirmed his receipt of the edition and fawningly praised Rosenthal for rescuing Modena's text from obscurity: "But you my friend and beloved master, do not worry and do not fret, for I will not reveal your name and will not say where the book came from; how well do I know how lovers of strife and haters of wisdom have increased in this generation, those who for the sake of temporary advantage will don the rough garment to deceive,⁵⁰ in order to appear before the people as holy and zealous for the glory of the kabbalists and their books."⁵¹ Goldenberg informed Rosenthal of his plans to travel to Ashkenaz, referring to German-speaking lands outside the Habsburg Empire, and signed off with an account of his pilgrimage to the dilapidated grave of Joseph Solomon Delmedigo in the Prague cemetery. For all their criticism, antikabbalists also made pilgrimages to the gravesites of their predecessors.

Rosenthal's desire to withhold his name from the edition of *Ari Nohem* was in keeping with the public persona he had to maintain in Pest. As a powerful and wealthy layman in the Jewish community, he played a central role in the educational and rabbinic politics of Pest and nearby cities in the

---

⁴⁸ Letter no. 15, *KH* 3 (Prague: Landau, 1838), 193. In the same issue, Joseph Almanzi mentioned his own copy of *Ari Nohem*. See letter no. 10, 141, n. 53. Almanzi's copy survives as MS E. For his poem in praise of Modena that mentions *Ari Nohem*, see *Higayon be-Khinor* (Vienna: Franz von Schmid, 1839), Poem 41, 70–78; as cited in Adelman, "Success and Failure," 48, n. 40.

⁴⁹ Letter dated 23 Shevat 5599 (7 February 1839), in Jekuthiel Greenwald, *Sefer Toldot misphahat Rosenthal* (Budapest, 1921), 103. Greenwald includes only 23 Shevat at the top of the letter without giving the year; however, Goldenberg's response cited below is dated 2 Adar 5599 and opens as an immediate reply to Rosenthal's letter of 23 Shevat.

⁵⁰ Zech. 13:4.

⁵¹ Greenwald, *Sefer Toldot*, 81–84. Letter dated 2 Adar 5599 (16 February 1839). The letter also appears in *Shai le-Moreh*, ed. Simeon Buechler (Budapest: Sternberg, 1895), 39–41.

early nineteenth century.⁵² Rather than risk alienating his contemporaries who were well disposed to Kabbalah and who might be offended by his edition, he preferred to remain anonymous.⁵³ Moses Landau, who transmitted Rosenthal's manuscript to Goldenberg, was a central figure in the Jewish Enlightenment in Prague. Their correspondence leaves little doubt that either of them had thought to print *Ari Nohem* in Prague.⁵⁴ They apparently had agreed that the work should appear at a press in "Ashkenaz," beyond the borders of the Habsburg Empire, so as to avoid the censorship that had stymied Reggio.

Rosenthal and Goldenberg had other concerns besides books. Their collective attempt to print *Ari Nohem* occurred in the midst of an elaborate campaign to secure an appointment for Rapoport as rabbi of Prague. After having spent much of his early life in Lemberg, Rapoport had been appointed rabbi of Tarnopol, a Galician town that was home to Goldenberg as well as Joseph Perl (1773–1839). A satirist and educational reformer who was one of the dominant figures of the Jewish Enlightenment in Galicia, Perl had triumphed over competing factions in Tarnopol in arranging Rapoport's appointment.⁵⁵ But it was a pyrrhic victory, as opposition to Rapoport among Hasidim and others in the town steadily mounted. Desperate to leave Tarnopol in the spring of 1839, Rapoport hoped to become rabbi of Prague and enlisted Rosenthal to secure the support of the great figure of nineteenth-century Hungarian Jewry, Rabbi Moses Sofer.⁵⁶ In a letter from Tarnopol in the early summer, Rapoport entreated Rosenthal to write to Sofer on his behalf and informed him in passing that Goldenberg had returned from Leipzig, where he had left *Ari Nohem* with a printer who planned to print his edition.⁵⁷ Six weeks later, an embarrassed Goldenberg wrote to Rosenthal that he still had not heard from Fürst but insisted that

---

⁵² Michael K. Silber, "Rosenthal Family," in *The YIVO Encyclopedia of the Jews of in Eastern Europe*, 2:1593–94.

⁵³ He had little compunction in attacking Reggio and Luzzatto for their ostensible defamation of Maimonides in a pamphlet that appeared at the same time. See Solomon Rosenthal, *Bet Owen* (Ofen, 1839).

⁵⁴ Landau's press printed editions of the Bible, Talmud, and much else, but little Kabbalah. See Bedřich Nosek, "Auswahlkatalog Hebräischer Drucke Prager Provenienz: Druckerei M. I. Landau, 1824–1853," *Judaica Bohemia* 15 (1979): 86–121. On Landau, see also Sharon Flatto, *The Kabbalistic Culture of Eighteenth-Century Prague: Ezekiel Landau (the "Noda Biyehudah") and his Contemporaries* (Oxford: Littman Library, 2010), 56–57.

⁵⁵ Haim Gertner, "Image and Reality in the Relationship between Maskilim and Hasidim: The Case of Shlomoh Yehudah Rapoport's Appointment to the Rabbinate of Tarnopol" (Hebrew), in Assaf and Rapoport-Albert, *Yashan mipnei Hadash*, 2:355–83.

⁵⁶ Jacob Katz, "Towards a Biography of the Hatam Sofer," in *Divine Law in Human Hands*, 403–43; Marc B. Shapiro, "Aspects of Rabbi Moses Sofer's Intellectual Profile," in *Be'erot Yitzhak*, 285–310; Michael K. Silber, "Sofer, Mosheh" in *The YIVO Encyclopedia of the Jews of in Eastern Europe*, 2:1775–78.

⁵⁷ Letter dated 13 Tammuz 5599 (25 June 1839). See Greenwald, *Sefer Toldot*, 84–85.

he had been promised that *Ari Nohem* would appear at the Tauchnitz press in Leipzig.[58] By the end of December, Goldenberg was exasperated and exclaimed to Rosenthal: "I sold one hundred copies of the book in the city of Leipzig; now I have received a letter from him [Fürst] that states he only wants to give me fifty copies and I have already exchanged words with him; but it seems he is not to be trusted, for to this day he has not sent me a single copy and I have not even seen a single page, and who knows if the book will reach our land."[59]

Fürst's edition had indeed appeared in Leipzig at the Tauchnitz press with a title page that bore the date 1840. A student of the Hebraist Wilhelm Gesenius, Fürst served as a *Privatdozent* in Oriental languages at the University of Leipzig. He refused to convert to Christianity to obtain a professorship and later had the dubious privilege of being the first of the *Wissenschaft* scholars to become an unsalaried honorary professor.[60] Fürst claimed that Goldenberg had given him a copy of *Ari Nohem* with the annotations of an unnamed individual and implored him to print it.[61] After jettisoning much of this scholarly apparatus, he agreed to print it at his own expense. Rosenthal's name did not appear anywhere, and his introduction bore the heading "Introduction of a Certain Man."[62] In his own preface, Fürst translated into Hebrew the description of Kabbalah in Leopold Zunz's *Die gottesdienstlichen Vorträge der Juden*.[63] In a note to his translation, Fürst concluded, "In our own times scholars of wisdom and science have risen up to fight against the sect of the Hasidim, who have inherited the delusion of Kabbalah from the sect of the Ba'al Shem Tov."[64] Fürst pointedly raised one of the polemical contexts into which he and other scholars hoped to place *Ari Nohem*: opposition to Hasidism. His translation of Zunz attempted to incorporate one the leading practitioners of *Wissenschaft des Judentums* in his own edition.

If Fürst's preface amounted to little more than a translation from Zunz, Rosenthal's unsigned introduction offered an excellent summary of *Ari Nohem*. He mentioned Modena's attack on the antiquity of Kabbalah, especially the critical treatment of kabbalistic texts, his ideal of Maimonidean rationalism, and his rejection of kabbalistic notions of prayer. The final paragraph described the popularity of Kabbalah among Christian theologians and mentioned the Latin translations of kabbalistic classics by Knorr

---

[58] Letter dated 3 Elul 5599 (13 August 1839). Ibid., 103–4.
[59] Letter dated 15 Tevet 5600 (22 December 1839). Ibid., 104.
[60] Schorsch, "The Emergence of Historical Consciousness in Modern Judaism," in *From Text to Context*, 194.
[61] *Ari Nohem*, ed. Fürst, iii.
[62] Ibid., xvii–xx.
[63] Leopold Zunz, *Die gottesdienstlichen Vorträge der Juden* (Berlin: A. Asher, 1832), 402–9.
[64] *Ari Nohem*, ed. Fürst, xiii, n.8.

von Rosenroth.⁶⁵ "The author [Modena] saw all this with a broken heart and spoke in anguish,"⁶⁶ Rosenthal exclaimed and pointed to Modena's opposition to Christian Kabbalah, without realizing that Knorr von Rosenroth's translation project took place well after Modena's death.

Rosenthal was happy to remain anonymous as long as no one else took credit for his work, but the publication of his own edition in Fürst's name left him incensed. In a letter to Luzzatto, Rosenthal accused Fürst and Goldenberg of conspiring against him:

> Samuel Leb Goldenberg of Tarnopol, who is known to you, deceived and cheated me and caused me great pain. With flattery and promises he took the exemplary book *Ari Nohem* from me, which I had copied from an old manuscript filled with errors. I had labored intensively in editing it and had it copied by a professional scribe. I had composed a frontispiece, an introduction, an index to each and every chapter that summarized its contents, as well as many explanatory notes, and sent it to him. He had promised not to change a single thing and as payment for my labor [agreed] to send me several copies after it was printed. But now it is obvious that he betrayed and deceived me, for he handed over the book as a gift to a foreign man, irascible and choleric, as well arrogant, Julius Fürst, ... [who] spoiled the book manuscript of *Ari Nohem* and plundered my work without any indication, and he added an introduction that had no relevance to the book.⁶⁷

In writing to Luzzatto, Rosenthal was addressing himself to one of the most distinguished Jewish scholars of the time. A contributor to Goldenberg's journal as a signed author and as an anonymous correspondent, Luzzatto took a similar stance to Modena's in his attitude toward Kabbalah. He was also addressing one of Rapoport's primary interlocutors in the Jewish Enlightenment at a point when the two were estranged from one another.⁶⁸ Luzzatto, who had corresponded with Rosenthal the year before about the antikabbalistic poetry of Jacob Frances, does not appear to have responded.⁶⁹

In addition to appealing to Luzzatto, Rosenthal expressed his outrage in a letter to Ludwig Philippson of Magdeburg, editor of the *Allgemeine*

---

⁶⁵ Andreas Kilcher, "Kabbalistische Buchmetaphysic: Knorrs Bibliothek und die Bedeutung des Sohar," in Schmidt-Biggemann, *Christliche Kabbala*, 211–23; Boaz Huss, "The Text and Context of the 1684 Sulzbach Edition of the *Zohar*," in Goodblatt and Kreisel, *Tradition, Heterodoxy, and Religious Culture*, 117–38.

⁶⁶ *Ari Nohem*, ed. Fürst, xx.

⁶⁷ Victorius Castiglioni, ed., *Sefer Igrot le-Shadal* (Trieste, 1899), letter no. 6, December 5, 1839, 55–56. Cited by Adelman, "Success and Failure," 50, n. 43.

⁶⁸ Shmuel Werses, "*Shadal* and *Shir*: Luzzatto and Rapoport through Their Letters" (Hebrew), in Bonfil, Gottlieb, and Kasher, *Samuel David Luzzatto*, 79–98.

⁶⁹ See letter no. 248 (5 July 1839) and letter no. 253 (September 20, 1839), in *S. D. Luzzatto's Hebraische Briefe*, ed. Eisig Gräber (Przemysyl: Zupnik & Knoller, 1882) (photo offset ed., Jerusalem, 1966), 631, 640–41.

Zeitung des Judentums, an important weekly German Jewish newspaper. Rosenthal asked him to publicize Fürst's theft in his newspaper.[70] A short notice from Pest about *Ari Nohem* appeared in the *Allgemeine Zeitung des Judentums*, but it mentioned neither Fürst nor Rosenthal.[71] Philippson's newspaper may not have mentioned Rosenthal, but Fürst's own journal, *Der Orient*, included fulsome praise for Rosenthal for his great diligence and identified him as the author of the introduction.[72] All this hardly mattered to the offended party. A letter from Rapoport a month later indicates just how outraged Rosenthal remained: "[Goldenberg] showed me your letter about the book *Ari Nohem*, where you specifically charged him 'not to mention my name on this book,' but now he is being assailed with complaints."[73] Rapoport and Goldenberg were evidently well aware that Rosenthal was furious about Fürst's edition.

Fürst was not the only who had engaged in scholarly theft in the edition of *Ari Nohem*. Rosenthal himself seems to have taken a lengthy section from Reggio's work and appended it to the conclusion without attribution. The last six pages of the edition contain a searing indictment of Kabbalah that was not part of Modena's text but had constituted the final chapter of Reggio's *Ha-Torah veha-filosofiya*. After having read this chapter in manuscript, Rosenthal appears to have appended it to the conclusion of his edition without ascription, and Fürst published it in this form. In this appendix Reggio had objected to the popularization of Kabbalah. He cited many of the sources adduced in *Ari Nohem*, including works by Bar Sheshet, Isserles, and Luria, and accused kabbalists of inconsistency, forgery, and deception. He too lamented the appearance of Kabbalah in print in the sixteenth century and in his own time and concluded with a short discussion of Sabbetai Zevi that pointed to Kabbalah as the source of his messianism.[74]

Neither the sloppiness of Fürst's edition nor the instances of scholarly theft went unnoticed. A short, scathing review signed only with the letter "R" appeared a year later in an issue of *Israelitische Annalen*, a weekly

---

[70] Two drafts of this letter are extant in Rosenthal's correspondence. See Warsaw, Jewish Historical Institute, MS 24, letters 35 and 36.

[71] *Allgemeine Zeitung des Judentums* no. 4, January 25, 1840, 51. On Philippson, see Hans Otto Horch, "'Auf der Zinne der Zeit': Ludwig Philippson (1811–1889)—der 'Journalist des Reformjudentums,'" *Bulletin des Leo Baeck Instituts* 82 (1989): 5–21.

[72] *Der Orient* no. 5, February 1, 1840, 79–80; cited by Adelman, "Success and Failure," 51, n. 47. Fürst seems to have habitually used the work of his colleagues without acknowledgment. In *Der Orient* he translated several of Rapoport's Hebrew essays into German and published them with minimal or no attribution. See Isaac Barzilay, *Shlomo Yehudah Rapoport (Shir), 1790–1867, and His Contemporaries* (Ramat Gan: Massada Press, 1969), 135–45.

[73] Letter dated 10 Adar 5600 (14 February 1840); Greenwald, *Sefer Toldot*, 93.

[74] *Ari Nohem*, ed. Fürst, 91–97. A version of this chapter later appeared in Isaac Reggio, *Yalkut Yashar* (Gorizia: Joh. Bapt. Seitz, 1854), 101–22.

journal edited by the historian I. M. Jost.[75] The reviewer censured Fürst for publishing a text filled with errors and for failing to compare the edition of *Ari Nohem* given to him by Goldenberg with the manuscript in Reggio's possession. After listing a number of these mistakes, he criticized Fürst for claiming that the author had been a rabbi in the town of Modena rather than Venice and for placing the table of contents between Modena's opening letter and the actual text of *Ari Nohem*. This paled, however, in comparison to the outright theft perpetrated by "a certain man" in the last several pages of the edition where a chapter from *Ha-Torah veha-filosofiya* was copied without attribution. Three months later a notice appeared in *Israelitische Annalen* that acknowledged Solomon Rosenthal as the author of the afterword to *Ari Nohem* but claimed that the accusations of plagiarism were exaggerated.[76] Reggio apparently took this as a confession.[77]

Reactions to *Ari Nohem*

Reggio in Gorizia, Fürst in Leipzig, Rapoport in Lemberg and Tarnopol, Luzzatto and Ghirondi in Padua, Della Volta in Mantua, Rosenthal and Kunitz in Pest, Goldenberg in Tarnopol and Prague: *Ari Nohem* circulated widely in northern Italy and central Europe in the two decades before it appeared in print. How the text was copied in manuscript and who did so in each instance has yet to be discovered. Reggio presented his copy to Kunitz in Vienna and made a second copy from Della Volta when his first was not returned. Luzzatto similarly obtained his copy from Mantua. It remains unclear how Rosenthal obtained his copy, although Kunitz may have been the source given that they lived in the same city; Rosenthal later gave his copy to Goldenberg in Prague, who traveled to Leipzig to deliver it to Fürst. No fewer than four scholars—Reggio, Bloch, Rosenthal, and Fürst—contemplated or prepared an edition of *Ari Nohem*. By 1840 *Ari Nohem* was well known among a small coterie of scholars.

When Fürst's edition finally appeared, it ignited the ire of his colleagues, but some were simply pleased that it had finally appeared in print. Luzzatto

---

[75] *Israelitische Annalen*, January 26, 1841, "Nachrichten und Correspondenzen," no. 9, 68–69; cited by Adelman, "Success and Failure," 51, n. 48. On Jost, see Schorsch, "From Wolfenbüttel to *Wissenschaft*: The Divergent Paths of Isaak Markus Jost and Leopold Zunz," in *From Text to Context*, 233–54. On the journal, see Reuven Michael, *Y. M. Yost: avi ha-historyografya ha-Yehudit ha-modernit* (Jerusalem: Magnes Press, 1983), 131–38.

[76] *Israelitische Annalen*, no. 18, April 30 1841, "Literarisches Eigenthum," 144. This notice identified the earlier reviewer as "our Italian correspondent." Given that this earlier reviewer signed his review with the letter "R" and was familiar with Reggio's manuscript, it may have been Reggio himself.

[77] *Mazkeret Yashar*, 11–12.

wrote to Jost in Frankfurt asking him for copies of *Ari Nohem* and Geiger's recent book on Joseph Solomon Delmedigo.[78] Jost responded about a week later that he would be delighted to send him the books for free.[79] Around the same time, Jacob Bodek in Lemberg tried to assuage Rosenthal: "I want to tell you that many of Lemberg's sages read the book *Ari Nohem*, and they were astonished and impressed by the wonderful notes but they didn't know who had written them. I explained to them that you had written them as Fürst had indicated" in *Der Orient*.[80] That same year Isaac Baer Levinsohn wrote to a colleague: "My soul yearns to see the book *Ari Nohem* printed in Leipzig, for a while ago I had the chance to examine it in manuscript for a short time, but I hadn't read it carefully," and he pleaded for a copy, claiming that no new books ever arrived in Kremenitz. Levinsohn mentioned that some had claimed it was better to believe *Ari Nohem* was a forgery than the *Zohar*. Although he doubted the idea, he pointed to positive evaluations of the *Zohar* in Modena's *Bet Yehudah* and left it an open question.[81] In an article on the origins of the *Zohar* printed the following year, Levinsohn exulted in the publication of *Ari Nohem* as having anticipated many of his own arguments against the antiquity of the *Zohar*.[82] In the period between his letter of 1840 and the publication of *Shorshe Levanon*, Levinsohn evidently had obtained a copy of *Ari Nohem* and put to rest any doubts about Modena's authorship.

For all this discussion in the Hebrew republic of letters before and after the printing of *Ari Nohem*, it would be more than a decade before sustained responses to Modena's work appeared: one by a Sephardic kabbalist in Livorno, Elijah Benamozegh (1823–1900), another by an Ashkenazi kabbalist and follower of Elijah of Vilna, Isaac Haver Wildmann (1789–1853), and

---

[78] Letter no. 274, May 4, 1840; *S. D. Luzzatto's Hebraische Briefe*, ed. Gräber, 686. See Geiger, *Melo Chofnajim*.

[79] Letter no. 12, May 12, 1840, in *Igrot le-Shadal*, 21–25.

[80] Letter dated May 17, 1840; Greenwald, *Sefer Toldot*, 101–3. The letter also appears in Buechler, *Shai le-Moreh*, 53–54.

[81] Isaac Baer Levinsohn, *Sefer ha-Zikhronot* (Warsaw, 1890), 50–51. Letter dated to 1840; as cited in Libowitz, *Rabi Yehudah Aryeh Modena*, 81, who refers to the 1886 edition of *Sefer ha-Zikhronot*. Levinsohn's letter is addressed to someone with the initials *tzadi heh gimmel bet*, who can tentatively be identified as Zvi Hirsch Grinboim, a participant in the Russian Jewish Enlightenment and correspondent of Levinsohn's. Shortly after this exchange, Grinboim was baptized in the Russian Orthodox Church and took the name Vladimir Fedorov. He later taught Greek in a gymnasium and served as a censor of Hebrew and Yiddish books in Kiev. On *tzadi heh gimmel* (without the *bet*) as indicative of Grinboim, see Abraham Baer Gottlober, *Zikhronot u-masaot*, ed. Reuven Goldberg (Jerusalem: Mossad Bialik, 1976), 2:115. For the information on Grinboim and the reference to Gottlober, see Michael Stanislawski, *Tsar Nicholas I and the Jews: The Transformation of Jewish Society in Russia, 1825–1855* (Philadelphia: JPS, 1983), 144–46.

[82] *Shorshei Levanaon* (Vilna, 1841), 239; as cited by Adelman, "Success and Failure," 52, n. 51. See also Levinsohn's note on 247.

a third by a scholar deeply committed to Jewish Reform, Abraham Geiger (1810–1874). Both Benamozegh and Wildmann devoted entire works to the rebuttal of *Ari Nohem*, while Geiger praised Modena's opposition to Kabbalah in his biography.

A rabbinic polymath whose intellectual interests defy easy summary, Benamozegh devoted one of his first publications to a refutation of Modena's work.[83] Having read *Ari Nohem* shortly after it was printed, Benamozegh had been deeply disturbed by it. At twenty-six he responded with *Eimat Mafgia al Ari*, which he issued at his own press in Livorno.[84] Its title alluded to a Talmudic passage as well as the object of his criticism: "these are the ... fears in which the strong succumb to the weak: the fear the *mafgia* instills in the lion."[85] Although written at a relatively young age, *Eimat Mafgia* concerned issues that occupied Benamozegh for the rest of his life: the antiquity of Kabbalah, the relationship between Judaism and Christianity, and the dissemination of esoteric knowledge. Like Reggio, Benamozegh wrote a philological and philosophical commentary to the Bible. Unlike Reggio, Benamozegh had profound respect for Kabbalah as a biblical hermeneutic and as an authentic strain of ancient Jewish esotericism. His biblical commentary, which historicized the text of the Bible, incensed his rabbinic colleagues in Aleppo, who deemed it heretical and ordered it destroyed.[86] Less than a decade after *Eimat Mafgia*, Benamozegh wrote another defense of Kabbalah, *Ta'am la-Shad*, in response to Luzzatto's *Vikuah al Hokhmat ha-Kabalah*.[87]

Benamozegh demonstrated a keen awareness of the intellectual assumptions and practices of contemporary historical scholarship and stressed their importance to any account of Kabbalah:

> If we seek to examine why enemies of this knowledge [Kabbalah] have become so numerous and why its adherents so few ... it is because believers [in Kabbalah] lack an awareness of other forms of knowledge.... Our obligation to engage

---

[83] Moshe Idel, "Kabbalah in Elijah Benamozegh's Thought," in Elijah Benamozegh, *Israel and Humanity*, trans. Maxwell Luria (New York: Paulist Press, 1995), 378–402; Alessandro Guetta, "Elia Benamozegh: Bibliografia" *RMI* 53 (1987), 67–81; Guetta, ed., *Per Elia Benamozegh* (Milan: Edizioni Thálassa de Paz, 2001); Guetta, "The Last Debate on Kabbalah in Italian Judaism: I. S. Reggio, S.D. Luzzatto, and E. Benamozegh," in Cooperman and Garvin, *The Jews of Italy: Memory and Identity*, 256–75; Guetta, *Philosophy and Kabbalah: Elijah Benamozegh and the Reconciliation of Western Thought and Jewish Esotericism* (Albany: SUNY Press, 2009).

[84] *Emat Mafgia al Ari* (Livorno: Benamozegh, 1855).

[85] BT *Shabbat*, 77B. Rashi defined *mafgia* as an insect whose voice was so powerful that when heard by a lion, it was mistaken for a large animal and caused the lion to flee.

[86] *Em la-Mikra* (Livorno: Benamozegh, 1862); Yaron Harel, "The Edict to Destroy *Em la-Mikra*—Aleppo 1865" (Hebrew), *HUCA* 64 (1993): 27–36.

[87] For references to Modena in this work, see *Ta'am la-Shad* (Livorno: Benamozegh, 1863) (photo offset ed., Tel Aviv, 1970), 1, 12, 29, 167.

with these [the human sciences] has become even greater now, when most of the opponents of the Torah have used them to construct a millstone and a stumbling block to the believer. But how can we topple the fortresses they have constructed if we are not as well versed in their stratagems? ... How can we prove to them the antiquity of this knowledge, of its books and its authors, if we do not know the *critical* scholarship that they use to bend their bow to fire?[88]

Benamozegh's response to a new mode of inquiry was not to withdraw but to master it and use it to his own advantage.

While Benamozegh did not return to a sustained discussion of critical scholarship, he employed historicist methods in his rebuttal of *Ari Nohem*. He rebuked Modena for failing to mention thinkers such as Menasseh ben Israel and Isaac Abravanel, who combined Kabbalah with philosophy.[89] In accord with accepted scholarly norms, Benamozegh examined Modena's other writings, particularly his sermons, and found numerous references to the *Zohar*.[90] He repeatedly contested Modena's reading of certain sources adduced in *Ari Nohem*. He challenged the characterization of Solomon ibn Adret and Yedaiah Bedersi as critical of the transmigration of souls and Solomon Luria and Moses Isserles as opponents to Kabbalah. In both cases he grounded his objections on the existence of evidence that Modena had ignored or misinterpreted. Modena had used Bedersi's writings to reconstruct Ibn Adret's opinions, when Ibn Adret's own writings offered ample evidence that contradicted this reconstruction; he had characterized Isserless as an opponent of Kabbalah, when Isserles' own works drew upon and explicated Kabbalah.[91] The effect of these corrective arguments was not only to contest an individual point or supply a neglected piece of evidence; Benamozegh sought to undermine the antikabbalistic tradition in Jewish thought, a tradition central to the modern reputation of *Ari Nohem*.

Benamozegh's treatment of the printing of Kabbalah offers an instructive instance of his attitude toward knowledge: "But the printing of kabbalistic books is of equal value to all, beloved, sweet, and pleasing to all sects and all opinions, for the publication of any form of knowledge is pleasant and beneficial to those who love it as well as to those who detest it, for it leads to study and examination, and from the debate [it generates] the issue will be clarified."[92] Unlike Modena's earlier readers, Benamozegh understood and emphasized the conservative approach to knowledge in *Ari Nohem*. By contrast, he was prepared to celebrate the public dissemination of Kabbalah and welcomed the open debate about its worth. Although

---

[88] *Emat Mafgia*, 1, 2B.
[89] Ibid., 2, 19A.
[90] Ibid., 15B.
[91] Ibid., 4B–5A, for Bedersi and Ibn Adret; 6A for Isserles; 6B for Solomon Luria.
[92] Ibid., 24B.

his argument seems like a model defense of the freedom of expression, Benamozegh was not immune from partisanship. In the very first line of *Eimat Mafiga*, he lamented the printing of *Ari Nohem* and wished it had never occurred.[93]

Benamozegh may have been aware of contemporary scholarship, and at times he may have even welcomed the diffusion of knowledge, but he hardly saw himself as a scholar in the mold of Luzzatto or Geiger. The form his writing took, particularly in response to Modena, reveals the limits of his intellectual engagement. Rather than compose a monograph, he wrote a chapter-by-chapter rebuttal of *Ari Nohem*. Modena thus set the agenda. Benamozegh's discussion of several issues crucial to his own theology, such as the ideas of Maimonides, the nature of the sefirot, and the antiquity of Kabbalah, remained scattered. Maimonides in particular presented Benamozegh with enormous difficulties. Early in the work, he wondered about Maimonides' centrality for contemporary thinkers: "But it is fitting to note that it has become widespread in our time to elevate, exalt, and praise to the very heights the book of the *Guide* by the rabbi, of blessed memory, and especially among those scholars who have not properly grasped the belief in the Oral Torah or the wisdom of Kabbalah. This is something that requires study and careful reflection, for it certainly did not happen by accident."[94] Benamozegh understood the centrality of Maimonides for Modena and for more contemporary thinkers but did not develop this insight into the revival of Maimonides any further.[95]

Elsewhere he identified the *Guide* as one of the crucial sources for Modena's arguments about Kabbalah. Maimonides' history of Jewish esoteric secrets, which centered on a rupture in their transmission followed by his own recovery through his intellect, played a central role in Modena's arguments against the antiquity of Kabbalah. Benamozegh pursued a familiar strategy in responding to Modena's use of Maimonides: Modena had misread the very book he claimed to champion.[96] For Benamozegh Maimonides would have readily agreed that allusions to the esoteric secrets of Kabbalah could be found in rabbinic literature. Modena had picked only those passages germane to his argument and discarded all others, particularly those that might have reflected a positive attitude toward Kabbalah.

Over and above the abuse of his sources, Modena had parodied kabbalistic ideas. Benamozegh responded to Modena's argument about the sefirot: "Even a one-day-old child can discern that ten is greater than one, and if he wants to glorify himself in front of a crowd, he will call out against

---

[93] Ibid., 1, 2A.
[94] Ibid., 5A.
[95] Harris, "The Image of Maimonides"; Nadler, "The 'Rambam Revival.'"
[96] *Emat Mafgia*, 1, 17A.

the kabbalists [and claim] that they are multiplying the divinity."[97] Benamozegh drew a parallel between the sefirot and ideas about God in other forms of philosophical theology, such as Pythagoras's *monad* and Plato's *idea*.[98] Like these philosophers, kabbalists did not multiply God by describing his many attributes, and it was a juvenile caricature of their arguments to claim that they had. Thus, while *Eimat Mafgia* effectively undermined Modena's arguments as specious and one-sided, the book did not counter Modena's assault on the antiquity of Kabbalah with new historical or philological evidence.

Eimat Mafgia appeared at same time as another response to Modena's criticism, *Magen ve-Zinah* by Isaac Haver Wildmann.[99] Like Benamozegh's work, Wildmann's took the form of a chapter-by-chapter refutation of *Ari Nohem*. Both authors made a range of similar claims: they defended the antiquity of Kabbalah, the validity of the sefirot, Kabbalah as a method of exegesis, and the unimpeachable piety of kabbalists. Each expressed shock that a rabbi of Modena's stature could have written something so critical of Kabbalah, a type of knowledge they conceived of as central to the Jewish tradition. Yet a crucial difference separated them: Benamozegh never situated himself within a particular school of contemporary rabbinic thought. His claims about Kabbalah as a fundamental aspect of rabbinic Judaism took the form of a defense of medieval and early modern kabbalists. In contrast, through his repeated emphasis on his connection to Elijah of Vilna, Wildmann asserted his allegiance to the greatest Talmudist of the eighteenth century, who was also a mystic and an opponent of Hasidism.[100] The rabbi of the small Polish town of Suwalk, Wildmann had studied with Menahem Mendl of Shklov, the most important kabbalist among Elijah of Vilna's disciples. According to his own testimony, Menahem Mendl had spent twenty months studying Kabbalah with Elijah of Vilna and had transcribed several of his master's works.[101] Wildmann placed enormous emphasis on having

---

[97] Ibid., 9B.

[98] Ibid., 10A.

[99] *Magen ve-Zinah* (Johannesburg, 1855). The title page of the book read Amsterdam. See Adelman, "Success and Failure," 86, n. 23. All references to the photo offset edition of *Magen ve-Zinah* (Bnei Brak: Nesah, 1984). On Wildmann, see Allan Nadler, *The Faith of the Mithnagdim: Rabbinic Responses to Hasidic Rapture* (Baltimore: Johns Hopkins University Press, 1997), 36.

[100] Immanuel Etkes, *The Gaon of Vilna: The Man and His Image* (Berkeley: University of California Press, 2002); Shmuel Werses, "The Gaon R. Elijah of Vilna in the Literature of the Jewish Enlightenment" (Hebrew), in *Hakitzah Ami: Sifrut ha-Haskalah be-idan ha-modernizasyah*, 25–66 (Jerusalem: Magnes Press, 2000); Moshe Hallamish, Joseph Rivlin, and Raphael Shuchat, eds., *Ha-Gera u-vet midrasho* (Ramat-Gan: Bar Ilan University Press, 2003). Eliyahu Stern, "Elijah of Vilna and the Making of Modern Rabbinic Judaism," Ph.D. diss., UC Berkeley, 2008.

[101] Nadler, *The Faith of Mithnagdim*, 8, n. 24.

been Menahem Mendl's disciple and repeatedly quoted the teachings of Elijah of Vilna and his student Hayim of Volozhin.[102]

Wildmann saw the publication of *Ari Nohem* as part of a larger trend among contemporary Jews to contest every aspect of rabbinic culture. He correctly understood that a central aspect of this criticism involved the recovery and publication of sources from earlier periods. Wildmann chastised his contemporaries for using Modena's work to challenge the authenticity of Kabbalah.[103] Like Azulai, who had dismissed *Ari Nohem* as a pamphlet, Wildmann referred to it derisively as a "notebook," but he pointed to its popularity and claimed that several poor souls clung to it as if it had been given at Sinai.[104] Unlike Benamozegh, who saw his book as a response to recent critical scholarship, Wildmann claimed not to address those who had already adopted such heretical views and imagined his audience as composed of those who believed in the authenticity of the Oral Torah.[105] His work was meant to ensure that *Ari Nohem* did not lead them astray. This difference in intended audience points to a further contrast in attitudes toward knowledge. If Benamozegh welcomed the publication of all types of books, Wildmann adopted a more restrictive view toward knowledge. Like Elijah of Vilna, who similarly charged Hasidim with discharging mystical secrets to the multitudes, Wildmann thought certain types of books should not be disseminated at all. Wildmann quoted Modena as having read all types of heretical literature in order to respond to potential critics and mentioned that other figures such as Maimonides had pursued similar strategies. Wildmann had little patience for such folly. "Our eyes can see in our own generation that anyone who begins to enter into their [the heretics] words and their books departs entirely and denies the essence of the Torah."[106] For corroboration Wildmann pointed to Joseph Yaavetz, a fifteenth-century Sephardic homilist, who claimed that all his contemporaries who had studied philosophy had converted to Christianity while those who had not were martyred.[107]

---

[102] *Magen ve-Zinah*, preface, unpaginated. For Elijah of Vilna, see 5A, 34A, 45A, 49A; for Hayim of Volozhin, see 15A, 16A, 21A, 41A.

[103] Ibid., 2A.

[104] Ibid., 25B.

[105] Ibid., 3A. Wildmann, however, was aware of developments within critical scholarship, even if he chose not to engage them. He referred to Abraham Geiger's book on Delmedigo as "harmful" and its author as "wicked." See 3B.

[106] Ibid., 6B–7A.

[107] Ibid., 7A. Wildman referred to Yaavetz's *Or ha-Hayim*. See Baer, *A History of the Jews in Christian Spain*, 2:509, n. 12. On the use of Yaavetz by the Hasid Zvi Elimelekh of Dinov to criticize participants in the Jewish Enlightenment, see Mendel Piekarz, "'Why Did the Spanish Exile Perish,' as a Forewarning of the Dangers of the Enlightenment" (Hebrew), *Daat* 28 (1992): 87–115; as cited in Nadler, "The 'Rambam Revival,'" 233, n. 7.

A final point of contrast between *Magen ve-Zinah* and *Eimat Mafgia* relates to content. Benamozegh may have believed in the antiquity of the *Zohar* and other kabbalistic classics, but he did not respond to Modena's historical criticism.[108] Wildmann devoted an extensive section to a rebuttal of Modena's theory of the origins of the *Zohar*. While he maintained that the *Zohar* reflected the ideas of Simeon bar Yohai, he acknowledged that he may not have written the work in its entirety. He proposed that Bar Yohai's thoughts were written down in antiquity on sequestered scrolls that were arranged according to the order of the pericopes of the Pentateuch in the Geonic period.[109] Wildmann offered no evidence to support this theory: his grudging admission that Bar Yohai may not have written the *Zohar* was part of a range of nineteenth-century apologia for the *Zohar*, such as Kunitz's *Ben Yohai* and Benamozegh's *Ta'am la-Shad*.[110]

A year after Wildmann's rebuttal of *Ari Nohem*, Abraham Geiger wrote a biography of Modena that included his work with the same title as Wildmann's polemic: *Magen ve-Zinah*.[111] One of the most significant Jewish intellectuals of his time, Geiger served as the driving force behind the Reform movement through his twin duties as congregational rabbi and academic theologian.[112] Although unable to hold a university post, he eventually lectured at a rabbinical school in Berlin. Unlike Reggio, who devoted much of his career to the study of Modena, or Benamozegh and Wildmann, who put their attack on *Ari Nohem* at the center of their defenses of Kabbalah, Geiger's chief intellectual interests lay elsewhere. At the height of his scholarly powers in the 1850s while serving as a communal rabbi in Breslau, Geiger wrote a series of scholarly monographs before publishing his great history of Judaism in the period of the Second Temple and Mishnah.[113]

One of these monographs was his study of Modena. The vast majority of his essay concerns *Kol Sakhal*, which had recently appeared in Reggio's edition, and *Magen ve-Zinah*, which was part of Geiger's book. While Geiger focused on Modena's works (or those attributed to him) that probed the limits of rabbinic Judaism, his biographical essay contains a précis of *Ari Nohem* that indicates he identified with and perhaps exceeded Modena's

[108] See *Ta'am la-Shad*.
[109] *Magen ve-Zinah*, 49B–50A.
[110] Wildman quoted Kunitz; see ibid., 46A. See also David Luria, *Kadmut Sefer ha-Zohar* (Königsberg, 1855). A note to the preface to the second edition referred to *Ari Nohem*. See Luria, *Kadmut Sefer ha-Zohar* (Warsaw, 1887) (photo offset ed., New York, 1951).
[111] Geiger, *Leon da Modena*. Modena's work was a response to criticism of the Oral Torah by "a certain heretic from Hamburg" who was none other than Uriel da Costa. See Fishman, *Shaking the Pillars of Exile*, 50.
[112] Jakob Petuchowski, ed., *New Perspectives on Abraham Geiger* (New York: Ktav, 1975); Heschel, *Abraham Geiger and the Jewish Jesus*.
[113] Abraham Geiger, *Urschrift und Uebersetzungen der Bibel* (Breslau: J. Hainauer, 1857).

criticism of Kabbalah.[114] After praising the work as "well ordered," he quoted Modena's description of Kabbalah as neither a source of wisdom nor coterminous with Jewish tradition. Geiger translated Modena's use of *hokhmah*, Hebrew for wisdom, as *Wissenschaft*, a term that referred to Geiger's own systematic pursuit of knowledge. In fact Geiger seems to have taken a particular relish in positing that Kabbalah had absolutely nothing to do with *Wissenschaft*. Thus, Geiger presented a fairly accurate summary of *Ari Nohem* even though he repeatedly stressed that he himself had little firsthand acquaintance with kabbalistic literature or with kabbalists themselves. More than any of the other scholars who engaged with *Ari Nohem* in the early nineteenth century, Geiger matched Scholem's description of someone who actively "disdained close acquaintance with the sources." His summary leaves the impression that *Ari Nohem* performed an intellectual task he supported as worthwhile, but one that he would not have wanted to undertake himself.

In the latter decades of the nineteenth century, *Ari Nohem* circulated among Jewish intellectuals but did not receive sustained treatment like it had in the two decades after its initial printing.[115] Moses Leib Lilienblum, an embattled Russian Jewish writer who lost faith both in the Jewish tradition and in the possibility of enlightenment, described his experience reading *Ari Nohem*:

> There were several books that I had never seen, among them *Behinat ha-Dat* of Elijah Delmedigo with the commentary of Yashar (Reggio), and *Ari Nohem*, and *Shorshe Levanon* [by Levinsohn]. I had already read the book *Ari Nohem* and it had not made any impression upon me, and what is more, I considered its author to be a disreputable man; but now that my mind had opened a little bit more, and I had read all three of the aforementioned books over a few days, all of which prove Kabbalah to be a forgery and to which I also included the book *Moreh Nevukhei ha-Zman* . . . I stopped believing in Kabbalah.[116]

Only after reading Reggio's commentary on *Behinat ha-Dat* and other works was Lilienblum convinced by Modena's arguments about Kabbalah. If someone like Lilienblum, who was so at pains to separate himself from the Jewish observance and the Jewish Enlightenment of his past, would

---

[114] Geiger, *Leon da Modena*, 12–15.

[115] It was mentioned in passing by Graetz in his excursus on the authorship of the *Zohar*. See Heinrich Graetz, *Geschichte der Juden*, vol. 7, n. 12 (Leipzig: O. Leiner, 1863), 493. See also the repeated references to Modena and *Ari Nohem* in Abraham Baer Gottlober, *Toldot ha-Kabalah veha-Hasidut* (Zhitomir, 1869), 9, 68, 69, 70–71, 85, 90.

[116] Moses Leib Lilienblum, *Hat'ot Ne'urim* (Tel Aviv, 1966), 238. See also the reference to *Ari Nohem* in *Shnei Yosef Ben Shimon*, a poem by Lilienblum's correspondent Judah Leib Gordon; *Kitve Yehudah Leib Gordon: Shirah* (Tel Aviv: Dvir, 1963), 161. Both as cited in Adelman, "Success and Failure," 111, nn. 9, 11. On Lilienblum, see Moseley, *Being for Myself Alone*, 368–76.

happen upon *Ari Nohem* and cease believing in Kabbalah, then the effort by earlier participants in the Jewish Enlightenment to recover *Ari Nohem* appears to have had a modest effect.

For Lilienblum, *Ari Nohem* functioned within a wider orbit of texts about Kabbalah, including *Moreh Nevukhei ha-Zman*, the unfinished philosophical masterpiece by Nachman Krochmal.[117] Kabbalah was hardly Krochmal's central concern in his attempt to write a contemporary *Guide for the Perplexed*, yet he included several prescient comments about the genealogy of Kabbalah and the history of Sabbatianism.[118] A century after *Ari Nohem* first appeared in print, Fischel Lachover wrote a study of Kabbalah in Krochmal's thought that highlighted these insights.[119] Lachover sent a copy of his article, which had appeared in a serial founded by Hayim Nachman Bialik and continued after his death as a memorial to him, to Scholem, who had published his celebrated "Redemption through Sin" in an earlier number of the same journal.[120] On April 27, 1941, Scholem responded to Lachover: "Krochmal did well to see the comparison between the radical Gnostics and the Sabbatians, and it's a pity this article was only known to me after I had written my work on this subject in 'Redemption through Sin,' for I would have been happy to rely upon Krochmal."[121] In May 1941, less than a month after writing to Lachover, Scholem wrote his celebrated preface to *Major Trends in Jewish Mysticism*, which characterized the study of Kabbalah prior to his own efforts as "a field strewn with ruins" and "scattered debris." Three years later, when he wrote his "Reflections on Modern Jewish Studies," a parricidal text if there ever was one, he characterized Krochmal as a marginal figure who exercised no "impact upon those engaged in scientific work."[122] Perhaps. Except it was Zunz, the very founder of the academic

---

[117] On the production of Krochmal's text, see Ismar Schorsch, "The Production of a Classic: Zunz as Krochmal's Editor," *LBIYB* 31 (1986): 281–315.

[118] David Biale, "The Kabbala in Nachman Krochmal's Philosophy of History," *Journal of Jewish Studies* 32 (1981): 85–97; Jay M. Harris, *Nachman Krochmal: Guiding the Perpexed of the Modern Age* (New York: New York University Press, 1991), 98–99.

[119] Lachover, "Revealed and Concealed."

[120] "Redemption through Sin" (Hebrew), *Keneset* 2 (1937). For an English translation, see *The Messianic Idea in Judaism*, 78–141. On Scholem's essay, see Steven M. Wasserstrom, *Religion after Religion: Gershom Scholem, Mircea Eliade, and Henry Corbin at Eranos* (Princeton: Princeton University Press, 1999), chap. 14; Benjamin Lazier, *God Interrupted: Heresy and the European Imagination between the World Wars* (Princeton: Princeton University Press, 2008), pt. 3.

[121] Cited and dated in Werses, "Hasidism and Sabbatianism," 119, n. 84. For a facsimile of the letter, see *Yediot Genazim* 8 (1983): 330. For another appreciation of Lachover's study, see the letter by S.Y. Agnon to Lachover, in *Mi-Sod Hakhamim: Mikhtavim, 1909–1970* (Jerusalem and Tel Aviv: Schocken, 2002), 159–60.

[122] Scholem, "Reflections on Modern Jewish Studies (1944)," 56. See also Ephraim E. Urbach, "Gershom Scholem and Judaic Studies," in *Gershom Scholem: The Man and his Work*, ed. Paul Mendes-Flohr (Albany: SUNY Press, 1994), 35, n. 10.

study of Judaism, who edited Krochmal's work.[123] It is hard not to wonder at Scholem's note to Lachover. Scholem was clearly aware of nineteenth-century studies of Kabbalah, much as he was aware of *Ari Nohem*. Yet he chose to fashion himself as a scholar without any predecessors and without any peers.

[123] See also the reference to Krochmal's theory of Gnosticism and Kabbalah in Gottlober, *Toldot ha-Kabalah veha-Hasidut*, 43.

EPILOGUE

History of a Failure

IN MODENA'S LIFE and in his death, *Ari Nohem* was a stunning failure. Five years before he composed his criticism of Kabbalah, Modena wrote the first of two wills, which included the following instruction for his funeral: "Let them march around my grave according to the custom of the Levantines."[1] And so the greatest antikabbalist of the early modern period, the critic who sought to extricate Kabbalah from Jewish practice, the theologian who sought to historicize Kabbalah, issued instructions to include a kabbalistic rite at his own funeral. History does not relate whether Modena knew the genealogy of this ritual he referred to as Levantine, but Scholem demonstrated that kabbalists created it to ward off demons from the dead.[2] Given Modena's discussion of this ritual in his *Riti*, a work in which Gaffarel publicly chastised him for presenting a Judaism cleansed of Kabbalah, it seems unlikely that he was aware of its kabbalistic origins.[3] The Judaism Modena thought he could free from Kabbalah was already so saturated with it that he unknowingly issued instructions to include one of its rituals at his own funeral.

But the antikabbalist's kabbalistic funeral was not the only irony that attended the author of *Ari Nohem*. No graveyard ritual, kabbalistic or otherwise, could keep the spirits at bay. Just over a decade after Modena's death, his grandson Isaac Levi was called before the Holy Office in Venice on charges of divination, magic, and the worship of demons.[4] Levi was accused of attempting to catch thieves on behalf of various Christian clients through the performance of a Venetian ritual called *esperimento dell' inghistera*. The ritual called for a bowl of water along with the presence of innocent people, whether children, virgins, or pregnant women. Levi had allegedly performed it while uttering Hebrew incantations and using Hebrew texts. As the investigation continued, Levi was subsequently accused of copying occult books and circumventing the law by offering them for sale.

---

[1] *Autobiography*, 178. See Elliott Horowitz, "Cohen's *Autobiography of Leon Modena*," *JQR* 81 (1991): 459–60. On his second will, which treats his literary estate, see chapter 1.

[2] Scholem, "Tradition and New Creation," 154–56; as cited in Horowitz, "Cohen's *Autobiography of Leon Modena*."

[3] *Riti*, 5.7.3 (Paris, 1637), 211; as cited in *Autobiography*, 272, with reference to the Venice edition of 1638.

[4] Pullan, *The Jews of Europe and the Inquisition of Venice*, 89–90; as cited in Adelman, "Leon Modena: the Autobiography and the Man," 40–41. On the identification of Isaac Levi mentioned in the file as Modena's grandson, see Ioly Zorattini, *Processi del S. Uffizio di Venezia*, 11:9.

Serious discrepancies between the testimonies of Levi's two Christian clients forced the Holy Office to drop its investigation. But before they had abandoned their work, inquisitors examined Levi's residence where they discovered a number of books, including his grandfather's *Sha'agat Aryeh*, a volume of Maimonides, and a book by Savonarola. Among Levi's Hebrew books was one that has tentatively been identified as *Sefer ha-Bahir*.[5] Considered the first kabbalistic text, the *Bahir* was the one pseudepigraphic work of Kabbalah criticized in *Ari Nohem* that had not appeared in print as a single book in the sixteenth century. Levi had evidently wasted no time in procuring a copy of the first edition printed in Amsterdam in 1651. To determine the contents of Levi's Hebrew books, the Holy Office had consulted none other than Giulio Morosini, Modena's former student who had converted to Catholicism.[6] One of the people who had accused Levi of practicing alchemy also claimed to have been in Levi's home, where he had seen the *Clavicula Salomonis* as well as a kabbalistic manuscript that Levi had declared had been composed by Urban VIII.[7] Inquisitorial documents are notoriously difficult to interpret, but a fair amount of corroborating evidence survives to mitigate the possibilities of unreliable testimony. Levi had indeed copied Modena's *Sha'agat Aryeh*; books by Savonarola and Maimonides appeared in the list of Modena's possessions composed upon his death; and the Isaac Levi examined by the Inquisition was a preacher in the Venetian Ghetto. A second irony thus attends the great early modern critic of Kabbalah: Isaac Levi may have preserved Modena's papers and prepared a fair copy of *Ari Nohem*, but he functioned as a channel of transmission, not an intellectual legacy.

Levi was not the only member of Modena's inner circle who spurned his criticism. Joseph Hamiz, Modena's prized student, the addressee of *Ari Nohem*, beloved to him like the son he hoped his own would have become, remained a committed kabbalist. The year that Isaac Levi was first brought before the Holy Office, Hamiz embarked upon a joint venture to compose a commentary to the *Zohar* and to reprint the *Zohar Hadash*, the same book that Modena had lamented had been brought to Venice from Salonika by Naftali Ashkenazi. His collaborator in the republication of the *Zohar Hadash* was Moses Zacut, the young correspondent of Samuel Aboab who had thought to challenge the aged Venetian critic of Kabbalah more than a decade earlier.[8] Hamiz was an equal opportunity kabbalist. In addition to reprinting the *Zohar Hadash* and initiating a commentary, he assiduously

---

[5] For the evidence, see ibid., 123; for the identification, see 10, n. 13.
[6] Ibid., 10, n. 10.
[7] Ibid., 117–18.
[8] *Zohar Hadash* (Venice: Bragadin, 1662). Hamiz's introduction to *Zohar Hadash* appears in Libowitz, *Seridim*, 31–32. On Hamiz's *Zohar* commentary, see Huss, *Ke-zohar ha-rakia*, 133–34, 254.

History of a Failure • 233

collected the writings of the medieval prophetic kabbalist Abraham Abulafia. After leaving Venice, he eventually settled on the island of Zante. When the messianic movement sprung up around Sabbatai Zevi a few years later, Hamiz became a committed believer.[9]

Owning a kabbalistic manuscript of the pope's work, practicing necromancy and divination on behalf of gentiles, printing a new edition of the *Zohar Hadash*, gathering the writings of a kabbalistic reader of Maimonides, embracing a Messiah who was deeply influenced by Kabbalah: within three decades of the composition of *Ari Nohem*, Modena's grandson and student had done it all. At the most basic level—the intended reader—*Ari Nohem* had failed. It could not convince Levi to live a life committed to Maimonidean rationalism or Hamiz to abandon Kabbalah and return to the *Guide of the Perplexed*.

If *Ari Nohem* could not persuade Modena's closest associates, it was even less successful in opposing the increasing popularity of Kabbalah in the decades and centuries after Modena's death. As an agent, the book was futile. The Jewish community in Venice at the turn of the seventeenth century witnessed the first of several waves in the spread of Kabbalah. Less than two decades after Modena's death, a messianic movement informed and guided by Kabbalah coalesced around Sabbatai Zevi. Whether Sabbatianism was a dialectical outcome of Lurianic Kabbalah, as maintained by Scholem, or the actual cause of its spread, as Scholem's critics have claimed, Sabbatian prophets and pamphlets transmitted Kabbalah throughout Europe and the Mediterranean. If their success was short lived, their kabbalistic message lingered long after their demise. The three great heresy hunters of the late seventeenth and early eighteenth centuries—Sasportas, Hagiz, and Emden—all pursued the Sabbatian believers for perverting what they thought was true Kabbalah, not for Kabbalah as such. In the late eighteenth century, a movement of religious enthusiasm emerged in Poland and Lithuania. This new movement, Hasidism, was deeply indebted to Kabbalah and became an exteremly popular form of religious piety by the turn of the nineteenth century.

The different ways the *Zohar* was read in the centuries after the composition of *Ari Nohem* provide one small measure of the popularity of Kabbalah. The very ways of reading that Modena had objected to in *Ari Nohem* continued: editions, translations, and abridgments of the *Zohar* appeared in print for the next several centuries, and the rabbinic elite, those custodians of Judaism that Modena had chastised for using the *Zohar* as a legal source,

---

[9] Ephraim Kupfer, "R. Joseph Hamiz in Zante and His Work" (Hebrew), *Sefunot* 2 (1971–1978): 199–216; Isaiah Tishby, "Documents about Nathan of Gaza in the Writings of Joseph Hamiz" (Hebrew), in *Netive Emunah ve-Minut: Masot u-Mehkarim be-Sifrut ha-Kabalah veha-Shabtaut*, 52–80 (Jerusalem: Magnes Press, 1982).

continued to draw on the *Zohar* in their formulation of the law.¹⁰ But the *Zohar* began to be read in new ways that Modena could never have foreseen. It began to be read not as a written text, but as a visual image and an architectural plan. Before the spread of Hasidism in the early eighteenth century, the Jews of Gwozdziec, a small trading town in the Polish Commonwealth, constructed and painted their synagogue with themes and motifs drawn from the *Zohar*.¹¹ The walls of this synagogue told a visual story, a kabbalistic one that would have been unthinkable without the *Zohar*. At the turn of the nineteenth century, participants in the Jewish Enlightenment described Hasidim liturgically reciting the *Zohar* as if it were a prayer book.¹² More than a century later, Jews in southern Morocco sacralized the *Zohar* and turned it into a ritual object.¹³ The *Zohar* was so important it had ceased to be read. In the contest between *Ari Nohem* and the *Zohar*, criticism had no chance.

Ari Nohem may not have become a Jewish classic, but how many books become classics? This was hardly its only failure. Modena's basic critical insight—the recent origins of Kabbalah—was knowledge that had to be rediscovered repeatedly over the next three centuries. For all that *Ari Nohem* circulated in manuscript and set the agenda for eighteenth-century apologists of Kabbalah, for all the efforts made by nineteenth-century scholars to see the work into print, and for all of the polemics that ensued from its eventual printing, the knowledge Modena had produced was lost and had to be repeatedly recovered. Jacob Emden, Samuel David Luzzatto, and Heinrich Graetz all posed variations on a question Modena had framed and basically solved in the early seventeenth century. But even their assaults on the antiquity of the *Zohar*—delivered in the form of a rabbinic compilation in Emden's *Mitpahat Sefarim*, a learned dialogue in Luzzatto's *Vikuah al Hokhmat ha-Kabalah*, and a historical narrative in Graetz's *Geschichte der Juden*—were not enough to convince Gershom Scholem. Scholem's inaugural address answered the question it posed—did Moses de Leon compose the book of the *Zohar*?—in the affirmative. Only twenty years later, in *Major Trends in Jewish Mysticism*, did Scholem come to accept Graetz's (and Modena's) position.

---

¹⁰ For one example, see Flatto, *The Kabbalistic Culture of Eighteenth-Century Prague*, 147–55.

¹¹ Thomas C. Hubka, "The *Zohar* and the Polish Synagogue: The Practical Influence of a Sacred Text," *JJTP* 9 (2000): 173–250.

¹² Ada Rapoport-Albert, "A Maskilic Tract in Defense of Hasidism in an Anonymous Manuscript from the Circle of E. Z. Zweifel" (Hebrew), in *Mi-Vilnah le-Yerushalayim: mehkarim be-toldotehem uve-tarbutam shel Yehude Mizrah Eropah mugashim li-Profesor Shmuel Werses*, ed. David Assaf et al., 114, n. 59 (Jerusalem: Magnes Press, 2002); as cited by Manekin, "Joseph Perl on *Hok le-Yisrael*," 348, n. 14.

¹³ Harvey E. Goldberg, "The Zohar in Southern Morocco: A Study in the Ethnography of Texts," *History of Religions* 29 (1990): 233–58.

The failure of *Ari Nohem* was manifold. Modena failed to convince his immediate audience, and by extension the Jewish community of Venice, and by further extension Jewish communities throughout Europe and the Mediterranean, to abandon their embrace of a new Jewish theology that masqueraded under the guise of tradition. This was hardly surprising: no critic, no matter how stinging or how subtle, can convince people to change their beliefs or to abandon their practices. Modena had also failed to convince other scholars and other critics, the very people who might have been most receptive to his argument. To describe *Ari Nohem* as a failure is neither to indict the book nor to celebrate it. It is an attempt to understand it as a work written by an author constrained by the limits of his own particular moment in history. And it is an attempt to restore a sense of contingency to the study of the early modern past.

Acknowledgments

I AM DEEPLY GRATEFUL to the following institutions and individuals:

The staff at the Van Pelt Library and the Center for Advanced Judaic Studies, University of Pennsylvania, Philadelphia; the Library of the Jewish Theological Seminary, New York; the Dorot Division of the New York Public Library, New York; the Main Reading Room and the African and Middle Eastern Reading Room of the Library of Congress, Washington, DC; the Klau Library, Hebrew Union College, Cincinnati; the University Library and the Library of St. John's College, Cambridge; the Bodleian Library, Oxford; the British Library, London; the Gershom Scholem Library, the Institute for Microfilmed Hebrew Manuscripts, and the National Library, Jerusalem; the Palatine Library, Parma; the Ambrosiana Library, Milan; the Firestone Library, Princeton University, Princeton.

The Wexner Foundation, the School of Arts and Sciences, the History Department, and the Program in Jewish Studies, University of Pennsylvania.

The Council for the Humanities, the Society of Fellows in the Liberal Arts, the Program in Judaic Studies, the University Committee on Research in the Humanities and Social Sciences, and the History Department, Princeton University.

The Cahnman Publication Subvention Grant awarded by the Association for Jewish Studies.

David Ruderman, Talya Fishman, Ann Moyer, Roger Chartier.

Peter Schäfer, Anthony Grafton, Leonard Barkan, William Jordan, Mary Harper.

Fred Appel, Diana Goovaerts, Debbie Tegarden, Anita O'Brien, Princeton University Press.

Daniel Abrams, Howard Adelman, Lucia Allais, Allan Arkush, On Barak, Leora Batnitzky, Elisheva Baumgarten, Andrew Berns, Malachi Beit-Arié, Yaron Ben-Naeh, Ann Blair, Robert Bonfil, Ra'anan Boustan, Piet van Boxel, Francesca Bregoli, Stephen Burnett, Elisheva Carlebach, Robert Chazan, D'Maris Coffman, Yosef Cohen, Marcie Citron, James Clark, Angela Creager, Sarah Diamant, Gad Freudenthal, Matt Goldish, Michael Gordin, Molly Greene, Joseph Hacker, Dirk Hartog, Sam Haselby, Martha Himmelfarb, William Horbury, Elliott Horowitz, Boaz Huss, Moshe Idel, Joshua Katz, Arthur Kiron, Michael Laffan, Matthias Lehmann, Lital Levy, Olga Litvak, Charles Manekin, Rachel Manekin, Sharon Liberman Mintz, Yair Mintzker, Sue Naquin, Yael Okun, Judith Olszowy-Schlanger,

Peggy Pearlstein, Mauro Perani, John Pollack, Amnon Raz-Krakotzkin, Ted Rabb, Eileen Reeves, Elchanan Reiner, Benjamin Richler, James T. Robinson, Marina Rustow, Pinchas Roth, Shalom Sabar, David Sclar, Raymond P. Scheindlin, Menahem Schmelzer, Esther Schor, Jerry Schwarzbard, Ezra Schwat, Adam Shear, Peter Stallybrass, Michael Stanislawski, Guy G. Stroumsa, Sarah Stroumsa, Michael Terry, Christine Walsh, David Wasserstein, Joanna Weinberg, Sean Wilentz, the late Yosef H. Yerushalmi, Julian Zelizer.

Jennifer Bradley, Lisa Cerami, Josh Dubler, David Dweck, Noam Elcott, Joseph Harari, Kaden Harari, Ben Huberman, Ruth Kaplan, M. Lindsay Kaplan, Joseph Levine, James Marrow, Emily Rose, Joey Shabot, Sari Shabot, Harold Snedcof, Melanie Snedcof, Mara Zepeda.

Leon Wieseltier.

Nicholas de Lange.

Peter Ochs, Vanessa Ochs, Elizabeth Ochs, Rochelle Dweck, Altoon Dweck, David Schorr, Irrit Dweck, Jeronimo Romero, Rachel Dweck, Moki Schwartz, Ezra Dweck.

Natalie Dweck.

Harry Dweck, Emanuella Dweck.

Juliana Ochs Dweck.

Works Cited

MANUSCRIPT SOURCES

In compiling this handlist of manuscripts with *Ari Nohem*, I have drawn on the catalogue at the Institute of Microfilmed Hebrew Manuscripts at the National Library in Jerusalem; the bibliography included in Adelman ("Success and Failure," 1146–57); and Benjamin Richler, *Guide to Hebrew Manuscript Collections* (Jerusalem: Israel Academy of Sciences and Humanities, 1994). Given the importance of the two manuscripts that appear to have Modena's authorization, I have listed them first. The remainder are listed in alphabetical order by location. References to the microfilm numbers at the JNUL appear below each entry. Where catalogues exist, I have provided references to the manuscript entry in the catalog.

Handlist of Manuscripts with *Ari Nohem*

Manuscript A
Moscow. Russian State Library, Günzburg Collection, Hebrew MS 1681.
Microform reel F 48694.

Manuscript B
Warsaw. Jewish Historical Institute, Hebrew MS 177.
Microform reel F 12001.

Manuscript C
Budapest. Jewish Theological Seminary, MS 105.
Microform reel F 47084.

Manuscript D
Holon, Israel. Zeituni Collection, MS 10.
Microform reel F 53661.

Manuscript E
London. British Library, Add. 27088.
Microform reel F 5733.
G. Margoliouth, *Catalogue of the Hebrew and Samaritan Manuscripts in the British Museum* (London, 1899–1935), 1075.

Manuscript F
Milan. Biblioteca Ambrosiana, X 277 Sup.
Microform reel F 34379.

Manuscript G
New York. Jewish Theological Seminary, MS 2098.
Microform reel F 11196.

Manuscript H
New York. Jewish Theological Seminary, MS 3552.
Microform reel F 29357.

Manuscript I
New York. New York Public Library, MS 184.
This manuscript was formerly London, Montefiore Collection, MS 455.
Microform reel F 5356.
H. Hirschfeld, *Descriptive Catalogue of the Hebrew Manuscripts in the Montefiore Library* (London, 1904), 455.

Manuscript J
Oxford. Bodleian Library, MS Mich. 497.
Microform reel F 20467.
A. Neubauer, *Catalogue of the Hebrew Manuscripts in the Bodleian Library* (Oxford, 1886), 2185.

Manuscript K
Oxford. Bodleian Library, MS Mich. 314.
Microform reel F 20469.
A. Neubauer, *Catalogue of the Hebrew Manuscripts in the Bodleian Library* (Oxford, 1886), 2187.

Manuscript L
Oxford. Bodleian Library, MS Reggio 34.
Microform reel F 20468.
A. Neubauer, *Catalogue of the Hebrew Manuscripts in the Bodleian Library* (Oxford, 1886), 2186.

Manuscript M
Ramat Gan, Israel. Bar–Ilan, MS 1137 (Moussaief, 6).
Microform reel F 22834.
Joseph Avivi, *Ohel Shem: Reshimat Kitve ha-Yad asher be-osef R. Shlomo Moussaief* (Jerusalem, 1995), 137.

Manuscript N
Warsaw. Jewish Historical Institute, MS 25.
Microform reel F 11839.
S. D. Loewinger and B. D. Weinryb, *Catalogue of the Hebrew Manuscripts in the Library of the Juedisch-theologisches Seminar in Breslau* (Weisbaden, 1965), 251.

Other Manuscripts

Ancona. Communità Israelitica.
Modena, Leon. "Notebooks." MS 7.
Microfilm Reel F 2532.

London. British Library.
Modena, Leon. "Letters." MS OR. 5395.
Modena, Leon. *Ziknei Yehuda*. MS Add. 27148.

London. Montefiore Collection. (The collection has since been sold and dispersed. Microfiche of the entire collection available at the Library of Congress.)
Isaac Levi. *Medaber Tahapukhot*. MS 517.
Samuel Aboab. Correspondence. MS 257–58.

Milan. Biblioteca Ambrosiana.
Modena, Leon. *Hayyei Yehudah*. MS X 119 Sup.
Modena, Leon. *Magen va-Herev*. MS Q 139 Sup.

New York. Jewish Theological Seminary.
Attributed to Leon Modena. *Kol Sakhal* and *Sha'agat Aryeh*. MS 10611.

Parma. Bibilioteca Palatina.
Modena, Leon. *Magen va-Herev*. Parma MS 2257 (Codex De Rossi 1141).
Collection of Polemical Works. Parma MS 2440 (Codex De Rossi 533).
Attributed to Leon Modena. *Kol Sakhal* and *Sha'agat Aryeh*. Parma MS 2238 (Codex de Rossi 85).

Warsaw, Jewish Historical Institute.
Solomon Rosenthal. Correspondence. MS 24. Microfilm Reel F 40157.

Works Printed before 1800

Agrippa von Nettesheim. *De incertitudine et vanitate scientarium*. Cologne, 1531.
———. *De occulta philosophia libri tres*. Cologne, 1533.
Alashkar, Moses. *Hasagot she-hisig he-Hakham Moshe Alashkar*. Ferarra: Usque, 1556.
Almalikh, Avraham ben Yehudah. *Likute Shikhehah u-Feah*. Ferrara: Usque, 1556.
Ashkenazi, Naftali. *Imre Shefer*. Venice: Zanetti, 1601.
Azulai, Hayim Joseph David. *Shem ha-Gedolim Helek Sheni*. Livorno, 1786.
Bacharach, Yair Hayim *Havot Yair: Teshuvot*. Frankfurt: Vaust, 1699.
Baer, Issachar. *Yesh Sakhar*. Prague, 1609.
———. *Mekor Hokhmah*. Prague, 1611.
Bartolocci, Giulio. *Bibliotheca Magna Rabbinica*. Rome: Sacræ congregationis de propaganda fide, 1675–1694.
Basilea, Aviad Sar Shalom. *Emunat Hakhamim*. Mantua, 1730.
Cohen de Herrera, Abraham. *Sefer Bet Elohim*. Amsterdam: Benvenisti, 1655.
Cordovero, Moses. *Pardes Rimonim*. Krakow, 1592.
De' Rossi, Azariah. *Meor Enayim*. Mantua, 1573–1575.
Delmedigo, Joseph Solomon. *Sefer Elim*. Amsterdam: Menasseh ben Israel, 1629.
———. *Sefer Ta'alumot Hokhmah*. Hanau, 1629–1631.
Emden, Jacob. *Mitpahat Sefarim*. Altona, 1768.
Ergas, Joseph. *Shomer Emunim*. Amsterdam, 1736.
Fano, Menahem Azariah da. *Sefer Teshuvot*. Venice: Zanetti, 1600.
Gaffarel, Jacques. *Codicum cabalisticorum manuscriptorum, quibus est usus Joannes Picus comes Mirandulanus index*. Paris: Blageart, 1651.
Galatino, Pietro. *Opus de arcanis catholicae veritatis*. Soncino: Ortona, 1518.
Ha-Levi, Judah. *Kuzari*. Venice: Di Gara, 1593.

Helm, Solomon ben Moses. *Mirkevet ha-Mishneh*. Frankfurt, 1750.
Ibn Gabbai, Meir. *Avodat ha-Kodesh*. Krakow, 1576.
——. *Marot Elohim*. Venice, 1567.
Ibn Gabirol. *Sefer ha-Tapuah*. Riva di Trento, 1562.
Ibn Habib, Jacob. *Ein Yisrael*. Venice, 1566
Ibn Shem Tov, Shem Tov. *Sefer ha-Emunot*. Ferrara: Usque, 1556.
Ibn Yahya, Gedalya. *Shalshelet ha-Kabalah*. Venice: Di Gara, 1587.
Ibn Zarza, Samuel. *Sefer Mekor Hayim*. Mantua, 1559.
Ibn Zimra, David ben Solomon. *She'elot u-Teshuvot*. Livorno, 1652.
Isserles, Moses. *Sefer Torat ha-Olah*. Prague, 1569.
Lampronti, Isaac. *Pahad Yitzhak*. Vol. 2. Venice, 1753.
Landau, Jacob. *Sefer Agur*. Venice: Giustinian, 1546.
Levi, Isaac. *Ma'ase Hakhamim*. Venice: Bragadin, 1646.
Luria, Solomon. *She'elot u-Teshuvot*. Lublin, 1599.
Luzzatto, Moses Hayim. *Hoker u-Mekubal*. Shklov, 1785.
Maimonides, Moses. *Moreh Nevukhim*. Venice: Bragadin, 1551.
——. *Moreh Nevukhim*. Sabbioneta: Cornelius Adelkind, 1553.
Mizrahi, Elijah. *Teshuvot She'elot*. Constantinople, 1559.
Modena, Leon. *Bet Lehem Yehudah*. Venice: Bragadin, 1625.
——. *Bet Yehudah*. Venice: Vendramin, 1635.
——. *Ceremonies et coustumes qui s'observent aujourd'huy parmy les juifs*. Translated by Richard Simon. Paris: Loüis Billaine, 1674.
——. *Historia de gli riti hebraici*. Paris, 1637.
——. *Historia de' riti hebraici*. Venice, 1638.
——. *The History of the Present Jews throughout the World*. Translated by Simon Ockley. London: E. Powell, 1707.
——. *The History of the Rites, Customes, and Manner of Life of the Present Jews throughout the World*. Translated by Edmund Chilmead. London: J. Martin and J. Ridley, 1650.
——. *Lev ha-Aryeh*. Venice: G. Sarzina, 1612.
——. *Midbar Yehudah*. Venice: Zanetti, 1602.
Morosini, Giulio. *Via della fede*. Rome: Sacræ congregationis de propaganda fide, 1683.
Reuchlin, Johannes. *Augenspiegel*. Tübingen: Thomas Anselm, 1511.
Sefer ha-Bahir. Amsterdam, 1651.
Sefer ha-Zohar al ha-Torah. Mantua, 1558–1560.
Sefer ha-Zohar al ha-Torah. Cremona, 1558–1560.
Sefer Ma'arekhet ha-Elohut. Ferrara: Usque, 1558.
Sefer Ma'arekhet ha-Elohut. Mantua, 1558.
Sefer Yetzirah. Mantua, 1562.
Sheshet, Isaac bar. *She'elout u-Teshuvot*. Riva di Trento, 1559.
——. *Teshuvot ha-Rav*. Constantinople, 1546.
Tikkunei ha–Zohar. Mantua, 1558.
Zacut, Abraham. *Sefer Yuhasin*. Constantinople, 1566.
——. *Sefer Yuhasin*. Krakow, 1581.
Zacut, Moses. *Igrot ha-Remez*. Livorno, 1780.
Zohar Hadash. Venice: Bragadin, 1662.

Works Printed after 1800

Abrams, Daniel. "Defining Modern Academic Scholarship: Gershom Scholem and the Establishment of a New (?) Discipline." *JJTP* 9 (2000): 267–302.
———. "The Invention of the *Zohar* as a Book: On the Assumptions and Expectations of the Kabbalists and Modern Scholars." *Kabbalah* 19 (2009): 7–142.
———. "Orality in the Kabbalistic School of Nahmanides: Preserving and Interpreting Esoteric Traditions and Texts." *JSQ* 3 (1996): 85–102.
———, ed. *Sefer ha-Bahir*. Los Angeles: Cherub Press, 1994.
Adelman, Howard E. "Leon Modena, *Homo Ludens*, and *Kol Sakhal* (Hebrew). In Malkiel, *The Lion Shall Roar*, 91–105.
———. "Leon Modena: The Autobiography and the Man." In *Autobiography*, 19–49.
———. "New Light on the Life and Writings of Leon Modena." In *Approaches to Judaism in Medieval Times II*. Edited by David R. Blumenthal, 109–22. Chico: Scholars Press, 1984.
———. "Rabbi Leon Modena and the Christian Kabbalists." In *Renaissance Rereadings*. Edited by Maryanne Cline Horowitz, 271–86. Urbana: University of Illinois Press, 1988.
———. "Success and Failure in the Seventeenth Century Ghetto of Venice: The Life and Thought of Leon Modena, 1571–1648." Ph.D. dissertation. Brandeis University, 1985.
Agnon, S.Y. *Mi-Sod Hakhamim: mikhtavim, 1909–1970*. Jerusalem and Tel Aviv: Schocken, 2002.
———. *Sefer, Sofer ve-Sipur*. Jerusalem and Tel Aviv: Schocken, 1937.
———. *Sefer, Sofer ve-Sipur*. Jerusalem and Tel Aviv: Schocken, 1978.
Alashkar, Yosef ben Moshe. *Sefer Tsafnat Paneah*. Introduction by Moshe Idel. Jerusalem: Misgav Jerusalem, 1991.
Almanzi, Joseph. *Higayon ba-Kinor*. Vienna: Franz von Schmid, 1839.
Altmann, Alexander. "Lurianic Kabbalah in a Platonic Key: Abraham Cohen Herrera's *Puerta del Cielo*." In Twersky and Septimus, *Jewish Thought in the Seventeenth Century*, 1–37.
———. "Maimonides's Attitude toward Jewish Mysticism." In *Studies in Jewish Thought: An Anthology of German Jewish Scholarship*. Edited by Alfred Jospe, 200–219. Detroit: Wayne State University Press, 1981.
———. *Moses Mendelssohn: A Biographical Study*. Philadelphia: JPS, 1973.
———. "On the Border of Philosophy: The Figure of the Kabbalist R. Elijah Hayim Genazzano" (Hebrew). *JSJT* 7 (1988): 61–101.
Ancona, Clemente E. "Attacchi contro il Talmud di Fra Sisto da Siena, e la riposta, finora inedita, di Leon Modena, rabbino in Venezia." *Bollettino dell'Istituto di Storia della Società e dello Stato Veneziano* 5–6 (1963–1964): 297–323.
———. "L'inventario dei beni appartenenti a Leon da Modena." *Bollettino dell'Istituto di Storia della Società e dello Stato Veneziano* 4 (1962): 249–67.
Anidjar, Gil. *"Our Place in al-Andalus": Kabbalah, Philosophy, Literature in Arab Jewish Letters*. Stanford: Stanford University Press, 2002.
Ariel, David S. "Shem Tob ibn Shem Tob's Kabbalistic Critique of Jewish Philosophy in the 'Commentary on the Sefirot.'" Ph.D. dissertation, Brandeis University, 1981.

Assaf, Simha. "A Contribution to the Biography of R. Solomon Luria" (Hebrew). In *Sefer ha-Yovel li-khevod Levi Ginsburg*, 45–63. Philadelphia: JPS, 1946.

———. "On the Controversy over the Printing of Kabbalistic Books" (Hebrew). *Sinai* 5 (1939): 360–68.

———. "From the Storehouses of the Library in Jerusalem" (Hebrew). In *Minhah le-David: Sefer ha-Yovel le-David Yelen*, 221–39. Jerusalem: Weiss, 1935.

Avivi, Joseph. *Kabalat ha-Ari*. 3 vols. Jerusalem: Ben-Zvi Institute, 2008.

———. "*Ma'amar ha-Vikuah* of Ramhal." (Hebrew). *Ha-Ma'ayan* (1974): 49–58.

———. "The Writings of Ari in Italy Up to the Year 1620" (Hebrew). *Alei Sefer* 11 (1984): 91–134.

———. "The Writings of R. Menahem Azariah da Fano on the Wisdom of Kabbalah" (Hebrew). *Sefunot* 4, 19 (1988): 347–76.

Azulai, Hayim Joseph David. *Ma'agal Tov ha-shalem*. Edited by Aron Freimann. Jerusalem: Mekize Nirdamim, 1934.

Bacher, Wilhelm. "Das Merkwort PRDS in der jüdischen Bibelexegese." *Zeitschrift für die alttestamentliche Wissenschaft* 13 (1893): 294–305.

Baer, Fritz. "Abner aus Burgos." *Korrespondenzblatt des Vereins zur Gründung und Erhaltung einer Akademie für die Wissenschaft des Judentums* 10 (1929): 20–37.

Baer, Yitzhak. *A History of the Jews in Christian Spain*. 2 vols. Philadelphia: JPS, 1992.

———. "Abner of Burgos' *Minhat Kenaoth* and Its Influence on Hasdai Crescas" (Hebrew). *Tarbiz* 11 (1940): 188–206.

———. "Kabbalistic Doctrine in the Christological Teachings of Abner of Burgos" (Hebrew). *Tarbiz* 27 (1958): 278–89.

Barbierato, Federico. *Nella stanza dei circoli: Clavicula Salomonis e libri di magia a Venezia nei secoli XVII e XVIII*. Milan: S. Bonnard, 2002.

———. "Tra attori e inquisitori: Manoscritti, commedia dell'arte e diffusione delle conoscenze magiche nella Venezia del seicento." In *I Luoghi dell'immaginario barrocco*. Edited by Lucia Strappini, 341–52. Naples: Liguori, 2001.

Barnai, Jacob. *Shabtaut: Hebetim Hevratiyim*. Jerusalem: Zalman Shazar Center, 2000.

Baron, Salo W. "Ghetto and Emancipation: Shall We Revise the Traditional View?" *Menorah Journal* 14 (1928): 515–26.

Baruchson, Shifra. *Sefarim ve-korim: tarbut ha-keriah shel Yehude Italyah be-shilhe ha-Renesans*. Ramat Gan: Bar-Ilan University Press, 1993.

Barzilay, Isaac. *Shlomo Yehudah Rapoport (Shir), 1790–1867, and His Contemporaries*. Ramat Gan: Massada Press, 1969.

———. *Yoseph Shlomo Delmedigo (Yashar of Candia): His Life, Works and Times*. Leiden: Brill, 1974.

Baumgarten, Jean. *Le peuple des livres: Les ouvrages populaires dans la société ashkénaze XVIe–XVIIIe siècle*. Paris: Albin Michel, 2010.

Beit-Arié, Malachi. "Publication and Reproduction of Literary Texts in Medieval Jewish Civilization: Jewish Scribality and Its Impact on the Texts Transmitted." In Elman and Gershoni, *Transmitting Jewish Traditions*, 225–47.

Ben-Menahem, Naftali. "Early Printed Editions of the *Shulhan Arukh*" (Hebrew). In *Rabi Yosef Karo*. Edited by Isaac Refael, 101–20. Jerusalem: Mossad ha-Rav Kook, 1969.

Ben-Sasson, Yonah. *Mishnato ha-iyunit shel ha-Rema*. Jerusalem: Israel Academy of Sciences, 1984.
Ben-Shalom, Ram. *Mul tarbut Notsrit: Toda'ah historit ve-dimuye avar bi-kerav Yehude Sefarad ve-Provens bi-Yeme ha-Benayim*. Jerusalem: Ben-Zvi Institute, 2006.
Ben-Shammai, Haggai. "The Transmigration of Souls in Jewish Thought in the East in the Tenth Century" (Hebrew). *Sefunot* 5, 20 (1991): 117–36.
Ben-Shlomo, Yosef. *Torat ha-Elohut shel Rabi Moshe Cordovero*. Jerusalem: Mossad Bialik, 1965.
Benamozegh, Elijah. *Emat Mafgia al Ari*. Livorno: Benamozegh, 1855.
———. *Em la-Mikra*. Livorno: Benamozegh, 1862.
———. *Israel and Humanity*. Translated by Maxwell Luria. New York: Paulist Press, 1995.
———. *Ta'am la-Shad*. Livorno: Benamozegh, 1863. Photo offset edition, Tel Aviv 1970.
Benayahu, Meir. "The Controversy Concerning the *Meor Enayim* of Azariah de' Rossi." (Hebrew) *Asufot* 5 (1991): 213–65.
———. *Dor Ehad ba'aretz: Igrot Rabi Shmuel Aboav ve-Rabi Moshe Zakut be-inyene Eretz Yisrael*. Jerusalem: Yad ha-Rav Nissim, 1988.
———. *Haskamah u-reshut bi-defuse Venetsyah*. Jerusalem: Ben-Zvi Institute, 1971.
———. *Kitve ha-Kabalah shela-Ramhal*. Jerusalem: Menachem Press, 1979.
———. "The Positions of Rabbi Moses Zacut and Rabbi Samuel Aboab on the Controversies about Conversos from Portugal Who Returned to Judaism" (Hebrew). In *Shlomo Simonsohn Jubilee Volume: Studies on the History of the Jews in the Middle Ages and Renaissance Period*. Edited by Daniel Carpi, 29–44. Tel Aviv: Tel Aviv University Press, 1993.
———. "Rabbi Israel Najara" (Hebrew). *Asufot* 4 (1990): 203–84.
———. "*Sefer ha-Emunot* by Rabbi Shem Tov ibn Shem Tov: Its Concealment and Revelation" (Hebrew). *Molad* 5 (1973): 658–62.
———. *Sefer Toldot Ha-Ari*. Jerusalem: Ben-Zvi Institute 1967.
———. "Sources Concerning the Printing and Distribution of Hebrew Books in Italy" (Hebrew). *Sinai* 34 (1954):156–202.
Berger, David. "How Did Nahmanides Propose to Resolve the Maimonidean Controversy?" In *Me'ah She'arim: Studies in Medieval Jewish Spiritual Life in Memory of Isadore Twersky*. Edited by Gerald Blidstein, Ezra Fleischer, Carmi Horowitz, and Bernard Septimus, 135–46. Jerusalem: Magnes Press, 2001.
———. "On the Uses of History in Medieval Jewish Polemic against Christianity: The Quest for the Historical Jesus." In Carlebach, Efron, and Myers, *Jewish History and Jewish Memory*, 25–39.
Berkovitz, Jay. "Custom in the Legal Thought of Rabbi Yair Hayim Bacharach" (Hebrew). In *Mehkarim be-toldot Yehude Ashkenaz: Sefer Yovel li-khevod Yitzhak Zimmer*. Edited by Gershon Bacon, Daniel Sperber, and Aharon Gaimani, 29–56. Ramat Gan: Bar–Ilan University Press, 2008.
Berliner, Abraham. "Causing the Lips of Those That Are Asleep to Speak" (Hebrew). In *Zikaron le-Avraham Eliyahu: Kevutsat ma'amarim be-hokhmat Yisrael li-khevod Avraham Eliyahu Harkabi*. Edited by Baron D. V. Günzburg and Isaac Markon, 484–504. St. Petersburg, 1908. Reprint, Jerusalem 1969.
Bernstein, Simon. *The Divan of Leo de Modena*. Philadelphia: JPS, 1932.

Biale, David. *Gershom Scholem: Kabbalah and Counter-History*. Cambridge: Harvard University Press, 1979.
——. "The Kabbala in Nachman Krochmal's Philosophy of History." *Journal of Jewish Studies* 32 (1981): 85–97.
Black, Crofton. *Pico's Heptaplus and Biblical Hermeneutics*. Leiden: Brill, 2006.
Blair, Ann. *The Theater of Nature: Jean Bodin and Renaissance Science*. Princeton: Princeton University Press, 1997.
Bland, Kalman P. "Elijah Del Medigo's Averroist Response to the Kabbalahs of Fifteenth-Century Jewry and Pico Della Mirandola." *JJTP* 1 (1991): 23–53.
——. "A Jewish Theory of Jewish Visual Culture: Leon Modena's Concept of Images and Their Effect on Locative Memory." *Ars Judaica* 5 (2009): 59–66.
Bloch, Phillip. "Der Streit um den Moreh des Maimonides in der Gemeinde Posen um die Mitte des 16. Jahrhundert." *MGWJ* 47 (1903): 153–69, 263–79, 346–56.
Blogg, Salomon Ephraim. *Aedificium Salomonis*. Hanover: E. A. Telgener, 1832.
Bodian, Miriam. *Dying in the Law of Moses: Crypto-Jewish Martyrdom in the Iberian World*. Bloomington: Indiana University Press, 2007.
Bonfil, Robert. "Change in the Cultural Patterns of a Jewish Society in Crisis: Italian Jewry at the Close of the Sixteenth Century." In *Essential Papers on Jewish Culture in Renaissance and Baroque Italy*. Edited by David B. Ruderman, 401–25. New York: New York University Press, 1992.
——. "Cultura e mistica a Venezia nel Cinquecento." In *Gli Ebrei e Venezia: Secoli XIV–XVIII*. Edited by Gaetano Cozzi, 469–506. Milan: Edizioni Communità, 1987.
——. "A Cultural Profile." In Davis and Ravid, *The Jews of Early Modern Venice*, 169–90.
——. "Halakhah, Kabbalah, and Society: Some Insights into Rabbi Menahem Azariah da Fano's Inner World." In Twersky and Septimus, *Jewish Thought in the Seventeenth Century*, 39–61.
——. "New Information on the Life of Menahem Azariah da Fano and His Time Period" (Hebrew). In *Perakim be-Toledot ha-Hevrah ha-Yehudit be-Yeme ha-Benayim u-ba'et ha-Hadasha: Mukdashim li-Profesor Yakov Katz*. Edited by Yosef Salmon and Immanuel Etkes, 98–135. Jerusalem: Magnes Press, 1980.
——. *Rabbis and Jewish Communities in Renaissance Italy*. Oxford: Littman Library, 1990.
——. "Rabbis, Jesuits, and Riddles: An Inquiry into the World of Moses Zacut" (Hebrew). *Italia* 13–15 (2001): 169–89.
——. "Some Reflections on the Place of Azariah de Rossi's *Meor Enayim* in the Cultural Milieu of Italian Renaissance Jewry." In Cooperman, *Jewish Thought in the Sixteenth Century*, 23–48.
Bos, Gerrit. "Jewish Traditions on Strengthening Memory and Leone Modena's Evaluation." *JSQ* 2 (1995): 39–58.
Brenner, Michael. *Prophets of the Past: Interpreters of Jewish History*. Princeton: Princeton University Press, 2010.
Breuer, Edward. *The Limits of Enlightenment: Jews, Germans, and the Eighteenth-Century Study of Scripture*. Cambridge: Harvard University Press, 1996.
Brody, Zipporah. "R. Moses Botarel: His Commentary on *Sefer Yetzirah* and the Image of Abu Aharon" (Hebrew). In *Sefer zikaron le-Gershom Scholem bi-mlot*

esrim ve-hamesh shanim le-petirato. Edited by Joseph Dan, 1:159–206. Jerusalem: Hebrew University 2007.

Buechler, Simeon, ed. *Shai le-Moreh.* Budapest: Sternberg, 1895.

Burke, Peter. "Early Modern Venice as a Center of Information and Communication." In *Venice Reconsidered: The History and Civilization of an Italian City-State, 1297–1797.* Edited by John Martin and Dennis Romano, 389–419. Baltimore: Johns Hopkins University Press, 2000.

Burnett, Stephen G. *From Christian Hebraism to Jewish Studies: Johannes Buxtorf (1564–1629) and Hebrew Learning in the Seventeenth Century.* Leiden: Brill, 1996.

Busi, Giulio. "Francesco Zorzi: A Methodical Dreamer." In Dan, *The Christian Kabbalah*, 97–125.

———. *The Great Parchment.* Turin: Nino Aragno, 2004.

———. "'Who Does Not Wonder at This Chameleon?' The Kabbalistic Library of Giovanni Pico della Mirandola." In *Hebrew to Latin, Latin to Hebrew: the Mirroring of Two Cultures in the Age of Humanism.* Edited by Giulio Busi, 167–96. Turin: Nino Aragno, 2006.

Campanini, Saverio. "Anima in itinere: Un'orazione funebre di Avraham da Sant'Angelo." In *La cultura ebraica a Bologna tra medioevo e rinascimento.* Edited by Mauro Perani, 129–68. Florence: Giuntina, 2002.

———, ed. *The Book of Bahir.* Turin: Nino Aragno, 2005.

———. "Eine späte Apologie der Kabbala: Die *Abdita divinae cabalae mysteria* des Jacques Gaffarel." In *Topik und Tradition: Prozesse der Neuordnung von Wissensüberlieferungen des 13. bis. 17 Jahrhunderts.* Edited by Thomas Frank, Urusla Kocher, and Ulrike Tarnow, 293–320. Gottingen: V & R Unipress, 2007.

———. "Le prefazioni, le dediche, e i *colophon* di Gershom Soncino." In *L'attività editoriale di Gershom Soncino 1502–1527.* Edited by Giuliano Tamani, 31–57. Cremona: Edizioni dei Soncino, 1997.

———. "Some Notes on Gershom Scholem and Christian Kabbalah." In Dan, *Sefer zikaron le-Gershom Scholem bi-mlot esrim ve-hamesh shanim le-petirato*, 2:13–33.

———. "Wege in die Stadt der Bücher. Ein Beitrag zur Geschichte der hebräischen Bibliographie: Die katholische bibliographische "Dynastie" Iona-Bartolocci-Imbonati." In *Reuchlin und seine Erbern.* Edited by Peter Schäfer and Irina Wandrey, 61–76. Ostfildern: Thorbecke, 2005.

Canart, Paul. "Jean Nathanaël et le commerce des manuscrit grecs à Venise au XVIe siècle." In *Venezia centro di mediazone tra Oriente e Occidente (secoli XV–XVI) aspetti e problemi.* Edited by Hans-Georg Beck, Manoussos Manoussacas, and Agostino Pertusi, 2:417–38. Florence: L. S. Olschki, 1977.

Caputo, Nina. *Nahmanides in Medieval Catalonia: History, Community, and Messianism.* Notre Dame: University of Notre Dame Press, 2007.

Carlebach, Elisheva. *The Pursuit of Heresy: Rabbi Moses Hagiz and the Sabbatian Controversies.* New York: Columbia University Press, 1990.

Carlebach, Elisheva, John M. Efron, and David N. Myers, eds. *Jewish History and Jewish Memory: Essays in Honor of Yosef Hayim Yerushalmi.* Hanover, NH: Brandeis University Press, 1998.

Cassuto, Umberto. "Leon Modena e l'opera sua." *RMI* 8 (1933): 132–42.

Castiglioni, Victorius, ed. *Sefer Igrot le-Shadal.* Trieste, 1899.

Celenza, Christopher S. "The Search for Ancient Wisdom in Early Modern Europe: Reuchlin and the Late Ancient Esoteric Paradigm." *Journal of Religious History* 25 (2001): 115–33.
Cermanová, Iveta. "The Censorship of Hebrew Manuscripts in Vienna in the Early 19th Century: The Case of Abraham Trebitsch." *Judaica Bohemiae* 39 (2003): 93–103.
———. "Karl Fischer (1757–1844). 1. The Life and Intellectual World of a Hebrew Censor." *Judaica Bohemiae* 42 (2006): 125–78.
———. "Karl Fischer (1757–1844). 2. The Work of a Hebrew Censor." *Judaica Bohemiae* 43 (2007–2008): 5–63.
Cohen, Jeremy. *Living Letters of the Law: Ideas of the Jew in Medieval Christianity*. Berkeley: University of California Press, 1999.
Cohen, Mark R. "Leone Da Modena's *Riti*: A Seventeenth-Century Plea for Social Toleration of Jews." In Ruderman, *Essential Papers on Jewish Culture in Renaissance and Baroque Italy*, 429–73.
———. "Who Wrote the Ambrosiana Manuscript of *Hayyei Yehudah*?" In *Autobiography*, 284–93.
Cohen de Herrera, Abraham. *Bet Elohim Sha'ar ha-Shamayim*. Translated by Nissim Yosha. Jerusalem: Ben-Zvi Institute, 2002.
———. *Gate of Heaven*. Translated by Kenneth Krabbenhoft. Leiden: Brill, 2002.
———. *Puerta del Cielo*. Edited by Kenneth Krabbenhoft. Madrid: Fundación Universitaria Española, 1987.
Cohen, Yosef Adichai. "Hananel da Foligno, the Man and His Time: Italy, the First Half of the Sixteenth Century" (Hebrew). Ph.D. dissertation, Bar Ilan University, 2004.
Cooperman, Bernard. "Eliahu Montalto's 'Suitable and Incontrovertible Propositions': A Seventeenth-Century Anti-Christian Polemic." In Twersky and Septimus, *Jewish Thought in the Seventeenth Century*, 469–97.
———, ed. *Jewish Thought in the Sixteenth Century*. Cambridge: Harvard University Press, 1983
———. "Political Discourse in a Kabbalistic Register: Isaac de Lattes' Plea for Stronger Communal Government." In *Be'erot Yitzhak: Studies in Memory of Isadore Twersky*. Edited by Jay M. Harris, 47–68; 79–93 (Hebrew appendices). Cambridge: Harvard University Press, 2005.
Cooperman, Bernard Dov and Barbara Garvin, eds. *The Jews of Italy: Memory and Identity*. Bethesda: University of Maryland Press, 2000.
Copenhaver, Brian P. "Maimonides, Abulafia and Pico. A Secret Aristotle for the Renaissance." *Rinascimento* 46 (2006): 23–51.
———. "Number, Shape, and Meaning in Pico's Christian Cabala." In *Natural Particulars: Nature and the Disciplines in Renaissance Europe*. Edited by Anthony Grafton and Nancy Siraisi, 25–76. Cambridge: MIT Press, 1999.
———. "The Secret of Pico's *Oration*: Cabala and Renaissance Philosophy." *Midwest Studies in Philosophy* 26 (2002): 56–81.
Cozzi, Gaetano, ed. *Gli Ebrei e Venezia: secoli XIV–XVIII*. Milan: Edizioni Comunità, 1987.
———. *Paolo Sarpi tra Venezia e l'Europa*. Turin: G. Einaudi, 1978.
Cozzi, Luisa. "La Tradizione settecentesca dei 'Pensieri' Sarpiani." *SV* 13 (1971): 393–450.

Dan, Joseph, ed. *The Christian Kabbalah Jewish Mystical Books and Their Christian Interpreters*. Cambridge: Harvard College Library, 1997.

———. "R. Judah Aryeh Modena and *Sefer ha-Yashar*." (Hebrew) *Sinai* 78 (1976): 197–98.

———, ed. *Sefer ha-Yashar*. Jerusalem: Mossad Bialik, 1986.

———. *The "Unique Cherub" Circle: A School of Mystics and Esoterics in Medieval Germany*. Tübingen: Mohr Siebeck, 1999.

Dane, Joseph A. *The Myth of Print Culture: Essays on Evidence, Textuality, and Bibliographical Method*. Toronto: University of Toronto Press, 2003.

Darnton, Robert. "'What Is the History of Books?' Revisited." *Modern Intellectual History* 4 (2007): 495–508.

Daston, Lorraine, and Peter Galison. *Objectivity*. New York: Zone Books, 2007.

Davidson, Herbert A. *Moses Maimonides: The Man and His Works*. New York: Oxford University Press, 2005.

Davidson, Nicholas. "Unbelief and Atheism in Italy, 1500–1700." In *Atheism from the Reformation to the Enlightenment*. Edited by Michael Hunter and David Wootton, 55–85. Oxford: Clarendon Press, 1992.

Davis, Joseph. "The Reception of the *Shulhan Arukh* and the Formation of Ashkenazic Jewish Identity." *AJS Review* 26 (2002): 251–76.

Davis, Robert C., and Benjamin Ravid, eds. *The Jews of Early Modern Venice*. Baltimore: Johns Hopkins University Press, 2001.

Del Bianco Cotrozzi, Maddalena. *Il Collegio rabbinico di Padova*. Florence: L. S. Olschki, 1995.

Delmedigo, Elijah. *Sefer Behinat ha-Dat*. Edited by Isaac Reggio. Vienna: Anton von Schmid, 1833.

———. *Sefer Behinat ha-Dat*. Edited by Jacob J. Ross. Tel Aviv: Tel Aviv University Press, 1984.

Del Torre, Maria Assunta. *Studi su Cesare Cremonini: Cosmologia e logica nel tardo aristotelismo padovano*. Padua: Antenore, 1968.

De' Rossi, Azariah *The Light of the Eyes*. Translated by Joanna Weinberg. New Haven: Yale University Press, 2001.

De' Rossi, Giovanni Bernardo. *Dizonario storico degli autori ebrei e delle loro opere*. 2 vols. Parma: Reale Stamperia, 1802.

———. *MSS Codices Hebraici Biblioth. I. B. De-Rossi*. 3 vols. Parma, 1803.

Desplanches, Luc. "Le monde de la Kabbale dans l'Italie du XVIIe siècle Léon de Modène: Ari Nohem." Thèse de doctorat, Université des Sciences Humaines de Strasbourg, 1985.

Dienstag, Jacob I. "Maimonides and Nahmanides: A Bibliography" (Hebrew). *Daat* 27 (1991): 125–39.

———. "Maimonides' *Guide for the Perplexed*: A Bibliography of Editions and Translations." In *Occident and Orient: A Tribute to the Memory of Alexander Scheiber*. Edited by Robert Dán, 95–128. Budapest and Leiden: Akadémiai Kiadó and Brill, 1988.

Divlitzki, Bezalel. "The Hasid R. Samuel Aboab and His Letters" (Hebrew). *Kovetz Etz Hayim* 2 (2008): 219–33.

Dooley, Brendan. *The Social History of Skepticism: Experience and Doubt in Early Modern Culture*. Baltimore: Johns Hopkins University Press, 1999.

Dubin, Lois C. *The Port Jews of Habsburg Trieste: Absolutist Politics and Enlightenment Culture*. Stanford: Stanford University Press, 1999.

Duran, Profiat. *Kitve Pulmus li-Profiat Duran*. Edited by Frank Talmage. Jerusalem: Zalman Shazar Center, 1981.

Elbaum, Jacob. *Petihut ve-histagrut: ha-yetsirah ha-ruhanit-ha-sifrutit be-Polin uve-artsot Ashkenaz be-shilhe ha-meah ha-shesh-esreh*. Jerusalem: Magnes Press, 1990.

Elbogen, Ismar. *Jewish Liturgy: A Comprehensive History*. Translated by Raymond P. Scheindlin. Philadelphia and New York: JPS and Jewish Theological Seminary of America, 1993.

Elior, Rachel. "The Dispute over the Status of Kabbalah in the Sixteenth Century" (Hebrew). *JSJT* 1 (1981): 177–90.

———, ed. *Ha-Halom ve-Shivro: ha-tenuah ha-Shabtait u-sheluhoteha*. 2 vols. Jerusalem: Magnes Press, 2001.

———. "Joseph Karo and Israel Ba'al Shem Tov" (Hebrew). *Tarbiz* 65 (1996): 671–709.

Elior, Rachel, and Peter Schäfer, eds. *Creation and Re-Creation in Jewish Thought: Festschrift in Honor of Joseph Dan on the Occasion of His Seventieth Birthday*. Tübingen: Mohr Siebeck, 2005.

Elman, Yaakov, and Israel Gershoni, eds. *Transmitting Jewish Traditions: Orality, Textuality, and Cultural Diffusion*. New Haven: Yale University Press, 2000.

Elqayam, Avraham. "The Sacred *Zohar* of Sabbetai Sevi" (Hebrew). *Kabbalah* 3 (1998): 345–87.

Elukin, Jonathan M. "A New Essenism: Heinrich Graetz and Mysticism." *JHI* 59 (1998): 135–48.

Emden, Jacob. *Torat ha-Kenaot*. Jerualem: Makor, 1970.

Etkes, Immanuel. *The Gaon of Vilna: The Man and His Image*. Berkeley: University of California Press, 2002.

Facchini, Cristiana. "Una insinuante modernità: Note su Leone Modena e l'ebraismo nel siecento: rassenga bibliografica." *Annali di storia dell'esegesi* 19 (2002): 467–97.

Fahn, Reuven "Rabbi Moses Kunitz" (Hebrew). In *Pirke Haskalah: Kitvei Reuven Fahn II*, 70–99. Stanisławów: 1937.

Farmer, S. A. *Syncretism in the West: Pico's 900 Theses (1486)*. Tempe, AZ: Medieval and Renaissance Texts and Studies, 1998.

Feiner, Shmuel. *The Jewish Enlightenment*. Philadelphia: University of Pennsylvania Press, 2004.

Fine, Lawrence. "The Art of Metoposcopy: A Study in Isaac Luria's Charismatic Knowledge." *AJS Review* 11 (1986): 79–101.

———. "Benevolent Spirit Possession in Sixteenth-Century Safed." In *Spirit Possession in Judaism: Cases and Context from the Middle Ages to the Present*. Edited by Matt Goldish, 101–23. Detroit: Wayne State University Press, 2003.

———. *Physician of the Soul, Healer of the Cosmos: Isaac Luria and His Kabbalistic Fellowship*. Stanford: Stanford University Press, 2003.

Fishbane, Eitan P. *As Light before Dawn: The Inner World of a Medieval Kabbalist*. Stanford: Stanford University Press, 2009.

Fishman, Talya. "Changing Early Modern Jewish Discourse about Christianity: The Efforts of Rabbi Leon Modena." In Malkiel, *The Lion Shall Roar*, 159–94.
———. "Forging Jewish Memory: *Besamim Rosh* and the Invention of Pre-emancipation Jewish Culture." In Carlebach, Efron, and Myers, *Jewish History and Jewish Memory*, 70–88.
———. *Shaking the Pillars of Exile: 'Voice of a Fool,' an Early Modern Jewish Critique of Rabbinic Culture*. Stanford: Stanford University Press, 1997.
Flatto, Sharon. *The Kabbalistic Culture of Eighteenth-Century Prague: Ezekiel Landau (the 'Noda Biyehudah') and His Contemporaries*. Oxford: Littman Library, 2010.
Fleischer, Ezra. "Review of *Kol Shirei Ya'akov Frances*" (Hebrew). *KS* 45 (1970): 177–87.
Fraenkel, Carlos. *Min ha-Rambam li-Shmuel Ibn Tibbon*. Jerusalem: Magnes Press, 2007.
Frances, Jacob. *Kol Shirei Ya'akov Frances*. Edited by Peninah Naveh. Jerusalem: Mossad Bialik, 1969.
Friedlander, Hayim. *Sha'are Ramhal*. Bnei Brak, 1986.
Funkenstein, Amos. *Perceptions of Jewish History*. Berkeley: University of California Press, 1993.
———. *Theology and the Scientific Imagination from the Middle Ages to the Seventeenth Century*. Princeton: Princeton University Press, 1986.
Galinsky, Judah. "Ashkenazim in Sefarad: The Rosh and the Tur on the Codification of Jewish Law." *Jewish Law Annual* 16 (2006): 3–23.
Geiger, Abraham. *Leon da Modena, Rabbiner zu Venedig (1571–1648), und seine Stellung zur Kabbalah, zum Thalmud und zum Christenthume*. Breslau: J. U. Kern, 1856.
———. *Melo Chofnajim*. Berlin, 1840.
———. *Urschrift und Uebersetzungen der Bibel*. Breslau: J. Hainauer, 1857.
Genazzano, Eliyyah Hayyim ben Binyamin da. *La lettera preziosa*. Edited by Fabrizio Lelli. Florence: La giuntina, 2002.
Gertner, Haim. "Image and Reality in the Relationship between Maskilim and Hasidim: The Case of Shlomoh Yehudah Rapoport's Appointment to the Rabbinate of Tarnopol" (Hebrew). In *Yashan mipnei Hadash: Shai le-Imanuel Etkes*. Edited by David Assaf and Ada Rapoport-Albert, 2:355–83. Jerusalem: Zalman Shazar Center, 2009.
Gilboa, Menuha. *Leksikon ha-Itonut ha-Ivrit ba-meot ha-shemoneh esreh ve-ha tesha-esreh*. Jerusalem: Mossad Bialik, 1992.
Giller, Pinchas. *Reading the Zohar: The Sacred Text of the Kabbalah*. New York: Oxford University Press, 2001.
Ginsburg, Elliot K. *Sod ha-Shabbat, the Mystery of the Sabbath: From the Tola'at Ya'aqov of Meir Ibn Gabbai*. Albany: SUNY Press, 1989.
Ginzburg, Simon. *Rabi Moshe Hayim Luzzatto u-Vene-Doro: Osef Igrot u-Te'udot*. 2 vols. Tel Aviv: Mossad Bialik, 1937.
Goetschel, Roland. "Elie Hayim de Genazzano et la Kabbale." *REJ* 142 (1983): 91–108.
———. *Meïr ibn Gabbay: Le discours de la Kabbale espagnole*. Leuven: Peeters, 1981.
———. "Providence et destinées de l'âme dans le Sefer ha-Emunot de Shem Tob Ibn Shem Tob (1380–1441)." In *Mehkere Misgav Yerushalayim be-Sifruyot am Yisrael*. Edited by Ephraim Hazan, 53–71. Jerusalem: Misgav Jerusalem 1987.

Goetschel, Roland. "Samuel David Luzzatto et David H. Joël: Deux Regards sur la Kabbale." In *Samuel David Luzzatto: The Bi-Centennial of His Birth*. Edited by Robert Bonfil, Isaac Gottlieb, and Hannah Kasher, 35–54. Jerusalem: Magnes Press, 2004.
Goldberg, Harvey. "The Zohar in Southern Morocco: A Study in the Ethnography of Texts." *History of Religions* 29 (1990): 233–58.
Goldish, Matt. *The Sabbatean Prophets*. Cambridge: Harvard University Press, 2004.
Goldman, Israel M. *The Life and Times of Rabbi David Ibn Abi Zimra*. New York: Jewish Theological Seminary of America, 1970.
Goldreich, Amos. *Sefer Meirat Enayim le-R. Yitshak de-min Ako: Mahudarah madait*. Jerusalem: Hebrew University, 1981.
Goodblatt, Chanita, and Howard Kreisel. *Tradition, Heterodoxy, and Religious Culture: Judaism and Christianity in the Early Modern Period*. Beer Sheva: Ben-Gurion University of the Negev Press, 2006.
Goodman-Thau, Eveline. "Meyer Heinrich Hirsch Landauer: Bible Scholar and Kabbalist." In *Mysticism, Magic, and Kabbalah in Ashkenazi Judaism*. Edited by Karl Erich Grözinger and Joseph Dan, 275–94. Berlin: Walter de Gruyter, 1995.
Gordon, Judah Leib. *Kitve Yehudah Leib Gordon: Shirah*. Tel Aviv: Dvir, 1963.
Gottlieb, Ephraim. "Shem Tov ibn Shem Tov's Path to Kabbalah" (Hebrew). In *Mehkarim be-Sifrut ha-Kabalah*. Edited by Joseph R. Hacker, 347–56. Tel Aviv: Tel Aviv University Press, 1976.
Gottlober, Abraham Baer. *Toldot ha-Kabalah veha-Hasidut*. Zhitomir, 1869.
———. *Zikhronot u-masaot*. Vol. 2. Edited by Reuven Goldberg. Jerusalem: Mossad Bialik, 1976.
Gräber, Eisig, ed. *S. D. Luzzatto's Hebraische Briefe*. Przemsyl: Zupnik and Knoller, 1882. Photo offset edition, Jerusalem, 1966.
———, ed. *S. L. Rappoport's hebräische Briefe an S. D. Luzzatto (1833–1860)*. Przemysl: 1886.
Graetz, Heinrich. *Geschichte der Juden*. Vol 7. Leipzig: O. Leiner, 1863.
Grafton, Anthony. *Defenders of the Text: The Traditions of Scholarship in an Age of Science, 1450–1800*. Cambridge: Harvard University Press, 1991.
———. *Forgers and Critics: Creativity and Duplicity in Western Scholarship*. Princeton: Princeton University Press, 1990.
———. "Giovanni Pico della Mirandola: Trials and Triumphs of an Omnivore." In *Commerce with the Classics: Ancient Books and Renaissance Readers*, 93–134. Ann Arbor: University of Michigan Press, 1997.
Grafton, Anthony, and Joanna Weinberg. *"I have always loved the Holy Tongue": Isaac Casaubon, the Jews, and a Forgotten Chapter in Renaissance Scholarship*. Cambridge: Harvard University Press, 2011,
Green, Arthur. *Keter: The Crown of God in Early Jewish Mysticism*. Princeton: Princeton University Press, 1997.
Greenberg, Joseph Zeev. "Responsa *Ziknei Yehudah* by Rabbi Judah Aryeh Modena as a historical source for the history of the Jews in Italy" (Hebrew). M.A. thesis, Bar–Ilan University, 1976.
Greenwald, Jekuthiel. *Sefer Toldot misphahat Rosenthal*. Budapest, 1921.
Grendler, Paul F. *The Roman Inquisition and the Venetian Press, 1540–1605*. Princeton: Princeton University Press, 1977.

Gries, Zeev. *Sifrut ha-hanhagot: Toldoteha u-mekomah be-haye haside R. Yisrael Ba'al Shem Tov*. Jerusalem: Mossad Bialik, 1989.
Guetta, Alessandro. "Anti-Catholic Apologetics in Leon Modena's *Magen va-Herev*: A Comparative Reading" (Hebrew). In Malkiel, *The Lion Shall Roar*, 69–89.
———. "Cabale et rationalisme en Italie à l'époque baroque." In *Réceptions de la Cabale*. Edited by Pierre Gisel and Lucie Kaennel, 109–26. Paris: Eclat, 2007.
———. "Elia Benamozegh: Bibliografia." *RMI* 53 (1987): 67–81.
———, ed. *Per Elia Benamozegh*. Milan: Edizioni Thálassa De Paz, 2001.
———. "The Last Debate on Kabbalah in Italian Judaism: I. S. Reggio, S. D. Luzzatto, and E. Benamozegh." In Cooperman and Garvin, *The Jews of Italy*, 256–75.
———. *Philosophy and Kabbalah: Elijah Benamozegh and the Reconciliation of Western Thought and Jewish Esotericism*. Albany: SUNY Press, 2009.
Gurfinkel, Eli. "Maimonides and Kabbalah: An Annotated Bibliography" (Hebrew). *Daat* 64–66 (2009): 417–85.
Hacker, Joseph. "The History of the Study of Kabbalah and Its Dissemination in Salonika in the 16th Century" (Hebrew). In Elior and Schäfer, *Creation and Re-Creation in Jewish Thought*, 165–80.
———. "A New Letter about the Controversy on the Printing of the *Zohar* in Italy" (Hebrew). In *Masuot: mehkarim be-sifrut ha-Kabalah uve-mahshevet Yisrael mukdashim le-zikhro shel Prof. Efrayim Gotlib*. Edited by Michal Oron and Amos Goldreich, 120–30. Jerusalem: Mossad Bialik, 1994.
———. "R. Jacob ibn Habib: Toward a Portrait of Jewish Leadership in Salonika in the Early Sixteenth Century" (Hebrew). *World Congress of Jewish Studies* 6, 2 (1976): 117–26.
Halbertal, Moshe. *Al derekh ha-emet: ha-Ramban vi-yetsiratah shel masoret*. Jerusalem: Mekhon Shalom Hartman, 2006.
———. *Concealment and Revelation: Esotericism in Jewish Thought and Its Philosophical Implications*. Princeton: Princeton University Press, 2007.
———. "What Is the *Mishneh Torah*? On Codification and Ambivalence." In *Maimonides after 800 Years: Essays on Maimonides and His Influence*. Edited by Jay M. Harris, 81–111. Cambridge: Harvard University Press, 2007.
Halivni, David Weiss. *Peshat and Derash: Plain and Applied Meaning in Rabbinic Exegesis*. Oxford: Oxford University Press, 1991.
Halkin, A. S. "Yedaiah Bedershi's Apology." In *Jewish Medieval and Renaissance Studies*. Edited by Alexander Altmann, 165–84. Cambridge: Harvard University Press, 1967.
Hallamish, Moshe. "A Document Concerning a Controversy about Kabbalah in Italy in the Early Seventeenth Century" (Hebrew). *Bar-Ilan* 22–23 (1987): 179–204.
———. "Kabbalah in the Adjudication of Joseph Karo" (Hebrew). *Daat* 21 (1988): 85–102.
Hallamish, Moshe, Joseph Rivlin, and Raphael Shuchat, eds. *Ha-Gera u-vet midrasho*. Ramat Gan: Bar–Ilan University Press, 2003.
Hames, Harvey J. "Elia del Medigo: An Archetype of the Halachic Man?" *Traditio* 56 (2001): 213–27.
———. *Like Angels on Jacob's Ladder: Abraham Abulafia, the Franciscans, and Joachimism*. Albany: SUNY Press, 2007.

Hamilton, Alastair. *The Apocryphal Apocalypse: The Reception of the Second Book of Esdras (4 Ezra) from the Renaissance to the Enlightenment.* Oxford: Clarendon Press, 1999.

Hansel, Joëlle. *Moïse Hayyim Luzzatto, 1707–1746: Kabbale et Philosophie.* Paris: Cerf, 2004.

Harari, Zev. "On the Problem of Joseph Solomon Delmedigo's Relationship to Kabbalah" (Hebrew). M.A. thesis, Hebrew University, 1980.

Harel, Yaron. "The Edict to Destroy *Em la-Mikra*—Aleppo 1865" (Hebrew). *HUCA* 64 (1993): 27–36.

Harrán, Don. "*Nomina Numina*: Final Thoughts of Rabbi Leon Modena on the Essence of Sacred Music." *Italia* 17 (2006): 7–63.

Harris, Jay M. *How Do We Know This? Midrash and the Fragmentation of Modern Judaism.* Albany: SUNY Press, 1995.

———. "The Image of Maimonides in Nineteenth-Century Jewish Historiography." *PAAJR* 54 (1987): 117–39.

———. *Nachman Krochmal: Guiding the Perplexed of the Modern Age.* New York: New York University Press, 1991.

Heller, Wendy. *Emblems of Eloquence: Opera and Women's Voices in Seventeenth-Century Venice.* Berkeley: University of California Press, 2003.

Herklotz, Ingo. *Cassiano dal Pozzo und die Archäologie des 17. Jahrhunderts.* Munich: Hirmer Verlag, 1999.

Heschel, Susannah. *Abraham Geiger and the Jewish Jesus.* Chicago: University of Chicago Press, 1998.

Hess, Jonathan M. *Germans, Jews and the Claims of Modernity.* New Haven: Yale University Press, 2002.

Horbury, William. "Judah Briel and Seventeenth-Century Jewish Anti-Christian Polemic in Italy." *JSQ* 1 (1993–1994): 171–92.

Horch, Hans Otto. "'Auf der Zinne der Zeit': Ludwig Philippson (1811–1889)—der 'Journalist' des Reformjudentums." In *Bulletin des Leo Baeck Instituts* 82 (1989): 5–21.

Horowitz, Elliott S. "Cohen's *Autobiography of Leon Modena*." *JQR* 81 (1991): 453–61.

———. "The Early Eighteenth Century Confronts the Beard: Kabbalah and Jewish Self-Fashioning." *Jewish History* 8 (1994): 95–115.

———. "Jewish Confraternities in Seventeenth-Century Verona: A Study in the Social History of Piety." Ph.D. dissertation, Yale University, 1982.

———. "Speaking of the Dead: The Emergence of the Eulogy among Italian Jewry of the Sixteenth Century." In Ruderman, *Preachers of the Italian Ghetto*, 129–62.

Horowitz, Isaiah. *The Generations of Adam.* Translated by Miles Krassen. New York: Paulist Press, 1996.

Horwitz, Rivka. "On Kabbala and Myth in 19th Century Germany: Isaac Bernays." *PAAJR* 59 (1993): 137–83.

———. "Kabbalah in the Writings of Mendelssohn and the Berlin Circle of Maskilim." *LBIYB* 45 (2000): 3–24.

Hubka, Thomas C. "The *Zohar* and the Polish Synagogue: The Practical Influence of a Sacred Text." *JJTP* 9 (2000): 173–250.

Hundert, Gershon David. *Jews in Poland-Lithuania in the Eighteenth Century: A Genealogy of Modernity.* Berkeley: University of California Press, 2004.

Hunter, Michael, ed. *Archives of the Scientific Revolution: The Formation and Exchange of Ideas in Seventeenth-Century Europe.* Rochester: Boydell Press, 1998.

Huss, Boaz. "Admiration and Disgust: the Ambivalent Re-Canonization of the *Zohar* in the Modern Period." In *Study and Knowledge in Jewish Thought*. Edited by Howard Kreisel, 203–37. Beer Sheva: Ben-Gurion University of the Negev Press, 2006.

———. *Ke-zohar ha-rakia: perakim be-hitkablut ha-Zohar uve-havnayat erko ha-simli.* Jerusalem: Mossad Bialik and Ben-Zvi Institute, 2008.

———. "NiSAN—The Wife of the Infinite: The Mystical Hermeneutics of Rabbi Isaac of Acre." *Kabbalah* 5 (2000): 155–81.

———. "The Text and Context of the 1684 Sulzbach Edition of the *Zohar*." In Goodblatt and Kreisel, *Tradition, Heterodoxy, and Religious Culture*, 117–38.

———. "Zohar Translations" (Hebrew). *Teuda* 21–22 (2007): 33–107.

Idel, Moshe. "Abraham Abulafia's Work and Doctrine" (Hebrew). Ph.D. dissertation, Hebrew University, 1976.

———. *Absorbing Perfections: Kabbalah and Interpretation.* New Haven: Yale University Press, 2002.

———. *Ben: Sonship and Jewish Mysticism.* New York: Continuum, 2007.

———. "Differing Conceptions of Kabbalah in the Early 17th Century." In Twersky and Septimus, *Jewish Thought in the Seventeenth Century*, 137–200.

———. "Introduction to the Bison Book Edition." In *Johann Reuchlin: On the Art of the Kabbalah: De Arte Cabalistica*, v–xxix. Lincoln: University of Nebraska Press, 1993.

———. "Italy in Safed, Safed in Italy: Toward an Interactive History of Sixteenth-Century Kabbalah." In *Cultural Intermediaries: Jewish Intellectuals in Early Modern Italy*. Edited by David B. Ruderman and Giuseppe Veltri, 239–69. Philadelphia: University of Pennsylvania Press, 2004.

———. "Jewish Thinkers versus Christian Kabbalah." In *Christliche Kabbala*. Edited by Wilhelm Schmidt-Biggemann, 49–65. Ostfildern: Thorbecke, 2003.

———. "Judah Moscato: A Late Renaissance Jewish Preacher." In Ruderman, *Preachers of the Italian Ghetto*, 41–66.

———. "Kabbalah and Ancient Philosophy according to R. Isaac and R. Judah Abravanel" (Hebrew). In *Filosofiyat ha-Ahavah shel Yehudah Abravanel*. Edited by Menahem Dorman and Zeev Levy, 73–112. Tel Aviv: Ha-Kibutz ha-Meuhad, 1985.

———. *Kabbalah: New Perspectives.* New Haven: Yale University Press, 1988.

———. "Kabbalah in Elijah Benamozegh's Thought." In Elijah Benamozegh, *Israel and Humanity*, trans. Maxwell Luria, 378–402. New York: Paulist Press, 1995.

———. *Language, Torah, and Hermeneutics in Abraham Abulafia.* Albany: SUNY Press, 1989.

———. "The Magical and Neoplatonic Interpretations of the Kabbalah in the Renaissance." In Cooperman, *Jewish Thought in the Sixteenth Century*, 186–242.

———. "Maimonides and Kabbalah." In *Studies in Maimonides*. Edited by Isadore Twersky, 31–81. Cambridge: Harvard University Press, 1990.

———. "Maimonides' *Guide of the Perplexed* and the Kabbalah." *Jewish History* 18 (2004): 197–226.

———. *Messianic Mystics.* New Haven: Yale University Press, 1998.

———. "Nahmanides: *Kabbalah, Halakhah*, and Spiritual Leadership." In *Jewish Mystical Leaders and Leadership in the 13th Century*. Edited by Moshe Idel and Mortimer Ostow, 15–96. Northvale, NJ: Jason Aronson, 1998.

Idel, Moshe. "On Adolf Jellinek and Kabbalah" (Hebrew). *Peamim* 100 (2004): 15–22.
———. "On Mobility, Individuals and Groups: Prolegomenon for a Sociological Approach to Sixteenth-Century Kabbalah." *Kabbalah* 3 (1998): 145–73.
———. "On the History of the Prohibition to Study Kabbalah before Age 40" (Hebrew). *AJS Review* 5 (1980): 1–20.
———. "'One from a Town, Two from a Clan': The Diffusion of Lurianic Kabbala and Sabbateanism: A Re-Examination." *Jewish History* 7 (1993): 79–104.
———. "PaRDeS: Some Reflections on Kabbalistic Hermeneutics." In *Death, Ecstasy, and Other Worldly Journeys*. Edited by John J. Collins and Michael Fishbane, 249–68. Albany: SUNY Press, 1995.
———. "Perceptions of Kabbalah in the Second Half of the 18th Century." *JJTP* 1 (1991): 55–114.
———. "Prisca Theologia in Marsilio Ficino and in Some Jewish Treatments." In *Marsilio Ficino: His Theology, His Philosophy, His Legacy*. Edited by Michael J. B. Allen and Valery Rees, 137–58. Leiden: Brill, 2002.
———. *Rabi Menahem Recanati ha-Mekubal*. Jerusalem: Schocken 1998.
———. "Rabbi Solomon ibn Adret and Abraham Abulafia: History of a Submerged Controversy about Kabbalah" (Hebrew). In *Atarah le-Hayim: Mehkarim ba-sifrut ha-Talmudit veha-rabanit li-khevod Profesor Hayim Zalman Dimitrovksi*. Edited by Daniel Boyarin, Shamma Friedman, Marc Hirshman, Menahem Schmelzer, and Israel Ta-Shma, 235–51. Jerusalem: Magnes Press, 2000.
———. "Transmission in Thirteenth-Century Kabbalah." In Elman and Gershoni, *Transmitting Jewish Traditions*, 138–65.
———. "We Have No Kabbalistic Tradition on This." In Twersky, *Rabbi Moses Nahmanides (Ramban)*, 51–73.
Infelise, Mario. "Le marché des information à Venise au 17e siècle." In *Gazettes et information politique sous l'Ancien Regime*. Edited by Henri Duranton and Pierre Rétat, 117–28. Saint Etienne: Université de Saint-Etienne, 1999.
Ioly Zorattini, Pier Cesare. "Derekh Teshuvah: La via del ritorno." In *L'identità dissumlata: giudaizzanti iberici nell'Europa cristiana dell'età moderna*. Edited by Pier Cesare Ioly Zorattini, 195–248. Florence: L. S. Olschki, 2000.
———, ed. *Processi del S. Uffizio di Venezia contro ebrei e giudaizzanti (1642–1681)*. Vol. 11. Florence: L. S. Olschki, 1993.
Israel, Jonathan I. *European Jewry in the Age of Mercantilism, 1550–1750*. London: Littman Library, 1998.
Jacobs, Louis. "Attitudes of the Kabbalists and Hasidim towards Maimonides." *The Solomon Goldman Lectures* 5 (1990): 45–55.
Jaffee Martin S. *Torah in the Mouth: Writing and Oral Tradition in Palestinian Judaism, 200 BCE–400 CE*. New York: Oxford University Press, 2001.
Jardine, Nicholas. *The Birth of History and Philosophy of Science: Kepler's "A Defence of Tycho against Ursus."* Cambridge: Cambridge University Press, 1984.
Johns, Adrian. *The Nature of the Book: Print and Knowledge in the Making*. Chicago: University of Chicago Press, 1998.
Jospe, Raphael. "Early Philosophical Commentaries on the *Sefer Yezirah*: Some Comments." *REJ* 149 (1990): 369–415.

Julius, Raphael. "Anton von Schmid: Royal Printer and Nobleman." *Jewish Book Annual* 51 (1993–1994): 195–202.
Katchen, Aaron L. *Christian Hebraists and Dutch Rabbis: Seventeenth-Century Apologetics and the Study of Maimonides' 'Mishneh Torah.'* Cambridge: Harvard University Press, 1984.
Katz, Jacob. *Halakha ve-Kabalah: Mehkarim be-toldot dat Yisrael al medoreha ve-zikatah ha-hevratit* . Jerusalem: Magnes Press, 1984.
———. "Halakhic Statements in the Zohar." In *Divine Law in Human Hands: Case Studies in Halakhic Flexibility*, 9–30. Jerusalem: Magnes Press, 1998.
———. "Post-Zoharic Relations between Halakhah and Kabbalah." In Cooperman, *Jewish Thought in the Sixteenth Century*, 283–307.
———, ed. *Toward Modernity: The European Jewish Model*. New Brunswick, NJ: Transaction Books, 1987.
———. "Towards a Biography of the Hatam Sofer." In *Divine Law in Human Hands*, 403–43.
Kaufmann, David. "Elia Menachem Chalfan on Jews Teaching Hebrew to Non-Jews." *JQR* 9 (1897): 500–508
———. "Jair Chaim Bacharach: A Biographical Sketch." *JQR* 3 (1891): 292–313, 485–536.
Kellner, Menachem. *Maimonides' Confrontation with Mysticism*. Oxford: Littman Library, 2006.
Kieszkowski, Bohdan. "Les rapports entre Elie del Medigo et Pic de la Mirandole." *Rinascimento* 4 (1964): 41–91.
Kilcher, Andreas. "Kabbalistische Buchmetaphysic: Knorrs Bibliothek und die Bedeutung des Sohar." In Schmidt-Biggemann, *Christliche Kabbala*, 211–23.
Kimelman, Reuven. *Lekhah dodi ve-kabalat shabat: Ha-mashma'ut ha-mistit*. Jerusalem: Magnes Press, 2003.
Koenigsberger, H. G. "Decadence or Shift? Changes in the Civilization of Italy and Europe in the Sixteenth and Seventeenth Centuries." In *Estates and Revolutions: Essays in Early Modern European History*, 278–97. Ithaca: Cornell University Press, 1971.
Kraye, Jill. "Daniel Heinsius and the Author of De Mundo." In *Classical Traditions in Renaissance Philosophy*. Aldershot: Ashgate, 2002.
Krutikov, Mikhail. *From Kabbalah to Class Struggle: Expressionism, Marxism, and Yiddish Literature in the Life and Work of Meir Wiener*. Stanford: Stanford University Press, 2011.
Kunitz, Moses. *Ben Yohai*. Vienna: 1815.
———. *Hamzaref*. Vol. 1. Vienna: Anton Strauss, 1820.
Kupfer, Ephraim. "New Documents on the Controversy over the Printing of the *Zohar*" (Hebrew). *Michael* 1 (1972): 302–18.
———. "R. Yosef Hamiz in Zante and His Work" (Hebrew). *Sefunot* 2 (1971–1978): 199–216.
———. "Strictures of a Scholar on the Writings of R. Joseph Ashkenazi" (Hebrew). *Kovez Al Yad* 21 (1985): 213–88.
Lachover, Fischel. "Revealed and Concealed in the Thought of Nachman Krochmal" (Hebrew). *Keneset* 6 (1941): 296–332.

Lachter, Hartley. "Spreading Secrets: Kabbalah and Esotericism in Isaac ibn Sahula's *Meshal ha-Kadmoni*." *JQR* 100 (2010): 111–38.
Lampronti, Isaac. *Pahad Yitshak*. Vol. 10. Lyck: Mekize Nirdamim, 1874.
Lasker, Daniel J. "Jewish Anti-Christian Polemics in the Early Modern Period: Change or Continuity?" In Goodblatt and Kreisel, *Tradition, Heterodoxy, and Religious Culture*, 469–88.
Lawee, Eric. "Abravanel in Italy: The Critique of the Kabbalist Elijah Hayyim Genazzano." *Jewish History* 23 (2009): 223–53.
Lazier, Benjamin. *God Interrupted: Heresy and the European Imagination between the World Wars*. Princeton: Princeton University Press, 2008.
Lehman, Marjorie. "The *Ein Ya'aqov*: A Collection of Aggadah in Transition." *Prooftexts* 19 (1999): 21–40.
Lehmann, James H. "Maimonides, Mendelssohn and the Me'asfim: Philosophy and the Biographical Imagination in the Early Haskalah." *LBIYB* 20 (1975): 87–108.
Lelli, Fabrizio. "Un collaboratore ebreo di Giovanni Pico della Mirandola: Yohanan Alemanno." *Homo Vivens* 5 (1994): 401–30.
———. "*Prisca Philosophia* and *Docta Religio*: The Boundaries of Rational Knowledge in Jewish and Christian Humanist Thought." *JQR* 91 (2000): 53–99.
Letteris, Meir. *Zikaron ba-sefer*. Vienna, 1869.
Levi, Isaac. *Medaber Tahpukhot*. Edited by Daniel Carpi. Tel Aviv: Tel Aviv University Press 1985.
Levi, Joseph. "A Jewish Academy for Sciences in the Early Seventeenth Century: The Effort of Joseph Solomon Delmedigo" (Hebrew). *Proceedings of the Eleventh World Congress of Jewish Studies*, Division B. Vol. 1 (1994): 169–76.
Levinsohn, Isaac Baer. *Sefer ha-Zikhronot*. Warsaw, 1890.
———. *Shorshe Levanon*. Vilna, 1841.
Libowitz, Nehemiah S. *Rabi Yehudah Aryeh Modena: Be-Komato ve-Tsivyono*. Second edition. New York: Harry Hirsh, 1901.
———. *Seridim mi-kitve ha-filosof ha-rofe veha-mekubal Yosef Hamits*. Jerusalem: Darom, 1937.
Liebes, Yehuda. "Hebrew and Aramaic as Languages of the Zohar." *Aramaic Studies* 4 (2006): 35–52.
———. "How the *Zohar* Was Written." (Hebrew) *JSJT* 8 (1989): 1–71.
———. "The Messiah of the *Zohar*: The Messianic Image of Simeon bar Yohai" (Hebrew). In *Ha-Ra'ayon ha-Meshihi be-Yisrael*. Edited by Shmuel Reem, 87–236. Jerusalem: Israel Academy of the Sciences, 1982.
———. "The Messianism of R. Jacob Emden and Its Relation to Sabbatianism." *Tarbiz* 49 (1980): 122–65.
———. "*Sefer Sheqel ha-Qodesh* of R. Moses de Leon" (Hebrew). *Kabbalah* 2 (1997): 271–85.
———. *Torat ha-Yetsirah shel Sefer Yetsirah*. Jerusalem and Tel Aviv: Schocken, 2000.
———. "The *Zohar* as a Halakhic Book." (Hebrew) *Tarbiz* 64 (1995): 581–605.
Lilienblum, Moses Leib. *Hat'ot Ne'urim*. Tel Aviv, 1966.
Love, Harold. *The Culture and Commerce of Texts: Scribal Publication in Seventeenth-Century England*. Amherst: University of Massachusetts Press, 1998.
Lowry, Martin. *The World of Aldus Manutius: Business and Scholarship in Renaissance Venice*. Ithaca: Cornell University Press, 1979.

Luria, David. *Kadmut Sefer ha-Zohar*. Königsberg, 1855.
———. *Kadmut Sefer ha-Zohar*. Warsaw, 1887. Photo offest edition, New York, 1951.
Luzzatto, Moses Hayim. *Hoker u-Mekubal*. Königsberg: E. J. Dalkowski, 1840.
———. *Milhemet Moshe*. Warsaw: Unterhendler, 1889.
———. *Le philosophe et le cabaliste*. Edited by Joëlle Hansel. Lagrasse: Verdier, 1991.
———. *Sefer Adir ba-Marom*. Warsaw: Y. Goldman, 1886.
———. *Yalkut Yediot ha-Emet*. 2 vols. Tel Aviv: Ahava, 1965.
Luzzatto, Samuel David. *Vikuah al Hokhmat ha-Kabalah*. Gorizia, 1852. Photo offset edition, Jerusalem, 1968.
Luzzatto, Simone. *Discorso circa il stato de gl'Hebrei et in particolar dimoranti nell'inclita città di Venetia*. Edited by Riccardo Bachi. Bologna: A. Forni, 1976.
———. *Ma'amar al Yehude Venetsyah*. Translated by Dan Lattes. Jerusalem: Mossad Bialik, 1950.
Luzzatto Voghera, Gadi, and Mauro Perani, eds. *Ramhal: Pensiero ebraico e Kabbalah tra Padova ed Eretz Israel*. Padua: Esedra, 2010.
Magid, Shaul. *From Metaphysics to Midrash: Myth, History, and the Interpretation of Scripture in Lurianic Kabbala*. Bloomington: Indiana University Press, 2008.
Mahler, Raphael. *Hasidism and the Jewish Enlightenment*. Philadelphia: JPS, 1985.
Maimonides, Moses. *The Guide of the Perplexed*. Translated by Shlomo Pines. Chicago: University of Chicago Press, 1963.
Malcolm, Noel, *De Dominis (1560–1624): Venetian, Anglican, Ecumenist and Relapsed Heretic*. London: Strickland and Scott, 1984.
Malkiel, David. "The Burden of the Past in the Eighteenth Century: Authority, Custom, and Innovation in the *Pahad Yitzhak*." *Jewish Law Annual* 16 (2006): 93–132.
———. "Christian Hebraism in a Contemporary Key: The Search for Hebrew Epitaph Poetry in Seventeenth-Century Italy." *JQR* 96 (2006): 123–146.
———, ed. *The Lion Shall Roar: Leon Modena and His World*. Jerusalem: Magnes and Ben-Zvi Institute, 2003.
———. "Leon Modena and His World: Past, Present, and Future." In *The Lion Shall Roar*, 7–15.
———. "New Light on the Career of Isaac Samuel Reggio." In Cooperman and Garvin, *The Jews of Italy*, 276–303.
———. "The Reggios of Gorizia: Modernization in Micro." In *The Mediterranean and the Jews: Society, Culture, and Economy in Early Modern Times*. Edited by Elliott Horowitz and Moises Orfali, 67–84. Ramat Gan: Bar-Ilan University Press, 2002.
———. *A Separate Republic: The Mechanics and Dynamics of Venetian Jewish Self-Government, 1607–1624*. Jerusalem: Magnes Press, 1991.
Manekin, Rachel. "Galicia." In *The YIVO Encyclopedia of the Jews of in Eastern Europe*. Edited by Gershon David Hundert, 1:560–67. New Haven: Yale University Press, 2008.
———. "Joseph Perl on *Hok le-Yisrael* and the Spread of Hasidism" (Hebrew). In *Yashan mipnei Hadash: Shai le-Imanuel Etkes*. Edited by David Assaf and Ada Rapoport-Albert, 2:345–54. Jerusalem: Zalman Shazar Center, 2009.
Margalit, David. "On Memory: Concerning *Lev ha-Aryeh* by Rabbi Judah Aryeh Modena" (Hebrew). *Korot* 5 (1972): 759–772.
Margoliouth, George. *Catalogue of the Hebrew and Samaritan Manuscripts in the British Museum*. 4 vols. London: British Museum, 1899–1935.

Martin, John. *Venice's Hidden Enemies: Italian Heretics in a Renaissance City.* Berkeley: University of California Press, 1993.
Martin, Julian. *Francis Bacon, the State, and the Reform of Natural Philosophy.* Cambridge: Cambridge University Press, 1992.
Marx, Moses. *Gershom Soncino's Wanderyears in Italy, 1498–1527 Exemplar judaicae vitae.* Cincinnati: Society of Jewish Bibliophiles, 1969.
McCagg, William O. *A History of Habsburg Jews, 1670–1918.* Bloomington: Indiana University Press, 1989.
McCuaig, William. *Carlo Sigonio: The Changing World of the Late Renaissance.* Princeton: Princeton University Press, 1989.
McKitterick, David. *Print, Manuscript, and the Search for Order, 1450–1830.* Cambridge: Cambridge University Press, 2003.
Mehlman, Israel. "Concerning the Book *Meor Enayim* by Azariah de' Rossi in Italy." In *Genuzot Sefarim,* 21–39. Jerusalem: JNUL Press, 1976.
Melamed, Abraham. "Conversion Myths: Maimonides and Aristotle" (Hebrew). *Daat* 64–66 (2009): 166–93.
Mendelssohn, Moses. *Jerusalem, or, On Religious Power and Judaism.* Translated by Allan Arkush. Hanover, NH: Brandeis University Press, 1983.
Meroz, Ronit. "Contrasting Opinions among the Founders of R. Israel Saruq's School." In *Expérience et écriture mystiques dans les religions du livre.* Edited by Paul B. Fenton and Roland Goetschel, 191–202. Leiden: Brill, 2000.
———. "Faithful Transmission Versus Innovation: Luria and His Disciples." In Schäfer and Dan, *Gershom Scholem's Major Trends in Jewish Mysticism 50 Years After,* 257–74. Tübingen: Mohr Siebeck, 1993.
———. "R. Israel Saruq, Student of the *Ari,* a Renewed Inquiry into the Issue" (Hebrew). *Daat* 28 (1992): 41–51.
———. "The Teachings of Redemption in Lurianic Kabbalah" (Hebrew). Ph.D. dissertation, Hebrew University, 1988.
———. "Zoharic Narratives and Their Adaptations." *Hispania Judaica Bulletin* 3 (2000): 3–63.
Meyer, Michael A. *The Origins of the Modern Jew: Jewish Identity and European Culture in Germany, 1749–1824.* Detroit: Wayne State University Press, 1967.
———. "Where Does the Modern Period of Jewish History Begin?" *Judaism* 24 (1975): 329–38.
Michael, Reuven. *Y. M. Yost: Avi ha-historyografya ha-Yehudit ha-modernit.* Jerusalem: Magnes Press, 1983.
Mieses, Judah Leib. *Kinat Ha-Emet.* Vienna: Anton von Schmid, 1828.
Mirandola, Giovanni Pico della. "Oration on the Dignity of Man." Translated by Elizabeth L. Forbes. In *The Renaissance Philosophy of Man.* Edited by Ernst Cassirer, Paul Oskar Kristeller, and John H. Randall Jr., 223–54. Chicago: University of Chicago Press, 1948.
Mithridates, Flavius. *Sermo de passione domini.* Edited by Chaim Wirszubski. Jerusalem: Israel Academy of Sciences and Humanities, 1963.
Modena, Leon. *Ari Nohem.* Edited by Julius Fürst. Leipzig: K. Tauchnitz, 1840.
———. *Ari Nohem.* Edited by Nehemiah S. Libowitz. Jerusalem: Darom, 1929.
———. "Ben David." In *Ta'am Zekenim.* Edited by Eliezer Ashkenazi, 61A–64B. Frankfurt: Kauffman, 1854.

———. *Hayyei Yehudah*. Edited by Daniel Carpi. Tel Aviv: Tel Aviv University Press, 1985.
———. *Igrot Rabbi Yehudah Aryeh Mi-Modena*. Edited by Yacov Boksenboim. Tel Aviv: Tel Aviv University Press, 1984.
———. *Jüdische Riten, Sitten, und Gebräuche*. Edited and translated by Rafael Arnold Wiesbaden: Marixverlag, 2007.
———. *Magen va-Herev*. Edited by Shlomo Simonsohn. Jerusalem: Mekize Nirdamim, 1960.
———. *She'elot u-Teshuvot Ziknei Yehudah*. Edited by Shlomo Simonsohn. Jerusalem: Mossad ha-Rav Kook, 1956.
———. *Shulhan Arukh le-Yehudah Aryeh mi-Modena*. Translated by Salomon Rubin. Vienna, Schlossberg, 1867.
Mopsik, Charles. *Les grands textes de la Cabale: les rites qui font Dieu*. Lagrasse: Verdier, 1993.
———. "Late-Judeo Aramaic: The Language of Theosophic Kabbalah." *Aramaic Studies* 4 (2006): 21–33.
———. "Moïse de Léon, le *Sheqel ha-Qodesh* et la rédaction du *Zohar*: Une réponse à Yehuda Liebes." *Kabbalah* 3 (1998): 177–218.
Moseley, Marcus. *Being for Myself Alone: Origins of Jewish Autobiography*. Stanford: Stanford University Press, 2006.
Muir, Edward. *The Culture Wars of the Late Renaissance: Skeptics, Libertines, and Opera*. Cambridge: Harvard University Press, 2007.
Mulsow, Martin. "Idolatry and Science: Against Nature Worship from Boyle to Rüdiger, 1680–1720." *JHI* 67 (2006): 697–711.
Myers, David N. "Philosophy and Kabbalah in Wissenschaft des Judentums: Rethinking the Narrative of Neglect." *Studia Judaica* 16 (2008): 56–71.
Nadler, Allan. *The Faith of the Mithnagdim: Rabbinic Responses to Hasidic Rapture*. Baltimore: Johns Hopkins University Press, 1997.
———. "The 'Rambam Revival' in Early Modern Jewish Thought: Maskilim, Mitnagdim, and Hasidim on Maimonides' *Guide of the Perplexed*." In Harris, *Maimonides after 800 Years*, 231–56.
Nahmanides. *Commentary on the Torah*. Translated by Charles B. Chavel. New York: Shilo, 1971.
Najara, Israel. *Mikveh Yisrael*. Edited by Shaul Regev. Ramat Gan: Bar-Ilan University Press, 2004.
Necker, Gerold. "Circle, Point and Line: A Lurianic Myth in the *Puerta del Cielo*." In Elior and Schäfer, *Creation and Re-Creation in Jewish Thought*, 193–207.
Neubauer, Adolf. "The Bahir and the Zohar." *JQR* 4 (1892): 357–68.
———. "Quelques notes sur la vie de Juda Léon de Modène." *REJ* 22 (1891): 82–86.
Nosek, Bedřich. "Auswahlkatalog Hebräischer Drucke Prager Provenienz: Druckerei M. I. Landau, 1824–1853." *Judaica Bohemia* 15 (1979): 86–121.
Ogren, Brian. *Renaissance and Rebirth: Reincarnation in Early Modern Italian Kabbalah*. Leiden: Brill, 2009.
Overfield, James H. "The Reuchlin Affair." In *Humanisim and Scholasticism in Late Medieval Germany*, 247–97. Princeton: Princeton University Press, 1984.
Pachter, Mordechai. "*Hazut Kasha* of Rabbi Moses Alsheikh" (Hebrew). *Shalem* 1 (1974): 157–93.

Paladini, Alba. *Il De Arcanis di Pietro Galatino: Traditio giudaica e nuove istanze filologiche*. Lecce: Congedo, 2004.
Pedaya, Haviva. *Ha-Ramban: Hit'alut, zeman mahzori ve-tekst kadosh*. Tel Aviv: Am Oved, 2003.
———. *Ha-Shem veha-mikdash be-mishnat R. Yitshak sagi nehor: Iyun mashveh be-kitve rishone ha-mekubalim*. Jerusalem: Magnes Press, 2001.
Peiresc, Nicolas-Claude Fabri de. *Lettres à Claude Saumaise et à son entourage (1620–1637)*. Edited by Agnès Bresson. Florence: L. S. Olschki, 1992.
Peleg, Erez. "Between Philosophy and Kabbalah: The Criticism of Jewish Philosophy in the Thought of Rabbi Shem Tov ben Shem Tov" (Hebrew). Ph.D. dissertation, Haifa University, 2002.
Pelli, Moshe. "The Beginnings of the Epistolary Genre in Modern Hebrew Literature: Isaac Euchel and His Letters" (Hebrew). *Bikoret u-Farshanut* 16 (1981): 85–101.
———. *Bikure ha-Itim: Bikure ha-Haskalah*. Jerusalem: Magnes Press, 2005.
———. *Kerem Hemed: Hokhmat Yisrael hi Yavneh ha-Hadasha*. Jerusalem: Magnes Press, 2009.
Penkower, Jordan S. "A Renewed Inquiry into the *Sefer Masoret ha-Masoret* of Elijah Bahur: The Lateness of Vocalization and Criticism of the *Zohar*" (Hebrew). *Italia* 8 (1989): 7–73.
———. "S. D. Luzzatto, Vowels and Accents, and the Date of the Zohar." In Bonfil, Gottlieb, and Kasher, *Samuel David Luzzatto*, 79–130.
Perani, Mauro. "Mistica e Filosofia: la mediazone di Nahmanide nella polemica sugli scritti di Maimonide." In *Nahmanide: esegetica e cabbalista*. Edited by Moshe Idel and Mauro Perani, 107–127. Florence: Giuntina, 1998.
Pettegree, Andrew. *The Book in the Renaissance*. New Haven: Yale University Press, 2010.
Petuchowski, Jakob, ed. *New Perspectives on Abraham Geiger*. New York: Ktav, 1975.
Pico della Mirandola, Giovanni, and Gian Francesco Pico. *Opera Omnia (1557–73)*. Hildesheim: Georg Olms, 1969.
Piekarz, Mendel. "'Why Did the Spanish Exile Perish,' as a Forewarning of the Dangers of the Enlightenment" (Hebrew). *Daat* 28 (1992): 87–115.
Pine, Martin L. *Pietro Pomponazzi: Radical Philosopher of the Renaissance*. Padua: Antenore, 1986.
Podet, Allen Howard. *A Translation of the Magen wa-Hereb by Leon Modena, 1571–1648*. Lewiston, NY: Mellen Press, 2001.
Pon, Lisa, and Craig Kallendorf, eds. *The Books of Venice*. Venice: La Musa Talìa, 2009.
Popkin, Richard H. *The History of Scepticism: From Savonarola to Bayle*. New York: Oxford University Press, 2003.
———. "Some Further Comments on Newton and Maimonides." In *Essays on the Context, Nature, and Influence of Isaac Newton's Theology*. Edited by James E. Force and Richard Popkin, 1–7. Dordrecht: Kluwer Academic Publishers, 1990.
Price, David H. *Johannes Reuchlin and the Campaign to Destroy Jewish Books*. New York: Oxford University Press, 2011.
Prijs, Joseph. *Die Basler Hebräischen Drucke (1492-1866)*. Edited by Bernhard Prijs. Olten: Urs-Graf Verlag, 1964.

Proietti, Omero. "'La Voce di De Acosta [=431]' sul vero autore del Qol Sakhal." *RMI* (70) 2004: 33–54.
Pullan, Brian. *The Jews of Europe and the Inquisition of Venice, 1550–1670.* Totowa, NJ: Barnes and Noble Books, 1983.
Raines, Dorit. "Judaism in the Eyes of the Venetian Patriciate in the Time of Leon Modena" (Hebrew). In Malkiel, *The Lion Shall Roar*, 19–54.
———. "Office Seeking, *Broglio*, and the Pocket Political Guidebooks in *cinquecento* and *seicento* Venice." *SV* 21 (1991): 137–94.
Rapoport, Solomon Judah. *Nahalat Yehudah*. Lvov, 1873.
Rapoport-Albert, Ada. "A Maskilic Tract in Defense of Hasidism in an Anonymous Manuscript from the Circle of E. Z. Zweifel" (Hebrew). In *Mi-Vilnah le-Yerushalayim: Mehkarim be-toldotehem uve-tarbutam shel Yehude Mizrah Eropah mugashim li-Profesor Shmuel Werses*. Edited by David Assaf, Israel Bartal, Shmuel Feiner, Yehuda Friedlander, Avner Holtzman, and Chava Turniansky, 71–122. Jerusalem: Magnes Press, 2002.
Rapoport-Albert, Ada, and Theodore Kwasman. "Late Aramaic: The Literary and Linguistic Context of the Zohar." *Aramaic Studies* 4 (2006): 5–19.
Ravid, Benjamin. "*Contra Judaeos* in Seventeenth-Century Italy: Two Responses to the *Discorso* of Simone Luzzatto by Melchiore Palontrotti and Giulio Morosini." *AJS Review* 7 (1982): 301–51.
———. *Economics and Toleration in Seventeenth Century Venice: The Background and Context of the Discorso of Simone Luzzatto*. Jerusalem: American Academy for Jewish Research, 1978.
———. "The Prohibition against Jewish Printing and Publishing in Venice and the Difficulties of Leone Modena." In *Studies in Medieval Jewish History and Literature*. Edited by Isadore Twersky, 135–53. Cambridge: Harvard University Press, 1979.
———. *Studies on the Jews of Venice, 1382–1797*. Aldershot: Ashgate, 2003.
Ravitzky, Aviezer. *History and Faith: Studies in Jewish Philosophy*. Amsterdam: J. C. Gieben, 1996.
———. "Samuel Ibn Tibbon and the Esoteric Character of the *Guide of the Perplexed*." *AJS Review* 6 (1981): 87–123.
Raz-Krakotzkin, Amnon. *The Censor, The Editor, and The Text: The Catholic Church and the Shaping of the Jewish Canon in the Sixteenth Century*. Philadelphia: University of Pennsylvania Press, 2007.
———. "From Safed to Venice: The *Shulhan Arukh* and the Censor." In Goodblatt and Kreisel, *Tradition, Heterodoxy, and Religious Culture*, 91–115.
Reggio, Isaac Samuel. *Behinat ha-Kabalah: Kolel Sefer Kol Sakhal ve-Sefer Sha'agat Aryeh*. Gorizia: Joh. Bapt. Seitz, 1852.
———. *Ha-Torah veha-filosofiya*. Vienna: Anton von Schmid, 1827.
———. *Igrot Yashar*. Vienna: Anton von Schmid, 1834.
———. *Mazkeret Yashar*. Vienna: Franz von Schmid, 1849.
———. *Torat Elohim*. Vienna: Anton Strauss, 1821.
———. *Yalkut Yashar*. Gorizia: Joh. Bapt. Seitz, 1854.
Reiner, Elchanan. "The Ashkenazi Elite at the Beginning of the Modern Era: Manuscript versus Printed Book." *Polin* 10 (1997): 85–98.
———. "The Attitude of Ashkenazi Society to the New Science in the Sixteenth Century." *Science in Context* 10 (1997): 589–603.

Reiner, Elchanan. "A Biography of an Agent of Culture: Eleazar Altschul of Prague and His Literary Activity." In *Schöpferische Momente des europäischen Judentums in der frühen Neuzeit.* Edited by Michael Graetz, 229–47. Heidelberg: C. Winter, 2000.

Reuchlin, Johann. *On the Art of the Kabbalah: De Arte Cabalistica.* Translated by Martin and Sarah Goodman. Bison book edition. Lincoln: University of Nebraska Press, 1993.

———. *Recommendation Whether to Confiscate, Destroy, and Burn All Jewish Books.* Translated by Peter Wortsman. Mahwah, NJ: Paulist Press, 2000.

Richardson, Brian. *Manuscript Culture in Renaissance Italy.* Cambridge: Cambridge University Press, 2009.

Richler, Benjamin. "Unknown Writings of R. Judah Aryeh Modena" (Hebrew). *Asufot* 7 (1993): 157–72.

Rivkin, Ellis. "Leon da Modena: Part 1." Ph.D. dissertation. Johns Hopkins University, 1946.

———. *Leon da Modena and the "Kol Sakhal."* Cincinnati: HUC Press, 1952.

———. "The Sermons of Leon da Modena." *HUCA* 23 (1950–1951): 295–317.

Rivkind, Isaac. "A Responsum of Leo da Modena on Uncovering of the Head" (Hebrew). In *Sefer ha-Yovel li-khevod Levi Ginsburg,* 401–23. Philadelphia: JPS, 1946.

Robinson, Ira. *Moses Cordovero's Introduction to Kabbalah: An Annotated Translation of His Or Ne'erav.* Hoboken: Ktav, 1994.

Robinson, James T. *Samuel Ibn Tibbon's Commentary on Ecclesiastes: The Book of the Soul of Man.* Tübingen: Mohr Siebeck, 2007.

Rosenberg, Shalom. "Emunat Hakhamim." In Twersky and Septimus, *Jewish Thought in the Seventeenth Century,* 285–341.

Rosenblatt, Jason P. *Renaissance England's Chief Rabbi: John Selden.* Oxford: Oxford University Press, 2006.

Rosenstock, Bruce. "Abraham Miguel Cardoso's Messianism: A Reappraisal." *AJS Review* 23 (1998): 63–104.

Rosenthal, Judah. "Elijah Hayim Genazzano's Disputation with a Franciscan Monk" (Hebrew). In *Mehkarim u-mekorot,* 1:431–56. Jerusalem: Rubin Mass, 1967.

———. "From the Hebrew Writings of the Apostate Abner of Burgos" (Hebrew). In *Mehkarim u-mekorot,* 1:324–67.

Rosenthal, Solomon. *Bet Owen.* Ofen, 1839.

Rosenzweig, Israel. *Hogeh yehudi mi-kez ha-Renesans: Yehudah Aryeh Modena ve-Sifro Midbar Yehudah.* Tel Aviv: Sifriyat Po'alim, 1972.

Rosman, Moshe. *How Jewish Is Jewish History?* Oxford: Littman Library, 2007.

Roth, Cecil. "Léon de Modène, ses *Riti Ebraici* et le Saint-Office à Venise." *REJ* 87 (1929): 83–88.

———. "Leone da Modena and his English Correspondents." *Transactions of the Jewish Historical Society of England* 17 (1951–1952): 39–43.

———. "Leone da Modena and the Christian Hebraists of His Age." In *Jewish Studies in Memory of Israel Abrahams,* 384–401. New York: Jewish Institute of Religion, 1927.

———. "Quatre lettres d'Elie de Montalte: contribution à l'histoire des Marranes." *REJ* 87 (1929): 137–65.

Rowland, Ingrid D. *The Scarith of Scornello: A Tale of Renaissance Forgery.* Chicago: University of Chicago Press, 2004.

Rubin, Zviah. "The Zoharic Works of R. Moses Hayim Luzatto and His Messianic Attitude" (Hebrew). *JSJT* 8 (1989): 387–412.
Ruderman, David B. *Early Modern Jewry: A New Cultural History*. Princeton: Princeton University Press, 2010.
———. *Jewish Thought and Scientific Discovery in Early Modern Europe*. New Haven: Yale University Press, 1995.
———. *Kabbalah, Magic, and Science: The Cultural Universe of a Sixteenth-Century Jewish Physician*. Cambridge: Harvard University Press, 1988.
———, ed. *Preachers of the Italian Ghetto*. Berkeley: University of California Press, 1992.
———. *The World of a Renaissance Jew: The Life and Thought of Abraham Ben Mordecai Farissol*. Cincinnati: HUC Press, 1981.
Rummel, Erika. *The Case against Johann Reuchlin: Religious and Social Controversy in Sixteenth-Century Germany*. Toronto: University of Toronto Press, 2002.
Saadia Gaon. *The Book of Beliefs and Opinions*. Translated by Samuel Rosenblatt. New Haven: Yale University Press, 1948.
Sack, Bracha. *Be-Sha'are ha-Kabalah shel Rabi Moshe Cordovero*. Beer Sheva: Ben-Gurion University of the Negev Press, 1995.
——— "The Influence of Cordovero on Seventeenth-Century Jewish Thought." In Twersky and Septimus, *Jewish Thought in the Seventeenth Century*, 365–79.
———, ed. *Ma'ayan En Ya'akov le-Rabi Moshe Cordovero*. Beer Sheva: Ben-Gurion University of the Negev Press, 2009.
Safran, Bezalel. "Leone da Modena's Historical Thinking." In Twersky and Septimus, *Jewish Thought in the Seventeenth Century*, 381–98.
Sahula, Isaac ben Solomon. *Meshal Haqadmoni: Fables from the Distant Past*. 2 vols. Translated by Raphael Loewe. Oxford: Littman Library, 2004.
Saperstein, Marc. *Exile in Amsterdam: Saul Levi Morteira's Sermons to a Congregation of "New Jews."* Cincinnati: HUC Press, 2005.
———. *Jewish Preaching 1200–1800: An Anthology*. New Haven: Yale University Press, 1989.
Sasportas, Jacob. *Zizat Novel Zvi*. Edited by Isaiah Tishby. Jerusalem: Mossad Bialik, 1954.
Saunders, J. W. "The Stigma of Print: A Note on the Social Bases of Tudor Poetry." *Essays in Criticism* 1 (1951): 139–64.
Schacter, Jacob J. "Rabbi Jacob Emden: Life and Major Works." Ph.D. dissertation, Harvard University. 1988.
Schäfer, Peter. "Gershom Scholem und die 'Wissenchaft des Judentums.'" In *Gershom Scholem: Zwischen den Disziplinen*. Edited by Peter Schäfer and Gary Smith, 122–56. Frankfurt: Suhrkamp Verlag, 1995.
———. "'Adversus cabbalam,' oder: Heinrich Graetz und die jüdische Mystik." In Schäfer and Wandrey, *Reuchlin und seine Erbern*, 189–210.
Schechter, Solomon. "Safed in the Sixteenth Century: A City of Legists and Mystics." In *Studies in Judaism: Second Series*, 202–85. Philadelphia: JPS, 1908.
Schmidt-Biggemann, Wilhelm, ed. *Christliche Kabbala*. Ostfildern: Thorbecke, 2003.
Schmitt, Charles B. "Perrennial Philosophy: From Agostino Steuco to Leibniz." *JHI* 27 (1966): 505–32.

Scholem, Gershom. "The Actual Author of the Commentary to *Sefer Yetzirah* Attributed to Rabad and His Books" (Hebrew). In *Mehkere Kabalah*. Edited by Yosef Ben-Shlomo, Tel Aviv: Am Oved, 1998, 112–36.

———. "The Actual Commentary of Nahmanides to *Sefer Yetzirah* and Other Kabbalah Attributed to Him" (Hebrew). In Ben-Shlomo, *Mehkere Kabalah*, 67–111.

———. *Avraham Kohen Herera: Ba'al "Sha'ar Ha-Shamayim."* Jerusalem: Mossad Bialik, 1978.

———. "The Beginnings of the Christian Kabbalah." In Dan, *The Christian Kabbalah*, 17–51.

———. *Das Buch Bahir*. Leipzig: W. Drugulin, 1923.

———. "*Devekut*, or Communion with God." In *The Messianic Idea in Judaism and Other Essays on Jewish Spirituality*, 203–27. New York: Schocken Books, 1995.

———. "Did Moses de Leon Compose the Book of the *Zohar*?" (Hebrew). *Madaei ha-Yahadut* 2 (1925/1926): 16–29.

———. "Die Erforschung der Kabbala von Reuchlin bis zur Gegenwart." In *Judaica III: Studien zur jüdischen Mystik*, 247–63. Frankfurt: Suhrkamp Verlag, 1973.

———. "From a Scholar to a Kabbalist: Kabbalistic Stories about Maimonides" (Hebrew). In Ben-Shlomo, *Mehkere Kabalah*, 189–200.

———. "*Gilgul*: The Transmigration of Souls." In *On the Mystical Shape of the Godhead: Basic Concepts in the Kabbalah*, 197–250. New York: Schocken Books, 1991.

———. "Israel Sarug, a Student of the *Ari*?" (Hebrew). *Zion* 5 (1940): 214–43.

———. *Major Trends in Jewish Mysticism*. Jerusalem: Schocken, 1941.

———. "A New Document about the History of the Beginnings of Kabbalah" (Hebrew). In Ben-Shlomo, *Mehkere Kabalah*, 7–38.

———. "New Information on Joseph Ashkenazi, the Tanna of Safed" (Hebrew). *Tarbiz* 28 (1959): 89–59, 201–235.

———. "On the Problem of the Book *Ma'arekhet ha-Elohut* and Its Commentators" (Hebrew). In Ben-Shlomo, *Mehkere Kabalah*, 171–88.

———. *Origins of the Kabbalah*. Philadelphia and Princeton: JPS and Princeton University Press, 1987.

———. "Redemption through Sin" (Hebrew). *Keneset* 2 (1937): 347–92.

———. "Redemption through Sin." In *The Messianic Idea in Judaism*, 78–141.

———. "Reflections on Modern Jewish Studies (1944)." In *On the Possibility of Jewish Mysticism in Our Time and Other Essays*. Edited by Avraham Shapira, 51–71. Philadelphia: JPS, 1997.

———. "Revelation and Tradition as Religious Categories in Judaism." In *The Messianic Idea in Judaism*, 282–303.

———. *Sabbatai Sevi: The Mystical Messiah, 1626–1676*. Princeton: Princeton University Press, 1973.

———. "*Shiur Komah*: The Mystical Shape of the Godhead." In *On the Mystical Shape of the Godhead*, 15–55.

———. "Tradition and New Creation in the Ritual of the Kabbalists." In *On the Kabbalah and its Symbolism*, 118–57. New York: Schocken Books, 1996.

Schorsch, Ismar. *From Text to Context : The Turn to History in Modern Judaism*. Hanover, NH: Brandeis University Press, 1994.

———. "The Emergence of Historical Consciousness in Modern Judaism." In *From Text to Context*, 177–204.
———. "From Wolfenbüttel to *Wissenschaft*: The Divergent Paths of Isaak Markus Jost and Leopold Zunz." In *From Text to Context*, 233–54.
———. "The Production of a Classic: Zunz as Krochmal's Editor." *LBIYB* 31 (1986): 281–315.
Schrijver, Emile G. L. "Saul of Berlin's *Besamim Rosh*: The Maskilic Appreciation of Medieval Knowledge." In *Sepharad in Ashkenaz: Medieval Knowledge and Eighteenth-Century Enlightened Jewish Discourse*. Edited by Resianne Fontaine, Andrea Schatz, and Irene Zwiep, 249–59. Amsterdam: Koninklijke Nederlandse Akademie van Wetenschappen, 2007.
Secord, James A. *Victorian Sensation: The Extraordinary Publication, Reception, and Secret Authorship of "Vestiges of the Natural History of Creation."* Chicago: University of Chicago Press, 2000.
Secret, François. *Les Kabbalistes Chrétiens de la Renaissance*. Paris: Dunod, 1964.
———. *Le Zôhar chez les Kabbalistes Chrétiens de la Renaissance*. Paris: Mouton, 1964.
———. "Notes pour une histoire du *Pugio Fidei* a la Renaissance." *Sefarad* 20 (1960) 401–7.
Septimus, Bernard. *Hispano-Jewish Culture in Transition: The Career and Controversies of Ramah*. Cambridge: Harvard University Press, 1982.
———. "'Open Rebuke and Concealed Love': Nahmanides and the Andalusian Tradition." In Twersky, *Rabbi Moses Nahmanides (Ramban)*, 11–34.
Sermoneta, Giuseppe. "Aspetti del Pensiero Moderno nell'Ebraismo Italiano tra Rinascimento e Età Barocca." In *Italia Judaica: Gli Ebrei in Italia tra Rinascimento ed Età Barocca*, 17–35. Rome, 1986.
Shapin, Steven. "The Invisible Technician." *American Scientist* 77 (1989): 554–63.
Shapiro, Marc B. "Aspects of Rabbi Moses Sofer's Intellectual Profile." In Harris, *Be'erot Yitzhak*, 285–310.
Shatz, Rivka. "Kabbalah: Tradition or Innovation" (Hebrew). In Oron and Goldreich, *Masuot*, 447–58.
Shatzmiller, Joseph. "Toward a Portrait of the First Controversy over the Writings of Maimonides" (Hebrew). *Zion* 34 (1969): 126–44.
Shear, Adam. *The Kuzari and the Shaping of Jewish Identity, 1167–1900*. Cambridge: Cambridge University Press, 2008.
Sheehan, Jonathan. "Sacred and Profane: Idolatry, Antiquarianism and the Polemics of Distinction in the Seventeenth Century." *Past and Present* 192 (2006): 35–66.
———. "Thinking about Idols in Early Modern Europe." *JHI* 67 (2006): 561–69.
Shmidman, Michael A. "On Maimonides' 'Conversion' to Kabbalah." In *Studies in Medieval Jewish History and Literature II*. Edited by Isadore Twersky, 375–86. Cambridge: Harvard University Press, 1984.
Shohat, Azriel. "Clarifications on the Episode of the First Controversy over the Books of Maimonides" (Hebrew). *Zion* 36 (1971): 27–60.
Shulman, David. "Is There an Indian Connection to *Sefer yesirah*?" *Aleph* 2 (2002): 191–99.
Siegmund, Stefanie B. *The Medici State and the Ghetto of Florence: The Construction of an Early Modern Jewish Community*. Stanford: Stanford University Press, 2006.

Silber, Michael. "The Historical Experience of German Jewry and Its Impact on Haskalah and Reform in Hungary." In Katz, *Toward Modernity: The European Jewish Model*, 107–57.

———. "Rosenthal Family." In Hundert, *The YIVO Encyclopedia of Jews in Eastern Europe*, 2:1593–94.

———. "Sofer, Mosheh." In Hundert, *The YIVO Encyclopedia of Jews in Eastern Europe*, 2:1775–78.

Silberman, Lou H. "The Magen V'hereb of R. Judah Aryeh of Modena (Leon Da Modena) Codex De Rossi 1141 with an Introductory Essay." Doctorate of Hebrew Letters, HUC, 1943.

———. "Scholem to Eisler on the Publication of *Das Buch Bahir*." *Studies in Bibliography and Booklore* 16 (1986): 5–12.

Silver, Daniel J. *Maimonidean Criticism and the Maimonidean Controversy, 1180–1240*. Leiden: Brill, 1965.

Simonsen, D. "Giulio Morosinis Mitteilungen über seinen Lehrer Leon da Modena und seine jüdischen Zeitgenossen." In *Festschrift Zum Siebzigsten Geburstage A. Berliner's*. Edited by Aron Freimann and Meir Hildesheimer, 337–44. Frankfurt: J. Kauffmann, 1903.

Simonsohn, Shlomo. "A Contract for the Printing of Hebrew Books in Cremona" (Hebrew). In *Scritti in Memoria di Umberto Nahon*. Edited by Robert Bonfil, Daniel Carpi, Maria Modena Mayer, Giorgio Romano, and Giuseppe B. Sermoneta, 143–50. Jerusalem: Sally Mayer Foundation 1978.

———. "Halakhah and Society in the Writings of Leone da Modena." In Twersky and Septimus, *Jewish Thought in the Seventeenth Century*, 435–45.

———. *History of the Jews in the Duchy of Mantua*. Jerusalem: Kiryath Sepher, 1977.

Smith, Gary. "Die Zauberjuden": Walter Benjamin, Gershom Scholem, and Other German Jewish Esoterics between the World Wars." *JJTP* 4 (1995): 227–43.

Snyder, Jon R. *Dissimulation and the Culture of Secrecy in Early Modern Europe*. Berkeley: University of California Press, 2009.

Socher, Abe. "The History of Nonsense." *AJS Perspectives* (Fall 2006): 32–33.

Sonne, Isaiah. "Church Use of the Kabbalah in Seventeenth-Century Missionary Work" (Hebrew). *Bitzaron* 36 (1957): 7–12, 57–66.

———. "Leon Modena and the Da Costa Circle in Amsterdam." *HUCA* 21 (1948): 1–28.

Sorotzkin, David. "The Timeless Community in Age of Change: The Emergence of Conceptions of Time and the Collective as the Basis for the Development of Jewish Orthodoxy in Early Modern and Late Modern Europe" (Hebrew). Ph.D. dissertation, Hebrew University, 2007.

Stanislawski, Michael. *A Murder in Lemberg: Politics, Religion, and Violence in Modern Jewish History*. Princeton: Princeton University Press, 2007.

———. *Tsar Nicholas I and the Jews: The Transformation of Jewish Society in Russia, 1825–1855*. Philadelphia: JPS, 1983.

Steinschneider, Moritz. *Catalogus Librorum Hebraeorum in Bibliotheca Bodleiana*. Facsimile edition. Hildesheim: Georg Olms, 1964.

Stern, Eliyahu. "Elijah of Vilna and the Making of Modern Rabbinic Judaism." Ph.D. dissertation, UC Berkeley, 2008.

Stern, Gregg. "What Divided the Moderate Maimonidean Scholars of Southern France in 1305?" In Harris, *Be'erot Yitzhak*, 347–76.
Stroumsa, Guy G. "John Spencer and the Roots of Idolatry." *History of Religions* 41 (2001): 1–23.
———. *A New Science: The Discovery of Religion in the Age of Reason*. Cambridge: Harvard University Press, 2010.
Stroumsa, Guy G., and Jacques Le Brun, eds. *Les Juifs Présentés aux Chrétiens par Léon de Modène Traduit par Richard Simon*. Paris: Les Belles Lettres, 1998.
Stroumsa, Sarah. *Reshito shel Pulmus ha-Rambam ba-Mizrah: Igeret ha-Hashtakah al Odot Tehiyat ha-Metim le-Yosef Ibn Shimon*. Jerusalem: Ben-Zvi Institute, 1999.
Stow, Kenneth. *Jewish Life in Early Modern Rome*. Aldershot: Ashgate, 2007.
———. *Theater of Acculturation: The Roman Ghetto in the Sixteenth Century*. Seattle: University of Washington Press, 2001.
Ta-Shma, Israel M. *Ha-Nigleh she-ba-nistar: Le-heker shekie ha-halakhah be-Sefer ha-Zohar*. Tel Aviv: ha-Kibutz ha-Meuhad, 2001.
———. *Ha-Sifrut ha-Parshanit la-Talmud be-Europah u-vi-Tsefon Afrikah: 1000–1200*. Vol 1. Jerusalem: Magnes Press, 1999.
———. *Ha-Sifrut ha-Parshanit la-Talmud be-Europah u-vi-Tsefon Afrikah: 1200–1400*. Vol. 2. Jerusalem: Magnes Press, 2000.
Talmage, Frank. "Apples of Gold: The Inner Meaning of Sacred Texts in Medieval Judaism." In *Jewish Spirituality: From the Bible through the Middle Ages*. Edited by Arthur Green, 313–55. New York: Crossroad, 1986.
———. *David Kimhi: The Man and the Commentaries*. Cambridge: Harvard University Press, 1975.
Tamani, Giuliano. "I libri ebraici di Pico della Mirandola." In *Giovanni Pico della Mirandola*. Edited by Gian Carlo Garfagnini. 2: 491–530. Florence: L. S. Olschki, 1997.
Tamar, David. *Mehkarim be-Toldot ha-Yehudim be-Erets Yisrael uve-Italyah*. Jerusalem: Rubin Mass, 1970.
Tishby, Isaiah. "The Conflict between Lurianic Kabbalah and Cordoverian Kabbalah in the Writings and Life of R. Aaron Berekhya of Modena" (Hebrew). In *Hikre Kabalah u-sheluhoteha*, 1:177–254. Jerusalem: Magnes Press, 1982.
———. "The Controversy over the Book of the *Zohar* in the Sixteenth Century in Italy" (Hebrew). In *Hikre Kabalah u-sheluhoteha*, 1:79–130.
———. "Documents about Nathan of Gaza in the Writings of Joseph Hamiz" (Hebrew). In *Netive Emunah ve-Minut: Masot u-Mehkarim be-Sifrut ha-Kabalah veha-Shabtaut*, 52–80. Jerusalem: Magnes Press, 1982.
———. "General Introduction." In *The Wisdom of the Zohar: An Anthology of Texts*, 1: 1–126. Oxford: Littman Library, 1989.
———. *Messianic Mysticism: Moses Hayim Luzzatto and the Padua School*. Oxford: Littman Library, 2008.
Trivellato, Francesca. *The Familiarity of Strangers: The Sephardic Diaspora, Livorno, and Cross-Cultural Trade in the Early Modern Period*. New Haven: Yale University Press, 2009.
Twersky, Isadore. "Law and Spirituality in the Seventeenth Century: A Case Study in R. Yair Hayyim Bacharach." In Twersky and Septimus, *Jewish Thought in the Seventeenth Century*, 447–67.

Twersky, Isadore ed. *Rabbi Moses Nahmanides (Ramban): Explorations in His Religious and Literary Virtuosity*. Cambridge: Harvard University Press, 1983.

Twersky, Isadore, and Bernard Septimus, eds. *Jewish Thought in the Seventeenth Century*. Cambridge: Harvard University Press, 1987.

Urbach, Ephraim E. *Ba'ale ha-Tosafot*, 2 vols. Jerusalem: Mossad Bialik, 1980.

——. "Gershom Scholem and Judaic Studies." In *Gershom Scholem: The Man and His Work*. Edited by Paul Mendes-Flohr, 29–39. Albany: SUNY Press, 1994.

Vajda, Georges. *Recherches sur la philosophie et la kabbale dans la pensée juive du Moyen Age* Paris: Mouton, 1962.

Valle, Carlos del. "La critique de la Qabbale chez Isaac ibn Polgar." In Fenton and Goetschel, *Expérience et écriture mystique dans les religions du livre*, 131–41.

Verman, Mark. *The Books of Contemplation: Medieval Jewish Mystical Sources*. Albany: SUNY Press, 1992.

Vivo, Filippo de. *Information and Communication in Venice: Rethinking Early Modern Politics* Oxford: Oxford University Press, 2007.

Wachstein, Bernhard. *Die hebräische publizistik in Wien*. Vienna: Selbstverlag der Historischen Kommision, 1930.

Walker, D. P. *The Ancient Theology: Studies in Christian Platonism from the Fifteenth to the Eighteenth Century*. Ithaca: Cornell University Press, 1972.

Wasserstrom, Steven M. "Further Thoughts on the Origins of *Sefer yesirah*." *Aleph* 2 (2002): 201–21.

——. *Religion after Religion: Gershom Scholem, Mircea Eliade, and Henry Corbin at Eranos*. Princeton: Princeton University Press, 1999.

Weinberg, Joanna. "Leon Modena and the *Fiore di Virtù*." In Malkiel, *The Lion Shall Roar*, 137–57.

——. "Preaching in the Venetian Ghetto: The Sermons of Leon Modena." In Ruderman, *Preachers of the Italian Ghetto*, 105–28.

Weinstein, Roni. *Juvenile Sexuality, Kabbalah, and Catholic Reformation in Italy: "Tiferet Bahurim" by Pinhas Barukh ben Pelatiyah Monselice*. Leiden: Brill, 2009.

Werblowsky, R. J. Zwi. *Joseph Karo: Lawyer and Mystic*. Oxford: Oxford University Press, 1962.

Werses, Shmuel. "The Dispute between Emden and Eibeschuetz in the Eyes of the Nineteenth-Century Maskilim" (Hebrew). In *Haskalah ve-Shabtaut: Toldotav shel Ma'avak*, 43–62. Jerusalem: Zalman Shazar Center, 1988.

——. "The Gaon R. Elijah of Vilna in the literature of the Jewish Enlightenment" (Hebrew). In *Hakitzah Ami: Sifrut ha-Haskalah be-idan ha-modernizasyah*, 25–66. Jerusalem: Magnes Press, 2000.

——. "Hasidism and Sabbatianism in the Estimation of Galician Maskilim" (Hebrew). In *Haskalah ve-Shabtaut*, 99–124.

——. "Magic and Demonolgy as Reflected in the Satirical Literature of Galician Maskilim" (Hebrew). In *Hakitzah Ami*, 353–84.

——. "Patterns in the Autobiographical Literature of the Haskalah" (Hebrew). In *Megamot ve-Zurot be-Sifrut ha-Haskalah*, 249–60. Jerusalem: Magnes Press, 1990.

——. "*Shadal* and *Shir*: Luzzatto and Rapoport through Their Letters" (Hebrew). In Bonfil, Gottlieb, and Kasher, *Samuel David Luzzatto*, 79–98.

———. "An Unknown Satiric Work of Joseph Perl" (Hebrew). *Hasifrut* 1 (1968–1969): 206–27.
Wieseltier, Leon. "*Etwas über die jüdische Historik*: Leopold Zunz and the Inception of Modern Jewish Historiography." *History and Theory* 20 (1981): 135–49.
Wilensky, Sara O. Heller. "Isaac Ibn Latif—Philosopher or Kabbalist?" In Altmann, *Jewish Medieval and Renaissance Studies*, 185–223.
Wildmann, Isaac Haver. *Magen ve-Zinah*. Johannisburg, 1855. Photo offset edition, Bnei Brak: Nesah, 1984.
Wilson, Bronwen. *The World in Venice: Print, the City, and Early Modern Identity*. Toronto: University of Toronto Press, 2005.
Wirszubski, Chaim. *Ben ha-Shitin: Kabalah, Kabalah Notsrit, Shabtaut*. Jerusalem: Magnes Press, 1990.
———. *Pico Della Mirandola's Encounter with Jewish Mysticism*. Cambridge: Harvard University Press, 1989.
Wolff, Larry. *The Idea of Galicia: History and Fantasy in Habsburg Political Culture*. Stanford: Stanford University Press, 2010.
Wolfson, Elliot R. *Abraham Abulafia—Kabbalist and Prophet: Hermeneutics, Theosophy, and Theurgy*. Los Angeles: Cherub Press, 2000.
———. "Beautiful Maiden without Eyes: *Peshat* and *Sod* in Zoharic Hermeneutics." In *The Midrashic Imagination: Jewish Exegesis, Thought, and History*. Edited by Michael Fishbane, 155–203. Albany: SUNY Press, 1993.
———. "Beneath the Wings of the Great Eagle: Maimonides and Thirteenth-Century Kabbalah." In *Moses Maimonides (1138–1204): His Religious, Scientific, and Philosophic Wirkungsgeschichte in Different Cultural Contexts*. Edited by Görge K. Hasselhoff and Otfried Fraisse, 209–37. Würzburg: Ergon Verlag, 2004.
———. "Beyond the Spoken Word: Oral Tradition and Written Transmission in Medieval Jewish Mysticism." In Elman and Gershoni, *Transmitting Jewish Tradition*, 166–224.
———. *The Book of the Pomegranate: Moses de Leon's Sefer Ha-Rimmon*. Atlanta: Scholars Press, 1988.
———. "By Way of Truth: Aspects of Nahmanides' Kabbalistic Hermeneutic." *AJS Review* 14 (1989): 103–78.
———. "Hai Gaon's Letter and Commentary on *Aleynu*: Further Evidence of Moses de León's Pseudepigraphic Activity." *JQR* 81 (1991): 365–409.
———. "The Influence of Luria on the Shelah" (Hebrew). *JSJT* 10 (1992): 423–48.
———. "Language, Secrecy and the Mysteries of Law: Theurgy and the Christian Kabbalah of Johannes Reuchlin." *Kabbalah* 13 (2005): 7–41.
———. *Luminal Darkness: Imaginal Gleanings from Zoharic Literature*. Oxford: Oneworld, 2007.
———. "Text, Context, and Pretext: Review Essay of Yehuda Liebes's *Ars Poetica* in *Sefer Yetsira*." *Studia Philonica Annual* 16 (2004): 218–28.
Woolf, Jeffrey. "The Responsa of Leon Modena: Continuity without Change" (Hebrew). In Malkiel, *The Lion Shall Roar*, 55–68.
Wootton, David. *Paolo Sarpi: Between Renaissance and Enlightenment*. Cambridge: Cambridge University Press, 1983.

Woudhuysen, H. R. *Sir Philip Sidney and the Circulation of Manuscripts, 1558–1640*. Oxford: Clarendon Press, 1996.
Yaari, Abraham. *Sheluhe Erets Yisrael*. Vol. 1. Jerusalem: Mossad ha-Rav Kook, 1997.
Yassif, Eli. "The Conflict over the Myth of Safed: Then and Now" (Hebrew). *Mikan* 4 (2005): 42–79.
———. "In the Fields and in the Open Spaces: On Space and Its Meaning in Stories about Safed" (Hebrew). *Katedra* 116 (2005): 67–102.
Yates, Frances A. *Giordano Bruno and the Hermetic Tradition*. Chicago: University of Chicago Press, 1964.
Yerushalmi, Yosef Hayim. *Zakhor: Jewish History and Jewish Memory*. New York: Schocken Books 1989.
Yosha, Nissim. *Mitos u-Metaforah: Ha-Parshanut ha-Filosofit shel R. Avraham Kohen Hererah le-Kabalat ha-Ari*. Jerusalem: Magnes Press and Ben-Zvi Institute, 1994.
Zacut, Moses. *Esa et Levavi: Shirim*. Edited by Dvora Bregman. Jerusalem: Ben-Zvi Institute, 2009.
The Zohar. Translated by Daniel C. Matt. Vol. 1. Stanford: Stanford University Press, 2004.
Zorzi, Marino. "Dal manoscitto al libro." In *Storia di Venezia*. Edited by Ugo Tucci and Alberto Tenenti, 4:817–958. Rome: Giovanni Treccani, 1996.
Zunz, Leopold. *Die gottesdienstlichen Vorträge der Juden*. Berlin: A. Asher, 1832.

Index

Note: Page numbers in italic type indicate illustrations

Abner of Burgos, 46, 154–55
Aboab, Immanuel, 188
Aboab, Samuel, 54, 178–82, 189, 193, 232
Abraham, 88–89, 142
Abravanel, Isaac, 45, 45n67, 46, 223
Abulafia, Abraham, 5, 117, 117n66, 212, 233
Abulafia, Jacob, 135
Agrippa von Nettesheim, 57, 156; *De incertitudine et vanitate scientiarum*, 156, 156n25
Akiva, 5, 68, 89
Alashkar, Moses, 110n35
Albo, Joseph, 180
Alemmano, Yohanan, 153
Alfasi, Isaac, 115, 115n54
Alkabetz, Solomon, 129
Allgemeine Zeitung des Judentums (newspaper), 218–19
Almanzi, Joseph, 215n48
Altschuler, Aaron Moses, 73n55
amanuenses, 36–37, 49
Amsterdam, 124, 181
Anabaptists, 163
anachronism, 87–95
annotations, 13, 22, 45–46, 176–77
antikabbalism, 12–13, 74, 108n23, 180, 203, 213, 214n47, 223
apostasy, 114
Arama, Isaac, 122, 141
Aramaic, 91
Ari Nohem (Modena): censorship fears concerning, 208, 210–11, 216; on Christian Kabbalah, 151–69; circulation of, 27, 58, 173, 175–76, 178, 184, 203, 209, 213, 220–21; as counterhistory, 11; as countertheology, 12; as critique of Kabbalah, 10–13, 24–25; dating of, 52n102; in early modern culture, 177–87; in eighteenth-century reference works, 198–200; and European intellectual tradition, 16; failures of, 231–35; Hamiz as immediate audience for, 12, 97–98, 103–4, 117–19, 121, 125, 131, 135–36, 140, 163, 166, 232–33; history of, 14, 18–19; on *Hokhmah*, 123–

24; legacy of, 203–4, 231–35; Levi's role in, 49, 52–55; and Maimonides, 103–26; Modena and, 31–32; Moscow manuscript of, 48–55; motivation for writing, 10; on myths about Safed, 131–39; overview of, 1–2; precursors of, 12; printing of, 27, 32, 33–34, 53–55, 181, 203–20, 224; reception of, 27, 173–200, 204, 214, 220–30; Reggio and, 206–13; responses of kabbalists to, 188–200, 204, 214, 221–27; Scholem and, 25n77; scribal copies of, 48–55, 174–77, 220; title of, 175–76; title pages to, *201, 212*; transmission of, 175; Warsaw manuscript of, 52–55; works circulated with, 176; on the *Zohar*, 61, 65–100
Aristotle, 99, 160
Ashkenazi, Joseph, 107n22
Ashkenazi, Naftali, 72–73, 73n54, 232
Ashkenazi, Samuel, 82
author's autograph, 33, 48–49
authorship, 87–95
autograph, 33, 48–49
Azulai, Hayim Joseph David, 177, 199–200, 206, 226; *Ma'agal Tov*, 126, 199; *Shem ha-Gedolim*, 126, 200

Bacharach, Samson, 185, 187; *Hut ha-Shani*, 185
Bacharach, Yair Hayim, 184–87, 199, 211; *Havot Yair*, *171*, 185; *Mekor Hayim*, 185
Bacon, Francis, 18n55
bareheadedness, among males, 87
Baron, Salo W., 202
Bar Sheshet, Isaac, 114–15, 120, 189, 196, 198, 219
Bar Tanhum, Mordechai, 78
Bartolocci, Giulio, 181–82
Bar Yedaiah ibn Raz, Amitai, 24
Bar Yohai, Simeon, 138; as author of *Zohar*, 5, 26, 61, 65n22, 66–67, 83, 84, 87–95, 97–98, 161, 189–90, 195, 206, 227; on law, 77–78, 81, 85; Modena's respect for, 87–88; not a kabbalist, 84–86; in

Bar Yohai, Simeon (cont'd)
  rabbinic literature, 24, 85–86; as subject of *Zohar*, 3
Basel, 73n56, 82, 124, 157
Basilea, Aviad Sar Shalom, 174, 188–91, 194, 198; *Emunat Hakhamim*, 188–92
Basola, Moses, 85n110
Bassan, Isaiah, 192–94
Battista, Giovanni, 182
Bedersi, Yedaiah, 180, 223
Benamozegh, Elijah, 27, 204, 221–27; *Eimat Mafgia al Ari*, 222–27; *Ta'am la-Shad*, 222, 227
Ben Asher, Bahya, 80n89
Ben Asher, Jacob, *Arba'ah Turim*, 76
Ben David, Abraham, 197
Ben ha-Kaneh, Nehuniah, 5
Ben Isaac, Samuel, of Verona, 72
Ben Israel, Menasseh, 223
Ben Meshulam, Samuel, 168
Benveneto, Baruch di, 153
Ben Yehiel, Asher, 199n111
Berekhya, Aaron, of Modena, 10, 57, 107, 146–47; *Magen Aharon*, 37
Berlin, Saul, 24n74, 177–78; *Besamim Rosh*, 177–78
Bialik, Hayim Nachman, 229
Bible, 2–3, 206, 222
biblical vocalization, 92–95
Bibliotheca magna rabbinica, 182
Bloch, Samson, 207–8, 220
Bodek, Jacob, 221
Bodin, Jean, *Theater of all of Nature*, 13–14
the book, history of, 17–18
Botarel, Moses, 75, 75n65
Briel, Judah, 188
Buxtorf, Johannes, 124; *Synagoga Judaica*, 157

Calvinists, 163
Casaubon, Isaac, 16, 17, 99, 156n22
Catholic Church, 16, 181–82
censorship, 19, 157, 208, 210–11, 216
Chilmead, Edmund, 200
Christianity: anti-Judaic writings of, 45–46; dissenting groups within, 163; Jews' relationship with, 9; and Kabbalah, 2, 8–9; Modena's polemics against, 45; Trinity doctrine of, 11, 146, 156, 165, 196
Christian Kabbalah: and Christian doctrine, 164–65, 165n59; critique of, 20, 26–27, 151–52; early adherents of, 154–56; in early modern Venice, 154–60; Jewish instruction in, 152–53; and Maimonides, 118n70; Modena's conception of, 151–52; Modena's critique of, 160–69; Pico and, 2, 154, 158–69; print dissemination of, 57; significance of, 8–9, 152–53
Clavicula Salomonis, 35, 232
Cohen, Gershon, 121n82
Cohen de Herrera, Abraham, 110, 141n56; *Puerta del Cielo*, 141n56
collective authorship, 90
Constantinople, 73n56, 97, 106, 140
Conti, Vincenzo, 72
conversion, 166–67, 169, 181–82, 226
Cordoverian Kabbalah, 138–39, 144, 146–47
Cordovero, Moses, 25, 107, 119, 129, 144–47; *Pardes Rimonim*, 3, 27, 57, 62, 99, *127*, 128, 130, 144–47, 185
Corpus Hermeticum, 99
counterhistories, 11
Cremona, 69, 72
Cremonini, Cesare, 35
Crescas, Hasdai, 141

Da Costa, Uriel, 227n111
Da Fano, Menahem Azariah, 10, 36–37, 57, 78, 107, 138–39, 144, 146–47, 189
Da Foligno, Hananel (Alessandro Franceschi), 166
deathbed repentance motif, 115n53, 126, 177
De Lattes, Isaac, 75
De Leon, Moses, 11, 24, 26, 59, 80, 80n89, 95–97, 161, 234
Della Torre, Hillel ha-Kohen, 210n29
Della Volta, Samuel, 209, 220
Delmedigo, Elijah, 12, 81–83, 89, 153; *Behinat ha-Dat*, 13, 24n75, 79–81, 83, 153, 185, 203, 208, 210, 210n29, 214, 228
Delmedigo, Joseph Solomon, 77, 78, 82–84, 96, 107, 134, 136, 139, 211, 215, 221, 226n105; "Ahuz Letter," 19n57, 175, 176; *Mazref le-Hokhmah*, 82–83, 97, 140, 186, 192; *Novlot Hokhmah*, 168; *Sefer Elim*, 83; *Ta'alumot Hokhmah*, 82–83, 113–14, 131, 134, *149*, 150
De' Rossi, Azariah, 89–90, 93, 96, 211; *Meor Enayim*, 93, *94*, *95*, 96n166
devekut (initiate's relationship to knowledge of the divine), 3
De Vidas, Elijah, 107

Donnolo, Shabbetai, 142
Dresnitz, Solomon Shlomel, 130–36
Drusius, Johannes, 80n88, 96, 97
Duran, Profiat, 165, 165n59

Egidius of Viterbo, 93, 153
ein sof (realm beyond existence), 145
Elbogen, Ismar, 91n139
Eleazar the Perfumer (Eleazar of Worms), 158, 197
Elijah of Vilna (the Gaon), 221, 225–26
emanations, Neoplatonic, 21
Emden, Jacob, 80n90, 183, 184, 233, 234; *Mitpahat Sefarim*, 203, 209, 214, 234
emunat hakhamim, 188
Ergas, Joseph, 174, 188, 196–98; *Shomer Emunim*, 188, 196–98
Esdras. *See* Ezra the Scribe
esotericism: Kabbalah and, 4–5, 10, 56, 70, 75, 81, 108–11, 161; language and, 91–92; and lost Jewish secrets, 81; Maimonides on, 121–22; writing as threat to, 70. *See also* secrets
exegesis: of Bible, 2–3; Kabbalah as source of, 2–3, 10–11; layers of meaning in, 62–63; levels of, 110–11; *Zohar* and, 62–64
exile, kabbalistic concept of, 7
existence, 145
Ezra the Scribe (Esdras), 159–63

Farrar, David, 64
Fedorov, Vladimir (Zvi Hirsch Grinboim), 221n81
Ferrara, 6, 22, 69, 106
Finzi, David, 194, 199
Fischer, Karl, 208
forgeries, 16–17, 99, 221, 228
Frances, Jacob, 184, 203, 213, 218
Franceschi, Alessandro (Hananel da Foligno), 166
Funkenstein, Amos, 11
Fürst, Julius, 27, 80, 203, 204, 216–21, 219n72

Gaffarel, Jacques, 107, 157–60, 169, 231
Galante, Yedidiah, 134–35
Galatino, Pietro, 9, 45–46, 155–56, 156n22, 190; *De arcanis catholicae veritatis opus*, 45, 156
Galicia, 203, 209, 216
Gedalya, Judah, 73

Geiger, Abraham, 204, 205, 221, 222, 224, 226n105, 227–28; *Magen ve-Zinah*, 227
Genazzano, Elijah, 116, 146
Gershon, Isaac, 38
Gesenius, Wilhelm, 217
ghetto, Venetian, 1, 2, 16, 20–21, 38, 232
Ghirondi, Mordecai Samuel, 193n89, 213–14, 220
Gikatilla, Joseph, 80n89; *Sha'arei Orah*, 57, 73–74, 74n57
gilgul. See transmigration of souls
Girondi, Jonah, 70
God: body of, 165; division vs. unity of, 3, 11, 120, 146, 224–25; names of, 119–20, 155, 156; secrets transmitted by, 4–5, 160–62
Goldenberg, Samuel, 207, 209, 214–20
Gordon, Judah Leib, 228n116
Gorizia, 205, 220
Gottlober, Abraham Baer, 204
Gozalo, Jacob, 84
Graetz, Heinrich, 59, 204, 234; *Geschichte der Juden*, 234
Greek manuscripts, 34
Grinboim, Zvi Hirsch (Vladimir Fedorov), 221n81
Guide of the Perplexed (Maimonides): Benamozegh on, 224; defense and promotion of, 11, 12, 15–16, 26, 102–4; on *Hokhmah*, 123; kabbalistic readings of, 3, 190–91; language of, 91–92; reception of, 124; title page to, *101*; and tradition, 17; on transmission of secrets, 108

Habsburg Empire, 203, 205, 208, 213
Hagiz, Moses, 183, 184, 188, 192–94, 233
Halevi, Judah, *Kuzari*, 142
Hamiz, Joseph, 10, 12, 57, 66, 97–98, 103–4, 117–19, 117n66, 121, 124–25, 131, 135–37, 139–40, 159–60, 163, 166, 169, 178, 199, 232–33
Hanau, 82
Hasidism, 27, 203, 204, 208, 216, 217, 225, 226, 233, 234
Haskalah. See Jewish Enlightenment
Hayim of Volozhin, 226
Hayyat, Judah, 67–68; *Minhat Yehudah*, 185
Hebrew language, 91
Heinsius, Daniel, 99
Hermes Trismegistus, 9, 16, 160, 161
historicist criticism, 99, 223
History of the Council of Trent (Sarpi), 16

Holy Roman Empire, 5, 155
Horowitz, Abraham, 107n22
Horowitz, Isaiah (Isaiah of Prague), 20, 168
Ibn abi Zimra, David, 76
Ibn Adret, Solomon, 50, 51, 86, 107–8, 117n66, 197, 223; *Perush ha-Haggadot*, 86n118
Ibn Ezra, Abraham, 143
Ibn Gabbai, Meir, 57, 105–13, 116, 117, 123, 124, 139, 169, 189; *Avodat ha-Kodesh*, 106, 106n17; *Derekh Emunah*, 107; *Tola'at Ya'akov*, 106
Ibn Habib, Jacob, *Ein Ya'akov*, 40, 40n48, 64, 86, 86n118, 180
Ibn Latif, Isaac, 141
Ibn Motot, Samuel, 141
Ibn Sahula, Isaac, 96, 96n166
Ibn Shem Tov, Shem Tov, 105–14, 110n35, 117, 139, 145; *Sefer ha-Emunot*, 57, 106–7
Ibn Shimon, Joseph, 121
Ibn Tamim, Dunash, 142
Ibn Tibbon, Samuel, 105, 124
Ibn Wakar, Joseph, 141
Ibn Yahya, Gedalya, 77, 116, 189
Imbonati, Carlo Giuseppe, 182
Immortality of the soul, 35–36
Innocent VIII, Pope, 153, 165
Inquisition, 35, 157, 231–32
interpretation. *See* exegesis
Isaac of Acre, 95–98; *Meirat Enayim*, 97
Isaac of Corbeil, 96, 96n166
Isaac the Blind, 70, 109n30
Isaiah of Prague (Isaiah Horowitz), 20, 168
Isbili, Yom Tov, 197
Islam, 183
Israelitische Annalen (journal), 219–20
Isserles, Moses, 12, 13, 50, 73–75, 78, 219, 223; *Torat ha-Olah*, 73–74, 73n55, 187

Jesus, 87, 155, 164, 182
Jewish books, controversy over, 155
Jewish Enlightenment (*Haskalah*), 14–15, 203, 205, 214, 216, 218
Jews: Ashkenazi, 6; expulsions of, 5; Sephardic, 6
Jost, I. M., 220, 221
Judah the Prince, 121, 161, 190
Judaism: Christians' relationship with, 9; Christian writings against, 45–46, 157, 167; Modena's defense of, 157–58; and philosophy, 206; Reform, 204, 222, 227. *See also* modern Judaism
Judeo-Arabic language, 91–92

Kabbalah: age of, 4; attitudes toward, 1, 204; censorship of, 208; Christian conversion and, 166; Christianity and, 2, 8–9, 20, 165n59 (*see also* Christian Kabbalah); concepts associated with, 3, 140, 165; Cordoverian, 138–39, 144, 146–47; critics of, 12–13, 15, 19, 50–52, 74, 184, 186–87, 219, 228–29 (*see also* Modena's critique of); defenses of, 174, 175, 176, 188–200, 204, 214, 221–27; esoteric nature of, 4–5, 10, 56, 70, 75, 81, 108–11, 161; exegesis based on, 2–3, 10–11; as *Hokhmah*, 123; innovations in, 7–8; intellectual inquiry inadequate for, 112–13, 123–24; as knowledge, 123–24, 222–23; and law, 11, 83–84; Lurianic, 8, 138–39, 144, 183, 183n45, 233; meanings of, 2–5; and messianism, 183; Modena's critique of, 1–2, 10–13, 16–17, 24–25, 50–52, 57–58, 80–86, 122–26, 136, 144–46, 160–63, 181–82; origins of, 10, 80–81, 160–63, 189–90, 204, 234; and philosophy, 75, 130, 139–43; popularity of, 69–74; print and, 7, 56–58, 223; and private religious experience, 10; and revelation, 111–12; ritual practices of, 4; scholarship on, 1, 229–30; Scholem and, 25; son-in-law's defense of, 37; spread of medieval, 5–10; success of, 4; and tradition, 110; transmission of, 57–58, 69–75, 108–12, 109n30, 160–62, 187, 189–90, 197. *See also* kabbalistic texts
kabbalistic texts: appropriation of Maimonides by, 115–18; authorship of, 87–88; critical of Maimonides, 105–12; in defense of Maimonides, 112–15; origins of, 67; printing and availability of, 6–7, 9, 56–58, 69–75, 187, 223
Kant, Immanuel, 149, 207
kapparot (penitential rite), 157
Karo, Joseph, 57, 76–78, 127, 131, 131n11; *Bet Yosef*, 76; *The Book of the Maggid*, 131–32; *Shulhan Arukh*, 8, 55–56, 76, 129, 185
Keneset (journal), 229, 229n120
Kepler, Johannes, 18n55
Kerem Hemed (journal), 207, 208, 209, 214, 215
Keter, 145

Keter Yitenu Lekha, 90, 90n139
Knorr von Rosenroth, Christian, 217–18
knowledge: Kabbalah and, 11, 123–24; Maimonides on, 123; reason as basis for, 11
Krochmal, Nachman, *Moreh Nevukhei ha-Zman*, 229–30
Kunitz, Moses, 206–7, 220; *Ben Yohai*, 214, 227

Lachover, Fischel, 229–30
Lampronti, Isaac, 176; *Pahad Yitzhak*, 198–99, 199n109, 211
Land, Aaron, 107n22
Landau, Jacob, 78; *Sefer Agur*, 76
Landau, Moses, 215–16
Landau Press, 208, 215, 216n54
language: and biblical vocalization, 92–95; esotericism and, 91–92; of *Zohar*, 91–95
law: anachronism in, 87; Kabbalah and, 11, 83–84; Karo's code of, 8, 55–56, 76–77, 129; *Zohar* and, 8, 76–78, 77n75, 81–85
Leipzig, 216–17
Lemberg, 216, 220, 221
Leon, Judah Messer, 12n38
Levi, Diana (née Modena), 37–38, 43, 66
Levi, Isaac, of Mantua, 36–37
Levi, Isaac (Yitzhak min Haleviyyim), 36n26; as amanuensis, 26, 32, 49; and *Ari Nohem*, 26, 32, 49, 52–55; autobiography of, 43–44; handwriting of, 48, 49; *Ma'ase Hakhamim*, 40; preservation of Modena's writings by, 22–23, 37–48; and printing, 40; relationship between Modena and, 37–38, 48; religious charges against, 231–32
Levi, Jacob (Ya'akov min Haleviyyim), 10, 37–38, 66, 98, 139, 146; *Nahalat Ya'akov*, 37, 66, 84, 90
Levinsohn, Isaac Baer, 204, 221, 221n81; *Shorshe Levanon*, 221, 228
Levita, Elijah, 12n38, 79–80, 93, 153; *Massoret ha-Massoret*, 93
Libowitz, Nehemiah, 25n77
Lieberman, Saul, 1
Lilienblum, Moses Leib, 204, 228–29
liturgy, 4, 7, 62, 129
Livorno, 126, 191, 199, 221–22
Locke, John, 200n115
Luria, David, 227n110
Luria, Isaac, 168, 219; contributions of, 7–8, 129; cult of personality around, 27; death of, 131; entry into Safed of, 131n11; and esotericism, 13; extraordinary powers of, 133–35; hagiographic narratives of, 57, 132–33; literary profile of, 19–20; as miracle worker, 8; Modena's critique of, 11, 13, 15, 27; Modena's knowledge of, 78n83; on philosophy, 140; reputation of, 131–32, 135–36; *Toledot Ari*, 196;
Luria, Solomon, 12, 189, 198, 223; on *Zohar* and law, 78, 78n83
Lurianic Kabbalah, 8, 138–39, 144, 183, 183n45, 233
Luzzattin, Moses, 43, 43n56
Luzzatto, Moses Hayim, 174–76, 174n4, 188, 191–96, 198, ; *Adir ba-Marom*, 196; *Hoqer u-Mekubal*, 175, 176, 195, 214; *Ma'amar ha-Vikuah*, 176, 188, 195; *Milhemet Moshe*, 176
Luzzatto, Samuel David, 203, 205, 209–10, 210n29, 216n53, 218, 220–21, 224, 234; *Vikuah al Hokhmat ha-Kabalah*, 222, 234
Luzzatto, Simone, 20–21, 43n56, 44; *Discorso*, 21
Lvov. *See* Lemberg

Ma'arekhet ha-Elohut, 57, 67, 69
maggid (celestial mentor), 131–32, 192
magic, 35, 135–37
Maimonides (Moses ben Maimon), 161, 232; authority of, 77; Benamozegh on, 224; *Code*, 124; and conversion to Kabbalah, 115–16, 190; defense and support of, 13, 80, 105–15, 124; *Guide of the Perplexed*, 3, 11, 12, 15–17, 26, 91–92, *101*, 102–26; kabbalistic appropriation of, 115–18, 141, 144; kabbalistic criticism of, 105–12; kabbalistic defenses of, 112–15; kabbalist responses to, 190, 197
Malkiel, David, 173
Mantua, 6, 36, 69, 72, 184, 188, 205, 207, 220
manuscript for circulation, 33
manuscripts: advantages of, 19, 34–35; of *Ari Nohem*, 48–55, 173–77, 220; composing practices for, 36–37; dissemination of, 173; Greek, 34; Modena and, 18–19, 31; persistence of, 18–19, 33; print's relationship to, 14, 18–20, 70–71; scholarly value of, 20; subject matter of, 34–36; in Venice, 34–37
Martin, Raymond, 93; *Pugio Fidei*, 156
Mendelssohn, Moses, 15n44; *Biur*, 206

278 • Index

Mendl, Menahem, of Shklov, 225–26
Messiah, 75–76, 122–23, 164
messianism, 8, 183–84, 191, 219, 233
Midrash, 190
Mieses, Judah Leib, *Kinat ha-Emet*, 209, 209n27
Min Haleviyyim, Yitzhak. *See* Levi, Isaac
Mishnah, 121, 131, 161, 189–90
Mithridates, Flavius, 153, 162
Mizrahi, Elijah, 50
Modena, Diana. *See* Levi, Diana
Modena, Esther, 43
Modena, Isaac, 43–44
Modena, Leon: activities of, 21–22; autobiography of, 23; *Ben David*, 31, 51, 87, 176, 178, 178n25, 198–99; *Bet Lehem Yehudah*, 40n48, 64, 181; *Bet Yehudah*, 40, 40n48, 46, 58, 180; birth of, 22; copybook of, *30*, 39; critical methods of, 98–99, 145; death of, 42n55, 231; gambling habit of, 23, 38; handwriting of, 48, 49; *Hayyei Yehudah* (The Life of Judah), 23, 31, 125–26; health of, 23; *Historia de gli Riti Hebraici*, 107; *Kol Sakhal*, 23–24, 31, 40–41, 87, 99, 178, 178n25, 194, 227; *Lev ha-Aryeh*, 104n3;; literary profile of, 19–20; livelihood of, 22, 45; *Magen va-Herev*, 31, 44–47, 87, 122, 156, 164n52, 169, 177, 178n25, 211; *Magen ve-Zinah*, 31, 178, 178n25, 227; manuscript form used by, 18–19, 31; marriage of, 23; *Midbar Yehudah*, 63, 65; and modern Judaism, 15–16; and printing, 31; as rabbi, 22; reception of, 58, 181–82, 184; *Riti Hebraici*, 19, 58, 157–58, 200, 200n115, 231; scholarship on, 23; Scholem on, 25n77; *Sha'agat Aryeh*, 40–41, *41*, *42*, 175–76, 175n11, 232; *Sha'agat Aryeh* as title for *Ari Nohem*, 193–94, 199; skepticism of, 16–17, 134–36; and tradition, 17; will prepared by, 41–44, 47, 231; writing practices of, 37–39, 44–45; writings of, 22, 31; *Ziknei Yehudah*, 46–47, *48*, 55. See also *Ari Nohem*
Modena, Mordecai, 23
Modena, Zebulun, 38
modernity, 10, 17
modern Judaism, 14–17
Montalto, Elijah, 134–35
Morin, Jean, 80n88
Morosini, Giulio, 181–82, 232; *Via della fede*, 181–82

Morpurgo, Samson, *Esh ha-Dat*, 189
Morteira, Saul Levi, 181, 181n37, 188
Moscato, Judah, 107; *Kol Yehudah*, 142
Moses, 4–5, 10, 68, 160–62

Nahmanides (Moses ben Nahman), 2, 51, 70, 74–75, 86, 97, 109, 109n30, 112–14, 123, 124, 161, 169, 197
Nahmias, David, 181
Nahmias, Jacob, 139–41, 166
Nahmias, Samuel. *See* Morosini, Giulio
Najara, Israel, 129
Nathan of Gaza, 178, 183
Neoplatonism, 21, 139. *See also* Plato and Platonism
newsletters, 34–35
Nietzsche, Friedrich, 149
Nishmat Kol Hai, 90, 90n139
Nissim, Rabbenu, 114–15
Norliengen, David ben Aharon, 72

Oral Torah: Kabbalah not part of, 57, 61, 69, 81, 109–10, 145; kabbalists' defense of, 226; Maimonides's history of, 121; Modena's defense of, 31; origins of, in revelation, 10, 109; sefirot and, 144–45. *See also* tradition
Der Orient (journal), 219, 219n72, 221
Orpheus, 161
Ottoman Empire, 5–6, 72–73

Pallavicino, Ferrante, 35
papacy, 16
Pardo, Joseph, 38
Pellicanus, Conrad, 93
Pentateuch, 3, 75, 205, 206
Perl, Joseph, 216
Pesaro, 66
Pfefferkorn, Johannes, 155
Philippson, Ludwig, 218–19
philosophy: and conversion, 226; Judaism and, 206; Kabbalah and, 75, 130, 139–43
phylacteries, 77–78
Pico della Mirandola, Giovanni, 2, 9, 12, 21, 27, 110n34, 151–54, 157–69, 160n37; *Apology*, 154, 154n12, 159, 160, 162, 163, 166; *Oration*, 153, 154n12, 159, 160, 162, 166
Plato and Platonism, 139–41, 160, 225. *See also* Neoplatonism
Polgar, Isaac, 12n38
Polish-Lithuanian Commonwealth, 5–6

Pomponazzi, Pietro, *On the Immortality of the Soul*, 35
Portugal, 5
Postel, Guillaume, 57
Prague, 129n3, 185, 208, 215–16
preaching, 9–10, 22, 64–65
primordial lights, 165
print/printing: costs of, 33, 70, 72; cultural history of, 18; of Hebrew texts, 6; of kabbalistic texts, 6–7, 9, 56–58, 69; of law code, 55–56; Levi and, 40, 46–48; manuscript's relationship to, 14, 18–20, 70–71; Modena and, 31, 46–48, 55–58; reasons for avoiding, 33; stigma of, 33; transmission of tradition affected by, 32, 56, 71–75, 167, 187, 191; in Venice, 34
Provençal, Moses, 70–72, 75, 92
Psalms, 63, 177
pseudepigraphy, 61, 67–68, 99, 162
Pythagoras and Pythagoreanism, 140, 156, 160, 225

Rapoport, Barukh Kahana, 194
Rapoport, Solomon Judah, 203, 208, 210, 213–14, 218–20, 219n72
Rashi, vii, 40, 74
reason: knowledge grounded in, 11; Modena's reliance on, 12
Recanati, Menahem, 73, 73n56, 145, 158, 160n37, 164
Reform Judaism, 204, 222, 227
Reggio, Isaac, 27, 117n65, 126n105, 203–13, 215, 216, 219–20, 222, 227, 228; *Ha-Torah veha-filosofiya*, 206, 219–20
Reuchlin, Johannes, 9, 26, 57, 93, 118n70, 155–56, 167; *Die Augenspiegel*, 155; *De arte cabalistica*, 156; *De verbo mirifico*, 155
revelation, 111–12
Richelieu, Cardinal, 158
Rosenthal, Solomon, 27, 203, 204, 210–11, 214–21, 216n53

Saadya Gaon, 50–51, 142, 180
Sabbatianism, 27, 174, 183–84, 183n45, 192, 198, 229, 233. *See also* Zevi, Sabbetai
Safed, 7–8, 27, 129–39, 147
Salonika, 73, 232
Sarpi, Paolo, 16, 17, 36, 36n24, 46, 59; *A History of the Council of Trent*, 16, 36; *Pensieri sulla religione*, 36
Saruq, Israel, 130, 136–41, 144
Sasportas, Jacob, 183, 184, 233

Savonarola, Girolamo, 160, 232
Scaliger, Joseph, 80
Schmid, Anton von, 207
Scholem, Gershom, 1, 25–26, 59, 183n45, 201, 204, 229–30, 233, 234; *Major Trends in Jewish Mysticism*, 1, 25, 229, 234; "Redemption through Sin," 229; "Reflections on Modern Jewish Studies," 229
Science of Judaism (*Wissenschaft des Judentums*), 14–15, 203, 217
scribal cultures, 34–37
secrets: Abraham and, 88–89; Kabbalah distinct from ancient Jewish, 133; lost, 81, 121–22; Maimonides on, 108, 121–22; Modena's distinction of Kabbalah from ancient Jewish, 81, 109, 122; publication of, 56, 70, 91, 121, 226; transmission of, 75, 108–10, 121; transmitted by God to Moses, 4–5, 122, 160–62. *See also* esotericism
Secrets of the Torah, 84, 108–10, 133, 168, 190
Sefer ha-Bahir, 3, 5, 7, 25, 67–69, 162, 232
Sefer ha-Yashar, 68
Sefer Yetzirah, 3, 5, 57, 67–69, 88, 142–43, 142n59, 162
sefirot (hypostases of divine being), 3, 11, 21, 120–21, 144–46, 196, 224–25
Selden, John, 124–25
sermons, 10, 38, 63, 223. *See also* Modena, Leon: *Midbar Yehudah*
shekinah, 7
Shiur Komah, 165, 197
Shivhei ha-Ari, 132
Shofar, 85
Shullam, Samuel, 97
Sibylline oracles, 9, 16
Sigonio, Carlo, 46
Simon, Richard, 200
Sixtus IV, Pope, 159, 161–62
Sixtus of Siena, *Bibliotheca Sancta*, 45–46
skepticism, 16–17, 134–36
slaves, 77
Sofer, Moses, 216
soul: immortality of, 35–36; transmigration of, 3, 31, 51, 54, 87, 108, 126, 126n105, 140, 157, 177, 179–80, 198–99; Venetian intellectuals on, 35–36
Spain, 5, 97
Spencer, John, 124
Spinoza, Baruch, *Theological-Political Treatise*, 17

spiritualists, 163
Steiner, George, 171
stigma of print, 33

Talmud, 3, 7, 77, 190; ban on printing of, 7, 69, 167; kabbalists ignorant of, 51–52; language and, 91; portrayal of Simeon bar Yohai in, 84–86, 190; printing of Kabbalah and, 69, 107n22; sermons and, 64; *Zohar* postdates the, 80
Tarnopol, 205, 216, 220
Tauchnitz press, 217
Tetragrammaton, 155, 156
Tikkunei ha-Zohar, 69, 84
Tishby, Isaiah, 72n52, 80n90, 173
Tosafists, 86
tradition: of antikabbalism, 12–13, 74, 108n23, 180, 203, 213, 214n47, 223; authorship and, 69; Kabbalah and, 2, 110; Modena's defense of, 17; transmission of, 32, 56, 71–75, 167, 187, 191. *See also* Oral Torah
transmigration of souls (*gilgul*), 3, 31, 51, 54, 54n109, 87, 108, 126, 126n105, 140, 157, 177, 179–80, 198–99
Treves, Isaac, 53n107
Treves, Jacob, 53n107
Trinity doctrine, 11, 146, 156, 163–65, 196

Uceda, Samuel, 107
Urban VIII, Pope, 232
Usque press, 110n35

Vendramin press, 40, 46
Venice: Christian Kabbalah in 154–60; culture of, 20–21; Jews in, 6; Modena in, 22; printing in, 34; reception of Kabbalah in, 129; Saruq in, 137; scribal cultures in, 34–37
Vera, Lope de, 156n22
vernacular languages, 91
Vienna, 205–8, 210
Vital, Hayim (Hayim Calabrese), 133, 136, 143, 147

vocalization, biblical, 79, 92–95
vowel points, 92–95

Wildmann, Isaac Haver, 27, 204, 221, 225–27, 226n105; *Magen ve-Zinah*, 225–27
Wissenschaft des Judentums. *See* Science of Judaism
working copy, 33
writing: compositional methods, 36–37; Modena's practice of, 37–39, 44–45

Ya'akov min Haleviyyim. *See* Levi, Jacob
Yaavetz, Joseph, 226
Yitzhak min Haleviyyim. *See* Levi, Isaac

Zacut, Abraham, 77; *Sefer Yuḥasin*, 80n88, 90, 96–98
Zacut, Moses, 54, 54n109, 176, 178–79, 181, 182, 188, 189, 194, 232
Zarza, Samuel, 50, 180
Zemah, Jacob, 156n25
Zevi, Sabbatai, 8, 178, 183–84, 219, 233. *See also* Sabbatianism
Zohar, 60; anachronism and, 87–95; antiquity of (*see* origins of); authorship of, 80, 80n89, 83, 95–97, 234; causes of Modena's criticism of, 65–79, 98; content of, 3, 61; critics of, 66–67, 79–86; and exegesis, 62–64; language of, 91–95; and law, 8, 76–78, 77n75, 81–85; Modena's attitude toward, 62–65; Modena's critique of, 26, 61, 65–100; origins of, 11, 13, 15, 24, 26, 59, 61, 65n22, 66–69, 79, 87–95, 161, 162, 195–96, 209, 221, 227, 234; positive aspects of, 62–65, 213; printing and dissemination of, 24, 56–57, 69–75, 72n52, 85n110, 153, 167, 232; reception of, 24, 61, 100, 233–34; transcription of, 5. See also *Tikkunei ha-Zohar*
Zohar Hadash, 73, 232
Zoroaster, 161
Zunz, Leopold, 59, 229–30; *Die gottesdienstlichen Vorträge der Juden*, 217

GPSR Authorized Representative: Easy Access System Europe - Mustamäe tee 50, 10621 Tallinn, Estonia, gpsr.requests@easproject.com

www.ingramcontent.com/pod-product-compliance
Lightning Source LLC
Chambersburg PA
CBHW030821230426
43667CB00008B/1317